THE BEST
AMERICAN
MAGAZINE
WRITING

2002

THE BEST AMERICAN MAGAZINE WRITING

2002

American Society of Magazine Editors

 Perennial

An Imprint of HarperCollins*Publishers*

HarperCollins books may be purchased for educational, business, or sales promotional use. For information please write: Special Markets Department, HarperCollins Publishers Inc., 10 East 53rd Street, New York, NY 10022.

FIRST EDITION

Library of Congress Cataloging-in-Publication Data is available upon request.

ISBN 0-06-051572-4

02 03 04 05 06 ❖/RRD 10 9 8 7 6 5 4 3 2 1

ASME Board of Directors 2001–2002

The American Society of Magazine Editors (ASME) is a nonprofit professional organization for editors of print and online magazines that are edited, published, and sold in the United States.

ASME's mission is to:

- Bring magazine editors together for the exchange of information on matters of mutual interest

- Encourage and reward outstanding and innovative achievement in the creation of magazines and their content

- Disseminate useful information on magazine editing to magazine staff members and others

- Attract young people of talent to magazine editorial work

- Safeguard the First Amendment

- Defend magazines against external pressures

- Acquaint the general public with the work of magazine editors and the special character of magazines as a channel of communication

ASME was founded in 1963, and currently has more than 900 members nationwide.

Contents

Introduction

Every endeavor has its particular demons, and journalism is no exception. I know journalists whose worst moment comes the minute they walk into a hotel room. They've just flown into some foreign country—not necessarily a country at war, just someplace they've never been before where the politics, the society, even the local food seems utterly baffling—and this is their first battle: homesickness. They sit on the bed wiped out by eighteen hours of travel and just think to themselves that they would rather be in almost any situation back home than where they are now. Others fear the phone. They have a call to make—to a political dissident, to a union boss, to the under-secretary of the ministry of health, whatever it is—and it takes them an hour to pick up the phone. Or a day. Or a week. Others fear interviews, or libraries, or the blank page that ultimately awaits all of us when we've finished our research.

For me, the worst demon is feeling irrelevant. I invariably spend the first few days of an assignment convinced that whatever I'm doing is futile and will never even coalesce into a story, much less a piece of journalism that people will want to read or that will have any effect upon the world. I suspect I'm not alone among magazine writers in this. It is virtually impossible for me to watch a wire service photographer filing his photos of the day's events, or a correspondent hammering out a 1,000-word

What interferes w or what do writers have to compete with?

story that will run in the next day's newspapers, without feeling that I'm getting left behind. From my perspective, there is a beautiful simplicity just to recording human events and transmitting them to the rest of the world. The information is guaranteed to be obsolete within days, if not hours, but that doesn't matter; you're already working on your next dispatch.

That sort of immediacy can leave magazine writers who are covering, say, the crisis in the Middle East, feeling hopelessly insecure. Their only refuge—their only hope of making their work compelling when it comes out a month or two later—is to write it so artfully that from the first paragraph the reader is caught like a fly in a Venus's-flytrap. When I first started writing, an old and very wise friend advised me to imagine my readers slumped on a couch with the television on. "Your job," he said, "is to make the first sentence of your article, and every sentence after that, even more distracting than the TV."

He was overstating his case, but not by much. One can pretty much assume that unlike newspaper readers, who primarily read for information, most of the people who pick up *Vanity Fair* or *Esquire* do not start out with a burning desire to know about last month's news stories. That's where the seduction comes in. How do you put down an article that begins, "In Afghanistan, nothing is ever what it seems. Including surrender," as Alex Perry's *Time* magazine article on the battle of Qala-i-Jangi did? Or Lauren Slater's article which begins, "Joe Rosen, plastic surgeon at the renowned Dartmouth-Hitchcock Medical Center, and by any account an odd man, has a cold. But then again, he isn't sure it's a cold. 'It could be Anthrax,' he says as he hurries to the car, beeper beeping, sleet sleeting, for it's a freezing New England midwinter day when all the world is white." Or William Langewiesche's superb article about EgyptAir Flight 990, which includes the passage: "The pilots were left to the darkness of the sky, whether to work together or to fight. I've often wondered what happened between those two men during the 114 seconds that remained of their lives. We'll never know."

A good magazine piece does not necessarily have to know. But it does have to inquire deeply, and it does have to describe vividly, and above all it does have to make one think. What would it be like in the cockpit of a doomed plane? What would have to happen in the life of a middle-aged pilot—not a terror-ist—to make him want to deliberately crash a commercial jet with 217 passengers on board? Asking such questions isn't going to help the poor people on that plane, but it may help others. It may expand our understanding of the world; it may illuminate something about airplanes or the laws of physics or why people commit the unthinkable; it may, in short, briefly allow us to exceed the direct experience of our lives.

At the opposite end of the spectrum from daily news—and equally important—are books. It's no coincidence that virtually every daily reporter I know aspires to write a book. A book is the last word, or at least an approximation of it, a work that comes out so long after the fact—hundreds of years afterwards, in some cases—that it has to offer a transcendent understanding of events in order to be relevant. A biography, for example, has to illumi-nate the psychological workings of its subject and, by extension, of humankind in general. A history book about a catastrophe has to explain not only what happened but also why—and, at least by implication, how to keep it from happening again.

The only problem with books is they take so damn long to write. That is where magazine writing comes in. After the September 11 terror attacks it became instantly and vitally important to under-stand the very complex relationship between the Muslim world and the United States. That is far beyond the scope of daily report-ing, so magazines stepped in. Both *Time* and *Newsweek* managed to get issues out within a couple of days of September 11, and at least one monthly—*Vanity Fair*—managed to add an extensive section on the attacks that appeared just three weeks later. The very diffi-cult task of these publications is to write something on deadline that at least aspires to—and occasionally achieves—something of lasting literary value. Not surprisingly, many important books start out as magazine articles. And this book collects the best examples of the year's magazine journalism in order to present them as a coherent whole—coherent not because of their topics, but because of their uniformly high quality.

Excellent magazine pieces have several things in common, it seems. First of all, to put it bluntly, they are all seductive and entertaining. I hesitate to use those words, given the grimness of some of the topics in this collection, but if we're going to read something that has already been covered ad nauseam in the daily press, it had better be damn hard to put down. An aspect of entertaining writing—I'm still cringing at the word—is quite simply that you feel like you're there, wherever "there" is. As with a good movie or novel, you can look up from a good magazine piece and be vaguely surprised that you're still safe on the couch in your living room. However superb *The New York Times* reporting was on the eight foreigners who were kidnapped in Ecuador in 2000, none of the *Times* readers felt as though they were there—that's not generally the job of the daily press. But it is always the job of a magazine journalist like Tom Junod, who hopes to coax readers into caring about a two-year-old kidnapping that will never, ever have a direct impact on their lives. "They worked in a seven-acre clearing, a nasty cut in the jungle cauterized against intrusion by a flimsy chain-link fence," writes Junod. "Outside the fence was the jungle, and on some days they worked and slept so hard that the only reason they knew it was there at all was that it got so freaking loud."

Another attribute of good magazine writing is that it broadly informs people about the world. You don't just learn that the plane went down; you learn why planes fly and why they crash and what happens when they pull out of a dive at more than Mach 1. (They break apart.) You learn how air traffic control works and how air disasters are investigated and how Muslims pray when they're about to die. The world is of such complexity that no one person can hope to know anything approaching a majority of things. It becomes the journalist's job to sift through the vast sea of human knowledge and to extract what seems useful and interesting and true. If the reader doesn't bite—if he simply doesn't care about the physics of flight—he's welcome to put the magazine down and continue watching TV. There's no helping the incurious, but then, there's little reason to try.

Finally, a truly great magazine piece erodes the illusion of psychological separateness that we are all tempted to hide behind. If there is one important task writers can perform, it is to promote the idea of a common humanity. I'm not a woman, I don't have a child; I'm certainly not responsible for anyone with muscular dystrophy. But that mattered little when I read Penny Wolfson's article about her son's struggle with the disease. All of human suffering, for me, was encapsulated in her description of how he stands up: "Ansel does not rise. He shifts sideways in the seat and pulls himself up heavily, propping his eighty pounds against the armrest for balance. . . . Actually he's sort of bent in half, with his hands still on the chair's joystick. There is a moment of imbalance. His feet are planted far apart, farther out than his hips, and he needs to bounce back and forth a few times to bring his feet together."

Where do people get the courage to face another day like that? Why don't they just give up? If I live into old age, I guess I'll find out, but in the meantime, Ansel and his mother may be two of the bravest people I've ever heard of. Their story makes me proud of the human race, gives me reason for optimism. If a child has the courage to do that, who knows what else is possible? And I would never have heard of him were it not for a magazine writer who chose to turn the tragic and the personal into something of universal value.

—Sebastian Junger

Acknowledgments

If you glance at the full list of National Magazine Award finalists at the back of this book, you may get the impression that for this edition of *The Best American Magazine Writing*, our third annual collection, the title is slightly misleading: The biggest story of the year (and possibly of our lifetimes) is treated only briefly in these pages.

Magazines did some of their finest work ever reporting on the September 11 terrorist attacks and their aftermath, lending context and perspective as the story unfolded. But the most extraordinary coverage spanned entire issues, which we obviously could not reproduce here. What we have included, however, is an enlightening and entertaining sample of the nearly 1,500 entries received for this year's National Magazine Awards, our industry's Oscars, which are sponsored by the American Society of Magazine Editors in association with the Columbia University Graduate School of Journalism.

Many thanks, of course, go to the writers and editors who crafted these pieces, and to the 200-odd editors who served as screeners and judges for the awards. From the opening of the very first submission packet to the scripting of the final citation, the awards process takes many long hours of reading and writing—but it never fails to reaffirm our faith in this medium. Keeping all the plates spinning, as ever, were Marlene Kahan, the up-early, up-late executive director of ASME, and her right and left hands, Andrew Rhodes and Stephanie Bukovac. Tom Goldstein, dean of the Columbia University Graduate School of Journalism, and his associate dean, Evan Cornog, provided valuable guidance and support. Meticulously tracking thousands of magazines and photocopied articles, longtime NMA director Robin Blackburn and her student helpers made sure the mammoth screening and judging operation went off without a hitch.

We are grateful to Daniel Menaker, our editor at HarperCollins, for enthusiastically adopting this project, and to our agent, David McCormick of Collins McCormick Literary Agency, for being ASME's champion. And we are indebted to Sebastian Junger, a frequent nominee and past NMA winner, who graciously agreed to share his marquee value by writing this volume's introduction.

Happy reading!

CYNDI STIVERS
President,
American Society of Magazine Editors
(2001–2002)

Contributors

KEN AULETTA has written the "Annals of Communications" column for *The New Yorker* since 1992. He is the author of eight books, including four national bestsellers, such as *Three Blind Mice: How the TV Networks Lost Their Way* and *Greed and Glory on Wall Street: The Fall of the House of Lehman;* and two national business bestsellers, *The Highwaymen: Warriors of the Information Superhighway* and *World War 3.0: Microsoft and Its Enemies.* Auletta has worked as the chief political correspondent for the *New York Post,* a staff writer and weekly columnist for the *Village Voice,* a contributing editor at *New York* Magazine, and weekly political columnist for the *New York Daily News.* He started writing for *The New Yorker* in 1977. Auletta has won numerous journalism awards, and has been selected as one of the twentieth century's top 100 business journalists by a distinguished national panel of peers.

E. L. DOCTOROW has been published in thirty languages. His novels include *Welcome to Hard Times, The Book of Daniel, Ragtime, Loon Lake, Lives of the Poets, World's Fair, Billy Bathgate,* and *The Waterworks.* Among his honors are the National Book Award, the National Book Critics Circle Award (twice), the PEN/Faulkner Award, the Edith Wharton Citation for Fiction, the William Dean Howells medal of the American Academy of Arts and Letters, and the presidentially conferred National Humanities Medal.

ANNE FADIMAN is the editor of *The American Scholar*. She is the author of *The Spirit Catches You and You Fall Down*, an account of cultural conflict between a Hmong refugee family and the American medical system, and *Ex Libris*, a collection of essays on books and reading. Fadiman has received a National Book Critics Circle Award for general nonfiction, a National Magazine Award for Feature Writing, a *Los Angeles Times* Book Award, a *Salon* Book Award, and a John S. Knight Fellowship in Journalism. She lives in rural western Massachusetts.

CAITLIN FLANAGAN lives in Los Angeles with her husband and children. She reviews books for *The Atlantic Monthly* and has worked as a college counselor.

JONATHAN FRANZEN was born in Western Springs, Illinois, in 1959, and grew up in Webster Groves, Missouri, a suburb of St. Louis. After graduating from Swarthmore College in 1981 he studied at the Freie Universität in Berlin as a Fulbright scholar and later worked in a seismology lab at Harvard University's Department of Earth and Planetary Sciences. In addition to winning a Whiting Writer's Award in 1998 and the American Academy's Berlin Prize in 2000, he has been named one of "Twenty Writers for the 21st Century" by *The New Yorker* and one of the "Best Young American Novelists" by *Granta*. Franzen is the author of *The Twenty-Seventh City*, *Strong Motion*, and *The Corrections*, winner of the National Book Award and *New York Times* Editors' Choice for 2001. He is a frequent contributor to *Harper's* Magazine and *The New Yorker*.

TOM JUNOD has written for *Esquire* and *GQ*. He lives in the Atlanta area with his wife, Janet, and their dogs, Hawk and Marco.

WILLIAM LANGEWIESCHE has been a correspondent for *The Atlantic Monthly* for over a decade and four of his articles have been finalists for National Magazine Awards. He has reported from South America, Asia, Africa, Europe, and the U.S., publishing pieces in *The New York Times*, *The New Yorker*, and many others. His years of work in the Middle East allowed him extensive contact with Islamic radicals, as did his tracking of the Algerian civil war, a conflict with Islamic roots. Langewiesche has published three books, *Cutting for Sign* (1995), *Sahara Unveiled: A Journey Across the Desert* (1996) and *Inside the Sky: A Meditation on Flight* (1998).

MARK LEVINE is a *Men's Journal* contributing editor who has also written frequently for *The New Yorker*. Levine's article "Killing Libby" appeared in the book *Wild Stories: The Best of "Men's Journal,"* published by Crown. He is the author of two award-winning books of poems, *Debt* and *Enola Gay*. He teaches poetry at the Iowa Writers' Workshop and divides his time between Iowa City and Brooklyn.

ALEX PERRY joined *Time* as a staff writer and travel editor in Hong Kong in February 2001. He now serves as the magazine's South Asia bureau chief, based in New Delhi, covering news across the region as well as Central Asia and Burma. A key member of *Time*'s coverage of the war in Afghanistan, Perry was the first reporter to reach Mazar-i-Sharif after it fell to the Northern Alliance. He was the only outside witness to the massacre of 300 Taliban at Mazar's Sultan Raziya School and broke the story of CIA agent Mike Spann's death in the prison uprising at Qala-i-Jangi. Perry also was the only reporter to stay inside the fort throughout the battle, providing eyewitness accounts of the uprising from the Alliance frontlines and from the positions of the American and British special forces. In March 2002, the Vietnam Veterans Memorial Fund honored Perry as the first-ever recipient of the Joseph L. Galloway War Correspondents Award, presented to a war correspondent for excellence in reporting while educating the public about conflicts throughout the world. Before joining *Time*, Perry was an editor for the news agency Agence France-Presse at its Asian headquarters in Hong Kong.

SAMANTHA POWER is the executive director of the Carr Center for Human Rights Policy at the John F. Kennedy School of Harvard University. She is a former Balkan war correspondent and a graduate of Harvard Law School. Power's book, *A Problem from Hell: America and the Age of Genocide* (Basic Books, March 2002) is a pathbreaking analysis of the last century of America's role in the history of genocide.

ANNA QUINDLEN joined *Newsweek* as a contributing editor in October 1999, succeeding the late Meg Greenfield. During the past twenty-five years, Quindlen's work has appeared in some of America's most influential newspapers and most widely-read magazines, and on both fiction and nonfiction bestseller lists. A columnist for *The New York Times* from 1981 to 1994, she became only the third woman in the paper's history to write a regular column for its influential Op-Ed page when she began the nationally-syndicated "Public and Private" in 1990. A collection of those columns, *Thinking Out Loud*, was published by Random House in 1993 and was on *The New York Times* bestseller list for more than three months. In 1992, Quindlen was awarded the Pulitzer Prize for commentary.

TERRENCE RAFFERTY has been *GQ*'s critic-at-large since 1997. Before that he was a staff writer at *The New Yorker* for ten years, contributing reviews and essays on movies and books. His work has also appeared in *Sight and Sound*, *The Atlantic Monthly*, *The Village Voice*, *The Nation*, *Film Quarterly*, *Film Comment*, *Vogue*,

The Boston Phoenix, Threepenny Review, Newsday, and *The New York Times.* In 1987, Rafferty was awarded a John Simon Guggenheim Memorial Fellowship for film criticism. In 1996 and 1997 he was the McGraw Professor of Writing at Princeton University. Rafferty's essays have appeared in many anthologies and college textbooks, including *Best Movie Writing 1999, Princeton Anthology of Writing, Cinema Nation, The A List,* and the Norton Critical Edition of E. M. Forster's *Howards End.* A collection of his writings on film, *The Thing Happens,* was published by Grove Press in 1993.

STEVE RUSHIN joined *Sports Illustrated* as a reporter after graduating from Marquette University in 1988. Within three years, at age twenty-five, he became the youngest senior writer on the *SI* staff. He currently writes the weekly column, "Air and Space." Born in Chicago, Rushin grew up in Bloomington, Minnesota, watching baseball and football games at Metropolitan Stadium, where he sold hot dogs and soft drinks to Twins and Vikings fans. Rushin has since moved up to the big leagues and now travels the world covering sporting events ranging from monster truck racing to the Olympics. His personal account of ice golfing in Greenland at fifteen degrees below zero was selected for *The Best American Travel Writing 2000.*

LEE SIEGEL was born in the Bronx, New York, in 1957 and graduated magna cum laude from Columbia University in 1984, with honors in comparative literature. He also holds a master's degree and a master's of philosophy from Columbia. Siegel is a writer for *Harper's* Magazine, a contributing editor of *The New Republic* and *ARTnews,* and has written for every distinguished magazine in the country. His essays, articles, reviews and reportage on literature, art, film, politics and culture have appeared in *The Atlantic Monthly, The New Yorker, Slate, The Nation, Dissent, Doubletake,*

Commonweal, Tikkun, the *Radical History Review, The New York Times Book Review, Newsday, The Daily News,* and *The Forward.* He is currently at work on essays for *Vanity Fair, The New York Review of Books,* and *Bookforum.*

LAUREN SLATER has a master's degree in psychology from Harvard University and a doctorate from Boston University. Her work was chosen for *The Best American Essays/Most Notable Essays* volumes of 1994, 1996, 1997, 1998, and 1999. Slater is the winner of the 1993 *New Letters* Literary Award in creative non-fiction and of the 1994 *Missouri Review* Award. She is the author of *Love Works Like This* (2002), *Lying* (chosen by *Entertainment Weekly* as one of the top ten nonfiction books of 2000), *Prozac Diary* (1999), and *Welcome to My Country* (1997). Slater lives with her family in Massachusetts.

JEFFREY STEINGARTEN is food critic at *Vogue* magazine and an occasional contributor to *Slate.* He is the author of the best-selling *The Man Who Ate Everything,* and of the forthcoming *It Must've Been Something I Ate.* Steingarten trained to become a food writer at Harvard College, Harvard Law School, M.I.T., and *The Harvard Lampoon.* "Salt Chic," Steingarten's essay in this collection, has also received awards from the James Beard Foundation and the International Association of Culinary Professionals. On Bastille Day, 1994, the French Republic made him a Chevalier in the Order of Merit for his writing on French gastronomy. As the man who ate everything, Chevalier Steingarten has no favorite food or flavor. His preferred eating destinations, however, are Memphis, Paris, Alba, Chengdu—and his loft in New York City.

AMY WALLACE is a senior writer at *Los Angeles Magazine.* For eleven years, she was a staff writer at the *Los Angeles Times* where she covered state politics, higher education, and the entertainment industry. Wallace's work has also appeared in *Vanity Fair*, *The Nation*, and *The New York Times*.

MICHAEL WOLFF writes "This Media Life," a weekly column about the media for *New York* Magazine, where he has taken on such figures as Rupert Murdoch, Michael Eisner, Barry Diller, Michael Ovitz, Tina Brown, Tim Russert, and Bill O'Reilly. He also writes regularly about national politics and extensively covered the 2000 presidential race and the impeachment of President Clinton. Wolff is the author of the bestselling book *Burn Rate*, a tale of the birth of the Internet industry and the rise and fall of Wolff New Media, the Web business he founded. Wolff began his career as a journalist with *The New York Times* and has written for many national publications. He is the author of *White Kids*, and *Where We Stand*, which became a multipart PBS series hosted by former Secretary of Labor Robert Reich.

PENNY WOLFSON has a B.A. and an M.F.A. in nonfiction writing from Sarah Lawrence College. A former reporter and editor, she has published essays about disability in *The Atlantic Monthly*, *The New York Times*, *Exceptional Parent*, and the literary magazines *Iris* and *Kaleidoscope*. Wolfson's book *Moonrise* will be released by St. Martin's Press in the spring of 2003.

THE BEST
AMERICAN
MAGAZINE
WRITING

2002

Tom Junod

Gone

The first American they met when they came out of the jungle? That's easy. It was a shrink. Of course it was. They spent 141 days with guns stuck up their asses. They were in dire and sweltering and abject captivity. They ate practically nothing but cat food and rice unless the occasional rat or snake happened by. They all lost significant percentages of their own precious mass, starting with body fat and eating into muscle. They all grew these huge, luxuriant beards. They had pieces of their flesh rotting away. They itched to the point of insanity. They all stunk to high heaven. Who else is going to meet them but the fellow dispatched to make them feel better about themselves? Who else is going to meet them—in Ecuador, of all places!—but the American hired to preach what they, as Americans, presumably were dying to hear, which was that healing and closure were just around the corner? Luckily, they didn't have to talk to him if they didn't want to. Luckily, they got to go home, to the little town of Gold Hill, Oregon, before they met with the counseling profession. When they got there, they couldn't tie their shoes; they found themselves getting lost on streets they had known most of their lives; they had to go to doctors because of the weird microbial shit that was still crawlingly alive inside of them; they found themselves crying when they looked at the sky and crying when they watched television and crying for no good reason at all; they were scared to be alone in the woods; and finally they looked around at the homes whose memory had sustained them against the punishing vagaries of time and distance and said to themselves the dread, unspeakable words: I don't even belong here. And you know what? The shrinks weren't too bad, once you got to know them. They tried hard. But you know what else? You know the shrinks' own secret? They were just like everybody else. They just wanted to know what happened, because they hadn't been there. They just wanted to hear the story. They just wanted to know what it was like.

·　　·　　·

But what *was* it like? Well, the thing was, they were all from the same town, the same company—Erickson Air-Crane Inc., of Central Point, Oregon—and they all went through the same basic experience, but it was very different for all three of them. Arnie Alford was very emotional about it. Jason Weber was very angry. And Steve Derry—well, Steve was like someone who looks into the terrible teeming heart of all existence and then has to behold that image whenever he looks at anything else.

What was it like for Arnie? The short answer is that it was like the episode with the *gusano*, because the episode with the *gusano* was when they all realized not only that they were in the jungle but that the jungle was somehow in *them*. *Gusano* means "worm," by the way. They were nine days in, nine days of the eventual 141. They were kidnapped on October 12, 2000, plucked in the wee hours from the clearing in the Ecuadoran jungle where they worked on Erickson's helicopters. They had been marched through the jungle at gunpoint. They slept on the ground until nine days in, when they were given some material for hammocks. That first night in his hammock, Arnie felt something nail him in the back of the neck, more like a slap than a bite. He figured he got stung and that whatever stung him left its stinger in. He tried to squeeze it out, but it wasn't going anywhere. Then it began swelling up. Then it grew into a lump on his neck. Then, after about a month, the lump began to move. He showed it to his captors, this band of self styled guerrillas who called themselves "the ninjas of the jungle." Ah, *gusano,* they said. The head ninja, the commandant, who was nothing but a freaking witch doctor, tried to fashion some sort of jungle remedy by blowing the smoke of his constant cigarette into a piece of gauze, then applying the gauze to Arnie's neck. When that didn't work, he just blew smoke directly into the lump, and when that didn't work, well, the commandant just squeezed as hard as he could, until finally this *creature* popped out, writhing on his finger, two knuckles long and alive. And that's what the kidnapping was like for Arnie Alford, if only because out of all the hostages— all eight of them—Arnie had, shall we say, the most symbiotic relationship with the jungle, and because it was through Arnie's poor trespassed person that the whole terrible situation revealed an almost miraculous capacity for getting worse.

Steve Derry? What was it like for Steve? Well, Steve is the quietest of all the guys from Gold Hill—he rarely greets the most outrageous or unexpected turn of fortune with anything more than "I'll be darned"—but also the funniest, so when you ask him, say, what monkey tastes like, he'll pause a few beats, and then answer in his Oregon deadpan, "Monkey," and then start laughing, a laugh so infectiously bitter and sardonic that it sounds almost sinister. But that's what captivity was like for Steve: It was like the taste of monkey. It was nonpareil. It was sui generis. He's an outdoorsman, Steve is, a hunter and fisherman, and he was used to spending long stretches of time alone in the splendor of nature, but he saw and heard shit in that jungle that he had never heard or seen before, and hopes never to hear or see again. A sloth, for example: He had the chance to see it close up, because the ninjas shook it down from its branch, then beat it to death, right in front of the hostages, as a display of their power. Then they ate it for dinner. It tasted like . . . sloth.

And Jason Weber? What was it like for Jason Weber? At twenty nine, he was the youngest, the angriest, the most impatient and reckless and conflicted, but it's easy to figure out what it was like for him because he wrote it down. He took a notebook with him and a pen, and the second night of his captivity, when they stopped in the jungle and set up an impromptu camp, he started writing: "Day Two. Heard helos [helicopters] again this morning. Bugs are every-where. We are camping in the same spot again tonight; tomorrow they told us we will go to another camp. They told us everyone knows we are gone and they are talking about money to get us back. So I guess we'll finally see how much we're worth. The worst thing about this whole ordeal is that I worry about my wife and kids. I know my wife is probably worried to death, I just wish I could tell her that I am fine. You never realize how much you need them until you can't have them. My little girl will probably forget who I am but as long as I get to see her again I will be sure to make up for it. Getting sad, time to change the subject."

And yet . . . it's still hard for any of them to say what it was like in a single anecdote, in a single story or image or diary entry. It's hard for them to say what it was like because of what they learned on their first day of freedom, which was that for all of them to live, one of them had to die.

·   ·   ·

The moon was full October 12 in the year 2000. None of them knew that at the time, or maybe they knew but didn't care. Who cares about a full moon? Who cares that rainstorms organize themselves around its waxing and waning; that in the absolute enclosure of jungle darkness, the night of the full moon is the only night that permits even a tingle of light; and that the full moon allows the movement of human traffic along jungle trails? Later, they would learn this by heart, but for now they cared no more for the significance of the full moon than they did for the cacophony of frogs that welled up at night out of the darkness. They had not come to Ecuador to commune with nature. They were workers; they'd come to work, but not so much for money—no one's getting rich working for Erickson—as for freedom. Three weeks on, three weeks off: That was the deal with Erickson. Three weeks working anywhere from twelve to eighteen hours every day on the giant Erickson helicopters that hoisted heavy equipment to an oil platform seventeen miles away in the jungle in exchange for three weeks with their families or three weeks hunting and fishing. Arnie Alford had seventeen years with the company, Steve Derry eleven, and Jason Weber almost six. They worked in a seven acre clearing, a nasty cut in the jungle cauterized against intrusion by a flimsy chain link fence. Inside the fence was something like civilization—a few barracks-style buildings, some campers, an office, a mess hall, a shack housing computers and radio equipment. Outside the fence was the jungle, and on some days they worked and slept so hard that the only reason they knew it was there at all was that it got so freaking loud.

Arnie was the first to wake up, or the first to be awakened. It was four in the morning. He was fifteen days into his tour, which meant he was six days away from home. He was forty-one years old, with a wife, Mindy, and a ten-year-old daughter, Kaitlin. He was in one of the campers. He was rooming with an Ecuadoran named John, who was in charge of the radio shack. He heard some banging, thought it was the cooks in the kitchen. Then the banging came to his door. John opened it; there was a guy standing in front of him wearing a ski mask and combat fatigues and carrying an AK-47. They followed him out into the clearing, where more guys with guns were rousting more people, and where everybody who worked in the compound was being herded together in the dust and the gravel. Arnie was the only

American at first. The rest were Ecuadorans, locals. The guy who seemed to be leading the guys with guns demanded that John give him the key to the radio shack. John said he didn't have it, so the guy broke down the door and then began smashing everything in sight, the computers, the radios, everything shattering and popping and making sounds like gunshots. Then the guy came out and said something in Spanish to one of the Ecuadorans, who said in response, "Oh, shit." "What did he say?" Arnie asked. "What did he say?" Now, you have to understand: Arnie weighed 230 pounds, on a frame of about five eight. He lifted weights, he came from a logging family, he worked on a fishing boat, he was extremely emotional, he was a sweet guy with a bad temper, he was someone you absolutely wanted for you and not against you—but he has a high voice, especially when he's excited, and he was excited now. "What did he say, what did he say?" Arnie said, and the Ecuadoran looked at him and said, "He wants all the gringos."

Jason was rooming with Steve in one of the barracks. He heard the banging, and he, like Arnie, thought it was coming from the kitchen, but unlike Arnie he was going to get up and tell them to shut the hell up. Then he heard what he thought were gunshots and someone knocking on his door, shouting, weirdly, inexplicably, "Taxi, taxi." He opened the door and saw a guy with a bandanna covering his face. He looked at Steve, who was his boss, and said, "Um, there's a guy here with a machine gun, and he says we should go with him." By the time they saw Arnie out in the clearing, another Erickson employee, Dennis Corrin, a fifty-two-year-old pilot from New Zealand, was standing next to him, and the men with the guns were in the process of herding the locals onto the porch of the office building, until the four gringos were standing together at gunpoint—standing revealed under the moon. Were they scared? Well, of course they were, but more than that, they were lonely. They were homesick instantly, cosmically. They were gringos, and they all thought they were going to die right there.

They never shook it, that feeling of loneliness. They didn't shake it when the men with the guns, much to Arnie's and Jason's and Steve's queasy relief, led them back to their bunks and had them pack bags—some clothes, some socks and underwear, a toothbrush and toothpaste, boots instead of tennis shoes—for the long march. They didn't shake it when they were herded into the back of a stolen pickup, along with a French pilot and a mechanic the gunmen had found in the camp, and the pickup zoomed out of the compound. There was silence in the truck as it banged and raced down a raddled jungle road trying to beat the dawn. Arnie and Steve and Jason didn't talk. What could they say? They didn't know anything. They didn't even know who had captured them, for although their captors called themselves guerrillas, they boasted no cause or affiliation. There were two of them in the back of the pickup guarding the six hostages. One pressed his gun hard into Steve's ribs, and when Steve finally complained, said, "Oh, excuse me," in English. The other stole their watches, threatening by universal gesture to cut their throats. The hostages didn't even think of trying to escape . . . or rather, they thought of it, they made *plans* for it, especially when the pickup took a turn on two wheels and nearly turned over, but that's *all* they did. And do you know why? Because they wanted to live. That was the first thing that they found out at gunpoint. That was the first of their discoveries. Hell, in the back of the pickup, that's all they knew, and all they needed to know: They just wanted to live. . . .

The truck stopped at a heliport and met other trucks. By the light of the moon, the kidnappers had scoured other camps in the jungle and stolen four other men who worked for the oil companies. There was German Scholz from Chile. There was Jorge Rodriguez from Argentina. There was Dave Bradley from Wyoming. And there was Ron Sander from Missouri. They didn't say anything, either. They were all stuffed into a Puma helicopter that the French pilot knew how to handle and the French mechanic knew how to service. Along with about thirteen kidnappers, eight hostages sat in the hold. They had no idea where they were going. They had no idea how long they would be gone. All they knew was that the sun was coming up over the jungle as the helicopter rose over the trees and that what they saw below them was endless and unintelligible and unimaginable and five thousand miles from home.

· · ·

But what was it like? You see, Lisa Weber hears it, too. They all do—the wives, the families—because it became their story when it became Jason's and Arnie's and Steve's. People want to know what they were doing, what they were thinking, when they found out. Well, this is what Lisa thought: that she was getting flowers. Jason liked to send them to her when he went away for Erickson, because he was away a lot. Of course, Lisa knew he had that in him, that restlessness, from the moment she met him. He was a marine. He courted her from a ship somewhere out at sea. They'd met at a country bar in southern California. Anaheim. Jason walked up to her and asked her to dance. He was from Oklahoma, so he knew what he was doing out on that dance floor. And he was cute—oh, boy, was he cute—dark, with short hair, not too big, but strong, with a presence about him, an energy. When he walked her out to her car, he just started talking, and Lisa was like, Will you just ask me for my number already? He did and then he was gone. He shipped out in three months, but then his letters began to arrive, from all over the world. Jason had grown up without a father. He felt he'd never gotten a good chance, and now he wanted to have a family so he could give a good chance to his kids. When he came home, he asked her to marry him. They were married in 1994. Jason started at Erickson in 1995. They had baby girl Jessica in 1996, and baby girl Kaitlyn in 1999. Jessica was Daddy's little girl. Not that she could keep Jason home any more than Lisa could.

Sometimes Lisa's girlfriends would ask her, Don't you miss Jason? And she was like, Sure, I miss him . . . but she was independent. Just as long as he loved her and loved his girls—and that's why, when she started getting those phone calls on October 12, she got it into her head about flowers. She had gotten a message that Connie called, from Erickson. Jason was friends with Buck, and Connie was Buck's wife. So Lisa called Connie and said, "What's wrong?" and when Connie said, Oh, nothing, she just wanted to talk, that's when Lisa started thinking something was up, because although she liked Connie, they just didn't have that kind of relationship. And when Connie said, Oh, by the way, can I have your new work address? Lisa was like, Okay, I get it. And when the receptionist phoned her, saying that a fellow named Buck was waiting for her in the lobby, Lisa was like, Isn't that sweet—Jason asked Buck to deliver them in person. And when Buck met her and began hugging her, Lisa was like, well, she was like, *Whaaat?*—because she saw the other Erickson people waiting there and figured that's an awful lot of manpower for a dozen roses.

•   •   •

A man goes to take a dump in the woods. He's been out in the woods for days now, on a hunting trip with his friends, and after some initial reluctance he has taken quite a liking to voiding his bowels in the great out of doors. Indeed, he has come to make a show of his gusto in this department, so much so that his hunting buddies decide to teach him a lesson. They gut a rabbit and pile the entrails in the hole over which their friend reliably squats. Sure enough, he repairs to his place in the woods, and some time later he returns, moving slowly, with a chastened waddle. "You wouldn't believe what happened," he says. "I shit my guts out, out there. Luckily, though, with a sharp stick and the grace of God, I got it all back in."

That was Dennis Corrin's. Dennis, the pilot from New Zealand, had a joke about everything, even the shit sticks, and by the time he told it, on the fourth night of their captivity—Day 4—well, they needed to hear a joke about shit sticks. They were forced to use them, you see. During the day, they beat the trail for hours at a time in rotten socks, drinking sugar water for strength, and during the night, they had to ask the ninjas to go with them when it came time to piss or shit in the woods. They had to ask for permission. They had to take their sticks and dig their holes and squat trembling while some asshole with a machine gun stood there smoking a cigarette. Back in the tent, they weren't allowed to talk; every time one of them spoke in a full voice, a ninja would shine a flashlight in his face and bark, *"Silencio!"* They learned to speak in a continual whisper, and so, when Dennis told the one about the shit stick and they all just started freaking *howling* in the middle of the jungle, they all figured they were going to get shot. . . .

They didn't, and the joke became the beginning of their . . . well, it's hard to know what to call it. Their resistance? Their rebellion? All those words sound so grand, when what really happened was so . . . incremental. They just began talking. They could tell one another what they had learned. They could start to figure things out. They could get their bearings.

Once the helicopter had disgorged the hostages, the ninjas had directed the Frenchmen to go back in the air and dump it a mile away in an effort to put the army off their trail. Nobody ever saw the Frenchmen again. They had gotten away. The ninjas never talked about them. There were eight of them now: the New Zealander, the Chilean, the Argentine, and the five Americans. During the day, they could hear planes and helicopters flying overhead, looking for them. From the ground, they couldn't see the sky through the canopy of trees; from the sky, they couldn't be seen. At first, of course, they wanted to be found; then they didn't. The ninjas had said that in any encounter with the army, they were under orders to shoot the hostages before they defended themselves. It was the first lesson in the mutability of hope: The planes and helicopters that they thought represented hope came to stand for throbbing terror. They decided that their only chance for survival was to preserve themselves, physically and psychologically, for the long haul. One of the ninjas told Jorge, the Argentine, that the last time they did this the negotiations had lasted six months. They could already sense the wasting of their flesh, and so on the morning of Day 6— two days after they mustered the courage to laugh at Dennis's joke—the guys from Gold Hill started doing sit ups and push ups. They wanted to see what they could get away with. The ninjas looked at them suspiciously, and then one of them tried doing exercises of his own, in both emulation and opposition. . . .

That's the one they called G. I. Jane. The one who'd shouted "Taxi" at Steve and Jason's door, they called him Taxi. The one who wore the ski mask was Ski Mask. The grizzled hard case with the red beard and the gold teeth always armed with a shotgun was Shotgun. There was also Wing Nut, who had big ears and was sometimes kind to them, and the Girl, who looked like a girl. There was Scarneck. The bandit who stole their watches was Watch-stealer, though later he morphed into Mini-Me because of his shameless adulation of the commandant, Qaddafi. Qaddafi was the one who made speeches about Ronald Reagan's criminality in Nicaragua and read revolutionary texts while the rest of them read self-help books in Spanish. The other commandant was Fernando, who was in charge of the radio. They packed a radio around, with a motorcycle battery. They had left a message behind, with the frequency the radio would be tuned to, they said. Someone from the oil companies would contact them, they said. . . .

The ninjas of the jungle. What a joke. They were stupid, they were dirty, they were venal, they were cruel, they were greedy, they stunk, and they lied. Without their guns, they were nothing. Without their guns, they were the fucking Girl Scouts. That's what Jason thought, anyway. That's what he obsessed about; that's what he wrote in his journal: I've been kidnapped by the Girl Scouts. Jason was a goddamn marine, a highly trained soldier from the U.S. of A. He had been to Somalia and Sudan. When the ninjas gave each of them their bowls—the bowls they were supposed to eat from and bathe with—Jason wrote LICK ME on his where his name was supposed to be. When he went to piss or squat, *two* ninjas went to guard him because he had no respect for them, and they knew it. But that was Jason's problem—he had no respect for anybody, early on. Oh, sure, he had respect for Steve and Arnie and Dennis, but the other guys? The guys from Schlumberger and from Helmerich & Payne? Jorge was a scaredy-cat. German was old—he was sixty—and he was lazy. Dave Bradley was forty-one years old, smart as hell, but he'd been to college and had nothing to show for it. Jason had no time for him.

As for the other guy, Ron Sander—well, Jason didn't know what to make of him. He was the oldest of the Americans, fifty-four, with silver hair and a little potbelly and bad legs. He was too quiet, too *peaceful.* When he talked, he talked about fishing with his wife back home on the Lake of the Ozarks, in Missouri. When Jason went off on German for pissing near the tarp—when German burned a hole in the tarp with his incessant cigarette and Jason said that if German's cigarette ever affected him again, he would stick it up his ass—Ron pulled him aside and told him to calm down, that they were all in this together. It was as if he'd decided to go through life without an enemy, and once he even asked Jason why he hated the ninjas so much. "They haven't done anything to you," he said. Oh, well, Jason thought: Maybe Ron was just scared.

Was Jason scared? No, never. The ninjas didn't deserve his fear. In fact, what bothered him, what ate him up, was something like the opposite of fear: the knowledge that he was better than his captors; the knowledge that he could get away from them if it weren't for Steve and Arnie and Ron and all the rest. It was something they all knew: that there was a hole in the jungle big enough for one man. One man could get away, if he was careless of the retribution that would surely be visited on those he left behind, and so early on, when Jason was hiking up a muddy trail and his guard fell facedown in the mud with a pack on his back and was helpless and all Jason had to do was break the guy's neck with a forearm and run into the trees—what Jason did instead, what he *had* to do, for the other seven, was help him up.

·　　·　　·

They were all brought up to believe. The girls. The ladies. The wives. Mindy Alford and Lisa Weber—they were all brought up to be well-mannered and very. . . well, nice. Lee Ramage seemed to appreciate that. Lee Ramage was the chief operating officer of Erickson Air-Crane Inc. He had a weekly meeting for the families of the hostages. Mindy Alford and Lisa Weber always went. So did Mike Derry and his wife, Edna. Mike wasn't like his brother Steve—he wasn't quiet. And he wasn't like Lisa and Mindy, either—he wasn't nice. He always got in Lee's face. He always wanted to know when Erickson was going to do something, and that made Lee nervous. He started twisting his ring when Mike Derry was around. You see, they were all supposed to be calm and patient; they were all supposed to be playing by the rules. At least, that's what the guy Lee brought in from Control Risks Group said. Each of the three companies whose employees had been kid-napped had hired a company to negotiate their release, and CRG was the company hired by Erickson, or rather by Erickson's insur-ance company. On October 27, a CRG negotiator spoke at the family meeting. There had not yet been any radio contact with the kidnappers, but he was very confident, very reassuring; he had done this before. Indeed, what he wanted to stress to Mindy and Lisa and Mike was that kidnapping had become a business in countries like Ecuador and that, like any business, it followed cer-tain rules and conventions. The first was that the hostages were the kidnappers' only assets, and so they would not be harmed.

They were too valuable. The second was that the kidnappers would try to use time against them—so the families had to be patient. They were not to contact the media—that would only make the kidnappers hold out for more. They were not to ask about money, for negotiations were almost like a game, and only companies with experience in the field—companies like CRG—knew how to play. The families just had to have faith in CRG, because CRG had never lost a hostage. They just had to believe.

Did Lisa and Mindy believe? Of course they did. Even Mike Derry believed at first. They had to. Their loved ones were hostages in a foreign land. How could they not believe in a company—an entire industry—built on the faith that all hostages come home alive?

. . .

To look at their calendars, to look at their notes and journals, you'd think that things started moving quickly for them once they got settled in the jungle. You'd think that there was improvement once the ninjas and the negotiators started, well, negotiating. On Day 9—October 20—they reached what they all called Camp One, which means that they didn't have to sleep on the ground anymore. They received some supplies, some fresh underwear, and some rope and black canvas for hammocks. On Day 21, the first day of November, the ninjas had German Scholz write a letter that included their VHF radio frequency and sent the letter to the Ecuadoran capital of Quito. On Day 23, negotiators made radio contact after one of the ninjas had scurried up a tree to hang the antenna. On Day 26, negotiations started. On Day 27, the ninjas asked "proof of life" questions—questions devised by the hostages' families requesting intimate information only they would know—and the answers were transmitted back home. On Day 29, the ninjas made their demand for ransom, and when the negotiators responded with *laughter,* literal *laughter,* they threatened to show their power by blowing up sections of Ecuador's oil pipeline. On Day 30, they all went to Camp Two, which had more food and more supplies than anything they had known so far in the jungle. On Day 32, the bomb squad was chosen, and on Day 37—November 17, 2000—the bomb squad was dispatched to do its work.

But the fact was, once they were settled into camps of provisional permanence, their hammocks became their prisons, and time itself—the saturation of time—became their enemy. They were sentenced to their hammocks. They *had* to be in them by sunset and couldn't leave them—except for relief, by request—until dawn. The night came, and they . . . oh, they would do anything to delay the coming of the night. They would have topics of discussion. They would have lectures. They would discuss the English monarchy with Dennis and trapshooting with Ron. They would discuss the universe with Dave Bradley. They would try to remember the speed of light and the distance between the earth and the sun and try to calculate how long it took for the sun's light to reach the earth. They'd do the calculations in their heads or on little scraps of paper. The answers were important to them because they hadn't seen the sun since they were kidnapped. The answers were important because they were starting to forget what they knew, they were starting to age in jungle time. Then the night would come anyway, so black under the seal of the jungle that they couldn't see the hands in front of their faces. They couldn't see the guards, and the guards couldn't see them. Everybody was jittery at night. The guards would shine flashlights in their faces to make sure they were there. They would tug the ropes of the hammocks. It didn't matter, because sleep was difficult anyway. Well, Steve couldn't sleep especially. He was trying to figure out ways to stop counting the days and wound up counting the minutes instead. He would listen to the rest of the guys fall asleep, one by one, and wonder how, night after night, Ron Sander would be the first to start snoring. He would listen to the changing of the guards. They changed every two hours, and sometimes he would make it through three changes before drifting off in his caul. He would just lay there thinking until he was thinking about thinking itself—thinking that thinking's not good. Thinking that men weren't meant to think so much when they have nothing good to think about—when the thoughts are unleavened by hope. And Steve had lost hope. They all had. They'd had to lose the conventional form of hope in order to survive, and so the hopes that started flowering in hope's absence became more and more exotic.

They pinned a lot of hopes on the bomb squad, for instance; they *rooted* for the bomb squad to bring Ecuador to a standstill, because maybe then someone would take the ninjas seriously and negotiate. And on Day 31, their first night in Camp Two, when Steve was trying to sleep with the blessing of the full moon, he heard something in the jungle, something coming from a long way off, the roar of the most pissed-off creature in the entire world. The next morning, he asked one of the ninjas what it was. "*Tigre*," the ninja said, and showed him its paw print, nine inches across, and the tree it had used as a scratching post, stripped of bark twelve feet from the ground. What's it like, being held captive in the jungle? This is what it's like: Hope starts to look like the tiger that stalks the camp, investing each dread night with the hope that there will be one fewer ninja in the morning.

•   •   •

They received proof of life on November 7. Day 27. That's what Mindy Alford wrote that day in her journal: "2:52, Kurt [from Erickson] called with proof of life." Mindy had asked for the name of one of Arnie's legendary dogs (Jagger) and the kind of car Arnie was restoring in the garage ('55 Chevy). Lisa Weber had asked . . . well, Lisa'd had a tough time with the proof-of-life questions. The negotiator from CRG had asked for ten, and Lisa's first involuntary reaction was that she didn't know ten. Mindy, of course, knew ten; she and Arnie were so *close*. They cooked together and canned vegetables they grew together in the garden. Lisa and Jason weren't like that, and so when Lisa was asked for personal questions—and wound up coming up with one about a baby gift they had sent Jason's friend Steve—she began to wonder if she knew her husband at all.

It was almost like being in the woods herself. It was almost like being in the jungle. She was in the dark all the time. Well, once the proof of life came back, she knew Jason was alive, but that was it. Everything else she had to ask for, beg for, plead for, from CRG or Erickson. She even had to beg and plead when she heard rumors that the kidnappers had made their demand. Finally, she was like, "You've asked me to trust you; you have to trust me. What is it?"

On November 17, Day 37, she found out. The ransom for her husband and seven other hostages was $80 million.

And that's when she knew that Jason wasn't coming home for the holidays.

•　　　•　　　•

The jungle was full of wonders. It was alive, and they were in the middle of it. There was a bird that sounded exactly human—that laughed in human tones. There was an insect that perched on their lips at night, breathing their breath. There were leaf-cutter ants whose jaws cut holes in their T-shirts. There was an animal they ate that had the tail of a rat, the body of a rabbit, the face of a pig. They also ate snake, turtle, jungle pig, jungle turkey, armadillo, tapir, and caiman, which is a kind of alligator, and which, Jason wrote in his journal, is "all white meat." They ate what they figured was piranha, scant and bony and toothsome. They ate monkey and sloth, and one morning, when they went to bathe, they saw, grinning at them, the head of the monkey they had eaten the night before.

They had been in Camp Two eighteen days when Arnie started to itch. Camp Two was dirty. They were dirty. Two days before,

Qaddafi had squeezed the *gusano* out of Arnie's neck, but now it was Arnie's belly button that itched. The next day, it began to emit some oil. The day after that, it began to hurt. The pain spread to his stomach. He was racked by contractions and could not get out of his hammock to take a piss. The next day—Day 51, the first day of December—Arnie passed into delirium with the pain. By nightfall, he was writhing and sweating and jabbering in his hammock, begging to go home. Ron asked one of the guards for a flashlight and used it to look into Arnie's navel. "Oh, God," he said. What it was, it was fucking *maggots*. They were deep in Arnie's belly button, thirty or forty of them, scurrying around. They were eating him alive, as though his flesh were rotten, as though he were already dead. Qaddafi began yelling at them, asking why they had let this go so far. He tried to pick out the maggots with his fingers, but they were in too deep. He tried flushing Arnie's navel with mouthwash, then whiskey, then gasoline, and then went back in with the point of his knife. Weight-lifting Arnie, tenor-voiced Arnie: Arnie was bucking in his hammock, crying, "Just let me go home, just let me go home," while the ninjas held him by the legs and Jason and Steve held his hands. "*Mi amigo necesita ayuda,*" Jason said to Qaddafi—trying to tell him that Arnie needed to go to the hospital—but Qaddafi kept saying, "One more day, one more day." In the morning, a ninja went to a local farm and came back with some veterinary medicine. Qaddafi put some in Arnie's navel, then took out a syringe from the first aid kit and shot him up with an antibiotic as thick as peanut butter. Five days later, when he gave Arnie a second injection and evicted the last of the maggots with his fingernails, Jason and Steve figured that he had never intended to take Arnie to the hospital at all—that all along he'd been giving Arnie one more day, either to get better or to be killed for convenience.

That was December 5: Day 55. Two days later, the bomb squad blew up a section of the oil pipeline. There was another bomb on December 9—"We are very happy they finally blew something up," Jason wrote in his journal—and another on the twelfth, with a full moon in between. The last explosion killed eight Ecuadorans on a bus, but what Jason recorded the next day was a kind of celebration among his captors: "Day 63. They are giving each other wacky haircuts. The Watchstealer has only got the top of his head cut and has hair all around the sides, while [another] has all the hair but the back shaved off. Juta [another ninja] cut his hair today and has a V on the top coming down the front. I guess it is some kind of jungle fashion statement. Heard they blew up pipeline again. Dream last night of escape."

· · ·

On Christmas morning 2000, Jessica Weber, four years old, found a letter delivered by Santa. It was signed "Daddy," and, oh, you should have seen her face light up. Of course, her father didn't write it; Lisa did. She had to—Jessica was getting accustomed to her father's absence. She had stopped asking Lisa where he was and why he wasn't home. She didn't talk about him anymore.

· · ·

Day 75. Christmas. Arnie so depressed he can't talk—thoughts of home like maggots of the mind. Steve's hand starting to rot with fungus. Dave Bradley starts to say what day it is, starts in with season's greetings, but who wants to hear that shit? When Jason hands out the candy he's been saving, he does so without a celebratory word. The ninjas are drunk and singing. The night before, they selected the new bomb squad; then half of them got drunk and shot their guns. Today, it's the other half. Festive breakfast drink of crushed banana, tree bark, and cloves.

Day 76. Jorge goes out with a guard and a shit stick into the jungle, and suddenly the ninjas are shouting and running toward the creek that serves as the boundary of the latrine. When they bring him back, he's shaking like a leaf, trembling all over—the guard says he tried to escape. Aw, he didn't try to escape—he doesn't have it in him. But the young captain who organizes the bomb squad orders him put in chains. Then night comes, and everybody else gets put in chains, except for Ron and German, who are too old to run. You want to know how low you can go? This is the lowest. They've taken everything now, not just freedom but also dignity. You're in chains. You're a captive, and that's all you are.

Day 77. Something's up. The bomb squad that went out last night comes back. Must have seen something they didn't like.

Day 78. Forty-eight days in Camp Two. The place is fetid, crawling with vermin, swarming with flies. Arnie goes out to the creek with his shit stick, with Mini-Me as his guard. Does his thing, then looks around—nobody's there. Mini-Me's disappeared—no sight of him, and when Arnie listens, no sound. Just the jungle, wide open in front of him. It's the biggest temptation out here—the temptation to just go, and get yourself shot. So Arnie doesn't run. He comes back and says, *"No guardia"* to the ninjas. That's when Mini-Me materializes behind him, smiling. He set up Jorge the other day, and now he wants to do the same to Arnie. Didn't make the bomb squad; figures he'll make his bones shooting a gringo in the back.

Day 79. Broke camp in the morning; ninjas say the next will be better, though it's five to fifteen days' hard hiking away. Everyone forced to carry his own chains, the lucky ones in their own backpacks, Dave and Jorge in homemade packs strapped to their shoulders with loops of tree bark. Everyone has to wade through creeks and marshes—and Ron's not built for this. His legs hurt him; he dreads the trail. At night ninjas pass hostages a bottle of booze, everyone's first taste of whiskey in three months.

Day 80. A clearing on the trail. First sight of the sky without trees in the way for eighty days. A half hour in the sun, and yet when you look around and see the jungle—the endlessness of it—that feeling of loneliness again.

Day 81. The seeds of incremental resistance. You save everything you can: pieces of rope, syringes from Arnie's sickness. On the trail, when there's a garish mushroom, you ask a ninja, *"Comida?"*; if he says, No, no, you scoop it up and save it in a water bottle, hoping to brew poison. Maybe these assholes will drink from it and get sick. Still in chains, but the ninja locking up drops the key, and Jason snags it, sleeps with it in his mouth.

Day 82. Happy New Year from near the Colombian border. The air heavy with herbicides from Plan Colombia.

Day 83. *Ambush.* In the morning, Ron and German leave early, with their own guards, because they've been lagging behind. Everybody else with heavy packs; Jason and Arnie and Steve all beasts of burden. They reach the river where they're supposed to wait for Ron and German, and a scouting party is sent out ahead. Seven shots from an AK-47, and utter chaos, utter confusion, utter terror, with Arnie and Steve and Jason and Dennis and Jorge and Dave ordered to lie down behind a log, guns pointed at their heads. So it's true, what they've said all along: They'd shoot the hostages before they'd defend themselves. Luckily, there is no army and no fight. What happened is that Ron and German made it to the meeting place early with their party. They surprised the scouting party, and the scouting party opened fire. G. I. Jane shot one of his own, and the bloodthirsty motherfucker is grousing that he only hit him in the leg. The wounded ninja is packed out on a horse commandeered from a local farm while the rest high-tail it on the trail till after dark. No food. Little sleep.

Day 84. A hard day on the trail and sardines for dinner—"the best meal I've ever had in my life," Jason writes. That evening, he looks at Ron's face and sees something he can't get out of his head: The man is white. Not like he's tired—like he's seen a ghost. Like he knows something about either himself or his captors. He has tried to foster nothing but goodwill in the camp, and now Arnie asks him if with all the talk of poisoning the ninjas and planning an escape, he's afraid he's going to get left behind. Don't worry, Arnie tells him. We won't leave you behind. We won't forget you.

· · · ·

Sheila Sander didn't get much information from Helmerich & Payne—not nearly as much as Lisa Weber and Mindy Alford got from Erickson, and they didn't get very much at all. She wasn't even told how much the guerrillas had demanded for ransom—she found out on her own, from reporters. You don't need to know that, is what she remembers H&P people saying when she asked questions. How much had the negotiators offered in response to the $80 million demand? She didn't need to know that. Had the hostages been threatened? Well, hostages are always threatened; it's part of the game. Of course, she didn't know—nobody knew except those with direct access to the negotiations—that the negotiators had decided to show the kidnappers the folly of their demands and had offered just $500,000, *total,* for all eight hostages. She didn't know that the negotiators had not increased the offer one penny, even when the kidnappers had broken off radio contact in the beginning of January, even when they came back on the radio on January 15 to issue a very specific threat, vowing that if the negotiators didn't come up with real money by January 30, a hostage would be killed. She'd heard rumors of the threat from a reporter, but she couldn't know how the negotiators had responded: with a counteroffer of $1 million, extended right before the deadline. All she knew, on the morning of January 31, was that Ron Sander, her husband, her fishing partner, the quiet man who shared her dream house on the Lake of the Ozarks—her man—was dead. He was the only man who had ever bothered to make her happy, and now he was gone. She didn't have to be told; she just knew. She didn't bother to comb out her hair that morning, didn't bother changing out of her housedress. She lit a cigarette, poured a cup of coffee, and waited.

Before too long, a car ferrying three executives from Helmerich & Payne—the company where Ron Sander worked for twenty-six years—pulled up in front of her house.

·   ·   ·

Day 105. January 24. It was odd who the ninjas decided to send as messenger, who acted as herald. This was supposed to be good news, right? For most of January, they didn't know what was going on. They were either packing hard through the bush, climbing to higher elevations, or else they were sitting around waiting. They went to one camp and then another; and although the ninjas reported no progress in the negotiations, they seemed weirdly calm—"better water, relaxed guerrillas," Jason wrote on January 10, Day 91. Of the negotiations, the hostages were told only that the negotiators had asked for one of them to be released, as a show of good faith, and the ninjas had refused. Then nine days later, on January 19, Qaddafi told them that he had changed his mind—that they should start preparing for one of them to go home. He asked them each another proof-of-life question and said that the hostage who was to be released would convey the answers to the negotiators in Quito. Not only that—he said that they should write letters to their families so that the freed hostage could deliver them. So they wrote letters to their wives and children and mothers and fathers and brothers. And they decided what they wanted said on their behalf when whoever got out talked to the press and the negotiators and the diplomats. And then, on the twenty-fourth of January, Shotgun came around, all smiles, and told Ron Sander that he had been selected, that he should get ready to leave. And they were all like, *Shotgun*? Not Qaddafi? Not Fernando? Not even the Young Captain of the bomb squads? But they didn't think too much of it because they were too busy priming Ron to be their representative. The last thing anyone remembers him saying was what he told German before he left—"I wish you were going instead of me. Your knees are worse than mine." Then he was gone, in the company of Fernando, the ninjas called Sota and Canario, and G. I. Jane. And the rest of them, seven men now smarting with the sense of being left behind—well, the next day, they were gone, too, bushwhacking through creeks and streams as fast as they could, humping for days for higher ground, moving so fast they didn't realize they walked right over a coral snake until they saw Shotgun beating it to death, with his goblin's grin.

· · · · ·

Lee Ramage asked them where they stood. Mindy and Lisa— he needed them now, to show their support. Mike Derry had been excommunicated from the family meetings. Mike Derry flipped when Ron Sander's body was found near the Colombian border. Well, so did Lisa and Mindy—Lisa especially. Lee had called her on the thirty-first, saying that a body had been found—but it wasn't one of their guys. That's what he kept saying. It wasn't Jason or Steve or Arnie. It wasn't Erickson. Lisa figured, Okay, one of them had a heart attack. She called Mindy, and they agreed: natural causes. He was old. Their husbands were young. She was at work the next day when she got a call from the U.S. ambassador to Ecuador. Autopsy report, she heard. Executed, she heard. Five bullets in the back. He was found dead by the side of a road with a sheet draped over him bearing the words, I AM A GRINGO. FOR NONPAYMENT OF RANSOM. HP COMPANY. She doesn't remember much after that—well, she remembers screaming. She remembers seeing the negotiator that night at Erickson and hearing him say, with tears in his eyes, "They never kill the hostages, they never kill the hostages," and she remembers telling him, "Don't tell that to me ever again! Don't tell that to anyone ever again! Because obviously they do!" Now, though, she was being asked to make a decision. Mike Derry had called a press conference. He had started a fund for the release of the hostages from Gold Hill. He had organized a demonstration in front of Erickson. Were Lisa and Mindy standing with Mike Derry or with Lee and Erickson? Of course, it was no choice at all. What power did Mike Derry have—or Lisa or Mindy—to get Steve and Arnie and Jason home? What connections? What money? "I'll stand with you, Lee, but you better get my husband home," Lisa said. "I promise," Lee said.

She flew in the Erickson jet to Ron Sander's funeral in Oklahoma on Tuesday, February 6. Just a flat-ass town in Oklahoma, like the one Jason had come from, with a closed casket, a burial in the winter wind, and a reception at a hall. Lisa introduced herself when people were leaving. Sheila Sander had figured her for one of Ron's distant relatives, but now Lisa came up to her and said, "My husband's Jason Weber. He was with your husband. He's still down there. He's one of the hostages." And Sheila Sander? She remembered, as she always did, that Ron didn't like to see her cry. She remembered how he calmed her and directed her to a purpose. So she hugged Lisa and introduced Lisa to Ron's family and comforted Lisa, and then took her aside and said: "You go back home and get your husband back. Because they say they're going to kill another one every two weeks until they get their money."

•   •   •

They did not tell their hostages, of course, that they had killed Ron Sander. They did not tell them the letters they wrote had gone undelivered, that the proof-of-life questions were simply part of their deception. They did not tell them that they had threatened to keep killing them until their demands were met. No, on February 10—Day 122—Fernando sat by the radio and flashed Arnie the thumbs-up. On February 12, Qaddafi told them the deal was 95 percent done—that the negotiators had offered 10.5 million, and the ninjas were deciding whether to hold out for 20. On February 14, Valentine's Day, the Young Captain broke the news that the negotiations were over, that the ninjas were just waiting for the money. A week later, on Day 133, a helicopter dropped seven bags filled with $13 million worth of $100 bills into a clearing near a river, the ninjas started slowly disbanding, and Jorge got on the radio to announce that the seven of them were still alive.

And yet . . . it wasn't good, February. They had no supplies in February. Food was rationed in February, and they were starving. They were wasting away, quickly now, as though they were in the end stages of a disease. Steve's hand was open and rotten and stinking—he was watching himself turn into meat. A few of them, Steve and Arnie included, began itching so badly that all they wanted to do was run. And Jason had stopped talking. Back in October, he had begun, for the first time in his life, to pray to God, but now he had not only stopped praying, he wrote that God, if there is a God, must be laughing at him. What sustained him now—his only prayer—was what he did every night before sleep, something he'd read about in a novel by Dean Koontz, oh, he couldn't remember the name, but it was about this retarded kid who had psychic ability, who imagined his thoughts as a string fed out into the world, and if anyone touched the string, he could talk to them, and so every night Jason would visualize his thoughts as a string floating through the air, and whoever touched it, well, it would always be Jessica. Kaitlyn was too young, but Jason figured that if he could just get Jessica to touch the string, she could always tell Kaitlyn that they once had a daddy, even if he never made it home. . . .

They broke camp on the twenty-fourth of February—Day 136—and began the last of their long marches, circling, walking back over the archaeology of their own buried garbage, on the way to the place where they were to be released. "Somebody better make a decision because I am tired of shitty sardine soup," Jason wrote. "I fucking want to go home. I AM DONE." They were eating the nuts that fell off a certain kind of tree; they were drinking the water from the blisters that bulged from a certain kind of vine. Then, suddenly, there were more of them than there were ninjas. The ninjas had dwindled down to four—Young Captain, Taxi, G. I. Jane, and Mini-Me—and on Day 138 Young Captain was asking permission to come under their tarp so that he could show them his stack of $100 bills and find out if they were real. On Day 139 they pissed and shat and then slept outside the shadow of a gun for the first time in nearly five months, and so when the storm came through on their last night in the jungle and lightning speared the camp and for an instant their world was once again split in two, Arnie said that it was God's judgment on the ninjas, but Jason knew it was the last rattling echo of divine laughter.

March 1, 2001. Day 141. Up early, hike for about an hour. YC's orders are changed, he says: He doesn't have to shoot them if they encounter the army. Then, at a trailhead, he stops and gives directions to the town of Santa Rosa, where a chopper from the Ecuadoran army is supposed to be waiting. And then, all at once: alone and free and scared to death. An empty farm with a field of pineapples: breakfast. A long, aching walk, through muddy fields churned up by pigs and cows . . . and then the walk seems to be taking too long, and at the next farmhouse Jorge asks a woman standing alone if they are going the right way. She is terrified by what she sees—seven bearded white men, gaunt and hungry-eyed, in filthy clothes—but manages to say no, they missed a turn, they have to go back to where they came from. Then behind them they hear gunshots—to this day they don't know where they came from—and it's off to the races. German is failing; they take turns carrying his pack, and after an hour on the open road, they come upon the blessed vision of a mother and a daughter scrubbing laundry on a washboard in front of their little house. The revelation of Santa Rosa. A man comes outside and the hostages tell him who they are, and he takes them to a house where they are served soda and a meal of bread and lemons. There is no helicopter waiting, but there is a local bus scheduled to come at 2:30, and Steve still has sixty dollars that he stashed away on October 12 and kept hidden on his person for 141 days, and they decide that if the bus comes, they will be on it no matter where it goes. Then a pickup comes barreling up the road and men jump out of it with television cameras, and another pickup comes and men in plainclothes identify themselves as Ecuadoran military and tell them all to get in. They do as they are told, and yet cars are coming at them from all directions, and they begin to think that maybe they're being kidnapped again, and it's all they can do not to choke the life out of the men who have taken them, but they hold on by the threads of their hope and their trust, and they're on the road to the military base when they hear that Ron Sander is not fishing with his good wife Sheila in Lake of the Ozarks but already one month dead.

•　　•　　•

It's hard, you know, waiting for that first phone call. It's sort of like the anxiety that went with the proof-of-life questions—because this is your one chance to say something and you haven't seen your husband in five months and what do you say? What does he say? And so Lisa waited and waited, and it was very late when the phone finally rang and she picked it up and there was Jason offering no preamble, no introduction, no hello, just saying, "I love you," instantly, immediately, before she had a chance to say a word.

•　　•　　•

The world is full of wonders. Gold Hill, Oregon, is full of wonders. Home is full of wonders, because, to be frank, when you come home you are *fucked up*. You can't believe how fucked up you are. You can't remember anything, so you have to write down the details of your life, exactly as you did in the jungle. The world is loud but your voice is soft, your vocal cords atrophied by 141 days of whispering. You're paranoid and dim-witted and ghostly. You can't bear to look at what you wore in the jungle, and you can't bear to throw it away. You're hungry, but when you eat you feel sick. You go to the bar to talk, but when you do, you don't say a goddamn word. Arnie? Arnie still itches. Arnie is crazy with guilt; he's certain he's done something to his family, no matter how often Mindy and Kaitlin insist that they are just happy to have him home. Steve? Steve's overwhelmed by how many people love him: the family members who suffered nearly as he suffered; the total strangers who say that he was never out of their prayers. For some reason, it kills him; it breaks his heart even as his heart is bolstered, for he is still captive to all those tears.

As for Jason: He wrote his last journal entry on March 30, 2001, twenty-eight days after coming home to Lisa and Jessica and Kaitlyn. "I wish I felt I was done with this nightmare," he wrote. "I'm starting to get back to a somewhat normal state of mind but it seems the more I try to find out what happened when we were gone the more pissed I get. All I want to get is a few answers and everything I want to know that is semi-important to me they can't talk about or won't tell the truth on. Sometimes I feel the negotiators really screwed up and they don't want us to know about that. All I want is to be healthy again and a little compensation and to be a helicopter mechanic.... I have worked my ass off for this company for six years and will continue to do so as long as they are fair and don't try to screw us.... Now is such a crazy time and I can't think straight. My concentration is horrible and everything I need to do I have to write down. The only good thing so far is how strong my wife is and what great kids I have. In that sense I am truly blessed."

But what was it like? Well, that's what it was like: They got screwed. They rejected Erickson's offer of compensation as an insult and wound up being paid with five months' time off in return for the time they spent in the jungle. Because of laws regarding workmen's compensation, they can't sue Erickson, although to a man they all say that if they could they would do so not for money but for answers. The negotiators had warned Lisa and Mindy that the kidnappers would try to use time as a weapon; as it turned out, it was the negotiators who tried to use time to bring down the ransom, but the time didn't belong to them: It belonged to Arnie and Steve and Jason, and now it's gone forever. In June, the Colombian government, acting in concert with the FBI's office in Bogotá announced that it had arrested fifty-seven people allegedly involved not only with the October 12 kidnapping but with kidnappings dating back several years. Reporters called and asked Jason and Steve and Arnie if the arrests promised closure. *Closure?* Hell, no—Ron Sander was dead. The gentle man who had gotten them home was dead. Sheila Sander was selling their dream house on the Lake of the Ozarks because she had no more dreams, no more plans; all her dreams and plans were with Ron. Ask *her* about closure. Ask Sheila if she has come to accept her husband's death, and this is what she says: "I could accept it if Ron had died of a heart attack. I could accept it if Ron had died of cancer. I cannot accept that he was executed. I cannot accept that his body was found by the side of the road. Because he didn't have to die. He didn't have to die. They just didn't want to pay the ransom. . . ."

So she is moving to Oklahoma to be close to her daughter, who two days before what would have been Ron's fifty-fifth birthday gave birth to a baby boy; she is moving to Oklahoma to be close to Ron's grave. There she gets to talk to the only man she could ever talk to, although he was so quiet; there she gets to see a gravestone already inscribed with her name and gets to read all about closure, in the language of stone.

•   •   •

September 6, 2001. Steve Derry slides his fishing boat out into the Rogue River, near Gold Hill; drops anchor; throws out a line. Cheeks pink as clouds at the end of the day; eyes like broken pieces of sky. He has done this all his life, but it's all different now. He's different. The river's different. The woods are different. The sun and the moon and the stars are different and so are the pleasures he takes from them. It's hard to explain, but everything has been ever so slightly rearranged and will never go back. That's why when he hears that Jason Weber is itching to return to Ecuador, to prove that the ninjas didn't beat him—when he hears that Jason would go back to Ecuador if not for the judgment of Lisa and the kids—Steve says quickly, "But they did beat him. They beat all of us. They beat the shit out of us. And now it's hard coming to terms with that. But you've got to. You have no choice. . . ." For five hours, he's out on the water, burning in the sun, in his slide; all day long, his line goes out and back in; and although his patience is endless, almost defiant, even he seems aware of the absurdity of casting his line one last time after he has said it's time to go home. Who catches a fish on the last cast of the day? But sure enough, his line snaps taut, and his rod doubles over, and he pulls a steelhead out of the water, green and silver and already dying as it tries to breathe in human hands.

"Well, I'll be darned," is all Steve Derry has to say before he sets free his prey in the cold, clear water.

The Atlantic Monthly

WINNER, FEATURE WRITING

Moonrise

In spare—yet unsparing—prose, writer Penny Wolfson describes her teenage son's battle with muscular dystrophy, the disease that will almost surely cut his life short. She paints his worsening condition in a series of memorable vignettes—sometimes wryly humorous, often painful, and always honest. The reader comes away from the piece understanding her belief that "human life is small, fragile and finite. And yet, still beautiful."

Penny Wolfson

Moonrise

A mother writes about her teenage son, afflicted with muscular dystrophy, and the life he leads, and the one he can look forward to.

At the Center for Creative Photography, in Tucson, Arizona, my husband, Joe, and I are looking at prints of *Moonrise, Hernandez, New Mexico,* by Ansel Adams. A slender young man in a suit has brought us, as requested, three versions of this famous photograph. He dons a pair of white gloves before removing the 14½" x 18½" enlargements from their Plexiglas sheaths, opens the hinged glass viewing case in front of us, and places the photographs carefully, lovingly, on a slanted white board inside. He stands there while we examine the pictures; when we are finished, he will repeat the process in reverse.

I don't know exactly where Hernandez, New Mexico, is, but it reminds me a bit of Sacaton, ninety miles northwest of here, the

Pima Indian village where Joe is a government doctor and where we have lived since July of 1983. Now it's December. We have made the trip to Tucson expressly to view the Ansel Adams photos, though we did not imagine that there would be so many prints from the same negative.

In *Moonrise* two thirds of the space is usurped by a rich black sky; a gibbous moon floats like a hot-air balloon in an other-worldly—and yet absolutely southwestern—landscape. A gauzy strip of low clouds or filtered light drifts along the horizon; distant mountains are lit by waning sun or rising moon. Only in the bottom third of the photo, among scrubby earth and sparsely scattered trees, does human settlement appear: a small collection of modest adobe houses and one larger adobe church. Around the edge of the village white crosses rise from the ground at many angles; at first glance they resemble clotheslines strung with sheets or socks, but on more-careful examination it is obvious that they mark graves.

The prints differ greatly in quality from the reproductions one usually sees, and also differ slightly from one another: here we see a more defined darkness, burnt in by the photographer, there a variation in exposure, a grainier texture. But that does not change the essential meaning of the photograph, a meaning one never forgets in the Southwest: Nature dominates. Human life is small, fragile, and finite. And yet, still, beautiful.

I. Falling, 1998

I am at the Grand Union in Dobbs Ferry, New York, with my son Ansel, who is thirteen years old. It's raining. He begged to come, so I brought him, not really wanting to, because I had to bring his wheelchair, too: it weighs more than 200 pounds and isn't easy to maneuver into the minivan, even with the ramp. I have to wrestle the motorized chair until it faces forward and then, bending and squeezing into the narrow confines of the van, I have to fasten it to the floor with several clasps. By the time I have done this even once, I'm irritable. A trip to the supermarket means doing it twice and undoing it twice.

Anyway, we've finished our shopping, and we leave the supermarket. Ansel is in his chair, without his hooded yellow raincoat from L. L. Bean, because he has decided that at his age a raincoat is babyish, not cool. He's afraid people at school will laugh at him. Maybe this is true, I say, but I think it's stupid. Why get wet when you can stay dry? Needless to say, I lose this argument.

Before loading the groceries I open the van door so that Ansel can get in the front seat, where he always sits if Joe isn't with us. He parks his chair at a distance from the minivan, so that I'll have room for the ramp, and starts to rise, laboriously. No, "rise" sounds too easy, like smoke going up a flue, airy, like yeast bread rising in the oven. Ansel does not rise. He shifts sideways in the seat and pulls himself up heavily, propping his eighty pounds against the armrest for balance. He leans with his left arm, twists his right shoulder around to straighten up, and brings his hip and buttocks to a partly standing position. Actually he's sort of bent in half, with his hands still on the chair's joystick. There is a moment of imbalance. His feet are planted far apart, farther out than his hips, and he needs to bounce back and forth a few times to bring his feet together. Finally he's up. He begins walking toward the door in his waddling, tiptoe way. His spine is curved quite a bit from scoliosis, his stomach is forward, his hands are out at his sides chest-high, his fingers outstretched.

His balance is so tenuous that his five-year-old brother, Toby, can knock him down. Sometimes Ansel will bellow, "I'm tired of everyone always leaving things all over the floor! Don't they know I'll fall?" It's true that we're a little careless about this. But Ansel will trip over anything—an unevenness in the sidewalk, the dog's water dish, some bits of food on the floor, things expected and unexpected—and sometimes over nothing. Sooner or later he falls. It's part of the routine. And the older he gets, the more he falls.

Now, in the Grand Union parking lot, he falls. Who knows why—it could be the wet ground. He's in the skinny aisle of asphalt between our car and the one parked next to us. He falls, and it's pouring, and I'm still loading grocery bags into the back.

"Mom!" he calls at me, half barking, half crying. "I fell!" There's such anguish, such anger, in his voice when he falls, and such resignation. He never thinks I hear him.

And why am I suddenly so angry? Such terrible impatience rises in me now. Am I really such a witch, such a bad mother, that when I'm loading groceries and my son falls, I don't have the time or patience to cope? Why am I so angry?

"Wait a minute," I say. "I'll be there in a minute."

So he sits on the wet pavement between the cars. I know his sweatpants are at this moment soaking through. I can see that the wheelchair, waiting to be rolled up the ramp, needing to be pushed and yanked into position, is also getting wet. Its foamy-nylon seat will need drying out later.

A middle-aged blonde woman has wheeled her shopping cart into the lot and approaches us. "Can I help?"

No, you definitely cannot help, runs through my head. This is both true and self-righteous. Physically, the job is not meant for two; it's easier for me to do on my own. How would we two, and Ansel, even fit between the cars?

I grit my teeth and smile and say, "No, no thanks, really. I can do it." People always seem puzzled and upset when they see him fall. It's so sudden, an instant crumpling, without warning. They can't see the weakness, the steady deterioration of his pelvis. Maybe someone would fall this way if he'd been hit hard in the solar plexus; I don't know. But Ansel's feet give way for no apparent reason, and he's down.

The blonde woman has heard me, but she keeps standing there, her hands clamped around the handle of her cart, her eyes moving from Ansel to the grocery bags to me. I know she means to be help-ful, and in a way I do want something from her—pity? an acknowl-edgment that I am more noble than she? But mostly I want her to go away. *Don't look at me. Don't watch this.*

"Mom! Where *are* you?"

I turn from the blonde woman; she fades away. "Okay, I'm coming," I say. I try to wedge myself between the cars so that I can retrieve Ansel. There's a special way to pick him up: you have to come from behind and grab him under the arms, raise him so that his toes dangle just above the ground, and then set his feet down precisely the right distance apart.

I'm in pretty good shape, but Ansel is dead weight. Another child could help you, could put his hands around your neck. His feet would come off the ground at even the suggestion of lifting. But Ansel is pulling me down, his limp shoulders, his heavy leg braces, his sodden pants, his clumsy sneakers. I can't hold him. My own sneakers slip on the wet pavement.

II. Chaos, 1999

The New York Academy of Medicine, on 103rd Street and Fifth Avenue, is not exactly in the slums, but it's not really the Upper East Side either. On a dreary, drizzly morning I park at the Metropolitan Museum garage, on Eightieth Street, and walk up Madison, past Banana Republic and Ann Taylor and patisseries and fancy meat purveyors and little French children's-clothing shops that display sashed dresses with hand-embroidered yokes in their windows. But above Ninety-sixth Street, near the Mount Sinai Hospital complex, the scenery and the people change abruptly; everything's older and more run-down. Street peddlers hawk books, batteries, Yankees caps, cheap scarves, acrylic ski caps, five-dollar handbags. I see an obese black man leaning on a cane, harried-looking workers with Mount Sinai badges, a woman exiting a hospital building through a revolving door carrying crutches.

Eleven years ago, when Ansel was three, doctors diagnosed in him a form of muscular dystrophy called Duchenne, which rapidly destroys muscle tissue, confining its victims to wheelchairs by adolescence and invariably resulting in early death. Like hemophilia, it is almost always transmitted to sons from asymptomatic "carrier" mothers. In my extended family, which produced an overwhelming number of daughters and almost no sons for two generations, the existence of the Duchenne gene—or, more correctly, the existence of an altered gene that doesn't properly code for a particular muscle protein—was unknown, a subterranean truth. My mother and sister and I, all carriers without outward signs, never guessed at this defect in our genetic heritage.

Joe and I gave our son, conceived and born in Arizona, the name of the great photographer we admired, Ansel Adams, who had died earlier that year. The name seemed apt; Ansel was, as people often told us, prettier than a picture, amber-haired and round-eyed, with a perpetually quizzical but serene countenance and the build of a slender but sturdy miniature football player. For two years he developed normally, reaching all the benchmarks on or close to schedule. He was an engaging and beautiful boy, gifted, one suspected, in some intangible way. When his teacher in nursery school began to point out Ansel's deficits in language and in gross motor skills (he couldn't master rudimentary grammar, couldn't alternate legs on the stairs), we refused to see any problem. It was impossible for us to believe that this perfectly wonderful child, our child, was not perfect at all, that he was in fact handicapped and would become progressively more handicapped.

It took a year for us to accept his differentness, to have him professionally evaluated, to reach a diagnosis. And although we have been to dozens of doctors and have dealt with every aspect of his disease, it has taken me eleven years to get up the nerve to come here, to the Academy of Medicine, and look squarely at what will happen to Ansel in a future I have not yet completely faced.

The library reading room is large and quiet, with a high ceiling and a faded tapestry on the wall behind me. At a long oak table beneath a grand chandelier, surrounded by busts of famous scientists, all men, who peer down from atop the bookshelves, I sit nervously waiting for the books I've requested. It makes sense, I suppose, that Louis Pasteur sits head and shoulders above the lesser-knowns.

But not even Pasteur, I remind myself, could have cured muscular dystrophy. Nor could any of the nineteenth-century doctors who described the disease, including the English physicians Charles Bell, Edward Meryon, and William Gowers and the French neurologist G.B.A. Duchenne, after whom the most common form of muscular dystrophy is named. And despite hundreds, perhaps thousands, of studies completed and articles written and compiled in prestigious journals such as *Muscle and Nerve* and *The Lancet* and *The Journal of the American Medical Association,* sitting right here in the bound volumes surrounding me in this rarefied room, no one, even in this century, has found a way to save my son.

A young woman arrives with my books: a general text on Duchenne muscular dystrophy from 1993 by a British geneticist named Alan E. H. Emery, and two books by Duchenne himself, one from the 1870s and crumbling with age, called *A Treatise on Localized Electrization* (*De l'électrisation Localisée,* first published in 1855), and one translated in the 1950s, *Physiology of Motion.* But I find the writings of the great doctor inscrutable and bizarre, filled with stuff about electrical impulses and pictures of strange apparatus; Duchenne devised such instruments as the "dynamometer," or strength gauge, and the harpoon biopsy needle, which he used to study muscles in his patients at different stages in their short lives (before that, muscle tissue was mostly observed at autopsy).

Duchenne's books have nearly no narrative; they consist mostly of pages and pages of minute drawings and observations of every muscle in the human body, with one- and two-page sections such as "Motions of the Thumb" and "Flexion of the Forearm." One forgets that before this century medicine was largely descriptive, and that one of the main questions about muscular dystrophy was whether it was primarily neurological—affecting the spine and nerves—or truly muscular. Duchenne confirmed that the disease had no neurogenic basis. Nevertheless, there was something obsessive if not downright nutty about him—or maybe my impatient twentieth-century mother's mind fails to grasp the connections between his results and his writings.

But when I open Emery's book, *Duchenne Muscular Dystrophy*, everything else vanishes. I read between lines; I am transfixed, by turns elated and restless. For the first time in eleven years I look at pictures of boys in the advanced stages of the disease. There are obese boys and skeletal boys looking like Auschwitz victims, their spines twisted and their emaciated arms and legs dangling. There is a boy with grotesquely enlarged muscles throughout his body; he resembles a deformed child body-builder, a waxy muscle-bound doll, a strange, surprised balloon boy. In many cases no attempt has been made to conceal the identities of these boys; their faces are in clear view, and their misshapen bodies are naked, so one can see the deterioration clearly. There is something vulgar and vulnerable about the nakedness of these boys, their genitalia seeming in some instances particularly underdeveloped compared with the rest of their bodies and often too frankly exposed. At home I don't see my son naked, as I used to when he was little; I glimpse only the outward signs of deterioration—the thick-veined calves, the legs bruised by falls, the callused, deformed feet, the increasingly swayed back, the heels that can no longer reach the floor. I focus on his face: despite its fleshy roundness, caused by steroids, it is still beautiful to me, with its alert, quizzical eyes and arched eyebrows, its stubborn mouth (how easily it registers disgust or frustration or delight!), its straight, broad nose with a suggestion of freckles, its crown of chestnut hair.

I study an engraving from 1879 of a boy in three positions rising from the floor, in what doctors call a Gowers' maneuver, named after the physician. In the first scene the boy is on his hands and knees; in the second his rump is raised into the air and his two hands press on the ground for support; in the third he rests a hand on his thigh to balance himself. Here I experience the oddest feeling—a thrill of identification. Yes! There it is, exactly. My child. So true, so utterly Ansel. But obviously true of other boys too, over hundreds or thousands of years. I feel less lonely, in a way, but I can't deny what's in the photographs. And there's no denying the statistics either: 90 percent of boys with Duchenne die by the age of twenty. At sixteen about half are dead. A nine-year-old we know who has Duchenne can no longer walk. Should I feel happy or sad knowing that Ansel is at the far end of the curve?

Some pages I barely glance at—I know the early symptoms, and I have already witnessed some of the decay in Ansel. I know that there is a "progressive weakness of movement, first affecting the lower limbs and then later the upper limbs" and "a gradual increase in the size of many affected muscles." I have seen that the "lumbar lordosis becomes more exaggerated and the waddling gait increases"; I see the shortening of the heel cords.

But as the disease progresses, Emery's book reminds me, the breakdown intensifies: "Muscle weakness becomes more profound, contractures develop, particularly . . . of the elbows, knees, and hips . . . movements of the shoulders and wrists also become limited. The talus bone [protrudes] prominently under the skin . . ." Finally all hell breaks loose: "Thoracic deformity . . . restricts adequate pulmonary airflow . . . a severe kyphoscoliosis [curvature of the spine] develops . . . a gradual deterioration begins in pulmonary function with reduced maximal inspiratory and expiratory pressures. By the later stages there is a significant reduction in total lung capacity." In other words, the spine contorts, compressing the chest cavity; the respiratory and heart muscles weaken; and eventually the child can't breathe. Less commonly, the heart gives out.

In a chapter called "Management," I review the paltry fixes: knee orthoses; braces that extend from ankle to groin; stretching exercises; steroids (the author, writing in 1993, downplayed their importance); wheelchairs; standing frames; rigid body jackets; the "Luque operation," which involves inserting two rods in the spine; tenotomy, or cutting the Achilles and other tendons; finally, assisted ventilation and drainage of the lungs. Some sound radical, some gruesome; at any rate, they are only Band-Aids, short-term measures that extend life perhaps one year, perhaps two. Sooner or later, usually by their mid-twenties, all boys with Duchenne succumb. Of 144 patients Emery studied, only sixteen made it to their twenty-fifth birthdays.

. . .

Every night, hands in his pockets for balance, on tiptoe, his jaw set in a grimace, his feet hesitantly reaching and shuffling, leaning longer on the right than on the left, Ansel stumbles along the hallway between his bedroom and the living room, willing himself to walk. It is unheard of—a fifteen-year-old with Duchenne walking. "Amazing," I tell him, "amazing," as he collapses in his wheelchair. We know it can't last forever, but we keep our fingers crossed.

Sunday morning I wake up, descend the stairs, begin boiling water for coffee. From the stove I get a glimpse of the cabinets that Joe fixed the day before: two low storage cupboards whose doors had been yanked off by the harsh sweep of Ansel's wheelchair. For weeks the jumble of our kitchen had been exposed, its internal disorder revealed. On Saturday, Joe finally mended them, filling in the holes and jimmying the hardware. The doors hung a bit askew, leaving an empty space like a knocked-out front tooth. Still, for the moment they stayed in place.

But now I see that one door has come loose at its hinges again; it hangs perilously from a single screw. Inside the darkness, chaos.

III. Moonrise, 2000

Ansel and I are on 165th Street in Washington Heights, on our way to the doctor at the Neurological Institute. I picked him up at school, and he told me he loves me, as he does at least once a day, and then we drove here and parked in the Kinney Lot, where, because of our "handicapped" placard, the attendants let us squeeze into a ground-level spot.

This is the neighborhood where Joe and I first lived together, in medical-school housing in one of the huge modern buildings making up The Towers, which overlook the George Washington Bridge. We did not particularly get along with our multiple roommates, and we did not always like each other, but it was our first home, and it holds memories: the "Man in the Pan" early-morning lectures at which the doctors-in-training studied dissected organs; the late Sunday nights when I searched for Joe and his friend Peter, who were studying for a Monday exam in the recesses of the vast Health Sciences Library; the white-coated world of the medical complex, with people waiting in line for treatment, and the marble floor of Columbia-Presbyterian Hospital, through which I walked when coming home from the subway. I had just read Malcolm X's great book about his life, and I was always aware of our closeness to the Audubon Ballroom, where Malcolm was shot, and also of the darkness and danger of the 168th Street subway station, where several rapes and murders had taken place. My sister's boyfriend, who worked in a microbiology lab at Presbyterian, had been stabbed in the heart on the train on his way to work. He recovered, because he was taken to the emergency room quickly, but he had a scary, knotty scar on his chest where the mugger's knife had gone in.

There are sweet memories, too, mostly associated with food: the French toast at the Haven coffee shop, around the corner, and the farmer's cheese from the old Daitch Dairy (a remnant of the aging Jewish community), and the old-fashioned luncheon-ette on Fort Washington, where a soda jerk whipped up choco-late malteds made with Breyer's ice cream. The apartment in The Towers was where I held a successful surprise party for Joe; I managed to concoct Julia Child's fanciest chocolate cake, le Mar-quis, without his ever noticing. It was also where I had to deliver the news to Joe that his adored stepfather had died suddenly, at forty-eight, of a heart attack.

We are supposed to see Dr. DeVivo at least once a year, but it has been a year and some months since our last visit. When Ansel and I arrive, we are told to sit in a secluded, empty waiting room, where he does his math homework and I glance at a mag-azine called *Healthy Kids*. Joe arrives—in a suit, because he is now the head of family practice at the Catholic Medical Centers, in Brooklyn and Queens—and a receptionist says that we are in the wrong waiting room. We go and sit for another twenty min-utes in a much more crowded room. A small boy in a stroller cries, seemingly overtired and cranky; his mother, in a foreign language, tries to soothe him. He has tiny white braces on his legs, but I can't make out what his problem is. I never ask, "Why are you here?" although I always want to know. It sounds too much like "What are you in for?"

When DeVivo, a white-haired, stocky man, enters the room, I am not sure I recognize him, it's been so long. But he is wearing a white coat, and he seems to be in charge, so we follow him into his large office at the end of the hallway. I am very conscious that on our last visit Ansel walked from the waiting room to the office, and I remember the look of surprise on the doctor's face: How amazing that a fourteen-year-old with Duchenne could still walk! Now Ansel wheels his way down the long corridor, and I am the one surprised that he could have walked so far so recently.

Joe, Ansel, and I sit in three upholstered chairs facing DeVivo, who sits behind a massive desk. I remember suddenly how poorly Joe did in his neurology rotation in medical school; how he didn't like the neurologists—they were too cerebral and academic, he felt. DeVivo's manner is restrained, and when he speaks, he addresses Ansel first. He asks Ansel about school, about his clarinet lessons (the doctor plays trombone), and gets only a typical teenager's grunts. The pleasantries aside, he gets to what's important: "Tell me, Ansel, how do you feel, physically, compared with the last time I saw you?"

"Well, I use the wheelchair more," Ansel says. "I get out of the wheelchair three or four times a day and stretch, and then I walk a few steps. That's all. I can't really walk more than that."

He doesn't say it sadly, just as fact; but Joe and I and the doctor know it is sad, and it sits heavy in the air, a presence among us. I think of Ansel at five, walking into town with me because he suddenly wanted to bake cookies and we had to buy cookie cutters. He walked slowly, but he walked all the way, a quarter of a mile in each direction.

For a moment no one else can speak. There isn't anything to say, is there? He gets worse. He will die. Even if it's slow, it will happen. It's a whole life, not a half-life, divided infinitely. Sooner or later it will not be there.

But in one way it's not sad. Ansel has spoken, after all, and we have all listened. He is no longer a small child but the voice of authority. Who can know the answers but Ansel? He has a deep voice and a little trace of a moustache on his upper lip. He and the neurologist discuss the best course of therapy, his medications (would Ansel agree to take three enzyme capsules a day, rather than the one he has been taking?), and his adherence to a low-salt, low-fat diet.

Joe, DeVivo, and Ansel retreat to the examining room that adjoins the office, where the table, made for small children, is too high for Ansel to mount. I stay behind, aware that he will not want his mother present when the doctor prods private parts or asks personal questions. I also don't want to see the fat that spills over the elastic of his underpants or the angry calluses on his feet when he removes his splints and shoes and socks. I'd rather look at the stack of magazines on luxury-home renovation, at the wall of books at the back of the room, at the color photos of racing sailboats—this must be one of the doctor's hobbies. I look out the dirty window of the Neurological Institute, half a block away from our old apartment at The Towers. It is strange to be here, looking out at a past that contained not even a flicker of Ansel. Why is it unthinkable to look at a future without him?

·   ·   ·

Joe and I are on the street on a Sunday afternoon, late. The forsythia is in bloom; there is yellow everywhere, and a dark sky with just a strip of light over the Palisades. Joe wants to know what I am writing: it is about Ansel's growing up and deteriorating all at once, the "unnaturalness" of a child's beginning to die just when he is beginning to flower.

Joe rejects this, furious. "What are you saying—because it's not average, not the norm, it's unnatural? That's like saying homosexuality is unnatural." I see his eyes flash behind his glasses. "What's unnatural about it?" he says. "It is in fact the natural order of things, that mutations occur. That's who we are, who we have to be, as humans."

"So you have no feelings about Ansel's getting worse?" I demand tearfully.

He purses his lips angrily, forcing air through them. "Of course I have feelings about it. But why is it necessarily sadder for someone to die young than old? Is it sadder for Ansel to die than a ninety-year-old man who's never done anything, who has nothing to show for his life? Anyway, Ansel's not dead. I can't mourn for him. And I refuse to see my life as a tragedy!"

"Well, that's what I'm writing about," I say. "And I'm sorry if you don't think it's sad!" Then I can't speak for ten minutes. I stride along next to Joe, up the hill beside the Food Emporium, and I don't look at him. I am too stubborn and angry. How can he say that a dying child is not heartrending? How about that boy Zachy, the only child of one of Joe's colleagues, who died at eight or nine of a brain tumor? Wasn't that worse, more tragic, than, say, my father's death at seventy-three? Wasn't my father's life, in concrete and substantial ways, long *enough*, whereas Zachy's was not?

At the top of the hill, thinking back on Zachy's death and its aftermath—his stunned parents sitting shiva in the apartment; the boy's baseball-card collection still visible in his bedroom—I can no longer hold on to my anger at Joe. I see him simply as a fellow sufferer: trying to construct meaning from ill fate, to find solace in the destruction of his first-born. He is just groping for a spiritual handhold. This is Joe, used to such loss (two fathers and a mother, all young, all loved), soothing himself, explaining to himself, as a child might, why death comes. And this is just the other half of me.

· · ·

In six months Ansel will be old enough to drive. In September he will be sixteen, able in New York State to take that step toward adulthood—obtaining a learner's permit. Even though we don't have the details yet, even though his father is not convinced that he can physically operate a motor vehicle, Ansel and I talk about driving as a reality—how he will take over the wheelchair van and I will buy a tiny red Miata, the car of my dreams. He is not as crazy about cars as some teenage boys are, but one day when he and I see a cab-yellow sixties Camaro idling at the corner of Cedar Street and

Broadway in the town where we live, his left eyebrow lifts, he peers at me sideways, and he says, "Wow." He's ready.

•   •   •

In the books on muscular dystrophy one learns that there are three markers: the onset of disease, confinement to a wheelchair, death. Ansel is approaching the date of confinement. He will be there, I am sure, by his sixteenth birthday.

I have panic attacks nearly every night. Awakened by some minor provocation—for instance, my daughter, Diana, enters the room to check the time—I turn over, sit up, and quite suddenly experience dread; there is no other word. I blink my eyes, because I am sure I'm going blind, and scratch my middle fingertip with my thumbnail, to assure myself that I'm not paralyzed. I try to take the pulse in my wrist but I'm too scared and can't count right. I am outside my body, physically detached, at the end of a long passageway, drowning—all those melodramatic scenarios of what it's like to die.

Seven years ago, when I was in labor with Toby, a nurse injected me with Stadol, a painkiller, and I became distant and paranoid like this. I held on to Joe's hand, literally for dear life. "Tell me I am not dying," I said over and over, to hear my own voice and to hear him respond. *What an irony,* I thought then, *to die giving birth!*

Now my heart seems to be racing in my head, but my blood is glacial, cold and slow. I have finally gone over the edge! The fear feeds on itself. I get dressed so that I can be ready to drive to the emergency room, if need be.

Sitting on the edge of the bed, sure of my own doom, I wonder suddenly, *Am I trying to experience my own death in place of Ansel's? Am I the sacrifice?*

•   •   •

It is the middle of March, and every moment pulls me two ways. In a community church in White Plains, New York, that looks like a cross between a pagoda and an airline terminal, I sit with Joe, Diana, and Toby in a fan-shaped room filled with folding chairs. It is a kind of backward room, because one enters by way of the stage and descends to the seats. Ansel who will be performing with an ensemble from his music school, can wheel onto the stage but not into the audience, so after he plays, Joe will have to carry him down the steps.

When the woodwinds come onstage and are seated, Ansel seems taller than the others, though he's actually quite short, because for the first time he is playing from his wheelchair. Usually he transfers, with difficulty, to a regular chair, but it was thought that the amount of time before the next group came on was too brief to allow for that. I can see Ansel now and then between the arms of the conductor. He is puffing out his big cheeks, like Dizzy Gillespie on the horn. He loves the clarinet, the instrument he chose when he began music lessons at school, in the fifth grade. Joe was against it. "What's the point," he asked, "when all boys with muscular dystrophy develop breathing difficulties? He won't be able to play for more than a couple of years; it will just be frustrating." As he does with nearly everything, Ansel stood firm, and got his way, and it is good that he did. Clarinet playing is his breathing therapy as well as his joy, and it may be the reason his lungs show no deterioration yet.

He progressed slowly when he took lessons at the public school, but as soon as he began at the music school, he flourished. Under the guidance of a gifted teacher Ansel has become a disciplined music student who, after many days and nights of mistakes, false starts, and practice, practice, practice, can be depended on to produce a fine sound. When he leaves his bedroom door open, I enjoy the lovely strains of the Weber clarinet concertino or of a Hindemith sonata. He is not a virtuoso; he is more of a plodder, but he plods well. He has learned to respect the difficulty of the task and the beauty of the result.

Sitting at the concert, I feel the pleasure of his playing, but seeing him in the wheelchair, I cannot shake the feeling of loss, a loss that feels sharpest when I love him most. I know that when boys become confined to their wheelchairs, their chests and lungs become constricted. Wind is the first thing to go. *Who knows which way the wind blows? Who knows where my love goes, how my love grows, where the time goes*? Despite my best efforts, despite my pride in Ansel (that serious, stubborn, laboring face!), a tear wells up in the corner of my eye. I shift my glasses so that Diana will not see. She does anyway.

"Mom, why are you crying?" she asks. I shake my head. "Ansel?" she whispers urgently. I nod, and wordlessly I put my arm around her shoulder—her bare, cool, pubescent shoulder, upon which I perhaps place too great a burden—and hold her close to me. Later Ansel sits with me, and Diana sits alone all the way in back. Joe has pulled Toby out, because he is complaining so much about being at a concert. The Festival Orchestra, sounding very professional despite being jerkily led by a very thin, very young conductor, plays Bach. In the midst of the quite proper, cultivated audience, Ansel and I dip and bounce our heads and shoulders to the rhythms. Near the end Ansel whispers, "Have you noticed everybody else here is completely still, no one else but you and me is moving to the music?" I have.

. . .

I keep with me much of the time a letter from a friend of a friend whose boy died of Duchenne at twenty-four. Even though I have never met her, I identify with this mother, because her boy did well; he must have been an outlier, like Ansel, to live to such a ripe old age. My son "was the absolute center of my life," she wrote. "Now I feel like the woman in the Hopper painting 'Cape

Cod Morning,' looking out the bay window, wondering what will come next."

. . .

Ansel has been away from the house for almost the entire weekend, attending a model UN at a nearby high school Friday night, all day Saturday, and Sunday morning. We are not used to his being away, and Diana and I both feel his absence. The question seems to be not "Is this what it will be like when he's away at college?" but "Is this what it will be like when he is dead?"

"Ansel is what makes the house happy," Diana says later that week, and I think back to the moment of his birth, when I heard a sound that reminded me of the popping of a champagne cork. I think of his name: a variation of Anschel, a diminutive of Asher which in Hebrew means "happy."

Diana and I try to think about what makes Ansel fun. "He's just a very up person," she says, which is odd, because he is also a big complainer, a class-A kvetch. "Puns," I say. "Remember when he wrote that story about the teenage monster who wasn't frightening enough because he didn't have enough 'scaritonin'?"

"Non sequiturs," Diana offers, and it's true. I used to call Ansel the king of non sequiturs. We might all be having a conversation about, say, the fact that the Lobster Roll is the only restaurant worth going to in the Hamptons. The rest of us might consider the topic exhausted and move rapidly on to two or three unrelated topics. We might be talking about the book I am reading for my psychology class in graduate school, or about how boring Toby finds the second grade. And then, maybe half an hour later, sometimes a day later, Ansel will pipe up with "There *is* that Mexican place in East Hampton," as though there has been not even a tiny break in the conversation. His neuroses are funny too, I say: For instance, he worries about global warming every time the temperature in winter is above average. Everyone else is enjoying the sun, but Ansel is worried! And he always worries about being worried: "Should I be worried?" He is so much like me, and like my father, that I can't help laughing at the reflection.

· · ·

I am aware that having a limited future makes Ansel freer. Next year, for example, he plans to enroll in the vocational-training program offered by the school system, even though he is on an academic track. The vocational program includes culinary arts, and Ansel knows that is what he wants. Isn't food what he thinks about all the time? The taste of a blood orange or a fresh fig may be the most important, most commented-on part of his day. In English he has chosen "luxury foods" for his special project; he writes of the high cost of hunting for truffles, of the packaging of caviar, of the pleasure of watching the guys behind the counter at Zabar's slice lox. He faithfully reads the "Dining Out" section of *The New York Times* and leafs through the Penzys Spices catalog.

He doesn't care that taking culinary arts each morning at a location in northern Westchester County will seriously limit his academic program. He does not want to sit through another year of science, even though it would "look better" on his college applications. He has no time to waste. Ansel calls a meeting with me and his guidance counselor and the director of the program, the last of whom he informs, "I can't do something without being serious about it. Otherwise I just don't think it's worth doing." When the director describes the culinary-arts program, which is almost completely hands-on cooking, the corners of Ansel's mouth curve into a little smile, and the guidance counselor, who knows him well, says, "I don't often see that look in Ansel's eyes."

It is apparent that cooking is what he must do. Being a public program, the vocational-training class must accommodate him, so he will probably have an aide for lifting heavy pots off the stove and similar tasks. It seems exciting, although I am a bit concerned that Ansel may miss out on two years of science, French, and math, which are given in the morning, when he will be off school grounds. After the meeting I stay behind to speak with his counselor.

"How would it be if he just does culinary arts for one year, not two?" I ask. Ansel would like to start the program this September, his junior year, but I think it will be better for college-admission purposes if he waits until his senior year.

"Yes, I assumed one year," the counselor says, adding, "Preferably his junior year."

I am surprised. "Because . . . ?"

"Because I know culinary arts will be in the morning next year; I'm not sure about the following year. And that would be better as far as academics go. Because he *has* to take history and English. Also . . ."

I know the other reason. She lets me say it. "Because we don't know where he will be physically in two years. This may be the only year he *can* do it."

·   ·   ·

I meet an old friend in the city for lunch. We walk to the restaurant, and she rattles on about the short story she is writing. I cannot open my mouth; I am sure I will start to cry. For two weeks I have been up every night with shoulder pain: a pinched nerve, probably brought on by a slipped disc. Yesterday my kitchen was gutted in advance of a major renovation for Ansel's benefit, and there are still bent nails sticking up from the floor every few inches.

My friend tells me about her latest challenge: her therapist has asked her, "What do you want?" As in life.

"Want," I say, almost sneering, and as I open my mouth, everything spills out, and in a little Vietnamese restaurant on Third

Avenue, I start weeping. "Who cares what you want?" I say accusingly, and I am frightened by my feeling, which comes out so raw and powerful and pitiless. "I want my son to live a long life. So what?" Every word is a choking effort, my tongue swollen and sore, my throat like gravel. Why bother wanting?

· · ·

I have two dreams. In the first one, two cars are driving fast in the left lane of the highway, in the wrong direction. Everyone in our car can see as we approach them that this is a very dangerous thing. But it's too late to stop. The cars crash head-on into other cars just in front of us, and I can see the drivers thrown aside, into the air, the cars tin-can crushed. But we are saved. We only witness the horror and move on. We don't even stop. What can we do?

In the second dream Ansel and I come upon a red-rock canyon in the middle of a southwestern desert. We are not really surprised; we have been expecting to find the canyon. It has a lip of rock across its entrance, so we cannot see beyond. Its contents are secret. But once we get inside, we are aware of water and sand, and a very beautiful light glinting off beach umbrellas. We are at the ocean. Ansel can walk. We stake out our place on the sand. We have brought our lunch and a blanket, and we sit together and eat: crusty French bread, a wedge of Parmigiano-Reggiano from Todaro Brothers, slices of ripe mango. We are happy.

· · ·

When Ansel rises from the table today, his legs tremble as he transfers to the wheelchair. Our house is in complete disorder: dining table and refrigerator and microwave are all sitting in the living room, because the kitchen renovation is not complete. The shelves in the living room hold two by fours; a sugar bowl; strips of insulation; our good silverware in a blue-felt Bloomingdale's bag; a tin candy box filled with paper clips, packing tape, nail clippers, misplaced trinkets and bits of toys, Pokémon cards and Monopoly hotels.

After dinner Ansel is sitting at the table drinking tea and trying to read *Treasure Island,* which he finds difficult because of the antiquated language and because he has been interrupted over and over again by Diana and Toby, who are bored. I am in the next room, also reading, when I hear a commotion: Ansel is screaming and weeping, "Stop! Stop! I can't stand it, stop!" in a weird, high, animal-like shriek. When I run in, I see that he has taken his empty teacup and begun to bang it over and over again on the table; while I watch, horrified he puts the cup down and begins to bang his forehead rhythmically.

"What happened?" I demand angrily of Diana. "What *happened*?!" I am stamping my foot, the rage spilling out of me. "What did you do?"

"I didn't do anything!" she retorts. "He was burping again—which he always does!—and I told him he was disgusting and he went crazy! God! You blame me for everything!"

Now Ansel begins to shriek again. "I'm an idiot! I'm an idiot! I did it because I'm an idiot!" His cheeks are big and red, and he can't catch his breath, and he begins to whimper. Embarrassment, comprehension, a normal sibling fight turned abnormal—a fifteen-year-old acting like a three-year-old.

"Pick him up," I say quietly to Joe, who has come in from the next room. "Pick him up and carry him into his room."

Later I ask Ansel, "What is it like—that anger? Are you on another planet, like I used to be when I had temper tantrums when I was a kid?" I know that anger is a locked box, but it is also freedom—a soaring, powerful white light.

"I don't know," he says. "I don't know. I just think if I scream and scream and scream maybe I'll stop being angry. Maybe I'll get it all out of me."

"Is there so much anger?" I ask. "What's it about?"

"Please, Mom." He turns his head away. "Please. Let's not talk about it anymore."

•　　•　　•

Another day he comes home from school depressed. "I'm worried about dying," he says. I honestly don't know what to say. Since when am I so wise anyway? I'm tired, and I worry about dying too. Driving home fast on the Saw Mill River Parkway, I sometimes think, *What will happen to my kids if I die?* It is always Ansel's face I see; how could he forgive me?

So I don't respond, not really, and later, when he is putting together the pieces of his clarinet, he wails melodramatically, "I'm so depressed, and no one cares!" Now I feel compelled to react, so I go into his room. He continues: "I was depressed in the first place, and then when I got to health class my teacher had written 'The Stages of Grief' up on the blackboard—we're studying death—and it just made me more depressed . . . And then we saw part of *Schindler's List,* clips of the movie . . ."

"Did you see the part with the little girl in the red coat who is wandering around the ghetto and then gets shot?" I ask, thinking this had upset him.

He looks at me. "She doesn't get shot, Mom. She hides in the building . . ."

"But she does, Ans. Eventually she does get shot."

"Nope," he says. "You're wrong, Mom. You forgot."

I don't want to contradict him again, though I know I'm right. I think of his great capacity for denial. I remember something the physician John Bach wrote in an article about boys with muscular dystrophy: "Successful adaptation does not depend upon an accurate perception of reality."

•   •   •

This morning I catch sight of Toby's torso while he is dressing. He is seven and a half, slender and small, built like a dancer. He has that nice square chest that a boy is supposed to have, with a line running down the center from breastbone to belly. Ansel would have been beautiful too, perhaps more so. I remember a photo from the summer before Ansel began taking prednisone to slow down the deterioration of his muscles, when he could still walk, ploddingly up the unrailed fronts steps. A blue-purple T-shirt, a sun-tinted face: a quite handsome eleven-year-old. Before the chipmunk cheeks, puffy from steroids. That must have been the summer before the wheelchair. My beautiful son.

•   •   •

Ansel's independent reading this month: Mark Twain's *Roughing It*; most of Phillip Lopate's *The Art of the Personal Essay*; "The Snows of Kilimanjaro" and other stories by Ernest Hemingway; M.F.K. Fisher's *A Cordiall Water*; *The Red Badge of Courage,* by Stephen Crane; *National Geographic*; S. J. Perelman's *Chicken Inspector no. 23.* His selection of a project for social studies, any "ism": Dadaism. Favorite music: Louis Armstrong, Thelonious Monk, show tunes, the Buena Vista Social Club.

•   •   •

Ansel and I are sitting in the living room, late. Everyone else has gone to sleep. He is doing his daily exercises: leaning with his palms against the back of the couch, pushing his heels down toward the floor, one at a time, to lengthen the Achilles tendons, trying to stay mobile for as long as possible. He has had a tough day, and he is very tired. Earlier he asked Joe to carry him to the bathroom (he usually walks), and when he got there he fell trying to reach the toilet.

"I don't know why I'm having so much trouble," he says to me later. "Do you think I'm just tired? Why should I be so tired?"

"I don't know, Ans. It may just be the disease. It's getting worse, I guess. That's really crummy, isn't it?"

He doesn't say anything. He is cutting his toenails, concentrating on the task of keeping all the parings in one pile on the coffee table.

"Isn't it?" I repeat.

He looks up. "No. I think everything that happens has a reason."

"I guess that's because you believe in God," I say.

"I used to get depressed thinking about this stuff," he continues, seeming to ignore my remark. "But then I realized it doesn't help. So I don't think about it anymore."

I ask him at another time, "Do you think about the fact that you may not have as many years as other people?"

"No, Mom. I just want to be happy."

• • •

Ansel says everything that happens has a reason. He uses the toilet in the middle of the night and flushes it, and the flood of water in the pipes wakes up our collie in the basement, and she begins barking, and I wake up, and it is a quarter to four.

In a way I'm not tired, so I get up and go down to the basement, where the dog is kenneled. She is wide awake and on her feet, waiting expectantly, as though we planned a rendezvous. She nips my heels and tries to push through my legs as we mount the stairs. Then she shoots outside, and I follow.

It's warm out, and completely calm; the three-quarters moon is immense and neon-yellow, hanging over the Palisades, nearly merging with the horizon. It seems otherworldly, like—and I know this is a ridiculous thought—an object from outer space.

In other words, it appears as it is—completely apart from, oblivious of, anything human.

I don't know if it's rising or setting. Joe will be able to tell me in the morning, but right now I don't want to know, not yet. I stand there with the mystery of the moon for some time, with the thrill of knowing its beauty—having it to myself for a few rare moments—while the dog sniffs under damp leaves, looking for a place to pee.

When she is finished, I take her back to the basement and give her a full bowl of water, which she drinks thirstily. I go to sleep easily, somehow fulfilled. Ansel says everything has a reason. He is fifteen. In two hours it will be daylight.

Time

FINALIST, REPORTING

Inside the Battle at Qala-i-Jangi

At a time when so much war coverage takes place on television, "Inside the Battle at Qala-i-Jangi" reaffirms the printed word's primacy and power. Alex Perry's heart-pounding account of how American soldiers crushed a Taliban uprising is old-fashioned battlefield reporting at its best.

Alex Perry

Inside the Battle at Qala-i-Jangi

From a ruined 19th century fortress, correspondent Alex Perry records the crushing of a Taliban revolt.

I n Afghanistan, nothing is ever what it seems. Including surrender.

On Nov. 24, a bright, warm Saturday, 300 Taliban soldiers who had fled the American bombardment of Kunduz, their last stronghold in the north of Afghanistan, laid down their weapons in the desert a few miles to the north of Mazar-i-Sharif. They surrendered to Northern Alliance General Abdul Rashid Dostum, who crowed that his forces had achieved a "great victory" as the POWs were herded 50 at a time onto flatbed trucks.

Even by the standards of Afghanistan's warlords, Dostum has

an unsavory reputation. In earlier episodes of Afghanistan's wars, he was reputed to have killed those of his soldiers who broke the rules by tying them to the tracks of his tanks. But outside Mazar, his soldiers told their prisoners that Dostum wanted to make a gesture of reconciliation to help unite Afghanistan's warring tribes. Afghan members of the Taliban would be free to return to their homes, while foreigners would be detained before being handed over to the U.N. Dostum didn't search his prisoners; that was a mistake, one he would bitterly regret. "If we had searched them, there would have been a fight," he said Wednesday, surveying hundreds of dismembered, blackened and crushed bodies. "But perhaps it wouldn't have been as bad as this."

The Taliban fighters, many of whom were foreigners, were transported from the field of surrender to a holding site in Qala-i-Jangi, a sprawling 19th century prison fortress to the west of Mazar, where Dostum stabled his horses. The convoy of prisoners had to pass through the city center; two weeks before, the Taliban had ruled the streets. The prisoners now peered out from under their blankets with shell-shocked, bloodshot eyes. The people of Mazar stared back at them with open hatred.

Things went wrong almost immediately. Once inside Qala-i-Jangi, the Taliban soldiers were asked to turn out their pockets. A prisoner, waiting until Alliance commander Nadir Ali was near, suddenly produced a grenade and pulled the pin, killing himself and the commander. In a similar attack the same night, another prisoner killed himself and senior Hazara commander Saeed Asad. The remaining men were led into underground cells to join scores of other captured Taliban fighters. Despite the grenade attacks, the Alliance guards were not reinforced.

SUNDAY MORNING The next morning, two Americans went to meet the prisoners at Qala-i-Jangi. Their mission at the fortress: to identify any members of al-Qaeda among the prisoners. But the Americans didn't conduct the interviews one by one—another mistake. Instead, at 11:15 a.m., the pair—Johnny Micheal Spann, 32, one of the CIA agents who had been active in Afghanistan since the war's beginning, the other identified by colleagues only as "Dave"—were taken to an open area outside the cells and a group of prisoners brought to meet them. According to members of a German television crew who were later trapped in the fort with Dave, Spann asked the prisoners who they were and why they joined the Taliban. They massed around him. "Why are you here?" Spann asked one. "To kill you," came the reply as the man lunged at Spann's neck. Spann drew his pistol and shot the man dead. Dave shot another, then grabbed an AK-47 from an Alliance guard and opened fire. According to eyewitness accounts given to the German team, the Taliban fighters launched themselves at Spann, scrabbling at his flesh with their hands, kicking and beating him. Spann killed two more with his pistol before he disappeared under the crush. An Alabaman with a wife and three children, Spann became the first American to die in combat in Afghanistan.

The Taliban then overpowered the Alliance guards, killing them with their own weapons. Dave mowed down three more Taliban, then sprinted to the main building along the north wall, where two Red Cross workers had just begun a meeting with the prison governor. "He burst in and told us to get out of there," says Simon Brooks, a Briton and a Red Cross staff member. "He was really shaken up. He said there were 20 dead Northern Alliance guys, and the Taliban were taking control of the fort." As Dave stayed behind to try to rescue Spann, the two Red Cross workers climbed up to the fort's parapet, hoisted themselves over the wall and slid 60 ft. down the other side. Meanwhile, the firing had alerted a pair of TV crews. They too ran to the main building; there they found Dave and were pinned down in the ensuing fire fight.

A few hundred yards to the south, in the prison block, the Taliban freed its comrades. Three escaped through a drain under the southern wall; all were soon shot by Alliance soldiers outside the fort. The Taliban fighters, trapped in the southwestern quarter of the fort, stormed a nearby armory, making off with AK-47s, grenades, mines, rocket launchers, mortars and ammunition. Alliance soldiers held on to the southeastern corner, which included an arched gateway, a courtyard and the gatekeeper's house. Other fighters took positions on the north wall and the roof of the main building. A vicious exchange of fire across the grassy parade ground followed. Two Alliance tanks along the north wall started firing into the Taliban area.

SUNDAY AFTERNOON At 2 p.m. two minivans and a pair of open-sided white Land Rovers mounted with machine guns pulled up outside the fortress gates. From the minivans jumped nine American special-operations men wearing wraparound sunglasses and baseball caps and carrying snub-nosed M-4 automatic rifles. The Land Rovers disgorged six British SAS soldiers armed with M-16s and dressed in jeans, sweaters, Afghan scarves and *pakuls,* the distinctive woolen hats of the Afghan *mujahedin.* The Americans and British quickly convened a conference with the Alliance leaders. "I want satcom [satellite communications] and JDAMS [guided munitions]," said the American commander. "Tell them there will be six or seven buildings in a line in the southwest half. If they can hit that, then that would kill a whole lot of these motherf_____."

A bearded American in a Harley-Davidson cap and mirrored sunglasses raised Dave on the radio. "Shit . . . shit . . . O.K. . . . Shit . . . O.K. Hold on, buddy, we're coming to get you," he said. Then, cutting the radio, he turned to his commander: "Mike is MIA. They've taken his gun and his ammo. We have another guy. He managed to kill two of them with his pistol, but he's holed up in the north side with no ammo." As a hurried discussion of tactics began, Harley-Davidson went back to his radio. Then he cut in: "Shit. Let's stop f___ing around and get in there." Pointing to the sky, he added, "Tell those guys to stop scratching their balls and fly."

Outside the fort, Alliance soldiers began pouring out of the northeast battlements, skidding over the walls and down the ramparts. The wounded were whisked away in commandeered taxis. A fire fight raged through the afternoon. Two American fighter planes began circling the area. Inside, TIME'S translator, Nagidullah Quraishi, was ordered to the gatekeeper's roof and told to translate conversations between the Western soldiers and their Afghan allies. Alliance General Majid Rozi told the Americans and the British that a white single-story building inside the Taliban area needed to be hit, and the visitors proceeded to spot the target for the planes far above. "Thunder, Ranger," said the American radio operator, speaking to the airplanes above. "The coordinates are: north 3639984, east 06658945, elevation 1,299 ft."

He turned to his comrades. "Four minutes."

"Three minutes."

"Two minutes."

"Thirty seconds."

"Fifteen seconds." From the sky, a great, arrow-shaped missile appeared, zeroing in on its target a hundred yards away and sounding like a car decelerating in high gear. The spotters lay flat. Alliance commanders and soldiers crouched against the door leading to the roof. The missile hit at 4:05 p.m. For a split second, as the concussive sound waves radiated outward, lungs emptied. Shrapnel whistled by. Then Alliance soldiers burst into applause. A U.S. soldier picked up a fallen piece of metal. "Souvenir," he said, grinning. Six more strikes followed before the British SAS commander re-established contact with Dave, still penned in with the TV crews. The SAS soldier told the Alliance commander that after two more strikes, his men should fire all their weapons. "Our guy is going to try to make a break for it," said the Briton. The conversation turned to Spann. "From what I understand, he was already gone before we got here," said an American.

"Three minutes," said the SAS guy. "Two minutes . . . 30 seconds." Everyone crouched once more against the wall. Again a glistening white arrow screamed down, again the split-second blackout. "One more," said the SAS man.

MONDAY The American and British teams stayed in position overnight. Fighting was constant, red tracers shooting off into Mazar city. Sometime after dark, Dave and the journalists escaped over the north wall. "He just climbed over and hitched a ride into town," a special-operations soldier later explained. "The first thing we have to do now is get our other guy out."

By Monday morning the Alliance had established a new command post at the northeast tower on top of what an American commander described as "10 tons of munitions, rockets, mortars, the works." A tank was driven onto the tower. From his seat on the garrison roof, commander Mohammed Akbar guided mortar and tank fire to Taliban positions in the southwest. "Excellent—right on the nose!" he shouted, as bullets from Taliban snipers whizzed just over his head. Then came the next mistake.

Around 10 a.m. four more special-operations soldiers and eight men from the 10th Mountain Division arrived at a position about 300 yds. outside the fort to the northeast. Inside the fort, bomb spotters were preparing three more strikes. A pilot circled overhead, radioing instructions to the spotters, his voice clearly audible on handsets held by the soldiers posted outside the fort. "Be advised," he said to the soldiers in the fort, "you are dangerously close. You are about a hundred yards away from the target." "I think we're perhaps a little too close," came the spotter's reply.

"But we have to be, to get the laser on the target." Pause. Bomb spotter: "We are about ready to pull back." Pilot: "We are about to release." Spotter: "Roger." Spotter: "Be advised we have new coordinates: north 3639996, east 06658866." Pilot: "Good. Copy." Spotter: "Mitch and Siberson are making their run now." Spotter again: "Two minutes."

At 10:53 a.m. the missile slammed into the north wall, perhaps 10 yds. from the Alliance's command center in the northeast tower. Much more powerful than previous strikes, it sent clouds of dust hundreds of feet into the air. "No, no!" Alliance commander Olim Razum yelled at the 10th Mountain soldiers. "This is the wrong place! Tell them to cut it!" A special-operations man glanced up at the cloud and shouted, "Incoming shrapnel—get down!" As the dust cloud cleared, a U-shaped hole the size of a small swimming pool appeared in the wall next to the northeast tower. The tank had flipped onto its back, its gun turret blown off. Alliance soldiers, bleeding, coated in dust, began sliding down the side of the fort and staggering across the surrounding cotton fields. "It missed," said a soldier named Afiz, blood dripping from his eyes and ears. "I don't know where my friends are." From under the fort's entrance arch, SAS and American soldiers emerged choking and spitting. "We have one down, semiconscious, no external bleeding," a radio crackled. "We have men down," a special-operations soldier told TIME. "Get out of here. Please."

Within 20 min., the casualties and walking wounded were loaded into seven jeeps and minibuses, which sped off to the U.S. base. Nine men were airlifted out. Nik Mohammed, 24, an Alliance soldier on the northeast tower at the time of the strike, said he helped pull three uniformed soldiers he believed to be Americans from the rubble of the collapsed wall and claimed that two of them were dead. On Tuesday the Pentagon said that there had been no military deaths but that five U.S. service members had been seriously injured and had been evacuated to Land-stuhl Regional Medical Center in Germany. Four British soldiers were also reported wounded over the previous 22 hours, one seriously, though British officials—who never comment on the SAS—will not confirm that they were wounded at Qala-i-Jangi. On the Alliance side, there were said to be as many as 30 dead and 50 injured.

At 4:50 p.m. a small group of special-operations soldiers returned. Dave was with them. He climbed up the northeast tower to confer with Alliance General Rozi. "You don't want to leave here tonight," an American soldier told TIME, checking his night-vision goggles. "There's going to be quite a show." The soldier used a reporter's satellite phone to call his wife and tell her he might be on the TV news that night—"Tape it all day, will you? O.K. Love you, babe." At midnight an American AC-130 gunship began lazily circling Qala-i-Jangi. It flew five times over the same spot, spraying the southern end of the fort with a golden stream of fire. Later a massive ball of flame lifted up from the fort, kicking off a fireworks display as mortar rounds and ammunition belts fired off into the night sky. Explosions sounded through the night; the blast blew open doors 10 miles away.

TUESDAY By the next morning the surviving Taliban troops were beginning to flag; Rozi estimated that there were only about 50 survivors from the original 600 or so in the fort and that they had no water or ammunition left. Their only food was horsemeat from Dostum's cavalry. A fighter who had escaped during the night was caught by local residents and hanged from a tree. Alliance forces were so confident of victory that at one frontline position, three shared a powerful joint of hashish. Others tucked into peanut butter and jelly from the American food drops. At 10 a.m. a group of 17 special-operations and SAS men returned to the gatekeeper's house. Harley-Davidson was there, along with

Dave, who was wearing a black *shalwar kameez* (the traditional Afghan pants and long shirt) and carrying an AK-47. After talking to Rozi, Dave told his men, "We're going to close in on these guys pretty hard. The one thing the general said to watch out for is a mortar still operating in there."

At 10:50 a.m. U.S. and British troops positioned themselves along the parapets to the east of the Taliban compound. "Did you see the show last night?" one asked TIME, grinning. "We watched for two hours. Really something." Around 100 Alliance soldiers scaled the southwest tower and lay down along the walls, firing on the Taliban below. Others manned the western tower. Before long, wounded and dead Alliance soldiers were being ferried through the gates. A U.S. soldier ran back to greet an SAS comrade who had felt the full force of Monday's air strike. "How's your hearing today?" he bellowed. Pause. "I said, 'How's your hearing?'"

By 1:25 p.m. from the southwest tower, commander Akbar estimated Taliban strength at "1½" men. On the field below lay hundreds of dead and dying. Two embraced in death. Alliance soldiers stepped gingerly over the bodies.

Some of the dead had their hands bound, and Alliance soldiers used scissors to snip off the strings. At 2:10 p.m. Akbar decided all the Taliban fighters were dead and walked down onto the field. His men, by now plainly spooked by the suicidal bravery of the Taliban, had to be forced to break cover. One wounded Taliban soldier, lying in the long grass, was shot to pieces. Alliance soldiers started looting, taking guns and ammunition and rifling the pockets of the dead for money, pens and cigarettes. The Taliban's new-looking sneakers were a particular target. Within minutes, the Alliance fighters had thrown away their shoes and yanked the sneakers from the cold, gray feet of the Taliban dead. The bloated carcasses of 30 horses, with entrails spilling, added a thick stench to the smoke and gunpowder. All the dead were described by the

Alliance as "terrorists" and "dangerous foreigners." "I killed four Chechens, four," said Mohammed Yasin excitedly. "I can show you the bodies." The occasional explosion from the smoldering arms depot sent Alliance men scampering across the field, hurdling bodies as they ran for cover.

In a basement under one pock-marked house, five Taliban fighters were trapped alive. Grenades were thrown in the tiny windows and AK-47s fired after them. With Alliance soldiers too afraid to enter the stables, a tank was brought in, crushing bodies under its tracks before firing five rounds into the block. In a ditch on the main parade ground, a young Taliban fighter, lying sprawled on his side, was still breathing. An Alliance soldier dropped a rock on his head. A few yards away lay a bloodied prayer book.

Even in the heat of battle, warriors can be rational; few fight to the death. But the Taliban at Qala-i-Jangi truly did, and beyond it. Spann's body, recovered by a special-operations squad, had been booby-trapped; a grenade had been hidden under the corpse of a Taliban fighter that lay on top of the American. As late as Thursday, those removing bodies were still taking fire from Taliban fighters who had somehow survived in the basements underneath the fort. On Saturday the basements were flooded; Northern Alliance observers expected perhaps five or six surviving Taliban to come out. In fact, at 11 a.m. no fewer than 86 filthy and hungry prisoners emerged; they were given bananas, apples and pomegranates, clothing and shoes. Three trucks took the wounded away. One of the 86 told Alliance fighters he was an American. The 20-year-old, who had been wounded in the leg, said he was from Washington. He would not give his name but said he was a convert to Islam who had come to Afghanistan—after a spell at a madrasah in Pakistan—to help the Taliban build a perfect Islamic government.

The battle was finally over. It had ended as it started, with a surrender. And its story held within its chapters a brutal lesson. The war against terrorism, they like to say, is a new form of war. But at Qala-i-Jangi, as the blood of horses and dead young men snaked into the dust, the oldest form of war imaginable seemed to have made a cruel and bitter return.

The American Scholar

FINALIST, ESSAYS

Moving

Anne Fadiman explores her family's move from city to country, turning a commonplace occurrence into an intricate emotional, intellectual, and social journey. Small and perfect in form, the essay reflects the sharp domestic eye of Jane Austen, the writer whom Fadiman quotes and evokes.

Anne Fadiman

Moving

From time to time, after we decided to move from New York City to western Massachusetts, my mind came to rest on the dispiriting example of James Montgomery Whitmore, my great-great-grandfather. Whitmore was a Mormon convert who traveled by covered wagon from Waxahachie, Texas, to Salt Lake City in 1857. Five years later, believing he had received a divine call to serve as a missionary in southern Utah, he sold his mercantile business, hauled his family down to Pipe Springs, bought livestock, planted grapevines, and started spreading the word. In 1866, a band of Paiute Indians stole a flock of sheep from his pasture, and when Whitmore and a hired hand followed their tracks onto the open plain, they were ambushed and shot. A posse of ninety men found their bodies twelve days later, buried under the snow.

Though the chances of ambush in western Massachusetts were slim, I did not feel my family history augured well. My great-great-grandfather should have stayed in Waxahachie; maybe we should stay in New York. But every time I walked past my husband's desk, I saw a yellow Post-it on his bulletin board that read, "The only safe thing is to take a chance." The quotation was attributed to Elaine May, who would have agreed with Wallace Stegner: "Why remain in one dull plot of earth when Heaven was reachable, was touchable, was just over there?"

.   .   .

My husband and I didn't think Manhattan was a dull plot of earth. I'd lived there for twenty-five years, George for twenty-one. We liked Mets games and New York accents. We liked Juilliard students who played Boccherini in subway stations and Sikh taxi drivers who wore turbans. We liked to walk from our loft in SoHo to Goody's, our favorite restaurant in Chinatown, and slurp Shanghai soup dumplings from large porcelain spoons. We liked our building, a turn-of-the-century box factory whose upper floors, when I moved there in 1978, were still served by a freight elevator that bore a hand-lettered sign: PLEASE RETURN THIS ELEVATOR TO THE GLUEING DEPARTMENT.

But as we grew older, we found ourselves inclining tropistically toward open spaces. It was impossible to describe our nature-cravings without sounding like Wordsworth, only more blubbery, so George and I avoided the subject around our friends, most of whom would have become seriously ill had they moved more than five blocks from the nearest bagel shop. We had both spent our early childhoods in New England, imprinted at tender ages by the smell of mown grass, the pea-green color of the air before a summer cloudburst, the taste of butter-and-sugar corn—the methods of whose eating my family had divided into two categories, Rotary (round and round) and Typewriter (left to right). (George and I added a third, Dot Matrix, for those who favor a back-and-forth approach.) We wanted those things again. Besides, our younger child was fond of projectiles—balls, slingshots, airplanes, rockets, arrows, torpedoes—and we were tired of shouting *"Not at the wedding pictures!"* Henry needed a yard.

We couldn't afford a weekend country house, and might not have wanted one anyway: too much like having a wife and a mistress. Serial monogamy seemed preferable. About ten years ago, we started talking about a second, rural phase. Since we were both writers, we could live anywhere we could plug in our modems. Cautiously, easing into the water by slow degrees, we visited college towns (bookstores, foreign films, possible teaching jobs) in Connecticut, Massachusetts, Vermont, and Maine. Some had houses priced beyond our means; some were too far from George's family, who live in Boston. We settled on the Pioneer Valley of Massachusetts, named for the Puritan frontiersmen of the late seventeenth and early eighteenth centuries, large numbers of whom, like my great-great-grandfather, were massacred by Indians who thought they should have stayed home.

.   .   .

When Sir Walter Elliot, the self-absorbed baronet in *Persuasion,* becomes "distressed for money," he decides to move out of his ancestral manor in Somersetshire. It is suggested that he might be able to stay put if he practiced certain economies, but he cannot imagine such a fall. "What! Every comfort of life knocked off! Journeys, London, servants, horses, table,—contractions and restrictions every where. To live no longer with the decencies of a private gentleman! No, he would sooner quit Kellynch-hall at once, than remain in it on such disgraceful terms."

Sir Walter is defined by his home. *The Baronetage,* the only book he ever reads, opens of its own accord to the page headed "ELLIOT OF KELLYNCH-HALL." When he becomes ELLIOT OF A-RENTED-HOUSE-IN-BATH, will he still be himself? (Yes, says Jane Austen. He's just as obnoxious as ever.) It makes Sir Walter uneasy to think of a tenant living in *his* bedchamber, taking walks through *his* grounds. "I am not fond," he observes, "of the idea of my shrubberies being always approachable."

We felt that way, too. Afraid to burn our bridges, we decided to rent out our loft, furnished, so we could creep back if we started missing soup dumplings too severely. We owned no shrubberies, but I wasn't sure that I wished strangers to approach the corner of the living room where we had exchanged our wedding vows, the bathtub that had soothed my first labor pains, the bed in which we had exchanged a thousand embraces and a thousand confidences. Would they appreciate "Nudes for Nudes," a series of four pencil sketches by George's mother that we had affixed permanently to the shower wall? (I have always believed that it is unsporting for fully clothed people to look at pictures of naked ones; the placement of this work was designed to even things up.) Would they be properly impressed by the dining-room lamp, a large black contraption that had formerly graced the Erie-Lackawanna railway station in Hoboken, New Jersey, and was still equipped with an anti-moth-immolation grille?

Sir Walter forbids anyone to mention that he is letting his house: "It was only on the supposition of his being spontaneously solicited by some most unexceptionable applicant, on his own terms, and as a great favor, that he would let it at all." We had no such qualms. We engaged a real estate agent who dressed in black and had an Italian first name and a last name that was half French and half Spanish. (It was hyphenated. Paolo was far too upscale to have only one name.) He walked around the loft. I'm not sure he appreciated "Nudes for Nudes." I saw him eyeing the aquamarine felt-tip-pen stain on the chair near the front door, the grungy sofa, the ancient gas stove. "It will be just right," he said in his expensive Italian-French-Spanish accent, "for a very special person."

Paolo wrote a display ad for the *New York Times* real estate section headlined "EXPRESS YOUR INTERIOR WORLD." At first I wasn't sure what this meant, but I hadn't spent all those undergraduate hours on *explication de texte* for nothing. Eventually I deconstructed it. It meant: "You—the very special person whose next address will be 150 Thompson Street—may look like an investment banker, but inside your three-piece suit there lives a starving poet who is crying to get out." The ad continued: "This bohemian loft [read: there are no Sub-Zero appliances] oozes charm & character [read: there are children's fingerprints on the walls] only found in original old

SoHo [read: there's only one bathroom]." In its favor, the loft did have "wd flrs, orig beamed ceils, and grt clsts."

Although there are pages and pages in *Persuasion* about whether Sir Walter will find the right tenants, there is not a word about cleaning up Kellynch-hall before its prospective occupants come to inspect it. Nineteenth-century novels never mention such matters. The servants take care of them. Even if the tenants were to drop in unannounced, the silver would already be polished, the floors waxed, the carpets beaten, and the ancestral portraits straightened. Paolo did not find our loft in a similar state of readiness.

"The animals will have to go," he observed. The animals! How thrilling! He made it sound as if we kept a pack of ocelots. In fact, our menagerie consisted of Silkie, Susannah's hamster, and Bunky, Henry's frog, both of whom lived in plastic boxes on the dining-room table, underneath the lamp from the Erie-Lackawanna railway station.

"The kitchen is cluttered," he added. Before Paolo's arrival, I had spent three hours de-cluttering it. There wasn't a single object on the counters. No one could toast, blend, or make coffee in this kitchen; it was apparently owned by people who had been born without digestive tracts. This met with Paolo's approval. The problem was the family photographs posted with magnets on the refrigerator. "No personal effects," he explained, using a phrase I had heard only on television detective shows, describing corpses that had been robbed before they were murdered.

We banished the animals to Henry's bedroom, expunged our personal effects, spread a patchwork quilt on the sofa, replaced the Revereware teakettle with an imported red enamel coffeepot you couldn't pick up without a potholder, replaced the potholder, repainted the kitchen cabinets, scrubbed the windows, mopped the floors, rolled out a Persian rug the children weren't allowed to walk on, moved nine bags of toys to our neighbor's loft, and propped the pillows vertically on our bed, which meant that all the comfortable ones—the soft, saggy blobs you could bury your cheek in—were

extradited to the closet. It could have been worse. If we'd been selling the loft instead of just renting it, we might have been tempted
to hire a fluffer. (*Fluffer* is a term borrowed from pornographic
filmmaking; he or she gets the male star ready for the camera.) In
the housing market, the fluffer—also known as a stager—induces a
temporary state of real-estate tumescence by removing much of
what the client owns and replacing it, from a private warehouse of
props, with new furniture, carpets, plants, paintings, towels, sheets,
shower curtains, throw pillows, lamp shades, ice buckets (to hold
champagne next to the Jacuzzi), breakfast trays (to hold tea and the
Sunday *Times*), and Scrabble sets (to spell out BEAUTIFUL HOME).
One fluffer ordered his client to remove a Georgia O'Keeffe painting from the wall and hide it under the bed. The colors were wrong.

Even though our loft was prepared by amateurs—self-fluffed,
as it were—it had never looked better. We rented it to a kindly
macroeconomist. The Elliots rent Kellynch-hall to a kindly admiral who keeps the house shipshape, though he moves the umbrellas from the butler's room to the hallway and strips Sir Walter's
dressing room of most of its looking glasses. "Oh Lord!" Admiral
Croft explains, "there was no getting away from oneself."

. . .

"No getting away from oneself": that is both the fear and the
hope of people who move. If you're pulling up stakes in order to
remake your life and your character, what if you go to all that
trouble and end up no more changed than Sir Walter? On the
other hand, what if your identity is stuck with such firm adhesive
to your old home that you leave little bits behind, and your new
self is tattered and diminished?

According to the sociologist James M. Jasper, it is no wonder that
Americans name their cars Quests and Explorers and Ventures and
Caravans. We move more than anyone else. In a typical year, 20 percent of all Americans relocate, as compared with 4 percent of all Germans, 8 percent of all British, and 10 percent of all Japanese. Each of

those one-in-five Americans flouts the law laid down by almost every book whose plot revolves around relocation: *Stay where you are!* Can you think of a happy book about moving? I can't. It's fine to hie yourself to Troy or Oz or Narnia or Wonderland, as long as you end up back where you started—and, indeed, a frequent theme in books about travel, whether real or imaginary, is the central character's strenuous efforts to get home. (Traveling is always thought to be more enjoyable than moving: we envy foreign correspondents but pity army brats.) A typical children's-book move is the one made by the orphaned heroines of *The Secret Garden* and *A Little Princess* from warm, fecund India to cold, dreary England. Even the *Little House* series, in which the Ingalls family stays intact and reasonably content as it moves from woods to prairie to creek to lake, becomes incrementally less idyllic with each volume. Most discouraging of all is the sort of educational volume, illustrated with photographs of cheerful moving men, that extols the joys of leaving your friends and starting a new school; you can tell the author is lying because the next title in the series is usually something like *Tonsillectomies Are Fun!*

And as we pass out of childhood, what do we read? *Martin Chuzzlewit*, in which young Martin moves to America, falls ill with fever, and loses all his money in a land swindle; *Main Street*, in which Carol Kennicott moves to Gopher Prairie and is suffocated by small-town life; *The Grapes of Wrath*, in which the Joads move to California and—well, you know the rest. From birth to adulthood, our lives are a journey away from Eden; and that—because it matches our own trajectory—is the only direction the literary moving van can go.

      •   •   •

When I was eight, our family moved from Connecticut to southern California. The weather was balmy, the beach broad, the incidence of runny noses low. But objective merit means little to a child. All I knew was that the light was too bright, the shadows were too hard, the landscape had too much brown.

I hoped that our move to Massachusetts would be not a deracination but a re-racination. During our last three months in New York, I was encouraged in this view by the e-mails I received from the owner of the place we were going to rent, a foursquare yellow clapboard farmhouse built in 1804, on the east bank of the Connecticut River, by Elijah and Resign Graves. (Those Puritans! It was coercive enough to name your daughter Felicity or Chastity, but Resign!) Our landlord, whose family was planning to spend a sabbatical year in London, was a science writer who had just completed the labels for an insect exhibition that featured a rare birdwing butterfly collected by a man who was eaten by cannibals. As the spring and summer progressed, she sent us frequent nature bulletins: The trillium was blooming. Two orioles had been spotted on the quince bushes. The red fox had trotted through the pasture. The hummingbirds had returned. The mother wrens were peering out of their nestbox. The boys had found two toads.

How familiar it all sounded! Frances Hodgson Burnett would never have sent Sara Crewe back to India, but our lives were not a novel. Might it be possible to journey backward instead of forward?

We'd find out soon enough. But first we had to deal with our To Do list: Fill out change-of-address forms. Re-glue kitchen cabinet knobs. Fix toilet. Unclog bathtub drain. Get sofa and chairs cleaned. Go to dentist. Get renter's insurance. Disconnect phone and utilities. Send transcripts to children's new school. Switch bank accounts. Duplicate keys. Write farewell note to neighbors. Cancel *New York Times.* We had to compile a list of instructions for our tenants: Put out garbage on Monday, Wednesday, and Friday, recycling on Wednesday only. Open the hall closet by pushing, not pulling. Remember to replace the water in the plastic lint catcher. (Our future landlord wrote us a similar list: Don't let the children touch the bat poop in the attic. Protect potato chips from mice by suspending bags from the ceiling. Feed suet to woodpeckers and thistle seed to finches.)

Our grt clsts held layers we hadn't seen for years. New Yorkers, lacking attics and basements and garages, treat their closets like trash compactors (or, to put it more charitably, like the squeezing machines that turn duck breasts into *canard pressé*). The byproducts of our shared lives had been compressed into a dense sediment that, when pried out and spread on the floor, expanded by a factor of ten. How could we have accumulated so many outgrown hiking boots, so many mateless mittens, so many letters from people who had once loomed large and now, like distant telephone poles, had shrunk to near-invisibility?

I had imagined that our final weeks would be sweet, a last hurrah of city-love, but we were too busy for sentiment. In our early days together, George and I had walked together down Prince Street every night, holding hands. Now we walked the same route every afternoon, dragging our cast-off possessions to Goodwill.

We packed 347 boxes. (I know the number because it is written on the moving company's invoice; the total weight was six tons.) We vowed we would never buy another book. We broke our nails peeling packing tape from slippery brown rolls. We kept losing our scissors, our Magic Markers, our color-coded dots (green for the new house, red for storage); later, we discovered that we had boxed them up.

When we left for Massachusetts, I had been awake for three days and three nights. Our rented car was so full that the rearview mirror was useless. Susannah held Silkie's terrarium between her knees. I held Bunky's aquarium between my feet. As we drove north on Interstate 91, I thought: This is the worst mistake I have ever made in my life. George and I will never get another writing assignment. Susannah will hang out at the mall. Henry will chew gum. The sushi will be frozen.

·   ·   ·

When I was younger, I spent several years studying the Hmong, a montagnard tribe whose entire culture had evolved around their frequent migrations. Their wood and bamboo houses could be taken apart, portaged in modular chunks, and put back together. Their great arts were textiles, jewelry, music, and storytelling. Everything was physically and psychologically portable, so it was possible to move without cutting off roots.

In the car, I was certain we could never do that: our reassembled lives would look nothing like our old ones. But when we drove down our new driveway, my despair lifted with a crazy whoosh that cannot be explained even by the lability of fatigue. My eyes filled with tears. The yellow house was beautiful. A few minutes later, the moving van pulled in, and I asked the driver to locate a box that I had labeled in red on all six sides: BALLS BALLS BALLS BALLS BALLS BALLS. At a school auction, we had been the high bidders on a set of balls of every conceivable genre—football, basketball, volleyball, softball, tennis, soccer, bocce. Henry spilled them out onto the back lawn and ran in circles, tossing and kicking and rolling.

That night, as we lay in bed, I murmured, "George! We're really in the country! Listen to the peepers on the riverbank!"

"Those aren't peepers on the riverbank," George said gently. "That's Bunky, on Henry's bureau. We're hearing him over the baby monitor."

As the weeks passed, we missed New York, sometimes acutely, but that did not make us love the Pioneer Valley any less. I reminded myself that the most happily remarried widows are the ones who had the best first marriages.

George and Susannah swam every day in the Connecticut River and reported what they had seen on the bottom (a golf bag, a glove, a potato). Henry and I bicycled to the corner store, which, unlike its SoHo analogue, had signs in the window offering night crawlers and chewing tobacco—but it also had seven brands of ice cream and a luxuriant hawthorn tree out front. On our fourth visit, Henry settled himself under the hawthorn and said, with a five-year-old's easily acquired sense of permanency, "This is where we always sit."

Last month, we signed the papers on an 1807 brick farmhouse

in a neighboring town. When we learned that it needed a new roof, we refused to look at any materials that were not guaranteed to last at least twenty-five years.

•   •   •

It is true that I had a great-great-grandfather who was killed by Indians, but these days I find myself thinking more often of another great-great-grandfather, also a Utah pioneer. John Sharp moved from Clackmannanshire, Scotland, where he had worked in a coal mine, to New Orleans, then to St. Louis, and finally, in 1850, to Salt Lake City. His journey to Utah was, I will grudgingly admit, even more arduous than our journey up Interstate 91. The first snows overtook his wagon train, and he and his party spent the winter in caves they dug in the side of Red Butte Canyon, roofing them with wagon boxes and walling them with stones.

When Sharp arrived in Salt Lake City, the skills he had acquired in the mines of Clackmannanshire won him the contract for quarrying and hauling, by ox-drawn wagon, the huge blocks of granite that were to form the foundation of the Mormon Tabernacle. He later became manager of the quarry, then superintendent of public works, and finally a director of the Union Pacific Railroad. In 1869, at Promontory Point, he helped drive the golden spike that completed the transcontinental railroad, enabling people to move across the country by train instead of covered wagon.

In 1904, an article about John Sharp was published in the monthly magazine of the Young Men's Mutual Improvement Association. It pointed out that had Sharp stayed in Scotland, he might never have left the coal pits. His life, noted the anonymous author, "teaches the lesson that to succeed one must struggle with circumstance, and overcome by faith and toil; that change, evolution, and action, secure mental and material progress; while, on the contrary, traveling self-satisfied in ruts, seeking sameness, and courting inaction, are conditions to be avoided."

The Atlantic Monthly

WINNER, REPORTING

The Crash of EgyptAir 990

Writer William Langewiesche, a pilot in his own right, explains why a jet packed with 217 passengers plunged 33,000 feet into the Atlantic Ocean in the dead of night—and why it took so long for the U.S. and Egyptian governments to issue an explanation. Using black-box transcripts and radar records, Langewiesche meticulously reconstructs the last minutes of the so-called suicide flight. In a feat of storytelling, he reveals the nasty combination of politics and culture clashes that delayed the official investigation.

William Langewiesche

The Crash of EgyptAir 990

Two years afterward the U.S. and Egyptian governments are still quarreling over the cause—a clash that grows out of cultural division, not factual uncertainty. A look at the flight data from a pilot's perspective, with the help of simulations of the accident, points to what the Egyptians must already know: the crash was caused not by any mechanical failure but by a pilot's intentional act.

I remember first hearing about the accident early in the morning after the airplane went down. It was October 31, 1999, Halloween morning. I was in my office when a fellow pilot, a former flying companion, phoned with the news: It was EgyptAir Flight 990, a giant twin-engine Boeing 767 on the way from New York to Cairo, with 217 people aboard. It had taken off from Kennedy Airport in the middle of the night, climbed to 33,000 feet, and flown normally for half an hour before mysteriously plummeting into the Atlantic Ocean sixty miles south of Nantucket. Rumor had it that the crew had said nothing to air-traffic control, that the flight had simply dropped off the New York radar screens. Soon afterward an outbound Air France flight had swung over the area, and had reported no fires in sight—only a dim and empty ocean far below. It was remotely possible that Flight 990 was still in the air somewhere, diverting toward a safe landing. But sometime around daybreak a Merchant Marine training ship spotted debris floating on the waves—aluminum scraps, cushions and clothing, some human remains. The midshipmen on board gagged from the stench of jet fuel—a planeload of unburned kerosene rising from shattered tanks on the ocean floor, about 250 feet below. By the time rescue ships and helicopters arrived, it was obvious that there would be no survivors. I remember reacting to the news with regret for the dead, followed by a thought for the complexity of the investigation that now lay ahead. This accident had the markings of a tough case. The problem was not so much the scale of the carnage—a terrible consequence of the 767's size—but, rather, the still-sketchy profile of the upset that preceded it, this bewildering fall out of the sky on a calm night, without explanation, during an utterly uncritical phase of the flight.

I don't fly the 767, or any other airliner. In fact, I no longer fly for a living. But I know through long experience with flight that such machines are usually docile, and that steering them does not require the steady nerves and quick reflexes that passengers may imagine. Indeed, as we saw on September 11, steering them may not even require much in the way of training—the merest student-pilot level is probably enough. It's not hard to understand why. Airplanes at their core are very simple devices—winged things that belong in the air. They are designed to be flyable, and they are. Specifically, the 767 has ordinary mechanical and hydraulic flight controls that provide the pilot with smooth and conventional responses; it is normally operated on autopilot, but can easily be flown by hand; if you remove your hands from the controls entirely, the airplane sails on as before, until it perhaps wanders a bit, dips a wing, and starts into a gentle descent; if you pull the nose up or push it down (within reason) and then fold your arms, the airplane returns unassisted to steady flight; if you idle the engines, or shut them off entirely, the airplane becomes a rather well behaved glider. It has excellent forward visibility, through big windshields. It has a minimalist cockpit that may look complicated to the untrained eye but is a masterpiece of clean design. It can easily be managed by the standard two-person crew, or even by one pilot alone. The biggest problem in flying the airplane on a routine basis is boredom. Settled into the deep sky at 33,000 feet, above the weather and far from any obstacle, the 767 simply makes very few demands.

Not that it's idiot-proof, or necessarily always benign. As with any fast and heavy airplane, operating a 767 safely even under ordinary circumstances requires anticipation, mental clarity, and a practical understanding of the various systems. Furthermore, when circumstances are *not* ordinary—for example, during an engine failure just after takeoff or an encounter with unexpected wind shear during an approach to landing—a wilder side to the airplane's personality suddenly emerges. Maintaining control then requires firm action and sometimes a strong arm: There's nothing surprising about this: all airplanes misbehave on occasion, and have to be disciplined. "Kicking the dog," I called it in the ornery old cargo crates I flew when I was in college—it was a regular part of survival. In the cockpits of modern jets it is rarely necessary. Nonetheless, when trouble occurs in a machine as massive and aerodynamically slick as the 767, if it is not quickly suppressed the consequences can blossom out of control. During a full-blown upset like that experienced by the Egyptian crew, the airplane may dive so far past its tested limits that it exceeds the very scale of known engineering data—falling off the graphs as well as out of the sky. Afterward the profile can possibly be reconstructed mathematically by aerodynamicists and their like, but it cannot be even approximated by pilots in flight if they expect to come home alive.

I got a feel for the 767's dangerous side last summer, after following the accident's trail from Washington, D.C., to Cairo to the airplane's birthplace, in Seattle, where Boeing engineers let me fly a specially rigged 767 simulator through a series of relevant upsets and recoveries along with some sobering replays of Flight 990's final moments. These simulations had been flown by investigators more than a year before and had been reported on in detail in the publicly released files. Boeing's argument was not that the 767 is a flawless design but, more narrowly, that none of the imaginable failures of its flight-control systems could explain the known facts of this accident.

But that's getting ahead of the story. Back on October 31, 1999, with the first news of the crash, it was hard to imagine any form of pilot error that could have condemned the airplane to such a sustained and precipitous dive. What switch could the crew have thrown, what lever? Nothing came to mind. And why had they perished so silently, without a single distress call on the radio? A total electrical failure was very unlikely, and would not explain the loss of control. A fire would have given them time to talk. One thing was certain: the pilots were either extremely busy or incapacitated from the start. Of course there was always the possibility of a terrorist attack—a simple if frightening solution. But otherwise something had gone terribly wrong with the airplane itself, and that could be just as bad. There are more than 800 Boeing 767s in the world's airline fleet, and they account for more transatlantic flights than all other airplanes combined. They are also very similar in design to the smaller and equally numerous Boeing 757s. So there was plenty of reason for alarm.

"EgyptAir Nine-Ninety, Radio Contact Lost"

One of the world's really important divides lies between nations that react well to accidents and nations that do not. This is as true for a confined and technical event like the crash of a single flight as it is for political or military disasters. The first requirement is a matter of national will, and never a sure thing: it is the intention to get the story right, wherever the blame may lie. The second requirement follows immediately upon the first, and is probably easier to achieve: it is the need for people in the aftermath to maintain even tempers and open minds. The path they follow may not be simple, but it can provide for at least the possibility of effective resolutions.

In the case of EgyptAir Flight 990 the only information available at first was external. The airplane had arrived in New York late on a flight from Los Angeles, and had paused to refuel, take on passengers, and swap crews. Because of the scheduled duration of the flight to Cairo, two cockpit crews had been assigned to the ocean crossing—an "active crew," including the aircraft commander, to handle the first and last hours of the flight; and a "cruise crew," whose role was essentially to monitor the autopilot during the long, sleepy mid-Atlantic stretch. Just before midnight these four pilots rode out to the airport on a shuttle bus from Manhattan's Pennsylvania Hotel, a large establishment where EgyptAir retained rooms for the use of its personnel. The pilots had been there for several days and, as usual, were well rested. Also in the bus was one of the most senior of EgyptAir's captains, the company's chief 767 pilot, who was not scheduled to fly but would be "deadheading" home to Cairo. An EgyptAir dispatcher rode out on the bus with them, and subsequently reported that the crew members looked and sounded normal. At the airport he gave them a standard briefing and an update on the New York surface weather, which was stagnant under a low, thin overcast, with light winds and thickening haze.

Flight 990 pushed back from the gate and taxied toward the active runway at 1:12 A.M. Because there was little other traffic at the airport, communications with the control tower were noticeably relaxed. At 1:20 Flight 990 lifted off. It topped the clouds at 1,000 feet and turned out over the ocean toward a half moon rising above the horizon. The airplane was identified and tracked by air-traffic-control radar as it climbed through the various New York departure sectors and entered the larger airspace belonging to the en-route controllers of New York Center; its transponder target and data block moved steadily across the controllers' computer-generated displays, and its radio transmissions sounded perhaps a little awkward, but routine. At 1:44 it leveled off at the assigned 33,000 feet.

The en-route controller working the flight was a woman named Ann Brennan, a private pilot with eight years on the job. She had the swagger of a good controller, a real pro. Later she characterized the air traffic that night as slow, which it was—during the critical hour she had handled only three other flights. The offshore military-exercise zones, known as warning areas, were inactive. The sky was sleeping.

At 1:47 Brennan said, "EgyptAir Nine-ninety, change to my frequency one-two-five-point-niner-two."

EgyptAir acknowledged the request with a friendly "Good day," and after a pause checked in on the new frequency: "New York, EgyptAir Nine-nine-zero heavy, good morning."

Brennan answered, "EgyptAir Nine-ninety, roger."

That was the last exchange. Brennan noticed that the flight still had about fifteen minutes to go before leaving her sector. Wearing her headset, she stood up and walked six feet away to sort some paperwork. A few minutes later she approved a request by Washington Center to steer an Air France 747 through a corner of her airspace. She chatted for a while with her supervisor, a man named Ray Redhead. In total she spent maybe six minutes away from her station, a reasonable interval on such a night. It was just unlucky that while her back was turned Flight 990 went down.

A computer captured what she would have seen—a strangely abstract death no more dramatic than a video game. About two minutes after the final radio call, at 1:49:53 in the morning, the radar swept across EgyptAir's transponder at 33,000 feet. Afterward, at successive twelve-second intervals, the radar read 31,500, 25,400, and 18,300 feet—a descent rate so great that the air-traffic-control computers interpreted the information as false, and showed "XXXX" for the altitude on Brennan's display. With the next sweep the radar lost the transponder entirely, and picked up only an unenhanced "primary" blip, a return from the airplane's metal mass. The surprise is that the radar continued to receive such returns (which show only location, and not altitude) for nearly another minute and a half, indicating that the dive must have dramatically slowed or stopped, and that the 767 remained airborne, however tenuously, during that interval. A minute and a half is a long time. As the Boeing simulations later showed, it must have been a strange and dreamlike period for the pilots, hurtling through the night with no chance of awakening.

When radar contact was lost, the display for EgyptAir 990 began to "coast," indicating that the computers could no longer find a correlation between the stored flight plan and the radar view of the sky. When Brennan noticed, she stayed cool. She said, "EgyptAir Nine-ninety, radar contact lost, recycle transponder, squawk one-seven-one-two." EgyptAir did not answer, so she tried again at unhurried intervals over the following ten minutes. She advised Ray Redhead of the problem, and he passed the word along. She called an air-defense radar facility, and other air-traffic-control centers as far away as Canada, to see if by any chance someone was in contact with the flight. She asked a Lufthansa crew to try transmitting to EgyptAir from up high. Eventually she brought in Air France for the overflight. The prognosis was of course increasingly grim, but she maintained her professional calm. She continued to handle normal operations in her sector while simultaneously setting the search-and-rescue forces in motion. Half an hour into the process, when a controller at Boston Center called and asked, "Any luck with the EgyptAir?" she answered simply, "No."

Government Lite Meets
Government Heavy

Among the dead were 100 Americans, eighty-nine Egyptians (including thirty-three army officers), twenty-two Canadians, and a few people of other nationalities. As the news of the disaster spread, hundreds of frantic friends and relatives gathered at the airports in Los Angeles, New York, and Cairo. EgyptAir officials struggled to meet people's needs—which were largely, of course, for the sort of information that no one yet had. Most of the bodies remained in and around the wreckage at the bottom of the sea. Decisions now had to be made, and fast, about the recovery operation and the related problem of an investigation. Because the airplane had crashed in international waters, Egypt had the right to lead the show. Realistically, though, it did not have the resources to salvage a heavy airplane in waters 250 feet deep and 5,000 miles away.

The solution was obvious, and it came in the form of a call to the White House from Egyptian President Hosni Mubarak, an experienced military pilot with close ties to EgyptAir, requesting that the investigation be taken over by the U.S. government. The White House in turn called Jim Hall, the chairman of the National Transportation Safety Board, an investigative agency with a merited reputation for competence. Hall, a Tennessee lawyer and friend of the Gores, had in the aftermath of the TWA Flight 800 explosion parlayed his position into one of considerable visibility. The Egyptians produced a letter formally signing over the investigation to the United States, an option accorded under international convention, which would place them in a greatly diminished role (as "accredited representatives") but would also save them trouble and money. Mubarak is said to have regretted the move ever since.

In retrospect it seems inevitable that the two sides would have trouble getting along. The NTSB is a puritanical construct, a small federal agency without regulatory power whose sole purpose is to investigate accidents and issue safety recommendations that might add to the public discourse. Established in 1967 as an "independent" unit of the Washington bureaucracy, and shielded by design from the political currents of that city, the agency represents the most progressive American thinking on the role and character of good government. On call twenty-four hours a day, with technical teams ready to travel at a moment's notice, it operates on an annual baseline budget of merely $62 million or so, and employs only about 420 people, most of whom work at the headquarters on four floors of Washington's bright and modern Loews L'Enfant Plaza Hotel. In part because the NTSB seems so lean, and in part because by its very definition it advocates for the "right" causes, it receives almost universally positive press coverage. The NTSB is technocratic. It is clean. It is Government Lite.

EgyptAir, in contrast, is Government Heavy—a state-owned airline with about 600 pilots and a mixed fleet of about forty Boeings and Airbuses that serves more than eighty destinations worldwide and employs 22,000 people. It operates out of dusty

Stalinist-style office buildings at the Cairo airport, under the supervision of the Ministry of Transport, from which it is often practically indistinguishable. It is probably a safe airline, but passengers dislike it for its delays and shoddy service. They call it Air Misère, probably a play on the airline's former name, Misr Air ("Misr" is Arabic for "Egypt"). It has been treated as a fiefdom for years by Mubarak's old and unassailable air-force friends, and particularly by the company's chairman, a man named Mohamed Fahim Rayan, who fights off all attempts at reform or privatization. This is hardly a secret. In parliamentary testimony six months before the crash of Flight 990, Rayan said, "My market is like a water pond which I developed over the years. It is quite unreasonable for alien people to come and seek to catch fish in my pond." His critics answer that the pond is stagnant and stinks of corruption—but this, too, is nothing new. The greatest pyramids in Egypt are made not of stone but of people: they are the vast bureaucracies that constitute society's core, and they function not necessarily to get the "job" done but to reward the personal loyalty of those at the bottom to those at the top. Once you understand that, much of the rest begins to make sense. The bureaucracies serve mostly to shelter their workers and give them something like a decent life. They also help to define Cairo. It is a great capital city, as worldly as Washington, D.C., and culturally very far away.

An official delegation traveled from Cairo to the United States and ended up staying for more than a year. It was led by two EgyptAir pilots, Mohsen al-Missiry, an experienced accident investigator on temporary assignment to the Egyptian Civil Aviation Authority for this case, and Shaker Kelada, who had retired from active flying to become a flight-operations manager and eventually vice-president for safety and quality assurance. These men were smart and tough, and managed a team primarily of EgyptAir engineers, many of whom were very sharp.

The U.S. Navy was given the job of salvage, and it in turn

hired a contractor named Oceaneering which arrived with a ship and grapples and remote-controlled submarines. The debris was plotted by sonar, and found to lie in two clusters: the small "west field," which included the left engine; and, 1,200 feet beyond it in the direction of flight, the "east field," where most of the airplane lay. From what was known of the radar profile and from the tight concentration of the debris, it began to seem unlikely that an in-flight explosion was to blame. The NTSB said nothing. Nine days after the accident the flight-data recorder—the "black box" that records flight and systems data—was retrieved and sent to the NTSB laboratory in Washington. The NTSB stated tersely that there was preliminary evidence that the initial dive may have been a "controlled descent." Five days later, on Sunday, November 14, a senior official at the Egyptian Transportation Ministry—an air force general and a former EgyptAir pilot—held a news conference in Cairo and, with Rayan at his side, announced that the evidence from the flight-data recorder had been inconclusive but the dive could be explained only by a bomb in the cockpit or in the lavatory directly behind it. It was an odd assertion to make, but of little importance, because the second black box, the cockpit voice recorder, had been salvaged the night before and was sent on Sunday to the NTSB. The tape was cleaned and processed, and a small group that included a translator (who was not Egyptian) gathered in a listening room at L'Enfant Plaza to hear it through.

"I Rely on God"

Listening to cockpit recordings is a tough and voyeuristic duty, restricted to the principal investigators and people with specific knowledge of the airplane or the pilots, who might help to prepare an accurate transcript. Experienced investigators grow accustomed to the job, but I talked to several who had heard the

EgyptAir tape, and they admitted that they had been taken aback. Black boxes are such pitiless, unblinking devices. When the information they contained from Flight 990 was combined with the radar profile and the first, sketchy information on the crew, this was the story it seemed to tell:

The flight lasted thirty-one minutes. During the departure from New York it was captained, as required, by the aircraft commander, a portly senior pilot named Ahmad al-Habashi, fifty-seven, who had flown thirty-six years for the airline. Habashi of course sat in the left seat. In the right seat was the most junior member of the crew, a thirty-six-year-old co-pilot who was progressing well in his career and looking forward to getting married. Before takeoff the co-pilot advised the flight attendants by saying, in Arabic, "In the name of God, the merciful, the compassionate. Cabin crew takeoff position." This was not unusual.

After takeoff the autopilot did the flying. Habashi and the co-pilot kept watch, talked to air-traffic control, and gossiped about their work. The cockpit door was unlocked, which was fairly standard on EgyptAir flights. Various flight attendants came in and left; for a while the chief pilot, the man who was deadheading back to Cairo, stopped by the cockpit to chat. Then, twenty minutes into the flight, the "cruise" co-pilot, Gameel al-Batouti, arrived. Batouti was a big, friendly guy with a reputation for telling jokes and enjoying life. Three months short of sixty, and mandatory retirement, he was unusually old for a co-pilot. He had joined the airline in his mid-forties, after a career as a flight instructor for the air force, and had rejected several opportunities for command. His lack of ambition was odd but not unheard of: his English was poor and might have given him trouble on the necessary exams; moreover, as the company's senior 767 co-pilot, he made adequate money and had his pick of long-distance flights. Now he used his seniority to urge the junior co-pilot to cede the right seat ahead of the scheduled crew change. When the junior man resisted, Batouti said, "You mean you're not going to get up? You will get up. Go and get some rest and come back." The junior co-pilot stayed in his seat a bit longer and then left the cockpit. Batouti took the seat and buckled in.

Batouti was married and had five children. Four of them were grown and doing well. His fifth child was a girl, age ten, who was sick with lupus but responding to treatment that he had arranged for her to receive in Los Angeles. Batouti had a nice house in Cairo. He had a vacation house on the beach. He did not drink heavily. He was moderately religious. He had his retirement planned. He had acquired an automobile tire in New Jersey the day before, and was bringing it home in the cargo hold. He had also picked up some free samples of Viagra, to distribute as gifts.

Captain Habashi was more religious, and was known to pray sometimes in the cockpit. He and Batouti were old friends. Using Batouti's nickname, he said, in Arabic, "How are you, Jimmy?" They groused to each other about the chief pilot and about a clique of young and arrogant "kids," junior EgyptAir pilots who were likewise catching a ride back to the Cairo base. One of those pilots came into the cockpit dressed in street clothes. Habashi said, "What's with you? Why did you get all dressed in red like that?" Presumably the man then left. Batouti had a meal. A female flight attendant came in and offered more. Batouti said pleasantly, "No, thank you, it was marvelous." She took his tray.

At 1:47 A.M. the last calls came in from air-traffic control, from Ann Brennan, far off in the night at her display. Captain Habashi handled the calls. He said, "New York, EgyptAir Nine-nine-zero heavy, good morning," and she answered with her final "EgyptAir Nine-ninety, roger."

At 1:48 Batouti found the junior co-pilot's pen and handed it across to Habashi. He said, "Look, here's the new first officer's pen. Give it to him, please. God spare you." He added, "To make sure it doesn't get lost."

Habashi said, "Excuse me, Jimmy, while I take a quick trip to the toilet." He ran his electric seat back with a whir.

There was the sound of the cockpit door moving.

Batouti said, "Go ahead, please."

Habashi said, "Before it gets crowded. While they are eating. And I'll be back to you."

Again the cockpit door moved. There was a *clunk*. There was a *clink*. It seems that Batouti was now alone in the cockpit. The 767 was at 33,000 feet, cruising peacefully eastward at .79 Mach.

At 1:48:30 a strange, wordlike sound was uttered, three syllables with emphasis on the second, perhaps more English than Arabic, and variously heard on the tape as "control it," "hydraulic," or something unintelligible. The NTSB ran extensive speech and sound-spectrum studies on it, and was never able to assign it conclusively to Batouti or to anyone else. But what is clear is that Batouti then softly said, "*Tawakkalt ala Allah*," which proved difficult to translate, and was at first rendered incorrectly, but essentially means "I rely on God." An electric seat whirred. The autopilot disengaged, and the airplane sailed on as before for another four seconds. Again Batouti said, "I rely on God." Then two things happened almost simultaneously, according to the flight-data recorder: the throttles in the cockpit moved back fast to minimum idle, and a second later, back at the tail, the airplane's massive elevators (the pitch-control surfaces) dropped to a three-degrees-down position. When the elevators drop, the tail goes up; and when the tail goes up, the nose points down. Apparently Batouti had chopped the power and pushed the control yoke forward.

The effect was dramatic. The airplane began to dive steeply, dropping its nose so quickly that the environment inside plunged to nearly zero gs, the weightless condition of space. Six times in quick succession Batouti repeated, "I rely on God." His tone was calm. There was a loud thump. As the nose continued to pitch downward, the airplane went into the negative-g range, nudging loose objects against the ceiling. The elevators moved even farther down. Batouti said, "I rely on God."

Somehow, in the midst of this, now sixteen seconds into the dive, Captain Habashi made his way back from the toilet. He yelled, "What's happening? What's happening?"

Batouti said, "I rely on God."

The wind outside was roaring. The airplane was dropping through 30,800 feet, and accelerating beyond its maximum operating speed of .86 Mach. In the cockpit the altimeters were spinning like cartoon clocks. Warning horns were sounding, warning lights were flashing—low oil pressure on the left engine, and then on the right. The master alarm went off, a loud high-to-low warble.

For the last time Batouti said, "I rely on God."

Again Habashi shouted, "What's happening?" By then he must have reached the left control yoke. The negative gs ended as he countered the pitch-over, slowing the rate at which the nose was dropping. But the 767 was still angled down steeply, 40 degrees below the horizon, and it was accelerating. The rate of descent hit 39,000 feet a minute.

"What's happening, Gameel? What's happening?"

Habashi was clearly pulling very hard on his control yoke, trying desperately to raise the nose. Even so, thirty seconds into the dive, at 22,200 feet, the airplane hit the speed of sound, at which it was certainly not meant to fly. Many things happened in quick succession in the cockpit. Batouti reached over and shut off the fuel, killing both engines. Habashi screamed, "What is this? What is this? Did you shut the engines?" The throttles were pushed full forward—for no obvious reason, since the engines were dead. The speed-brake handle was then pulled, deploying drag devices on the wings.

At the same time, there was an unusual occurrence back at the tail: the right-side and left-side elevators, which normally move together to control the airplane's pitch, began to "split," or move in opposite directions. Specifically: the elevator on the right remained down, while the left-side elevator moved up to a healthy recovery position. That this could happen at all was the result of a design feature meant to allow either pilot to over-power a mechanical jam and control the airplane with only one elevator. The details are complex, but the essence in this case seemed to be that the right elevator was being pushed down by Batouti while the left elevator was being pulled up by the captain. The NTSB concluded that a "force fight" had broken out in the cockpit.

Words were failing Habashi. He yelled, "Get away in the engines!" And then, incredulously, ". . . shut the engines!"

Batouti said calmly, "It's shut."

Habashi did not have time to make sense of the happenings. He probably did not have time to get into his seat and slide it forward. He must have been standing in the cockpit, leaning over the seatback and hauling on the controls. The commotion was horrendous. He was reacting instinctively as a pilot, yelling, "Pull!" and then, "Pull with me! Pull with me! Pull with me!"

It was the last instant captured by the on-board flight recorders. The elevators were split, with the one on the right side, Batouti's side, still pushed into a nose-down position. The ailerons on both wings had assumed a strange upswept position, normally never seen on an airplane. The 767 was at 16,416 feet, doing 527 miles an hour, and pulling a moderately heavy 2.4 gs, indicating that the nose, though still below the horizon, was rising fast, and that Habashi's efforts on the left side were having an effect. A belated recovery was under way. At that point, because the engines had been cut, all nonessential electrical devices were lost, blacking out not only the recorders, which rely on primary power, but also most of the instrument displays and lights. The pilots were left to the darkness of the sky, whether to work together or to fight. I've often wondered what happened between those two men during the 114 seconds that remained of their lives. We'll never know. Radar reconstruction showed that the 767 recovered from the dive at 16,000 feet and, like a great wounded glider, soared steeply back to 24,000 feet, turned to the southeast while beginning to break apart, and shed its useless left engine and some of its skin before giving up for good and diving to its death at high speed.

Conflicting Realities

When this evidence emerged at the NTSB, the American investigators were shocked but also relieved by the obvious conclusion. There was no bomb here. Despite initial fears, there was nothing wrong with the airplane. The apparent cause was pilot error at its extreme: Batouti had gone haywire. Every detail that emerged from the two flight recorders fit that scenario: the sequence of the switches and controls that were moved, the responses of the airplane, and the words that were spoken, however cryptic and incomplete. Batouti had waited to be alone in the cockpit, and had intentionally pushed the airplane to its death. He had even fought the captain's valiant attempt at recovery. Why? Professionally, the NTSB didn't need to care. It was up to the criminal investigators at the FBI to discover if this was a political act, or the result of a plot. Even at the time, just weeks after the airplane went down, it was hard to imagine that Batouti had any terrorist connections, and indeed, the FBI never found any such evidence. But in pure aviation terms it didn't really matter why Batouti did it, and pure aviation is what the NTSB is all about. So this was easy—Crash Investigation 101. The guy to blame was dead. The NTSB wouldn't have to go after Boeing—a necessary task on occasion, but never a pleasant prospect. The wreckage, which was still being pulled out of the ocean, would not require tedious inspection. The report could be written quickly and filed away, and the NTSB could move on to the backlog of work that might actually affect the future safety of the flying public.

When Jim Hall, the NTSB chairman, held a news conference to address the initial findings, on November 19, 1999, he was culturally sensitive, responsible, and very strict about the need to maintain an open mind. There had been leaks to the press about the content of the cockpit voice recorder. It was being said that Batouti's behavior had been strange during the dive and that he had recited Muslim prayers. Hall scolded the assembled reporters for using unofficial information and exciting the public's emotions. He made a show of being careful with his own choice of words. He said that the accident "might and I emphasize *might*, be the result of a deliberate act." He did not say "suicide" or "Arab" or "Muslim." He did not even say "Batouti." He said, "No one wants to get to the bottom of this mystery quicker than those investigating this accident, both here and in Egypt, but we won't get there on a road paved with leaks, supposition, speculation, and spin. That road does not lead to the truth, and the truth is what both the American people and the Egyptian people seek." It was standard stuff, a prelude to a quick wrapping up of the investigation. The Egyptian delegation, which had moved into rooms at the Loews L'Enfant Plaza Hotel, might have felt grateful to have such a man at the NTSB to guide them through these difficult times. Instead the Egyptians were outraged.

At the NTSB this came as a surprise. Looking back, it's possible to see signs of a disconnect, especially the Egyptian government's baffling speculation about a bomb in the forward lavatory; but just the day before Hall's press conference the Egyptian ambassador had heaped praise on the NTSB and the investigation. Now, suddenly and with startling vigor, the Egyptian delegation went on the offensive. The leader of the charge, Shaker Kelada, later told me about running across one of the American investigators in the halls of the NTSB. When the investigator mentioned with satisfaction that the work might wrap up within a few weeks, Kelada brought him up short with the news that he'd better change his plans—because far from being over, the investigation had hardly begun.

First the Egyptians had to prepare the ground: the delegation started to loudly criticize the performance and intentions of Boeing, the FBI, and the entire NTSB. Kelada said that Batouti was the scapegoat, and that this was happening because it was an *Egyptian* airliner that had gone down. It did not escape Kelada's attention that the legendary head of aviation investigations at the NTSB—a brilliant and abrasive engineer named Bernard Loeb, who was overseeing the Flight 990 inquiry—was Jewish and something of a Zionist.

Loeb retired last spring; Kelada implied to me last summer that this was a deception, and that Loeb continued to pull the strings. Loeb laughed when I mentioned it to him afterward. He was looking forward to spending time with his grandchildren. But at the same time, he was angry that Egypt, after receiving $1.3 billion in American assistance every year, would have used any of its budget to cause the United States unnecessary expense by prolonging an investigation that for the NTSB alone had so far cost $17 million. As to Zionism, Loeb did seem bothered by aspects of the Egyptian culture. I got the feeling, though, that his opinion was fresh—that it stemmed from his contacts with EgyptAir, rather than from experiences that had preceded them.

But it didn't really matter who at the NTSB was in charge of the investigation. In faraway Cairo, inevitably, it was seen as unfair. From the day that Flight 990's recorder tape was transcribed and word of its contents began to leak out, the feeling in Egypt was that all Arabs were under attack, and that the assault had been planned. More than a year after the crash I met a sharp young reporter in Cairo who continued to seethe about it. He said, "For many Egyptians it was a big example of this business of dictating the reality. What made many people question the authenticity of the U.S. claims was the rush to conclusions . . . The rush, the interpretation of a few words, it left no chance. The whole thing seemed to apply within a framework of an American sort of soap opera, one of those movies you make. You know—this is a fanatic, he comes from the Middle East, he utters a few religious words, he brings the plane down." But what if Batouti really had brought the plane down—where did the reporter's reaction leave Egypt? Earlier the reporter had written critically about the corruption at EgyptAir, but he refused even to think critically about it anymore.

The reporter's anger was similar, at least superficially, to the anger that was seething through Shaker Kelada and the rest of the Egyptian delegation in November of 1999. For Jim Hall, Bernard Loeb, and others at the NTSB, the source of the problem seemed at first to be the media coverage, which was typically overeager. Rumors of suicide had circulated in the press almost since the airplane hit the water, but it was only after the voice recorder was recovered that the reports began to make uninformed reference to Muslim prayers. Three days before Hall's press conference *The Washington Post* ran a headline saying, "PILOT PRAYED, THEN SHUT OFF JET'S AUTOPILOT." Television stations speculated that the "prayer" was the *shahada* ("There is no god but God; Muhammad is the messenger of God"), as if this were what one might say before slaughtering infidels. When the actual Arabic words—*Tawakkalt ala Allah*—became public, some news outlets gave the following translation: "I have made my decision. I put my fate in God's hands." This was reported so widely that the NTSB took the unusual step of announcing that "I have made my decision" had never been spoken. By implication, "I place my fate . . ." had.

When NTSB investigators explained their lack of control over the American press, the Egyptians scoffed and pointed out—correctly—that the reporters' sources were people inside the investigation. And anyway, the Egyptians added, what Batouti had said was not "I put my fate in God's hands"—as the NTSB's interpreter had claimed—but, rather, "I rely on God." The investigators blinked at the subtlety of this distinction, and made the necessary changes to the transcript. Then the Egyptians produced a letter from an Islamic scholar in Cairo who certified that the meaning of *Tawakkalt ala Allah* is "I depend in my daily affairs on the omnipotent Allah alone." The Egyptians wanted the letter inserted into the record, but were willing to allow "I rely on God" to remain in the transcript. Again, the investigators blinked. This was not the sort of thing they normally dealt with. They tried sometimes to bridge the gap as they might have with Americans, with a nudge and a smile, but it got them nowhere.

In essence the Egyptians were making two intertwined arguments: first, that it was culturally impossible for Batouti to have done what the NTSB believed; second, that the NTSB lacked the cultural sensitivity to understand what was on the cockpit voice recorder. With those arguments as a starting point, the Egyptians tore into the complexities of the evidence, disputing any assumptions or conclusions the NTSB put forward and raising new questions at every possible turn—a process that continues to this day. They were tenacious. For example (and this is just a small sample of the Egyptians' arguments): When Batouti said *"Tawakkalt ala Allah,"* he was not preparing to die but responding in surprise to something wrong with the flight. He said it quietly, yes, but with emotion that the Americans lacked the cultural sensitivity to hear. When he started the dive, he was trying to avoid a plane or a missile outside. If not that, then the airplane went into the dive on its own. When he idled the engines, it was to keep from gaining speed. When he cut the engines, he was going through the required restart procedure, because he erroneously believed—on the basis of the low-oil-pressure warning light that flashed in the cockpit—that the engines had flamed out. Apparently Habashi made the same mistake, which is why he discussed engine cuts. When Habashi called "Pull with me!," Batouti did exactly that. The split elevators were like the upswept ailerons—either an aerodynamic anomaly, resulting from the unknown pressures of ultra-high-speed flight on the 767, or, more simply, an error in the flight-data recorder. Whichever way, the Egyptians argued that expensive wind-tunnel testing was necessary at high Mach numbers near the speed of sound.

Meanwhile, most of the wreckage had been recovered and

spread out in a hangar in Rhode Island. A second salvage operation was mounted in the spring to coincide with a state visit by
Mubarak to Washington. It went to the west debris field and
brought up the left engine and a boatload of worthless scraps. At
the NTSB a story circulated about Al Gore, who was said to have
angered Mubarak by making a casual reference to "the suicide
flight." There was a short flap about that. The investigation continued. The documentation grew. The possibilities multiplied
and ran off in a hundred directions. An airline pilot observing the
scene said to me, "It could have been this, it could have been that.
Bottom line is, it could have been anything except their guy."

The Search for a Motive

While the Egyptians were proposing theory after theory to
absolve Batouti, the FBI was conducting a criminal investigation,
collecting evidence that provided for his possible motive. Mostly
through interviews with employees of the Pennsylvania Hotel, the
FBI found that Batouti had a reputation for sexual impropriety—
and not merely by the prudish standards of America. It was
reported that on multiple occasions over the previous two years he
had been suspected of exposing himself to teenage girls, mastur-
bating in public, following female guests to their rooms, and listening at their doors. Some of the maids, it was said, were afraid of
him, and the hotel security guards had once brought him in for
questioning and a warning. Apparently the hotel had considered
banning him. The FBI learned that EgyptAir was aware of these
problems and had warned Batouti to control his behavior. He was
not considered to be a dangerous man—and certainly he was more
sad than bad. In fact, there was a good side to Batouti that came out
in these interviews as well. He was very human. Many people were
fond of him, even at the hotel.

But a story soon surfaced that an altercation may have

occurred during the New York layover before the fatal departure. The FBI was told that there had been trouble, and possibly an argument with the chief pilot, who was also staying at the hotel. It was hypothesized that the chief pilot might have threatened disciplinary action upon arrival back in Cairo—despite the public humiliation that would entail. Was that perhaps Batouti's motive? Did the killing of 217 people result from a simple act of vengeance against one man? The evidence was shaky at best. Then, in February of 2000, an EgyptAir pilot named Hamdi Hanafi Taha, forty-nine, landed in England and requested political asylum, claiming that he had information on the accident. FBI and NTSB investigators flew immediately to interview him, hoping that he would provide the answers they needed. They were disappointed. Taha told a story that seemed to confirm that Batouti had been confronted by the chief pilot, and he added some new details, but he turned out to be an informant of questionable utility—a radical Muslim who, along with others in the ranks of EgyptAir pilots, had forced the airline to ban the serving of alcohol, and who now went on at length about corruption at EgyptAir, and also what he claimed was rampant alcoholism and drug use among his secular peers. The request for asylum was itself a little flaky. The American investigators flew home without solid information. Most of this came out in the press when the story of Batouti's sexual improprieties was leaked, further angering the Egyptians. They countered, eventually producing a Boeing 777 captain named Mohamed Badrawi, who had been with the other pilots in New York on the fateful night, and who testified at length that they were like a band of brothers—that Batouti and the chief pilot got along well and had had no direct confrontations. Rather, Badrawi said, he had acted at times as a "mediator" between the two men, cautioning Batouti on behalf of the chief pilot to "grow up" in order to avoid legal problems in the United States.

With that on the record, assigning a motive to Batouti became all the more difficult. For a variety of reasons, Bernard Loeb thought the FBI was wasting everyone's time. He did not really oppose the search for a motive, but he was against entering such speculative and easily countered discussions into the NTSB's public record. Privately he believed in the story of the fight. But as he later emphasized to me, "We just didn't need to go there."

Loeb thought the same about much of the investigation. Month after month, as the NTSB chased down the theories that EgyptAir kept proposing, Loeb worried about all the other projects that were being put aside. He tried to keep a sense of distance from the work, driving from suburban Maryland to his office dressed in a sports jacket and tie, just like any other Washingtonian with a quiet job. But it was a hopeless ambition. Most mornings the Egyptian delegation was there too. Later Loeb said to me, his voice strangled with frustration, "You had to be there! You had to live through this! Day in and day out! It was as if these people would go back to their rooms at night and then identify some kind of reason . . . And then it would start all over again. It was insane! It was just insane!"

To bolster their arguments the Egyptians had hired some former accident investigators and also the retired NTSB chairman Carl Vogt, whose willingness to legitimize the Egyptian campaign was seen by many within the NTSB as a betrayal. The Egyptians also turned to the American pilots' union—in principle to improve their communication with the NTSB, but in practice probably just to add weight to their side. In the spring of 2000 the union sent to Washington a man named Jim Walters, a U.S. airline pilot with long experience in accident investigations. Walters thought he could patch things up. Later he said to me, "The Egyptians appeared to be listening to me. But as it turned out, they weren't." Then he said, "I thought I was there to give them advice . . ." It was a disappointment. He liked the Egyptians personally, and remained sympathetic to their side even after he left.

I asked him to describe the scene in Washington. He said, "The

NTSB isn't terribly tolerant of people who don't follow good investigative procedure. And they weren't used to dealing with a group like this, right in their back yard, with offices in the same building, there *every* day. I thought, The first thing we have to do is calm everybody down. I thought I could explain to the Egyptians, 'This is how the NTSB operates,' and explain to Jim Hall, 'Hey, these guys are Egyptians. You've got to understand who these guys are, and why they're doing things the way they are, and maybe we can all just kiss and make up and get along from here.'"

But it didn't work out that way. Walters was naive. Kiss and make up? The Egyptians no more needed his advice about investigative procedure than they had needed the NTSB's opinions about the nature of a free press.

A small war had broken out between Egypt and the United States on a battlefield called Loews L'Enfant Plaza Hotel. On one side stood Shaker Kelada and his men, fighting for the honor of their nation against the mysterious forces of American hegemony, and specifically against an agency whose famed independence they believed had been compromised. On the other side stood Bernard Loeb and his people, fighting just as hard—but to set a schedule, write the report, and disengage. Jim Hall was scurrying in between. And Boeing was off in Seattle, not quite out of range, trying unsuccessfully to look small.

The irony is that Loeb, too, thought the agency's independence had been compromised, though for the opposite reason: there were meetings at the White House, and phone calls to Jim Hall, in which concern was expressed about accommodating the Egyptian view, and in which it was implied that there should be no rush to finish a report that inevitably would offend Mubarak. Loeb was disgusted and typically vocal about his opinion. When I asked him if the influence was necessarily so wrong, he said, "Next they ask you to *change* the report—to say Batouti didn't do it." He added, however, that no one had ever suggested such a change—and it was a good thing, too.

Egypt Versus the West

By late last May the fight had slowed, and Shaker Kelada was able to spend most of his time back home in Cairo. The NTSB had just issued a draft report, and Egypt was preparing an opposing response. I found Kelada in his expansive new office at the Cairo airport, where we talked several times over the course of a week. These were not good conversations. Kelada insisted on repeating the official Egyptian positions, and would go no further. At one point he began to attack the New York air-traffic controllers, and specifically Ann Brennan, for having walked away from her display. He implied that her absence had a bearing on the accident, or perhaps sparked a subsequent cover-up by the American government. He said, "It was very sloppy air-traffic control, and not what the U.S. wants to show. They're number one at everything, and they don't want *anyone* to know that they have a sloppy operation in New York."

I tried to reach him as one pilot to another. I said, "Come on, I think of that as being a normal operation, don't you?"

He said, "Well, if it is, I don't want to fly in the New York area!"

It was nonsense. And in aviation terms, a lot of what he said to me was equally unconvincing. Eventually I stopped taking notes.

Even when he was being reasonable, the party line kept showing through. He said, "I cannot say it's a mechanical failure. I don't have enough evidence, but I cannot dismiss the possibility of a mechanical failure . . . If I want to be careful."

I said, "On the other hand, you *do* have enough evidence to dismiss the human factor?"

And he said, "Yes."

"To dismiss the intentional act?"

"Yes." He paused. He said, "We search for the truth."

It was late in the day. Kelada sat behind his desk—a man in a big office with jets outside, a smart man, a careful man. I thought of the question that had plagued me all along: not whether the Egyptians were right or wrong but whether they really believed their own words. Loeb had said to me, "Do they *believe* it? I believe they believe in fear."

I went downtown, to an old coffeehouse near the Nile, and spent a few hours with Hani Shukrallah, a columnist and one of the more thoughtful observers of the Egyptian scene. Shukrallah is a small, nervous man, and a heavy smoker. He said, "I know that as far as the Egyptian government was concerned, the point that this was *not* pilot error, and that the Egyptian pilot did *not* bring it down—this was decided before the investigation began. It had to do with Egypt's image in the outside world . . . The government would have viewed this exactly as it would, for example, an Islamic terrorist act in Luxor—something that we should cover up. So it got politicized *immediately.* And this became an official line: You are out there to prove that EgyptAir is not responsible. It became a national duty. It was us versus the West. And all the history played into it, from Bonaparte's campaign until now." In the minds even of people on the street, Shukrallah said, it became "an all-out war."

Following Flight 990's Path

If so, the United States was in such a strong position that it could lose the struggle only by defeating itself. This is why from the very start of the difficult process it was all the more important for the NTSB to consider the evidence fairly and keep an open mind. The problem was that so many of the scenarios the Egyptians posited were patently absurd—stray missiles, ghost airplanes, strange weather, and the like. Yet that didn't mean that everything they said was wrong. As long as Batouti's motive could not be conclusively shown, the possibility remained that the dive of Flight 990 was unintentional, just as Kelada maintained. And in the background the Egyptians had some very smart engineers looking into the various theories.

The 767's elevator movements are powered by three redundant hydraulic circuits, driving a total of six control mechanisms called "actuators," which normally operate in unison. Given the various linkages and cross-connections, the system is complex. The Egyptians thought it through and realized that if two of the six actuators were to fail on the same side of the airplane, they would drive both elevators down, forcing the 767 to pitch into a dive that might match the profile that had emerged from EgyptAir 990's flight-data recorder. Furthermore, if such a failure happened and either pilot tried to right it, that could conceivably explain the "splitting" of the elevators that occurred during 990's attempted recovery.

As might be expected, the discussion about dual actuator failures grew complicated. It also grew political. The NTSB had salvaged most of the actuators from the ocean floor and had found no clear evidence of failure, but with perceptions of public safety at stake, the agency asked Boeing for further information. Boeing engineers calculated that a dual actuator failure would not have deflected the elevators far enough down to equal the known elevator deflections of Flight 990, and that such a failure therefore would not have caused as steep a dive. To explore the question they performed a series of ground tests of a 767 elevator, inducing dual actuator failures and "splits" on a parked airplane in Seattle. After adjusting the measured effects for the theoretical aerodynamic pressures of flight, they found—as they had expected—poor correlation with the known record of Flight 990 elevator positions. They believed in any case that either pilot could quickly have recovered from a dual actuator failure by doing what comes naturally at such moments—pulling back hard on the controls.

The NTSB was satisfied; the Egyptians were not. They poked

holes in the conclusions and requested basic and costly aerodynamic research, at speeds well beyond the 767's limits, toward Mach One. The question was, of course, To what end? But for Boeing this was a delicate thing, because Egypt kept buying expensive airplanes and was influential in the Arab world. A bit of additional research would perhaps be in order.

Meanwhile, the company's engineers had moved on to flight simulations of the accident, a series of dives set up to be flown in Boeing's highly programmable 767 engineering simulator—a "fixed cab" without motion, capable of handling extremes. These were the profiles that I flew when I went to Seattle last summer. On that same trip I went to Everett, Washington, where the airplanes are made, and in a cockpit with a company test pilot split the elevators in a powered-up 767, as the Egyptian crew presumably had. In order to do this we needed to break the connection between the left and right control yokes, which are mechanically joined under the floorboards, and usually move together. He pushed on his, I pulled on mine, and at fifty pounds of pressure between us the controls were suddenly no longer working in tandem. Far behind us, at the tail, the elevators separated smoothly. On a cockpit display we watched each elevator go its own way. The airplane shuddered from the movement of the heavy control surfaces. We played with variations. Toward the end the pilot laughed and said I was compressing his bones.

But when I got to the simulations, they felt too real to be a game. The simulator was a surrogate cockpit already in flight—humming and warm, with all the controls and familiar displays, and a view outside of an indistinct twilight. It was headed east at 33,000 feet and .79 Mach—just as Flight 990 had been. The first set of profiles were "back-driven" duplications of the fatal dive, generated directly from Flight 990's flight-data recorder. Another Boeing test pilot sat in Batouti's seat, and the engineers clustered around behind. I let the simulation run on automatic the first few times, resting one hand on the controls to feel the beast die—the sudden pitch and shockingly fast dive, the clicking of a wildly unwinding altimeter, the warbling alarm, the loss of most displays at the bottom after the engines were gone, and the dark, steep, soaring climb up to 24,000 feet, the control yoke rattling its warning of an aerodynamic stall, the airplane rolling southeast to its end. I watched this several times and then flew the same thing by hand, matching the pressure I put on the control yoke to a specially rigged indicator, which, after the elevators' split had occurred, allowed me to match the force required to achieve Habashi's "pull" and Batouti's "push" as captured by the flight-data recorder. First I stood and flew Habashi's "Pull with me!" from behind the seat—up to ninety pounds of force, which under those conditions seemed like not very much. It was the other intention, the pushing, that was dramatic. What was required was not only pushing but then pushing harder. The idea that someone would do that in an airplane full of passengers shocked me as a pilot. If that's what Batouti did, I will never understand what was going on in his mind.

The second set of simulations were easier to fly. These were the dual actuator failures, which EgyptAir proposed might have overcome Batouti when he was alone in the cockpit. The purpose was to test the difficulty or ease of recovery from such an upset. Again the simulations began at 33,000 feet and .79 Mach. I flew by hand from the start. The airplane pitched down strongly and without warning. I hauled back on the controls and lost 800 feet. It was an easy recovery, but not fair—I had been ready. The engineers then made me wait before reacting, as they had made other pilots—requiring delays of five, ten, and finally fifteen seconds before I began the recovery. Fifteen seconds seems like an eternity in a 767 going out of control. Even so, by hauling hard on the yoke and throttling back, I managed to pull out after losing only 12,000 feet; and though I went to the maximum allowable dive speed, the airplane survived. This was not unusual. Airplanes are meant to be flown. During the original simulation sessions done for the NTSB every pilot with a dual actuator failure was able to recover, and probably better than I. So what was wrong with Batouti? The simplest explanation is that he was trying to crash the airplane. But if he wasn't, if the Egyptians were right that he couldn't recover from a dual actuator failure, what was wrong with him as an aviator?

I posed the question to Jim Walters, the airline pilot who despite his disappointment remained sympathetic to the Egyptians' position. He had a ready answer. He called Batouti "the world's worst airline pilot."

But how good do you have to be?

Bernard Loeb would have none of it. He said, "Sure. In the end they were willing to sell him down the river. They said, 'He panicked!' Bottom line is, if the actuator drops the nose, you can pull it up. They know that. They *admit* it. Pulling the nose up is the most intuitive, reflexive thing you can do in an airplane. So when you start hearing arguments like that, you *know* people are blowing smoke."

"Look, first we sit through this cockpit voice recording in which . . ." He shook his head. "How many cockpit voice recordings have I heard? Hundreds? Thousands? When someone has a problem with an airplane, you know it. One of our investigators used to say to me, 'These damned pilots, they don't tell us what's happening. Why don't they say, "It's the rudder!"' They don't do that. But I'll tell you what they do say. They make clear as hell that there's something really wrong. 'What the *hell's* going on? What is *that*?' Every single one of them. When there's a control problem of some sort, it is so crystal clear that they are trying desperately to diagnose what is going on. Right to when the recorder quits. They are fighting for their lives.

"But this guy is sitting there saying the same thing in a slow, measured way, indicating no stress. The captain comes in and asks what's going on, and he doesn't answer! That's what you start with. Now you take the dual actuator failure that doesn't match the flight profile, and is also fully recoverable. Where do you want to go after that?"

. . .

The NTSB's final report on Flight 990 was expected for the fall of this year, and it was widely presumed in aviation circles that the report would find no mechanical failure or external cause for the crash. It also seemed likely that the report would at least implicitly blame Batouti for the disaster—a conclusion that would, of course, be unacceptable within Egypt. Nonetheless, by last May, when I met him in Cairo, Shaker Kelada was looking pleased, and I later found out why. His engineers had gotten busy again, and had come up with new concerns—certain combinations of tail-control failures that might require further testing. Now Boeing had come to town for a quiet talk with its customers, and had agreed to do the tests. Boeing was going to inform the NTSB of the new work, and the end would again be delayed.

Sitting in his office, Kelada could not help gloating. He said, "Jim Hall told me, 'I've learned a very good lesson. When you deal with a foreign carrier in an investigation, before you go anywhere with it, you have to study the history and culture of the country.' These were his own words to me! He said, 'I knew nothing about Egypt or its culture before we got into EgyptAir 990.'"

I said, "What would he have learned?"

"Not to underestimate people. To think that he's way up there, and everybody's way down here."

Fair enough. But in the end there was the question of the objective truth—and there was the inclination not to seek real answers for even such a simple event as a single accident nearly two years before.

I knew that at the start of the investigation the Egyptian delegation had included a man named Mamdouh Heshmat, a high official in civil aviation. When the cockpit voice recording first arrived at L'Enfant Plaza, Heshmat was there, and he heard it through with a headset on. According to several investigators who listened alongside him, he came out of the room looking badly shaken, and made it clear he knew that Batouti had done something wrong. He may have called Cairo with that news. The next day he flew home, never to reappear in Washington. When NTSB investigators went to Cairo, they could not find him, though it was said that he was still working for the government. I knew I wouldn't find him either, but I wanted to see how Kelada would react to the mention of him. Kelada and I had come to the end. I said I had heard about a man who had been one of the first to listen to the tape—who could it have been? Kelada looked straight at me and said, "I don't recall his name." There was no reason to continue, from his perspective or mine.

GQ

FINALIST, COLUMNS
AND COMMENTARY

Eminem: A Fan's Notes

Whether exploring the literary antecedents of Eminem or lamenting the chiseled form of the modern diva, Terrence Rafferty brings to his GQ column on popular culture a sharp eye and a lucid, occasionally pyrotechnic, prose style. But what distinguishes his witty pieces is a marvelously original point of view, unswayed by conventional wisdom—or, indeed, by conventions of any kind.

Terrence Rafferty

Eminem:
A Fan's Notes

**Stop fuming and
fussing. Chill out
and enjoy the
outrageous brilliance.**

I 'm now making myself as scummy as I can," wrote Arthur
Rimbaud, age sixteen, in a letter to his friend and teacher
Georges Izambard. "Why? I want to be a poet, and I'm
working at turning myself into a *seer*." He enclosed an obscene
poem ("The Stolen Heart"), whose scatological and sexual
imagery perhaps—reasonable people may differ on this point—
describes his gang rape by a group of soldiers. It's always hard to
tell, with Rimbaud, how much is autobiography, how much is
fantasy, how much is merely provocative verbal play. "The idea,"
he wrote in that same letter, "is to reach the unknown by the
derangement of *all the senses*," and in his brief life (he died at
thirty-seven in 1891) and even briefer poetic career (he appears
to have given up the verse game, forever, before his twentieth

birthday) he managed to achieve an impressive level of derangement both on the page and in the world. His poems, which went
even further into the darkness of nature (and the poet's own
mind) than Baudelaire's *Flowers of Evil* had, shook up French literature. His life, while he was writing, was wild, deliberately
unruly; the teenager's liaison with the older, married poet Paul
Verlaine scandalized Paris, in part because Rimbaud chose not to
be discreet about it and in part because the relationship was so
often characterized by drunkenness and violence. After throwing
poetry over, Rimbaud spent the remainder of his days in a kind
of nomadic existence, enlisting in—and then deserting from—
an army of mercenaries and then making his way to the only
partially explored region of equatorial East Africa, where he
became a trader. In those later years, the masterpieces of his adolescence—"The Drunken Boat," "Vowels," *Illuminations*—began
to be published, and they attracted a passionate following. Rimbaud resented all attempts to locate him. He just didn't care.

By chance, I was reading Graham Robb's superb recent biography, *Rimbaud*, when I heard the news that the rapper who calls
himself Eminem (real name: Marshall Mathers) had been nominated for several Grammy awards, immediately sparking loud
protests by organizations representing groups of people he's
offended—notably, gays and women. Michael Greene, the president of the Grammy-granting National Academy of Recording
Arts and Sciences, fence-straddled amusingly, both defending
the musical "craft" of Eminem's album *The Marshall Mathers LP*
and condemning its lyrical content as "repugnant," "nauseating"
and "indefensible." Serious political talk shows such as *Hardball*
and *The Point*, sensing a possible remedy for their post-Florida-
recount blues, chewed over the Eminem issue and looked very
queasy, as if they were tasting some exotic dish they weren't
entirely sure they wanted to swallow. It's always entertaining, in a
mean-spirited sort of way, to watch sober, responsible-seeming
pundits attempting to analyze the head-splitting ambiguities of

our increasingly violent popular culture. Listening to ordinarily sensible commentators like Chris Matthews and Greta Van Susteren quoting particularly vicious Eminem lyrics and then, with wry, pained expressions on their faces, trying to figure out why anyone would say this stuff, why anyone would buy it (8 million or so have) and why the recording industry would want to honor it, I wondered, suddenly, what all the earnest talking heads would have made of Rimbaud.

What if, instead of quoting Eminem's lurid fantasies of killing his wife or his sneering homophobic one-liners, they were reciting lines from, say, Rimbaud's poem "My Little Lovers" *(How I hate you! / Plaster with painful blisters / Your ugly tits)* or from "Squattings," in which, in thirty-five impeccably rhymed Alexandrines, the poet savors the agonies of an elderly monk on his chamber pot, taking a midnight dump? No, I'm not really insane enough to suggest that the talented, shocking, deeply juvenile Eminem is the second coming of the teenage genius Rimbaud, but reading about a sense-deranging nineteenth-century French poet while listening to the consciously disturbing lyrics of a young Detroit rapper has somehow stimulated in me all sorts of questions about the bumpy progress of culture and consciousness in the nearly 130 years since Rimbaud's oracular pronouncement (in *A Season in Hell*) "It is necessary to be absolutely modern."

•   •   •

No one has ever quite got to the bottom of that line (much less charted reliably the tenebrous depths of the blasphemous, self-deprecating, hallucinatory prose poem that contains it). But whatever absolute modernity meant to the 19-year-old—or, rather, to the fragmented persona whose voice is the medium of *A Season in Hell's* fevered visions—it was clearly nothing simple, or comforting, or, finally, articulable, even by one who has done his damnedest to become "a seer." What Rimbaud appears to have arrived at, at the conclusion of his swift, blazingly intense adolescent expedition in search of the unknown, is a state of perfect, inviolable unknowability, of pure alienation from the very possibility of objective truth. (Without which it's kind of difficult to be a credible seer.) "The derangement of all the senses" turns out to have been not the means but the end of his artistic explorations. Is that "absolute modernity," then—or just nihilistic pathology? Rimbaud made it hard to tell the difference and, a century and a quarter on, we're still spinning our spiritual wheels in that dilemma, getting no traction in the muddy ground a ruthless, verbally intrepid, fearsomely illusionless teenager left behind him.

And we keep sinking deeper into that muck. I don't mean that the cultural artifacts of our time are inherently "worse" than Rimbaud's poems. The shocks to the system *A Season in Hell* generates are, if anything, more powerful (and less easily reversible) than those produced by even the rawest moments of *The Marshall Mathers LP.* I mean that Rimbaud's visionary aesthetic of derangement, whose influence was once confined to the small audience for high art, has gradually descended the cultural scale, to the lowest levels of mass entertainment: Shock and alienation are now embedded in the soil of pop culture, where good, unclean fun like Eminem's music grows and flourishes. It's trickle-down aesthetics, the destabilizing principles of Rimbaud and his heirs, the modernists, seeping drop by drop into mass culture, to the point where an album like *Marshall Mathers* can sell millions using the scabrous content and deliberately disorienting techniques that not so long ago were the exclusive property of the avant-garde. When Luis Buñuel and Salvador Dali made their notorious surrealist film *Un Chien Andalou,* in 1929, it was not embraced by millions (or even thousands) of moviegoers, nor was it nominated for any awards. Its first scene, of an eyeball being slit open by a razor blade, was designed to elicit outrage and revulsion, and did; Buñuel amused himself by referring to the film as "a passionate call to murder." The filmmakers worked hard to be inflammatory, but the fire was confined to a few Left Bank cafés, and the general public never smelled the smoke.

These days you can witness violence far more graphic and visceral than *Un Chien Andalou*'s in any horror movie, hear statements more casually bloodthirsty than Buñuel's on any rap album and experience imagery more disjointed and irrational than that once daring film's on MTV, twenty-four hours a day. Shock—the guiding principle of the most advanced, most "difficult" art of the past century—has been so thoroughly domesticated that the very concept of an avant-garde is senseless: We're all way ahead of ourselves now. (Or is it way behind?) Culture sure was a lot easier to deal with when the sordid, upsetting stuff could be left to the artists and the intellectuals, and everyone else could relax, after a hard day's work, with pleasant, inoffensive "escapist" entertainment. *The Marshall Mathers LP* is obviously not *Ulysses,* but what kind of *entertainment* is it? What could these foul, hate-drenched rants possibly be an escape from?

•   •   •

Boredom, for starters. Eminem's songs are exciting—outrageous, funny, eventful, rhythmically inventive. Adults (especially those of the "thoughtful" variety, who dominate the airwaves and the op-ed pages) tend to forget that teenagers crave excitement above all else and aren't picky about where they get it. We grown-ups may also forget that kids often have very warped senses of humor (which they're extremely proud of): Numbers like "'97 Bonnie and Clyde"—from Eminem's first album, *The Slim Shady LP* (1999)—in which a man who has killed his wife takes his little daughter for a ride to dispose of Mommy's corpse, are great sick jokes. There's no more point in parents railing against Eminem's sort of humor than there was when the object of their indignation was horror comics or *Mad* magazine or *South Park*. This is what your children want, and the more you hate it the more they want it. (As Eminem admits on *Slim Shady*, *I only cuss to make your mom upset.*) It's not altogether a bad thing, either. Becoming a grown-up has always been a fairly rugged process, and one of the ways in which adolescents inure themselves to the nasty shocks of adulthood is by reveling in them, laughing at them in order to prove, to themselves as well as to their equally confused peers, that they are perfectly at ease with the most brutal facts of life: murder, suicide, bad drugs, whatever. Eminem sums up the attitude succinctly in the introduction to his recently published volume of collected raps, *Angry Blonde*: "At the end of the day . . . it's all a joke." Music to the ears of, at least, his young white middle-class fans, for whom his verbal abandon and utter irresponsibility function as potent fantasies of escape from their parents' high expectations.

Outlaw fantasies have been a key element of youth culture for a long, long time. Eminem's anthemic numbers on *Slim Shady*, "Just Don't Give a Fuck" and "Still Don't Give a Fuck," are latter-day versions of Brando's biker cool in *The Wild One* (1954): "What are you rebelling against?" was the question; "What have you got?" was the answer. Brando, of course, turned out to be a sensitive guy underneath it all, which made him eligible to be a romantic hero—not a role that Eminem appears to aspire to. Sensitivity is high on his list of what there is to rebel against at the beginning of the new millennium; hence, the gay bashing, the misogyny, the rude cracks about Christopher Reeve. They're marks of integrity, of the pure, depraved indifference of a born loser.

And that callousness is one of the hallowed conventions of his chosen form, rap, at least since the late '80s, when the gangsta rap of West Coast groups like N.W.A. (one of whose founding members, Dr. Dre, is Eminem's producer) began to overshadow other approaches—the witty sexual braggadocio of LL Cool J, the goofy eclecticism of De La Soul, even the fierce political militancy of Public Enemy. Eminem's albums are in fact less sociopathic than many of the products of the gangsta school, including, notably, Dr. Dre's classic *The Chronic,* a peerlessly depressing brew of brilliant music and cheerful viciousness. What's disheartening about *The Chronic* is that it makes L.A.'s gang violence, which has killed God knows how many young blacks, sound like a terrific party. Eminem has the minimal good grace to let his Jerry Springer world sound as bleak and soul-crushing as it actually is: He makes jokes about how bad things are because he *knows* how bad things are. (As punk rock demonstrated, the loser strain in pop music requires at least a modicum of healthy self-loathing.) But the fact that he's white may, I'm sorry to say, have something to do with why his music, which obviously speaks to a huge constituency of similarly pigmented teenagers, upsets white parents more than malignancies like *The Chronic* upset them: Did they tolerate their children's interest in rap only as long as they could dismiss its more disturbing aspects as "black," safely other? (Gangsta rap, like the minstrel shows of old, has had the effect of reinforcing the most noxious stereotypes.)

But even if Ozzie and Harriet happen not to be racist in that way, adolescent outlaw fantasies are less frightening when they're more remote: Although white suburban boys may affect the killer machismo of Dr. Dre or Snoop Dogg, it's not likely that they're going to move to South Central and join the Bloods or the Crips. Eminem's violent scenarios, less movie-ish and more intimate, represent a somewhat more plausible alternative lifestyle for white kids. You can be confident your son will not become a Glock-toting L.A. gangsta, but you can't really be sure he won't turn into Richard Speck.

Eminem, that is, has made it awfully hard for white grown-ups to sustain the illusion that their children's music is somehow separate from who they really are. (Black parents have endured this anxiety for quite a while.) Who are these kids, anyway? The artist himself is scrupulously unhelpful on questions of identity. *I am whoever you say I am,* he announces in one song; in another, he jokes, *How the fuck can I be white? I don't even exist.* And in the introduction to *Angry Blonde,* he blithely muddies the waters with statements like "This book is made by Slim Shady, from the mind of Marshall Mathers, as seen from Eminem's point of view." Later he clarifies the matter a little: "The more I started writing and the more I slipped into this Slim Shady character, the more it just started becoming me. . . . I needed some type of persona. I needed an excuse to let go of all this rage, this dark humor, the pain and the happiness." This sort of uncertainty about the identity of the speaker is also a hallmark of rap, whose manner is confessional but whose genuine autobiographical content is often dubious: How much of Eminem's music is the "real" Marshall Mathers, how much the "fictional" Slim Shady? The titles of the albums increase the confusion: *The Marshall Mathers LP* is, if anything, more impersonal than *The Slim Shady LP.* At the end of the day, the whole concept of a fixed identity is "all a joke," too.

·   ·   ·

And that, I have to say, strikes me as an attitude that Arthur Rimbaud would have recognized and appreciated. In a sense, he invented it. It was he, after all, who wrote *"Je est un autre"*—"I is another"—and, with those irreducibly ambiguous words, suggested the polyphonic strategies of Joyce's and Eliot's modernism: techniques that are now accessible to millions in the roiling sonic density of the best rap music. All this chaos and derangement, and all generated by a French teenager's identity crisis. (The young Rimbaud was scarily intelligent and supremely arrogant: If *he* couldn't figure out who he was, then, he figured, identity itself must be an illusion.) In his poetry, Rimbaud perfected a voice in which the line between irony and passion—between pose and confession—has disappeared, because the self, which is the ground on which such distinctions are built, has slipped away, sometime during the long night of adolescence.

Is Eminem consciously inspired by Rimbaud's example? Of course not. The range of reference in his songs is extremely narrow, confined to other rappers, pop-culture celebrities and a select few products of kindred sensibility, such as *South Park*. Rimbaud, who was a voracious reader, had digested pretty much the entirety of French literature by the time he was 15, or perhaps *ingested* is the more precise word, since he wound up regurgitating everything in the next four years. That deliberate rejection of the past necessarily produces a more complex art than Eminem's simple ignorance of it, but whether Marshall Mathers knows it or not, he's following in the footsteps of Rimbaud—and Lautréamont and the surrealists and Allen Ginsberg and Bob Dylan and Jim Morrison and the Velvet Underground and Patti Smith and Johnny Rotten and Kurt Cobain—as well as in those of LL Cool J and Public Enemy and Tupac Shakur. And Eminem's apparent indifference to everything but the culture of the moment and his own immediate needs is a kind of extension-by-reduction of Rimbaud's notion of derangement: The rapper has achieved a state of perpetual infancy, all squall and spew and appetite. In the infinite regress of culture in the past century, this makes sense. The sound of *The Slim Shady LP* and *The Marshall Mathers LP* is a whine—the whine of a self that never knew it was a self, and maybe never will. This is what a season in hell feels like in the year 2001.

I just remembered: It's National Poetry Month. (April, the cruellest.) Let's celebrate the ways in which verse can derange the senses. Read some Rimbaud. Listen to Eminem. Be—if you can stand it—absolutely modern.

The New Yorker

WINNER, ESSAYS

My Father's Brain

In this article, Jonathan Franzen evokes the emotional trauma of watching a father lose first his identity and then his life to Alzheimer's. Throughout this very personal story, told with unstinting honesty and not a trace of sentimentality, Franzen weaves in current medical thinking about a disease that is destined to become only more prevalent as the vast Baby Boom generation ages.

Jonathan Franzen

My Father's Brain

What Alzheimer's takes away

Here's a memory. On an overcast morning in February, 1996, I received in the mail from my mother, in St. Louis, a Valentine's package containing one pinkly romantic greeting card, two four-ounce Mr. Goodbars, one hollow red filigree heart on a loop of thread, and one copy of a neuropathologist's report on my father's brain autopsy.

I remember the bright-gray winter light that morning. I remember leaving the candy, the card, and the ornament in my living room, taking the autopsy report into my bedroom, and sitting down to read it. *The brain* (it began) *weighed 1,255 gm and showed parasagittal atrophy with sulcal widening.* I remember translating grams into pounds and pounds into the familiar shrink-wrapped equivalents in a supermarket meat case. I remember putting the report back into its envelope without reading any further.

Some years before he died, my father had participated in a study of memory and aging at Washington University, and one of the perks for participants was a post-mortem brain autopsy, free of charge. I suspect that the study offered other perks of monitoring and treatment which had led my mother, who loved freebies of all kinds, to insist that my father volunteer for it. Thrift was also probably her only conscious motive for including the autopsy report in my Valentine's package. She was saving thirty-two cents' postage.

My clearest memories of that February morning are visual and spatial: the yellow Mr. Goodbar, my shift from living room to bedroom, the late-morning light of a season as far from the winter solstice as from spring. I'm aware, however, that even these memories aren't to be trusted. According to the latest theories, which are based on a wealth of neurological and psychological research in the last few decades, the brain is not an album in which memories are stored discretely like unchanging photographs. Instead, a memory is, in the phrase of the psychologist Daniel L. Schacter, a "temporary constellation" of activity—a necessarily approximate excitation of neural circuits that bind a set of sensory images and semantic data into the momentary sensation of a remembered whole. These images and data are seldom the exclusive property of one particular memory. Indeed, even as my experience on that Valentine's morning was unfolding, my brain was relying on pre-existing categories of "red" and "heart" and "Mr. Goodbar"; the gray sky in my windows was familiar from a thousand other winter mornings; and I already had millions of neurons devoted to a picture of my mother—her stinginess with postage, her romantic attachments to her children, her lingering anger toward my father, her weird lack of tact, and so on. What my memory of that morning therefore consists of, according to the latest models, is a set of hardwired neuronal connections among the pertinent regions of the brain, and a predisposition for the entire constellation to light up—chemically, electrically—when any one part of the circuit is stimulated. Speak the words "Mr. Goodbar" and ask me to free-associate, and if I don't say "Diane Keaton" I will surely say "brain autopsy."

My Valentine's memory would work this way even if I were dredging it up now for the first time ever. But the fact is that I've re-remembered that February morning countless times since then. I've told the story to my brothers. I've offered it as an Outrageous Mother Incident to friends of mine who enjoy that kind of thing. I've even, shameful to report, told people I hardly know at all. Each succeeding recollection and retelling reinforces the constellation of images and knowledge that constitute the memory. At the cellular level, according to neuroscientists, I'm burning the memory in a little deeper each time, strengthening the dendritic connections among its components, further encouraging the firing of that specific set of synapses. One of the great adaptive virtues of our brains, the feature that makes our gray matter so much smarter than any machine yet devised (my laptop's cluttered hard drive or a World Wide Web that insists on recalling, in pellucid detail, a "Beverly Hills 90210" fan site last updated on 11/20/98), is our ability to forget almost everything that has ever happened to us. I retain general, largely categorical memories of the past (a year spent in Spain; various visits to Indian restaurants on East Sixth Street) but relatively few specific, episodic memories. Those memories that I do retain I tend to revisit and, thereby, strengthen. They become—morphologically, electrochemically—part of the architecture of my brain.

This model of memory, which I've presented here in a rather loose layperson's summary, excites the amateur scientist in me. It feels true to the twinned fuzziness and richness of my own memories, and it inspires awe with its image of neural networks effortlessly self-coordinating, in a massively parallel way, to create my ghostly consciousness and my remarkably sturdy sense of self. It seems to me lovely and postmodern. The human brain is a web of a hundred billion neurons, maybe as many as two hundred billion, with trillions of axons and dendrites exchanging quadrillions of messages by way of at least fifty different chemical transmitters. The organ with which we observe and make sense of the universe is, by a comfortable margin, the most complex object we know of in that universe.

And yet it's also a lump of meat. At some point, maybe later on that same Valentine's Day, I forced myself to read the entire pathology report. It included a "Microscopic Description" of my father's brain:

> Sections of the frontal, parietal, occipital, and temporal cerebral cortices showed numerous senile plaques, prominently diffuse type, with minimal numbers of neurofibrillary tangles. Cortical Lewy bodies were easily detected in H&E stained material. The amygdala demonstrated plaques, occasional tangles and mild neuron loss.

In the notice that we had run in local newspapers nine months earlier, my mother insisted that we say my father had died "after long illness." She liked the phrase's formality and reticence, but it was hard not to hear her grievance in it as well, her emphasis on "long." The pathologist's identification of senile plaques in my father's brain served to confirm, as only an autopsy could, the fact with which she'd struggled daily for many years: like millions of other Americans, my father had had Alzheimer's disease.

This was his disease. It was also, you could argue, his story. But you have to let me tell it.

•   •   •

Alzheimer's is a disease of classically "insidious onset." Since even healthy people become more forgetful as they age, there's no way to pinpoint the first memory to fall victim to it. The problem was especially vexed in the case of my father, who not only was depressive and reserved and slightly deaf but also was taking strong medicines for other ailments. For a long time, it was possible to chalk up his non sequiturs to his hearing impairment, his forgetfulness to his depression, his hallucinations to his medicines; and chalk them up we did.

My memories of the years of my father's initial decline are vividly about things other than him. Indeed, I'm somewhat appalled by how large I loom in my own memories, how peripheral my parents are. But I was living far from home in those years. My information came mainly from my mother's complaints about my father, and these complaints I took with a grain of salt; she'd been complaining to me pretty much all my life.

My parents' marriage was, it's safe to say, less than happy. They stayed together for the sake of their children and for want of hope that divorce would make them any happier. As long as my father was working, they enjoyed autonomy in their respective fiefdoms of home and workplace, but after he retired, in 1981, they commenced a round-the-clock performance of "No Exit" in their comfortably furnished suburban house. I arrived for brief visits like a U.N. peacekeeping force to which each side passionately presented its case against the other.

In contrast to my mother, who was hospitalized nearly thirty times in her life, my father had perfect health until he retired. His parents and uncles had lived into their eighties and nineties, and he, Earl Franzen, fully expected himself to be around at ninety "to see," as he liked to say, "how things turn out." (His anagrammatic namesake Lear imagined his last years in similar terms: listening to "court news," with Cordelia, to see "who loses and who wins; who's in, who's out.") My father had no hobbies and few pleasures besides eating meals, seeing his children, and playing bridge, but he did take a *narrative* interest in life. He watched a staggering amount of TV news. His ambition for old age was to follow the unfolding histories of the nation and his children for as long as he could.

The passivity of this ambition, the sameness of his days, tended to make him invisible to me. From the early years of his mental decline I can dredge up exactly one direct memory: watching him, toward the end of the eighties, struggle and fail to calculate the tip on a restaurant bill.

Fortunately, my mother was a great writer of letters. My father's passivity, which I regarded as regrettable but not really any of my business, was a source of bitter disappointment to her. As late as the fall of 1989—a season in which, according to her letters, my father was still playing golf and undertaking major home repairs—the terms of her complaints remained strictly personal:

> It is extremely difficult living with a very unhappy person when you know you must be the major cause of the unhappiness. *Decades* ago when Dad told me he didn't believe there is such a thing as love (that sex is a "trap") and that he was not cut out to be a "happy" person I should have been smart enough to realize there was no hope for a relationship satisfactory to *me*.

This letter dates from a period during which the theatre of my parents' war had shifted to the issue of my father's hearing impairment. My mother maintained that it was inconsiderate not to wear a hearing aid; my father complained that other people lacked the consideration to "speak up." The battle culminated Pyrrhically, in his purchase of a hearing aid that he then declined to wear. Here again, my mother constructed a moral story of his "stubbornness" and "vanity" and "defeatism"; but it's hard not to suspect, in hindsight, that his faulty ears were already serving to camouflage more serious trouble.

A letter from January, 1990, contains my mother's first written reference to this trouble:

> Last week one day he had to skip his breakfasttime medication in order to take some motor skills tests at Wash U. where he is in the Memory & Ageing study. That night I awakened to the sound of his electric razor, looked at the clock & he was in the bathroom shaving at 2:30 A.M.

Within a few months, my father was making so many mistakes that my mother was forced to entertain other explanations:

> Either he's stressed or not concentrating or having some mental deterioration but there have been quite a few incidents recently that really worry me. He keeps leaving the car door open or the lights on & twice in one week we had to call triple A & have them come out & charge the battery (now I've posted signs in the garage & that seems to have helped). . . . I really don't like the idea of leaving him in the house alone for more than a short while.

My mother's fear of leaving him alone assumed greater urgency as the year dragged on. Her right knee was worn out, and, because she already had a steel plate in her leg from an earlier fracture, she was facing complicated surgery followed by prolonged recovery and rehab. Her letters from late 1990 and early 1991 are marked by paragraphs of agonizing over whether to have surgery and how to manage my father if she did:

> Were he in the house alone more than overnight with me in the hospital I would be an absolute basket case as he leaves the water running, the stove on at times, lights on everywhere, etc. . . . I check & recheck as much as I can on most things lately but even so many of our affairs are in a state of confusion & what really is hardest is his resentment of my intrusion—"stay out of my affairs!!!" He does not accept or realize my *wanting* to be *helpful* & that is the hardest thing of all for me.

At the time, I'd recently finished my second novel, and so I offered to stay with my father while my mother had her operation. To steer clear of his pride, she and I agreed to pretend that I was coming for her sake, not his. What's odd, though, is that I was only half-pretending. My mother's characterization of my father's incapacity was compelling, but so was my father's portrayal of my mother as an alarmist nag. I went to St. Louis because, for her, his incapacity was absolutely real; once there, I behaved as if, for me, it absolutely wasn't.

My mother was in the hospital for nearly five weeks. Strangely, although I'd never lived alone with my father for so long and never would again, I can now remember almost nothing specific about my stay with him; I have a general impression that he was somewhat quiet, maybe, but otherwise completely normal. Here, you might think, was a direct contradiction of my mother's earlier reports. And yet I have no memory of being bothered by the contradiction. What I do have is a copy of a letter that I wrote to a friend while in St. Louis. In the letter, I mention that my father has had his medication adjusted and now everything is fine.

Wishful thinking? Yes, to some extent. But one of the basic features of the mind is its keenness to construct wholes out of fragmentary parts. We all have a blind spot in our vision where the optic nerve attaches to the retina, but our brain unfailingly registers a seamless world around us. We catch part of a word and hear the whole. We see expressive faces in floral-pattern upholstery; we constantly fill in blanks. In a similar way, I think I was inclined to interpolate across my father's silences and mental absences and to persist in seeing him as the same old wholly whole Earl Franzen. I still needed him to be an actor in my story of myself. In my letter to my friend, I describe a morning practice session of the St. Louis Symphony that my mother insisted my father and I attend so as not to waste her free tickets to it. After the first half of the session, in which the very young Midori *nailed* the Sibelius violin concerto, my father sprang from his seat with miserable geriatric agitation. "So," he said, "we'll go now." I knew better than to ask him to sit through the Charles Ives symphony that was coming, but I hated him for what I took to be his philistinism. On the drive home, he had one comment about Midori and Sibelius. "I don't understand that music," he said. "What do they do—memorize it?"

.   .   .

Later that spring, my father was diagnosed with a small, slow-growing cancer in his prostate. His doctors recommended that he not bother treating it, but he insisted on a course of radiation. With a kind of referred wisdom about his own mental state, he became terrified that something was dreadfully wrong with him: that he would not, after all, survive into his nineties. My mother, whose knee continued to bleed internally six months after her operation, had little patience with what she considered his hypochondria. In September, 1991, she wrote:

> I'm relieved to have Dad started on his radiation ther-
> apy & it forces him to get out of the house *every* day
> [inserted here a smiley face]—a big plus. . . . Actually, being
> so sedentary now (content to do nothing), he has had too
> much time to worry & think about himself—he NEEDS dis-
> tractions! . . . More & more I feel the greatest attributes
> anyone can have are (1), a positive attitude & (2), a sense of
> humor—wish Dad had them.

There ensued some months of relative optimism. The cancer was eradicated, my mother's knee improved, and her native hope-fulness returned to her letters. She reported that my father had taken first place in a game of bridge: "With his confusion cleared up & his less conservative approach to the game he is doing remarkably well & it's about the only thing he enjoys (& can stay awake for!)." But my father's anxiety about his health did not abate; he had stomach pains that he was convinced were caused by cancer. Gradually, the import of the story my mother was telling me migrated from the personal and the moral toward the psychiatric. "The past six months we have lost so many friends it is very unsettling—part of Dad's nervousness & depression I'm sure," she wrote in February, 1992. The letter continued:

> Dad's internist, Dr. Rouse, has about concluded what I have felt all along regarding Dad's stomach discomfort (he's ruled out all clinical possibilities). Dad is (1) terribly nervous, (2) terribly depressed & I hope Dr. Rouse will put him on an anti-depressant. I *know* there has to be help for this. . . . If he won't go for counseling (suggested by Dr. Weiss) perhaps he now will accept pills or whatever it takes for nervousness & depression.

For a while, the phrase "nervousness & depression" was a fixture of her letters. Prozac briefly seemed to lift my father's spirits, but the effects were short-lived. Finally, in July, 1992, to my surprise, he agreed to see a psychiatrist.

My father had always been supremely suspicious of psychiatry. He viewed therapy as an invasion of privacy, mental health as a matter of self-discipline, and my mother's increasingly pointed suggestions that he "talk to someone" as acts of aggression—little lobbed grenades of blame for their unhappiness as a couple. It was a measure of his desperation that he had voluntarily set foot in a psychiatrist's office.

In October, when I stopped in St. Louis on my way to Italy, I asked him about his sessions with the doctor. He made a hopeless gesture with his hands. "He's extremely able," he said. "But I'm afraid he's written me off."

The idea of anybody writing my father off was more than I could stand. From Italy, I sent the psychiatrist a three-page appeal for reconsideration, but even as I was writing it the roof was caving in at home. "Much as I dislike telling you," my mother wrote in a letter faxed to Italy, "Dad has regressed terribly. Medicine for the urinary problem a urologist is treating in combination with medication for depression and nervousness blew his mind again and the hallucinating, etc., was terrible." There had been a weekend with my Uncle Erv in Indiana, where my father, removed from his familiar surroundings, unleashed a night of madness that culminated in my uncle's shouting into his face, "Earl, my God, it's your brother, Erv, we slept in the same bed!" Back in St. Louis, my father had begun to rage against the retired lady, Mrs. Pryble, whom my mother had engaged to sit with him two mornings a week while she ran errands. He didn't see why he needed sitting, and, even assuming that he did need sitting, he didn't see why a stranger, rather than his wife, should be doing it. He'd become a classic "sundowner," dozing through the day and rampaging in the wee hours.

There followed a dismal holiday when my wife and I finally intervened on my mother's behalf and put her in touch with a geriatric social worker, and my mother urged my wife and me to tire my father out so that he would sleep through the night without psychotic incident, and my father sat stone-faced by the fireplace or told grim stories of his childhood while my mother fretted about the expense, the prohibitive expense, of sessions with a social worker. But even then, as far as I can remember, nobody ever said "dementia." In all my mother's letters to me, the word "Alzheimer's" appears exactly once, in reference to an old woman I worked for as a teen-ager.

• • •

I remember my suspicion and annoyance, fifteen years ago, when the term "Alzheimer's disease" was first achieving currency. It seemed to me another instance of the medicalization of human experience, the latest entry in the ever-expanding nomenclature of victimhood. To my mother's news about my old employer I replied, "What you describe sounds like the same old Erika, only quite a bit worse; and that's not how Alzheimer's is supposed to work, is it? I spend a few minutes every month fretting about ordinary mental illness being trendily misdiagnosed as Alzheimer's."

From my current vantage, where I spend a few minutes every month fretting about what a self-righteous thirty-year-old I was, I can see my reluctance to apply the term Alzheimer's to my father as a way of protecting the specificity of Earl Franzen from the generality of a nameable condition. Conditions have symptoms; symptoms point to the organic basis of everything we are. They point to the brain as meat. And, where I ought to recognize that, yes, the brain is meat, I seem instead to maintain a blind spot across which I then interpolate stories that emphasize the more soul-like aspects of the self. Seeing my afflicted father as a set of organic symptoms would invite me to understand the *healthy* Earl Franzen (and the healthy me) in symptomatic terms as well—to reduce our beloved personalities to finite sets of neurochemical coordinates. Who wants a story of life like that?

Even now, I feel uneasy when I gather facts about Alzheimer's. Reading, for example, David Shenk's excellent new book, "The Forgetting: Alzheimer's: Portrait of an Epidemic," I'm reminded that when my father got lost in his own neighborhood, or forgot to flush the toilet, he was exhibiting symptoms identical to those of millions of other afflicted people. There can be comfort in having company like this, but I'm sorry to see the personal significance drained from certain mistakes of my father's, like his confusion of my mother with her mother, which struck me at the time as singular and orphic, and from which I gleaned all manner of important new insights into my parents' marriage. My sense of private selfhood turns out to have been illusory.

Senile dementia has been around for as long as people have had the means of recording it. While the average human life span remained low and old age was a comparative rarity, senility was considered a natural by-product of aging—perhaps the result of sclerotic cerebral arteries. The German neuropathologist Alois

Alzheimer believed he was witnessing an entirely new variety of mental illness when, in 1901, he admitted to his clinic a fifty-one-year-old woman, Auguste D., who was suffering from bizarre mood swings and severe memory loss and who, in Alzheimer's initial examination of her, gave problematic answers to his questions:

"What is your name?"
"Auguste."
"Last name?"
"Auguste."
"What is your husband's name?"
"Auguste, I think."

When Auguste D. died in an institution, four years later, Alzheimer availed himself of recent advances in microscopy and tissue staining and was able to discern, in slides of her brain tissue, the striking dual pathology of her disease: countless sticky-looking globs of "plaque," and countless neurons engulfed by "tangles" of neuronal fibrils. Alzheimer's findings greatly interested his patron Emil Kraepelin, then the dean of German psychiatry, who was engaged in a fierce scientific battle with Sigmund Freud and Freud's psycho-literary theories of mental illness. To Kraepelin, Alzheimer's plaques and tangles provided welcome clinical support for his contention that mental illness was fundamentally organic. In his "Handbook of Psychiatry" he dubbed Auguste D.'s condition *Morbus Alzheimer.*

For six decades after Alois Alzheimer's autopsy of Auguste D., even as breakthroughs in disease prevention and treatment were adding fifteen years to life expectancy in developed nations, Alzheimer's continued to be viewed as a medical rarity à la Huntington's disease. David Shenk tells the story of an American neuropathologist named Meta Neumann who, in the early fifties, autopsied the brains of two hundred and ten victims of senile dementia and found sclerotic arteries in few of them, plaques and tangles in the majority. Here was ironclad evidence that Alzheimer's was far more common than anyone had guessed; but Neumann's work appears to have persuaded no one. "They felt that Meta was talking nonsense," her husband recalled.

The scientific community simply wasn't ready to consider that senile dementia might be more than a natural consequence of aging. In the early fifties, there was no self-conscious category of "seniors," no explosion of Sun Belt retirement developments, no A.A.R.P., no Early Bird tradition at low-end restaurants; and scientific thinking reflected these social realities. Not until the seventies did conditions become ripe for a reinterpretation of senile dementia. By then, as Shenk says, "so many people were living so long that senility didn't feel so normal or acceptable anymore." Congress passed the Research on Aging Act in 1974, and established the National Institute on Aging, for which funding soon mushroomed. By the end of the eighties, at the crest of my annoyance with the clinical term and its sudden ubiquity, Alzheimer's had achieved the same social and medical standing as heart disease or cancer—and had the research-funding levels to show for it.

•   •   •

What happened with Alzheimer's in the seventies and the eighties wasn't simply a diagnostic paradigm shift. The number of new cases really is soaring. As fewer and fewer people drop dead of heart attacks or die of infections, more and more survive to become demented. Alzheimer's patients in nursing homes live much longer than other patients, at a cost of at least forty thousand dollars annually per patient; until they're institutionalized, they increasingly derange the lives of family members charged with caring for them. Already, five million Americans have the disease, and the number could rise to fifteen million by 2050.

Because there's so much money in chronic illness, drug companies are investing feverishly in proprietary Alzheimer's research while publicly funded scientists file for patents on the side. But because the science of the disease remains cloudy (a functioning brain is not a lot more accessible than the center of the earth or the edge of the universe) nobody can be sure which avenues of research will lead to effective treatments. Early-onset Alzheimer's is usually linked to specific genes, but the vastly more common late-onset variety cannot be traced to a single factor. And the disease's etiology is like the proverbial elephant—it looks like an inflammation of the brain but also like a neuro-chemical imbalance but also like a disease of abnormal-protein deposition of the kind that occasionally strikes the heart and kidneys.

Treatments currently under study target each of these aspects. People taking cholesterol-reducing drugs or nonsteroidal anti-inflammatory drugs (like aspirin or Celebrex) may enjoy a lower risk of Alzheimer's. Those who already have the disease can sometimes be helped for a while with acetylcholine-boosting medications or antioxidants like Vitamin E. There is intense competition among drug companies to develop enzyme inhibitors that zero in on the abnormal proteins. On the immunological front, researchers at Elan Pharmaceuticals recently came up with the seemingly outlandish idea of a vaccine for Alzheimer's—of teaching the immune system to produce antibodies that attack and destroy amyloid plaques in the brain—and found that the vaccine not only prevented plaque formation in transgenic mice but actually reversed the mental deterioration of mice already addled by it. Over all, the feeling in the field seems to be that if you're under fifty you can reasonably expect to be offered effective drugs for Alzheimer's by the time you need them. Then again, twenty years ago, many cancer researchers were predicting a cure within twenty years.

David Shenk, who is comfortably under fifty, makes the case in "The Forgetting" that a cure for senile dementia might not be an unmitigated blessing. He notes, for example, that one striking peculiarity of the disease is that its sufferers often suffer less and less as it progresses. Caring for an Alzheimer's patient is gruellingly repetitious precisely because the patient himself has lost the cerebral equipment to experience anything as a repetition. Shenk quotes patients who speak of "something delicious in oblivion" and who report an enhancement of their sensory pleasures as they come to dwell in an eternal, pastless Now. If your short-term memory is shot, you don't remember, as you stoop to smell a rose, that you've been stooping to smell the same rose all morning.

As the psychiatrist Barry Reisberg first observed twenty years ago, the decline of an Alzheimer's patient mirrors in reverse the neurological development of a child. The earliest capacities a child develops—raising the head (at one to three months), smiling (two to four months), sitting up unassisted (six to ten months)—are the last capacities an Alzheimer's patient loses. Brain development in a growing child is consolidated through a process called myelinization, wherein the axonal connections between neurons are gradually strengthened by sheathings of the fatty substance myelin. Apparently, since the last regions of the child's brain to mature remain the least myelinated, they're the regions most vulnerable to the insult of Alzheimer's. The hippocampus, which processes short-term memories into long-term, is very slow to myelinize. This is why we're unable to form permanent episodic memories before the age of three or four, and why the hippocampus is where the plaques and tangles of Alzheimer's first appear. Hence the ghostly apparition of the middle-stage patient who continues to be able to walk and feed herself even as she remembers nothing from hour to hour. The inner child isn't inner anymore. Neurologically speaking, we're looking at a one-year-old.

Although Shenk tries valiantly to see a boon in the Alzheimer's patient's childish relief from responsibility and childlike focus on the Now, I'm mindful that becoming a baby again was the last thing my father wanted. The stories he told from his childhood, in northern Minnesota, were mainly (as befits a depressive's recollections) horrible: brutal father, unfair mother, endless chores, backwoods poverty, family betrayals, hideous accidents. He told me more than once, after his retirement, that his greatest pleasure in life had been going to work as an adult in the company of other men who valued his abilities. My father was an intensely private person, and privacy for him had the connotation of keeping the shameful content of one's interior life out of public sight. Could there have been a worse disease for him than Alzheimer's? In its early stages, it worked to dissolve the social connections that had saved him from the worst of his depressive isolation. In its later stages, it robbed him of the sheathing of adulthood, the means to hide the child inside him. I wish he'd had a heart attack instead.

Still, shaky though Shenk's arguments for the brighter side of Alzheimer's may be, his core contention is harder to dismiss: senility is not merely an erasure of meaning but a source of meaning. For my mother, the losses of Alzheimer's both amplified and reversed long-standing patterns in her marriage. My father had always refused to open himself to her, and now, increasingly, he *couldn't* open himself. To my mother, he remained the same Earl Franzen napping in the den and failing to hear. She, paradoxically, was the one who slowly and surely lost her self, living with a man who mistook her for her mother, forgot every fact he'd ever known about her, and finally ceased to speak her name. He, who had always insisted on being the boss in the marriage, the maker of decisions, the adult protector of the childlike wife, couldn't help behaving like the child. Now the unseemly outbursts were his, not my mother's. Now she ferried him around town the way she'd once ferried me and my brothers. Task by task, she took charge of their life. And so, although my father's "long illness" was a crushing strain and disappointment to her, it was also an opportunity to grow slowly into an autonomy she'd never been allowed: to settle some very old scores.

As for me, once I accepted the scope of the disaster, the sheer duration of Alzheimer's forced me into unexpectedly welcome closer contact with my mother. I learned, as I might not have otherwise, that I could seriously rely on my brothers and that they could rely on me. And, strangely, although I'd always prized my intelligence and sanity and self-consciousness, I found that watching my father lose all three made me less afraid of losing them myself. I became a little less afraid in general. A bad door opened, and I found I was able to walk through it.

·   ·   ·

The door in question was on the fourth floor of Barnes Hospital, in St. Louis. About six weeks after my wife and I had put my mother in touch with the social worker and gone back East, my oldest brother and my father's doctors persuaded him to enter the hospital for testing. The idea was to get all the medications out of his bloodstream and see what we were dealing with underneath. My mother helped him check in and spent the afternoon settling him into his room. He was still his usual, semi-present self when she left for dinner, but that evening, at home, she began to get calls from the hospital, first from my father, who demanded that she come and remove him from "this hotel," and then from nurses who reported that he'd become belligerent. When she returned to the hospital in the morning, she found him altogether gone—raving mad, profoundly disoriented.

I flew back to St. Louis a week later. My mother took me straight from the airport to the hospital. While she spoke to the nurses, I went to my father's room and found him in bed, wide awake. I said hello. He made frantic shushing gestures and beckoned me to his pillow. I leaned over him and he asked me, in a husky whisper, to keep my voice down because "they" were "listening." I asked him who "they" were. He couldn't tell me, but his eyes rolled fearfully to scan the room, as if he'd lately seen "them" everywhere and were puzzled by "their" disappearance. When my mother appeared in the doorway, he confided to me, in an even lower whisper, "I think they've gotten to your mother."

My memories of the week that followed are mainly a blur, punctuated by a couple of life-changing scenes. I went to the hospital every day and sat with my father for as many hours as I could stand. At no point did he string together two coherent sentences. The memory that appears to me most significant in hindsight is a very peculiar one. It's lit by a dreamlike indoor twilight, it's set in a hospital room whose orientation and cramped layout are unfamiliar from any of my other memories, and it returns to me now without any of the chronological markers that usually characterize my memories. I'm not sure it even dates from that first week I saw my father in the hospital. And yet I am sure that I'm not remembering a dream. All memories, the neuroscientists say, are actually memories of memory, but usually they don't feel that way. Here's one that does. I remember remembering: my father in bed, my mother sitting beside it, me standing near the door. We've been having an anguished family conversation, possibly about where to move my father after his discharge from the hospital. It's a conversation that my father, to the slight extent that he can follow it, is hating. Finally, he cries out with passionate emphasis, as if he has had enough of all the nonsense, "I have *always* loved your mother. *Always.*" And my mother buries her face in her hands and sobs.

This was the only time I ever heard my father say he loved her. I'm certain the memory is legitimate because the scene seemed to me immensely significant even at the time, and I then described it to my wife and brothers and incorporated it into the story I was telling myself about my parents. In later years, when my mother insisted that my father had never said he loved her, not even once, I asked if she remembered that time in the hospital. I repeated what he'd said, and she shook her head uncertainly. "Maybe," she said. "Maybe he did. I don't remember that."

My brothers and I took turns going to St. Louis every few months. My father never failed to recognize me as someone he was happy to see. His life in a nursing home appeared to be an endless troubled dream populated by figments from his past and by his deformed and brain-damaged fellow-inmates; his nurses were less like actors in the dream than like unwelcome intruders on it. Unlike many of the female inmates, who at one moment were wailing like babies and at the next moment glowing with pleasure while someone fed them ice cream, my father never cried, and the pleasure he took in ice cream never ceased to look like an adult's. He gave me significant nods and wistful smiles as he confided to me fragments of nonsense to which I nodded as if I understood. His most consistently near-coherent theme was his wish to be removed from "this hotel" and his inability to understand why he couldn't live in a little apartment and let my mother take care of him.

For Thanksgiving that year, my mother and my wife and I checked him out of the nursing home and brought him home with a wheelchair in my Volvo station wagon. He hadn't been in the house since he'd last been living there, ten months earlier. If my mother had been hoping for a gratifying show of pleasure from him, she was disappointed; by then, a change of venue no more impressed my father than it does a one-year-old. We sat by the fireplace and, out of unthinking, wretched habit, took pictures of a man who, if he knew nothing else, seemed full of unhappy knowledge of how dismal a subject for photographs he was. The images are awful to me now: my father listing in his wheelchair like an unstrung marionette, eyes mad and staring, mouth sagging, glasses smeared with strobe light and nearly falling off his nose; my mother's face a mask of reasonably well-contained despair; and my wife and I flashing grotesquely strained smiles as we reach to touch my father. At the dinner table, my mother spread a bath towel over him and cut his turkey into little bites. She kept asking him if he was happy to be having Thanksgiving dinner at home. He responded with silence, shifting eyes, sometimes a faint shrug. My brothers called to wish him a happy holiday, and here, out of the blue, he mustered a smile and a hearty voice; he was able to answer simple questions and thanked them both for calling.

This much of the evening was typically Alzheimer's. Because children learn social skills very early, a capacity for gestures of courtesy and phrases of vague graciousness survives in many Alzheimer's patients long after their memories are shot. It wasn't so remarkable that my father was able to handle (sort of) my brothers' holiday calls. But consider what happened next, after dinner, outside the nursing home. While my wife ran inside for a geri chair, my father sat beside me and studied the institutional portal that he was about to re-enter. "Better not to leave," he told me in a clear, strong voice, "than to have to come back." This was not a vague phrase; it pertained directly to the situation at hand, and it suggested an awareness of his larger plight and his connection to the past and to the future. He was requesting that he be spared the pain of being dragged back toward consciousness and memory. And, sure enough, on the morning after Thanksgiving, and for the remainder of our visit, he was as crazy as I ever saw him, his words a hash of random syllables, his body a big flail of agitation.

For David Shenk, one of the most illuminating aspects of Alzheimer's is its slowing down of death. Shenk likens the disease to a prism that refracts death into a spectrum of its otherwise tightly conjoined parts—death of autonomy, death of memory, death of self-consciousness, death of personality, death of body—and he subscribes to the most common trope of Alzheimer's: that its particular sadness and horror stem from the sufferer's loss of his or her "self" long before the body dies.

This seems mostly right to me. By the time my father's heart stopped, I'd been mourning him for years. And yet, when I consider his story, I wonder whether the various deaths can ever really be so separated, and whether memory and consciousness have such secure title, after all, to the seat of selfhood. I can't stop looking for meaning in the two years that followed his loss of his supposed "self," and I can't stop finding it.

I'm struck, above all, by the apparent persistence of his *will*. I'm powerless not to believe that he was exerting some bodily remnant of his self-discipline, some reserve of strength in the sinews beneath both consciousness and memory, when he pulled himself together for the statement he made to me outside the nursing home. I'm powerless as well not to believe that his crash on the following morning, like his crash on his first night alone in a hospital, amounted to a relinquishment of that will, a letting go, an embrace of madness in the face of unbearable emotion. Although we can fix the starting point of his decline (full consciousness and sanity) and the end point (oblivion and death), his brain wasn't simply a computational device running gradually and inexorably amok. Where the subtractive progress of Alzheimer's might predict a steady downward trend like this—

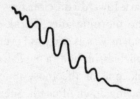

—what I saw of my father's fall looked more like this:

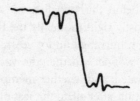

He held himself together longer, I suspect, than it might have seemed he had the neuronal wherewithal to do. Then he collapsed and fell lower than his pathology may have strictly dictated, and he chose to stay low, ninety-nine per cent of the time. What he *wanted* (in the early years, to stay clear; in the later years, to let go) was integral to what he *was*. And what I want (stories of my father's brain that are not about meat) is integral to what I choose to remember and retell.

One of the stories I've come to tell, then, as I try to forgive myself for my long blindness to his condition, is that he was bent on concealing that condition and, for a remarkably long time, retained the strength of character to bring it off. My mother used to swear that this was so. He couldn't fool the woman he lived with, no matter how he bullied her, but he could pull himself together as long he had sons in town or guests in the house. The true solution of the conundrum of my stay with him during my mother's operation probably has less to do with my blindness than with the additional will he was exerting.

After the bad Thanksgiving, when we knew he was never coming home again, I helped my mother sort through his desk. (It's the kind of liberty you take with the desk of a child or a dead person.) In one of his drawers we found evidence of small, covert endeavors not to forget. There was a sheaf of papers on which he'd written the addresses of his children, one address per slip, the same address on several. On another slip he'd written the birth dates of his older sons—"BOB 1-13-48" and "TOM 10-15-50"—and then, in trying to recall mine (August 17, 1959), he had erased the month and day and made a guess on the basis of my brothers' dates: "JON 10-13-49."

Consider, too, what I believe are the last words he ever spoke to me, three months before he died. For a couple of days, I'd been visiting the nursing home for a dutiful ninety minutes and listening to his mutterings about my mother and to his affable speculations about certain tiny objects that he persisted in seeing on the sleeves of his sweater and the knees of his pants. He was no different when I dropped by on my last morning, no different when I wheeled him back to his room and told him I was heading out of town. But then he raised his face toward mine and—again, out of nowhere, his voice was clear and strong—he said, "Thank you for coming. I appreciate your taking the time to see me."

Set phrases of courtesy? A window on his fundamental self? I seem to have little choice about which version to believe.

⋅   ⋅   ⋅

In relying on my mother's letters to reconstruct my father's disintegration, I feel the shadow of the undocumented years after 1992, when she and I talked on the phone at greater length and ceased to write all but the briefest notes. Plato's description of writing, in the Phaedrus, as a "crutch of memory" seems to me fully accurate: I couldn't tell a clear story of my father without those letters. But, where Plato laments the decline of the oral tradition and the atrophy of memory which writing induces, I at the other end of the Age of the Written Word am impressed by the sturdiness and reliability of words on paper. My mother's letters are truer and more complete than my self-absorbed and biased memories; she's more alive to me in the written phrase "he NEEDS distractions!" than in hours of videotape or stacks of pictures of her.

The will to record indelibly, to set down stories in permanent words, seems to me akin to the conviction that we are larger than our biologies. I wonder if our current cultural susceptibility to the charms of materialism—our increasing willingness to see psychology as chemical, identity as genetic, and behavior as the product of bygone exigencies of human evolution—isn't intimately related to the postmodern resurgence of the oral and the eclipse of the written: our incessant telephoning, our ephemeral E-mailing, our steadfast devotion to the flickering tube.

Have I mentioned that my father, too, wrote letters? Usually typewritten, usually prefaced with an apology for misspellings, they came much less frequently than my mother's. One of the last is from December, 1987:

> This time of the year is always difficult for me. I'm ill at ease with all the gift-giving, as I would love to get things for people but lack the imagination to get the right things. I dread the shopping for things that are the wrong size or the wrong color or something not needed, and anticipate the problems of returning or exchanging. I like to buy tools, but Bob pointed out a problem with this category, when for some occasion I gave him a nice little hammer with good balance, and his comment was that this was the second or third hammer and I don't need any more, thank you. And then there is the problem of gifts for your mother. She is so sentimental that it hurts me not to get her something nice, but she has access to my checking account with no restrictions. I have told her to buy something for herself, and say it is from me, so she can compete with the after-Christmas comment: "See what I got from my husband!" But she won't participate in that fraud. So I suffer through the season.

In 1989, as his powers of concentration waned with his growing "nervousness & depression," my father stopped writing letters altogether. My mother and I were therefore amazed to find, in the same drawer in which he'd left those addresses and birth dates, an unsent letter dated January 22, 1993—unimaginably late, a matter of weeks before his final breakdown. The letter was in an envelope addressed to my nephew Nick, who, at age six, had just begun to write letters himself. Possibly my father was ashamed to send a letter that he knew wasn't fully coherent; more likely, given the state of his hippocampal health, he simply forgot. The letter, which for me has become an emblem of invisibly heroic exertions of the will, is written in a tiny pencilled script that keeps veering away from the horizontal:

> Dear Nick,
> We got your letter a couple days ago and were pleased to see how well you were doing in school, particularly in math. It is important to write well, as the ability to exchange ideas will govern the use that one country can make of another country's ideas.
> Most of your nearest relatives are good writers, and thereby took the load off me. I should have learned better how to write, but it is so easy to say, Let Mom do it.
> I know that my writing will not be easy to read, but I have a problem with the nerves in my legs and tremors in my hands. In looking at what I have written, I expect you will have difficulty to understand, but with a little luck, I may keep up with you.
> We have had a change in the weather from cold and wet to dry with fair blue skies. I hope it stays this way. Keep up the good work.
>
> Love, Grandpa
>
> P.S. Thank you for the gifts.

•   •   •

My father's heart and lungs were very strong, and my mother was bracing herself for two or three more years of endgame when, one day in April, 1995, he stopped eating. Maybe he was having trouble swallowing, or maybe, with his remaining shreds of will, he'd resolved to put an end to his unwanted second childhood.

His blood pressure was seventy over palpable when I flew into town. Again, my mother took me straight to the nursing home from the airport. I found him curled up on his side under a thin sheet, breathing shallowly, his eyes shut loosely. His muscle had wasted away, but his face was smooth and calm and almost entirely free of wrinkles, and his hands, which had changed not at all, seemed curiously large in comparison to the rest of him. There's no way to know if he recognized my voice, but within minutes of my arrival his blood pressure climbed to 120/90. I worried then, worry even now, that I made things harder for him by arriving: that he'd reached the point of being ready to die but was ashamed to perform such a private or disappointing act in front of one of his sons.

My mother and I settled into a rhythm of watching and waiting, one of us sleeping while the other sat in vigil. Hour after hour, my father lay unmoving and worked his way toward death; but when he yawned, the yawn was *his*. And his body, wasted though it was, was likewise still radiantly *his*. Even as the surviving parts of his self grew ever smaller and more fragmented, I persisted in seeing a whole. I still loved, specifically and individually, the man who was yawning in that bed. And how could I not fashion stories out of that love—stories of a man whose will remained intact enough to avert his face when I tried to clear his mouth out with a moist foam swab? I'll go to my own grave insisting that my father was determined to die and to die, as best he could, on his own terms.

We, for our part, were determined that he not be alone when he died. Maybe this was exactly wrong—maybe all he was waiting for was to be left alone. Nevertheless, on my sixth night in town I stayed up and read a light novel cover to cover while he lay and breathed and loosed his great yawns. A nurse came by, listened to his lungs, and told me he must never have been a smoker. She suggested that I go home to sleep, and she offered to send in a particular nurse from the floor below to visit him. Evidently, the nursing home had a resident angel of death with a special gift for persuading the nearly dead, after their relatives had left for the night, that it was O.K. for them to die. I declined the nurse's offer and performed this service myself. I leaned over my father, who smelled faintly of acetic acid but was otherwise clean and warm. Identifying myself, I told him that whatever he needed to do now was fine by me, he should let go and do it.

Late that afternoon, a big early-summer St. Louis wind kicked up. I was scrambling eggs when my mother called from the nursing home and told me to hurry over. I don't know why I thought I had plenty of time, but I ate the eggs with some toast before I left, and in the nursing-home parking lot I sat in the car and turned up the radio, which was playing the Blues Traveler song that was all the rage that season. No song has ever made me happier. The great white oaks all around the nursing home were swaying and turning pale in the big wind. I felt as though I might fly away with happiness.

And still he didn't die. The storm hit the nursing home in the middle of the evening, knocking out all but the emergency lighting, and my mother and I sat in the dark. I don't like to remember how impatient I was for my father's breathing to stop, how ready to be free of him I was. I don't like to imagine what he was feeling as he lay there, what dim or vivid sensory or emotional forms his struggle took inside his head. But I also don't like to believe that there was nothing.

Toward ten o'clock, my mother and I were conferring with a nurse in the doorway of his room, not long after the lights came back on, when I noticed that he was drawing his hands up toward his throat. I said, "I think something is happening." It was agonal breathing: his chin rising to draw air into his lungs after his heart had stopped beating. He seemed to be nodding very slowly and deeply in the affirmative. And then nothing.

After we'd kissed him goodbye and signed the forms that authorized the brain autopsy, my mother sat down in our kitchen and uncharacteristically accepted my offer of undiluted Jack Daniel's. "I see now," she said, "that when you're dead you're really dead." This was true enough. But, in the slow-motion way of Alzheimer's, my father wasn't much deader now than he'd been two hours or two weeks or two months ago. We'd simply lost the last of the parts out of which we could fashion a living whole. There would be no new memories of him. The only stories we could tell now were the ones we already had.

Vogue

WINNER, LEISURE INTERESTS

Salt Chic

In this essay, Vogue *food writer Jeffrey Steingarten sets out to find the world's finest salt. Employing extensive (verging on obsessive) research and drawing on his tremendous culinary expertise, Steingarten not only confirms that differences* do *exist but also explains—in minute yet readable detail—what accounts for them. Along the way, he charms the reader with a dry wit that leaves food insiders and grazers alike deeply satisfied.*

Jeffrey Steingarten

Salt Chic

**Do different salts
taste different?
Jeffrey Steingarten
travels to the ends
of the earth to track
down the reason one
salt smells of violets,
another costs $65 a
pound, and whether
it even matters.**

M y first step was to buy a pocket-size electronic scale capable of weighing one-thousandth of a gram, the kind of scale you might find at a major drug deal in, say, the Everglades. Next, I took thirteen different kinds of salt from my pantry, packaged them up, and sent them off to the AmTest laboratory near Seattle for the most minute analysis. And then I reserved a seat on the next day's flight to

Palermo, Sicily. Within days I was installed in the exquisite medieval mountaintop city of Erice, feasting on hillocks of freshly made sheep's-milk ricotta and broad platters of hand-rolled cous-cous moistened with rich fish broth. But that wasn't the point of my visit. Far from it. The point was pure science. Before I was through, I would solve the mystery surrounding the taste of salt.

Nothing in the food world today is cooler than salt, and despite an excess of God-given modesty, I must admit that I got there very, very early. Now every gourmet store sells expensive brands of salt in a rainbow of colors from the world over. Food fans who once brought back unusual olive oils to their friends at home now come bearing bags of exotic salt. Chefs plan special dinners in which each course is paired with a particular type of salt. Food writers compete to demonstrate their disdain for Diamond Crystal Salt and Morton's. Said one owner of a Manhattan gourmet shop, "I don't even use regular salt anymore. It's like cooking with sour wine."

It is a rare day when I feel that I stand at the very forefront of fashion, at the cutting edge of chic. But this is one of them. Just look at my countertop. There is a jar of Sicilian sea salt from the vast salt flats at Trapani, and pouches of powder-fine Indian black salt, which is really a beautiful, indescribable lavender, and Thai salt, which is simply white. There's regular table salt and kosher salt (which should be called "koshering salt," as it is used to prepare meat in accordance with Jewish dietary laws). My Maldon sea salt from England comes in lovely square flakes; the Korean salt has been roasted in vessels of bamboo; one type of Hawaiian salt is coral-colored because of the red *alae* clay lining the salt pools and the other is black from the lining of lava rock. I am not sure how the rose-tinted salt from Maras, Peru, got that way. Please remind me to place a call to Maras, Peru. And, as you'd expect, there are bags of fleur de sel, the most delightful type of sea salt because, after evaporation by the sun, it is collected by hand from the fluffy and ephemeral top layer of the salt pools, almost like snowflakes; mine are from Guérande and from the Île de Ré in Poitou-Charentes and from the Camargue in southern France. Each crystal of fleur de sel is said to form around a single alga (the singular form of *algae*), giving it what some sniffers perceive as the aroma of violets. Maybe someday I'll smell the violets, too.

And if this isn't chic enough for you, let me tell you about Oshima Island Blue Label Salt, one of the rarest in the world and among the most expensive. It is evaporated from the primordial seawater around Oshima Island, in the middle of the vast and empty ocean, 45 minutes by plane from Tokyo. It is available for purchase in small amounts only by members of a club called the Salt Road Club. And I am a card-carrying member—without doubt the only member with whom you are acquainted and the only American granted admission. The membership card is a lovely shiny plastic ocean blue, and I carry it always in my wallet, next to my heart. My friend Nafumi Tamura, who had helped me last year by translating some Japanese materials on the history of sashimi, arranged for my membership through her mother's home address in Osaka. In a remarkable twist of fate, Nafumi now works in the kitchen of a hot new restaurant in Manhattan named Fleur de Sel.

There is about a half pound of Oshima Island Blue Label Salt in a bag on my counter, and it is currently my favorite salt of all— only in part because of its rarity and dizzyingly high status—but I use it infrequently so as not to squander it all before next year's harvest. In fact, I don't use it at all. How chic is that?

Now somebody has thrown a stink bomb into our midst. He is Robert L. Wolke, a retired chemistry professor who has written a series of three articles in *The Washington Post* claiming that all salt tastes the same! If two salts seem to differ, he says, this is due only to their differing crystal shapes and sizes. But their chemical composition is essentially identical. When texture is not a factor—

when, as in cooking, the salts are dissolved in liquids—their tastes are completely indistinguishable. No salt is chemically saltier than any other. Wolke makes lots of clumsy fun of people who think otherwise. His series of articles won two important awards for newspaper food journalism.

The food world was in an uproar. If Wolke is right, all the time, money, and pride we have devoted to exotic salts have been completely wasted, and are now exposed as pretense and fraud. My single claim to chic would be washed down the drain. Somebody has to prove Wolke wrong!

I was surprised both that the series won any journalism awards at all and that *The Washington Post* printed the articles in the first place. For one thing, Wolke had published an article very similar to the first two installments of the *Post* series in *The San Francisco Chronicle* eight years ago, on December 30, 1992! This is not what I call journalism. Second, in making his argument that all salts taste alike, Wolke needed two crucial pieces of evidence—a chemical analysis of various types of salt, and a scientifically conducted, comparative taste test of them. Wolke did not mention any tests already conducted (I know of two, both unpublished) or any plans to conduct one. He simply asserts that the amounts of the other minerals mixed in with the sodium chloride are too small to taste. Wolke may be right, but he surely doesn't prove it.

We can all certainly agree on some basic facts about salt. All salt comes from the sea, including inland salt deposits left by prehistoric seas. Evaporate water from the open ocean, and you will end up with a sludge containing about 75 percent sodium chloride and the rest a wide variety of minerals, dominated by magnesium and calcium. Refine the sludge further and you will get edible white table salt, mainly sodium chloride but with about 1 percent in other minerals. Different refining methods produce salt crystals that look entirely different from each other—some are like snowflakes, others like dense cubes. Koshering salt forms hollow stepped pyramids. So, they all melt at different rates on the tongue and in food. (Shirley Corriher, food scientist and author of *Cook Wise: The Hows and Whys of Successful Cooking* [William Morrow Cookbooks], tells me that some salts dissolve nine times faster than others.) Fluffy crystals of fleur de sel or thin flakes of Maldon salt sprinkled on dry food will melt immediately on the tongue, delivering a powerful hit of saltiness. The compact cubes of Diamond Crystal and Morton's melt slowly on the tongue, reluctantly releasing their salty taste over a longer span of time, to which one writer attributes the bitterness of common table salt. In dishes like tuna tartare, fleur de sel will dissolve quickly, where Diamond Crystal may remain in crunchy form for some time, possibly an advantage.

. . .

These are the taste effects of texture, which Wolke acknowledges, at least in principle. But what about the 1 percent of other minerals? Can we taste them? Do they help explain the different tastes of various salts? Wolke says no, they are too dilute to taste. His is a remarkable assertion, considering that everybody can taste the difference between bottled mineral water and ordinary water. And mineral water contains only one-twentieth of 1 percent of dissolved minerals.

So, Wolke must be wrong, I figured, but could I prove it? I made plans to give it a try, which is one reason I traveled to Erice.

In Erice is the Majorana Centre, which hosts scientific conferences. There were two of them in early May, one concerned with gravity and black holes, which are not my specialties, and the other with "molecular gastronomy," which is, sort of. The biennial workshops in molecular gastronomy were begun eight years ago by my friends Hervé This, Ph.D., now at the Collège de France, and the late Nicholas Kurti, once professor of physics at

Oxford University and secretary of the Royal Society. The meetings attract scientists, chefs, and some journalists, from England, France, Italy, and to a lesser extent the United States. This year, the topic was the texture of food. (Do you realize that a slice of bread is a fractal?) But Hervé gave me a green light to conduct a salt tasting. Two scientists were corralled into helping me— David Kilcast and Alan Parker. David Kilcast, Ph.D., is the head of Sensory and Consumer Science at the Leatherhead Food Research Association (a leading food-research center) in England. Alan Parker, Ph.D., is a scientist who specializes in food texture at Firmenich, S.A. (among the world's largest flavor and perfume companies), in Geneva.

We met for lunch at the restaurant Monte San Giuliano, the only good place to eat in Erice, which you reach through a flowered courtyard and up an old stone stairway, all with views of the salty Mediterranean. When I brought out my thirteen Ziploc bags of white crystals and my gram scale, we sensed a gathering momentum among management, staff, and a neighboring table of diners to throw us back down the antique stairway. After flashing our badges from the Majorana Centre, we were reluctantly allowed to proceed with our power lunch.

The idea was that we would compare pairs of salts using what is known as the Duo-trio method. David and Alan sketched out the general procedure. We would dissolve each type of salt in water, to eliminate the influence of texture—and therefore Wolke's major claim. In each trial, a subject would be given three little plastic cups of salt water. He would sip from the first cup, a "reference sample" containing American table salt. Next he would sip from the other two cups, one containing the same table salt and the other containing one of the chic, expensive, and exotic salts I had brought from America. Then the subject would try to pair the two samples of table salt—or pick the one that didn't match the other two. If he succeeded this would be a sign that table salt tastes different from its upscale cousins. If the overall outcome was random, with just as many wrong pairings as correct ones, then we would have failed to prove that different salts taste different.

David and Alan regrettably decided that four salts were the maximum we could compare with table salt, considering the available time. I chose the four: fleur de sel from Guérande and from the Île de Ré; the famous Sicilian sea salt from Trapani, a city on the plain directly below Erice; and Oshima Island Blue Label salt because of its price, rarity, and the major role it has come to play in my shaky self-esteem. We dissolved the American table salt to various concentrations and tasted them; for some reason we all arbitrarily agreed that the amount in seawater, with 3 percent salt, was ideal.

David and Alan organized everything, with the help of a charming young French taste scientist named Christine Fayard. The experiment would be conducted in a double-blind fashion, meaning that the scientist conducting each tasting would be ignorant of which was the chic-salt solution and which two came from the supermarket. They would conscript eight or ten subjects, and each would taste all four salt solutions. The next day, everything went as planned, except that nearly everybody wanted to be a subject and the atmosphere in the tasting room tilted toward chaos. The scientists withdrew to tabulate the outcome, which they announced at the group's next session. *The results were random!* Only one taster got them all right, the identity of whom modesty prevents me from disclosing. (This outcome will randomly occur an average of one in every sixteen trials, a rare event but sadly not rare enough to justify hubris on my part.) We had failed to disprove Wolke!

Noticing that I had climbed up on a low stone wall and was teetering over a sheer drop down to the salt flats of Trapani, David Kilcast very generously volunteered the taste laboratories at Leatherhead to repeat the experiment soon after he returned to England using trained (though not specifically salt-sensitive) subjects and the same five salts, plus two others I slipped in. I suggested that we decrease the concentration of salt. Seawater overwhelms the palate, I argued, preventing one from tasting the other minerals. Aren't we humans genetically programmed to gag when we swallow seawater? David did not react to the evolutionary argument, but his staff in England favored a 2 percent concentration. Back in Manhattan after a few days of very fine eating in Palermo (including the best pasta with sea urchins I've tasted, a new and dazzling type of gelato named Cremolata, and the famous Palermitan sandwich of sliced cow's spleen and lung stewed in lard and nestled, dripping, in a crisp roll between a slab of fresh ricotta and shreds of cacciocavalo cheese, at the Focacceria San Francesco), I played around with salt solutions and voted for 1 percent. They ignored me.

While I nervously awaited news from England, the chemical analysis from AmTest arrived. I had given them a list of all the minerals in seawater, and this is what I had asked AmTest to measure in my salt samples. I had high hopes for my lovely Hawaiian red salt and black salt—until I read the labels. The colors are supposed to come from the red clay or lava rock lining the ponds where the Hawaiian seawater is evaporated: now the labels concede it's regular sea salt mixed with clay or lava. Please! This is little different from garlic salt or seasoning salt or that fancy salt from Venice that's mixed with herbs and spices. It is not really salt. I eliminated Hawaii from the competition.

All thirteen salts turned out to be about 99 percent sodium chloride and 1 percent other things. Overall, the weightiest "impurities" were sulfate (the rotten-egg smell!), followed by nearly equal parts of calcium and magnesium, plus smaller amounts of potassium, silicon (what sand is made of), iron, phosphorus, strontium, and aluminum.

Can these be tasted? I retired with my calculator for some

serious figuring. Rearranging the numbers from AmTest, I estimated that the average chicken soup seasoned with about 1 percent salt will contain 224 parts per million of bitter minerals and metals. Can you taste an amount as small as this? Of course we can taste an amount as small as this—it's the same as the difference between ordinary water and bottled water containing a moderate quantity of minerals. Or just dissolve some table salt in water and dilute it down to 250 parts per million. Anybody who can't distinguish this weak salt solution from ordinary water should see a doctor. Plus, bitter tastes are said to be even more obvious than salty ones. Wolke has to be wrong. But would we be able to prove it?

Two days later, my fertile musings were interrupted by an E-mail from David Kilcast with the results. This time there were 20 tasters, "panelists," sitting in individual booths at a constant room temperature of 72°F., all under Northlight illumination. Panelists who correctly distinguished the chic salt were asked if they liked it and why.

As it turned out, some chic salts were indistinguishable in taste from ordinary table salt and others were quite distinct. This means that Wolke is wrong in principle, though it is obvious that some quite plain-tasting salts are promoted with unfounded enthusiasm. The Sicilian sea salt confused everybody. (Of the many available types, ours was unfortunately excessively white and refined.) Otherwise, a majority of panelists identified the chic salt in every case. But a bare majority is not enough to be statistically significant. To my chagrin, the fleur de sel from the Île de Ré did not score much differently from table salt. I'd better refill my saltcellar.

Two chic salts were marginal, distinguished by thirteen out of 20 panelists, which would happen by chance 13 percent of the time, certainly a rare event but not rare enough for statistical significance. These were Oshima Island Blue Label Salt (oops!) and the fleur de sel from Guérande. The panelists generally preferred

Oshima Island over table salt, finding it milder but not less salty. They did not prefer the salt from Guérande, which some found sulfurous.

The roasted Korean salt was detected fourteen out of 20 times, which is nearly significant, but panelists were particularly unsure and some used words like *astringent, fizzy*, and *strange* to describe what must reflect the bamboo-roasting technique.

The winner and clear champion was a sea salt from Okinawa, which a friend named Kathryn had brought back from Japan, and which I decided to slip in at the last minute, as its feeling on the tongue seemed so much like that of fleur de sel. Sixteen out of 20 panelists could tell it from Diamond Crystal, which could happen by chance only 1 percent of the time. And panelists were unusually certain about their decisions. The bad news is that a strong majority of those with a preference liked the Diamond Crystal better, describing the Okinawa salt as bitter, astringent, or acidic.

Whew! What have we accomplished? The salt skeptics have been sort of defeated, I feel, but ours is a Pyrrhic victory. The textures of various chic salts have a powerful effect on their taste—but mainly when they reach the tongue with their crystals intact. More than a majority of the chic salts could be distinguished just by their taste, but not always with a high level of statistical significance and not always to the detriment of Diamond Crystal. I wonder what a 1 percent dilution of the salts would have turned up.

Nafumi Tamura had reported from the kitchen at Fleur de Sel that different salts seem to act differently in tuna tartare, and probably in other foods, as well. Even if the minerals in less refined salts may be difficult to taste when dissolved in water, can they still change in other ways the taste or texture of things we eat? That is the question. I have begun looking into this, which means I have E-mailed Harold McGee for help. (Harold is probably the leading authority on food science in this country and author of the classic *On Food and Cooking: The Science and Lore of the Kitchen* [Scribner]. It was he who forced that spleen, lung, and lard sandwich on me in Palermo.) Harold's immediate response was yes, that even at low levels minerals can affect taste and texture. Sulfates might contribute an unpleasant smell; iron can split fatty acids into smaller, more volatile (and aromatic?) molecules. Then Harold actually looked it up and quickly discovered two more examples. Magnesium and calcium can free up some of the sodium that is bound to other food molecules, *making the salt taste saltier*. And they can prevent aroma molecules from getting stuck in thickeners—things like the pectin in jams—keeping them available for our sensual pleasure.

I looked back at the thirteen chemical analyses from AmTest. Common American table salt has the smallest amounts of both calcium and magnesium. Oshima Blue Label is highest in calcium (by quite a margin), trailed by Maldon, the French fleurs de sel, and Diamond Crystal Kosher salt. Fleur de sel de Guérande and Thai salt have the most magnesium, trailed by all three salts from Japan and then the other fleurs de sel.

That's just a start, but I think we've got them on the run.

Men's Journal

FINALIST, FEATURE WRITING

Killing Libby

A huge conglomerate, bent on profit at any cost. A small mining town, which the company virtually owns and runs, wallowing in an environmental disaster that has killed (and continues to kill) many of its citizens. It's a story we've all read and watched unfold onscreen before. But rarely are such tragic, complex tales told in such a simple and profound way. Mark Levine presents both sides of the story of Libby, Montana, which one resident dubs "America's Chernobyl." Levine's clean writing style never interferes with the telling, even though he is a part of the story: It's only as he is leaving Libby that he realizes he can breathe freely again—and so can we.

Mark Levine

Killing Libby

The EPA calls it the most severe exposure to a hazardous material in American history. The only people in Libby, Montana, who didn't see it coming were the victims, who are dying to know if it's really possible to poison an entire town and get away with it.

A s U.S. Highway 2 crosses Montana, it is dotted along its six-hundred-mile length with signposts bearing white crosses. They flicker past like small anonymous advertisements, punctuating the mostly empty road, which stretches across the sparsely populated top of the state— from the wheat fields of Wolf Point in the east, past the wind- scoured town of Chinook, where the plains collide with the Rocky Mountains, skirting the lower fringes of Glacier National Park, and continuing through a claustrophobic corridor of ragged hills. The crosses mark the sites of highway fatalities. Some of them are hung with plastic wreaths; some have names scratched on their surfaces; some are bent by wind and ice; many are rusted.

For a while, as if playing a child's game with myself, I keep a tally of the roadside body count, which lends me the impression that I am being shepherded along my route by specters, that death forms the backdrop of this journey. Near Libby, a hamlet on the northwestern edge of the state, the white crosses begin to multiply, like rogue vegetation. In one innocuous stretch, just outside town, there is a cross every hundred yards or so; a cross stands beside a sign announcing the town limits, in view of the great charred steel skeleton of a former sawmill; yet another one decorates the lawn outside the Libby Area Chamber of Commerce, whose officials have spent the past few years battling the notion that the town, population 2,675, has become, as one resident put it, "America's Chernobyl."

Directly behind the Chamber of Commerce sits a charmless rectangle about the size of a pair of football fields, hemmed in by a chain-link fence. This is Libby's cemetery, adorned with its own bland rows of crosses. Diane Keck knows this place. Until 1954, when she was fifteen and her family moved away, her father was the town undertaker. "In the course of my father's job, he noticed something strange," she says. "A lot of the men who worked up at the mine just outside town were dying young. He made a connection. He told us kids to stay away from the stuff from the mine." Some of that stuff—a micalike mineral of a thousand uses called vermiculite, which is tinged with tremolite, a naturally occurring and particularly virulent form of asbestos—was forever drifting through the air around Libby. The mineral hung in dust clouds over the town and accumulated on the ground at a plant where ore was processed and shipped. "They would dump it into open boxcars and there would be a big poof of smoke," Keck remembers. "And there were big piles of it, like mountains, and we would play blindman's bluff around them."

Ten years ago, Keck started coughing, and she hasn't stopped since. When she hikes in the woods, she gets short of breath. Doctors tell her that she has signs of asbestosis, an incurable lung disease that is caused almost exclusively by industrial exposure to asbestos. A few years ago, Keck learned that most of the children from her old neighborhood had also been diagnosed with asbestos-related lung disease. Her brother has it; so does her nephew, who grew up nearby; so too, it seems, does nearly everyone in town.

It takes little more than five minutes to drive through Libby, but I have no intention of passing through. The town is the site of a toxic contamination that is unprecedented in American history, and I have followed a trail of white crosses here to meet the people and to hear their stories. Libby has always been remote and rugged, even by Montana standards, and until recently it was a tightknit, seemingly idyllic community, shadowed by the rough peaks of the Cabinet Mountains, their slopes drenched in blue light. You don't have to hike very far into the hills around town to come upon a chain of secluded lakes, and you can still spend days at those heights without crossing paths with another person. Grizzlies roam the woods, and trout cluster in the shallows of the Kootenai River, which cuts through town. But the fresh, folkloric Rocky Mountain air has become a burden rather than a

blessing for many of Libby's residents, who, like Keck, are endur-
ing the effects of a lung-thickening disease and opening their
homes to hazardous-waste workers in hooded Tyvek suits who
are equipped with respirators and sensitive monitors.

This is the short form of the telling: Just north of Libby stands a
hill that once looked like any other hill. For sixty-seven years, the
shape of this hill was altered by explosives and earthmovers, and by
the labor of men who were brought up the hill on clattering buses.
The men came up, and the rock they dug out was brought down,
tens of thousands of pounds of rock each hour. It was hard work,
removing the top of the hill, but it was good work. It paid well. It
supported generations of families. True, the miners died young, but
danger was an accepted part of their daily routine; grousing about
pain and misfortune was not. Miners kept their suspicions about
the vermiculite dust that coated their work clothes to themselves.

Then, in 1990, the hill was vacated by W.R. Grace, the multi-
national corporation that had operated the mine since 1963.
Although the company possessed detailed knowledge of the
asbestos hazards to which its workers had been exposed, it had
kept that knowledge to itself. State and federal governments had
also been aware of the risks. Ironically, Marc Racicot, Montana's
attorney general from 1989 to 1993, and its governor from 1993
to 2001, was raised in Libby. But even that didn't compel state
officials to inform the community.

By 1995, a few families had noticed that miners' wives were dying
of their husbands' ailment, and the miners' children, too, had
learned that they often shared it, as if the hazards of the trade were
genetically passed on. But not until 1999 did residents begin to
notice that asbestosis was showing up in people who had never been
at the mine and had never lived with miners. Still, there was no
organized outcry about the contamination until the end of that
year, when the Environmental Protection Agency began a belated
full-scale investigation of the town's legacy of pollution.

The EPA discovered that asbestos has probably shortened the

lives of most of the 1,898 workers who toiled at the mine between 1940 and 1990. What's more, the effects are ongoing. An astounding one third of Libby's residents are believed to have contracted asbestos-related lung disease. "We haven't begun to count the number of people who have been, or will be, killed by this," an EPA scientist, protective of his identity, told me, before adding with disgust, "This was deliberate murder."

Soon after I arrive in Libby, I meet a man named Les Skramstad, whose thin, wavering voice barely rises above a whisper. Skramstad, sixty-four, is grizzled and bowlegged and wears a camouflage cap with a dirty feather stuck in its side. A toothpick often hangs from his mouth when he speaks. Although Skramstad didn't receive a high school diploma until he was in his forties, he is as forceful and eloquent a man as I have met. He has worked as a rancher and a logger and a mechanic. Once, for barely three years, he worked as a miner in Libby and as a result has full-blown asbestosis. "Full-blown is when you got a death sentence," he says. "You better put your affairs in order." In 1997, Skramstad sued W.R. Grace for personal injury. His was the first of only three cases in Libby to reach a jury, and he won a judgment of $660,000 against the company, which has made him something of a pariah in town. But his victory didn't dispel his bitterness about what he and his community have suffered. "Should a person have to die just because they live in Libby?" he asks.

"It was more or less like a brotherhood at the mine. The first day of work, I got on the bus downtown and they hauled us up on the hill. There was a guy named Tom DeShazer, and I walked over to him and said, 'Here I am,' and he said, 'Yeah, you're going to go be a sweeper in the mill.' He sent me over to the warehouse to get a respirator. I'd never seen a respirator before. A guy named Shorty Welch handed it to me, and I said, 'What am I supposed to do with this?' and he kind of laughed and said, 'Well, wear it if you can.' It was a little aluminum gadget, about the size of your hand, that fit over your nose and mouth.

"I got on the man-lift and rode up to the top floor of that mill, and, my God, I'd never seen anything like it in my life. I guess a guy has seen a dust storm before. The dust was probably three, four inches deep. It was almost like walking on a real plushy carpet. It was so dusty that it was hard to see what the heck was going on.

"I believe I was getting $2.10 an hour. I really wanted that job, so, boy, I started sweeping with all my might. After about fifteen minutes, Jesus, I couldn't breathe. So I threw that respirator off, and it was plugged with dust. I thought I was going to suffocate. Everyone who worked up there looked the same after a few hours. We all looked brown.

"I was beating this dust off myself so I could eat lunch when Tom DeShazer said, 'Oh, don't pay any attention to that. It's just a nuisance dust. It won't hurt you. You can eat a ton of it and it'll never hurt you.'"

—LES SKRAMSTAD

• • •

I am standing on the porch of a whitewashed house three miles from W.R. Grace's defunct mine. The house is owned by history buff, gentleman farmer, and amateur toxic-contamination expert Mike Powers. Powers, sixty-four, came to Libby twenty years ago and restored a lush turn-of-the-century homestead on the banks of the Kootenai, where he tends his small herd of exotic Swiss cattle and lives in an old farmhouse built from hand-hewn logs.

Once, long ago, Powers's farm played host to the workshop in which the potent dust that helped build and bury Libby was first stirred up. The wizard of Libby, a man named E.N. Alley, who died two years before Powers's birth, slept in the house where

Powers now sleeps, and left traces of his handiwork all over the property.

In 1921, Alley ventured into a disused forty-foot-deep shaft that had been dug into a hill near his ranch. He carried a torch to light his way. Before long, he heard a sizzling sound. His flame had roasted some of the loose rock in the tunnel, and the pebbles had puffed up, like popcorn, and drifted before his eyes. Alley had found the world's largest deposit of vermiculite, whose peculiar exfoliating properties are due to the evaporation of water molecules between the rock's layers. Alley staked his miner's claim, came up with the suitably Jazz Age name Zonolite for his product, and christened the mountain after the brand. What he didn't know was that the vermiculite was inextricably braided with asbestos fibers, and that inhaling those fibers—especially in high concentration, especially over long stretches of time—would kill a man.

Zonolite was marketed as a lightweight, nonflammable additive to construction materials, and by 1926 a hundred tons of it were being produced in Libby daily. Its most widespread application would be in home insulation—today, as many as 15 million attics in the United States may contain asbestos-laced Zonolite. A mill was built on top of Zonolite Mountain to separate valuable ore from waste rock. The mill stood ten stories tall, higher by far than any building in Libby, and featured a tangle of grinders, steel screens, conveyor belts, and chutes. Ore would be poured in at the top, and by the time it tumbled to the bottom, being crushed as it fell, it had been sifted into a granular residue. The milling produced plumes of thick, white dust—containing up to five thousand pounds of asbestos each day—that billowed from atop the mountain, settling on the hillside and in creek beds and hovering over Libby like a fog. Children in town would write their names in the dust on sidewalks.

By 1942, when the state of Montana first contacted the Zonolite Company to express its concern about the dust at the mine, there was already ample medical knowledge about the dangers of asbestos. The author of a 1937 article in *The New England Journal of Medicine* did not mince words. "Asbestos," he wrote, "is extremely dangerous and fatal." Such warnings did not deter W.R. Grace, then based in Cambridge, Massachusetts, from buying Zonolite in 1963, or from doubling the mine's daily output—to 15,000 tons of ore, containing 900,000 pounds of asbestos—between then and 1990, when the mine closed after mounting signs of a future filled with asbestos-related litigation had become impossible to ignore.

Although Powers never worked in the mine, he recently learned that his lungs are diseased from inhaling asbestos. "My only exposure," he says, "is living here." We tour his farm, and everywhere we go he points out glittering flecks of vermiculite. Standing in the former chicken house, Powers tells me, "The carpenter who helped me work on this building—his lungs are full of asbestos. The guy that worked on the furnace shield has it. The electrician, the plumber—they have it." Powers figures that the property into which he has sunk his savings and his labor is unsalable. "Maybe," he says, "W.R. Grace will buy this farm and turn it into an asbestos theme park." As he talks, Powers bangs on a wall and jolts a puff of vermiculite dust loose into the air.

"Look there," he says. "Strange how it catches in the cobwebs."

"I'd come home from work pretty well laden with dust, and my kids were little at that time, and they'd meet me at the door and grab my legs, and they'd get a blast of it. Then my wife, Norita, would give me a hug at the door, and she'd get a dose of it, too. I contaminated them every single day. If it had just took the lives of us miners, that would have been bad enough. But I carried it home and gave it to my wife and three of our five children. That's a pretty poor percentage. My daughter Laurel, she's got six kids. She's got it. And my boy Brent, he's got it real bad, like me, full-blown. My grandfather lived to be eighty-eight. My dad lived to be seventy-eight. I may not make sixty-eight. Brent, he may not make forty-eight. Any man should look out for his family first, and being that I had a hand in their destiny, that's pretty grim."

—LES SKRAMSTAD

•   •   •

Chris Weis, a forty-seven-year-old toxicologist, was not, at first, alarmed. Based in Denver, Weis specializes in emergency response for the EPA's Region 8 office, which covers the northern Rockies. Just before Thanksgiving 1999, while attending a meeting in Helena, Montana, Weis was paged by his managers. The agency had seen an inflammatory report in the *Seattle Post-Intelligencer* concerning a small town that Weis had never heard of where close to two hundred deaths and another four hundred cases of fatal illness were being attributed to exposure to mine contaminants.

"Look," he tells me, in the EPA's field office in Libby, "I've got a doctorate in toxicology and a doctorate in medical physiology. My first reaction to the reports was, This doesn't happen."

Weis nonetheless went to Libby to investigate, visiting the former mine and a number of sites where ore was processed and handled. He contacted a pulmonologist in Spokane, Washington, two hundred miles to the west, who had treated hundreds of Libby residents for asbestos-related lung disease, which occurred in town at sixty times the national average rate. He learned of at least nineteen local cases of an invariably fatal cancer called mesothelioma, whose only known cause is exposure to asbestos, and which is so rare that, as Weis says, "one case in a population of a million is considered an epidemic." He spent some time talking to residents. "Libby is a small town," he points out, "so if you talk to forty or fifty people and every one of them has a neighbor or family member with an asbestos-related disease—to say the least, that's unusual." Weis returned to Denver persuaded that Libby had the distinction of hosting "the most severe human exposure to a hazardous material this country has ever seen."

Within two days, the EPA descended on Libby in full force, bringing in a team of scientists, physicians, geologists, and toxic-cleanup experts. None of them were prepared for the dimensions of the disaster they would discover. They learned that W.R. Grace had "pumped so much asbestos fiber into the airshed here, it hung in the center of town in concentrations that were probably twenty times higher than the present occupational-exposure limit," Weis says. They learned that when W.R. Grace left town in 1990, the company had done a sloppy job cleaning up its former properties, which remained highly contaminated. And there was more. "We found disturbing evidence that the material had been readily accessible to the general public in Libby. Ore was often free for the taking. Kids played in it; it was in sandboxes and on ball fields. People would load up their pickup trucks and take it home to use in their gardens as a soil amendment and on their driveways as a surfacing material. When the high school track needed resurfacing in the 1970s, W.R. Grace brought down truckloads of raw ore—almost, in some cases, pure asbestos— and covered the track with it. Kids ran on mine tailings until 1983."

Finally, the EPA called in the Agency for Toxic Substances and Disease Registry, a division of the Centers for Disease Control and Prevention, which invited the residents of Libby and the surrounding valley, past and present, to undergo screening for signs of asbestos-related disease. As Weis recalls, "We anticipated that, given the severity of exposures in Libby, we might see possibly as much as 10 or 12 percent of the population come back with scarring on their lungs." Chest X-rays were taken of 6,144 people. Preliminary results released this March, representing 1,078 of those examined, revealed that 30 percent showed symptoms of lung disease. "We just weren't prepared for that," Weis says. "What's unprecedented is that so many of these sick people had no known source of exposure to asbestos. They only lived in Libby."

Weis was also shocked to discover that his predecessors at the EPA and other federal agencies had been well informed of the dangers in Libby. "The pieces of this situation were put together in the seventies," he says. "Very detailed studies were done. The results were unequivocal." While it's true that until 1970, when Congress passed the Occupational Safety and Health Act, regulatory oversight of workplaces was severely limited, rarely had a year passed since the mid-fifties in which some government agency did not visit Libby and come back with troubling findings. In 1968, for instance, the U.S. Public Health Service warned W.R. Grace that "the dust concentrations are from 10 to 100 times in excess of the safe limit."

Nonetheless, a series of EPA memos in the early eighties addressing the health risks at the mine were allowed to languish. At that time, President Reagan, in his first term, was intent on reducing government spending in order to cut taxes. (In a report issued this spring, the office of the EPA's inspector general acknowledged that the "EPA did not place emphasis on dealing with asbestos-contaminated vermiculite due to funding constraints and competing priorities.") It's worth noting that in 1982, Reagan convened a closed-door gathering of advisers to come up with suggestions for where to trim the budget. The group, called the Grace Commission, was chaired by an old friend of the president's, J. Peter Grace, the president and CEO of W.R. Grace.

The EPA is still cleaning up Libby, having spent $12 million on its efforts in 2000, with another $16 million budgeted for 2001. Sixty to seventy percent of Libby's homes are thought to contain vermiculite insulation. Most yards have vermiculite in the soil. At dusk, the streets downtown still glisten with a sheen of powdery ore. Nights at my motel, I often pass hazardous-waste workers in the hallway. They have been brought to Libby by the EPA. By day, they can be seen entering sealed houses around town, beating pillows, vacuuming curtains, and dusting mantels in an effort to measure how much asbestos fiber has worked its way into the fiber of daily life in Libby.

Naturally, the ore that was taken from W.R. Grace's mine did not all stay in Libby for long. It was transported to more than 250 processing plants around the country. The EPA has barely started examining these sites. In Minneapolis, though, the agency tracked down fifty-seven former employees of a factory that had received its share of Libby's vermiculite. Twenty-four of those workers either had died or were dying of asbestos-related disease.

"You can still go to your local Kmart and buy gardening supplies that contain Libby vermiculite," says Weis, who is in charge of gathering and evaluating scientific data on Libby's contamination. "Speaking purely as a toxicologist, I've never seen as hideous a poison as this material."

"Around the last part of 1960, a boss at the experimental lab come down and told us, 'I want you to get in the pickup and go up on the hill and get a load of asbestos.' That was the first time I ever heard the word. I'd seen a lot of it up there, but I didn't know what it was. We got shovels and picks and dug it out of the hill. We brought it down to town, and spread it out as thin as possible in our work area, and put electric heaters on it to dry out. We got on our hands and knees to pick out rocks from it, because we'd been told they wanted 100 percent asbestos. We worked every day on it, all day long, for a couple of weeks. When the stuff got dry, the wind would blow through the door and scatter it all over the building. We didn't want to lose any of it, so we sealed up all the doors with rags. I had no idea what they wanted it for. But like I say, we were just paid to do a job. There was not a peep about it being dangerous."

—LES SKRAMSTAD

• • •

Its name comes from a Greek word meaning "inextinguishable," and it endures fire, flood, and frost as fiercely as it clings to a person's lungs. A human hair is well over a thousand times as thick as one of its strands. It can be woven like cotton, which cannot be said of any other mineral. It has been an ingredient in at least three thousand products, common and rare, and, despite the widespread and mistaken impression that it has been banned—efforts by the EPA to do so, in 1989, were overturned on legal technicalities—it remains ubiquitous, not only in insulation but in clutch and brake linings, in pipe and boiler insulation, in wallboard and floor tiles, in oven mitts and plastic pot handles, and in baby powder.

Its advocates and apologists will dispute it, but over the past century, a vast medical literature has exhaustively described the means by which asbestos has killed, according to EPA estimates, 259,000 people in the United States, with another 166,000 deaths anticipated over the next thirty years. Among the proud array of carcinogenic products, natural and fabricated, only tobacco has contributed to a higher death toll. Most of its victims will never know what caused their death, because they are unaware they have been exposed to it, and the lapse between exposure and the onset of illness is typically longer than ten years. In this way, it maims not like a gun, inflicting harm at the moment of contact, but rather like a land mine, which lies dormant for years.

"There's something about this fiber that's not average," says Dr. Brad Black, the director of Libby's new Center for Asbestos-Related Disease. Black's job is not what he bargained for when he opted to be a small-town doctor in a place served by a twenty-four-bed hospital and fewer than ten physicians. Since the "asbestos clinic," as everyone in town calls it, opened last year, Black has seen, he estimates, four or five hundred asbestos-diseased patients, including the construction worker whose chest X-ray he has put on display for me.

"See those large patches of white?" Black says, pointing to blocks of washed-out-looking glare that rim the dark crescents of lung. "They wouldn't be there in a healthy lung. It's scarring." Black explains that tremolite asbestos fibers, once inhaled, embed themselves in the lining of the lung—the pleura—like needles, and stay there. The body can't flush them out; medicine can't destroy them; surgery can't cut them out. Surrounding tissue responds to the irritation by calcifying. A healthy pleura is as thick as Saran Wrap; in a person with asbestosis, it may be as thick as an orange peel. Then the lung itself gets covered with calloused tissue; oxygen struggles to find its way into the lung, and carbon dioxide struggles to find its way out. "It's just a progressive scarring," Black explains, "until respiratory or heart failure."

If one were to attempt to devise the perfect suffering, death by asbestosis would come close to fitting the bill. It is slow and incapacitating. It steadily wastes the patient. It brings the patient to the very verge of suffocation and allows him to remain there for months, even years, on end, to reflect on his situation. A typical patient will cough until he vomits. His lungs will fill with fluid. He will feel as if he is swimming in the fluid, drowning.

Just ask Don Kaeding, who survived four years as an artilleryman during the Second World War, but is paying for his twenty-eight months of service on behalf of Zonolite. I find Kaeding yoked by a fifty-foot length of tube to a noisy machine in the corner of his living room. The tubing fits snugly in his nostrils, curls over his ears, runs down his shirt, and snakes its way along the wall to a canister that feeds Kaeding his breath. "God damn, but this is an irritating disease," he says apologetically. "I got these cords to drag around, and they're always in everybody's way. My wife's mother tripped on them one night and broke her arm." Kaeding is seventy-eight. His skin is ashen, his hair waxy, his lips blue. He's been on supplemental oxygen for five years, like a puppet on a life-giving string, and, as he tells me, "ain't no one volunteers for this."

Kaeding—who filed a personal-injury suit against W.R. Grace, only to have his claim dismissed for exceeding the three-year statute of limitations—is one of a cadre of Libby residents being kept alive by mechanical means. Most of them don't leave the house much, because the effort of slipping into a portable oxygen unit, which weighs down a frail body and which gets unpleasantly frosty, tends to consume as much energy as an oxygen-deprived person can muster on a given day. Nonetheless, I spot shoppers resting their air tanks in their carts at the local grocery store. I see an oxygen-outfitted man wheeling a bicycle around town, stowing his gear as others would their Gatorade. And one of my new circle of asbestos-diseased acquaintances tells me the tale of an old woman in Libby who, not long ago, while hooked up to her air supply, put her head beneath her bedcovers, lit a furtive cigarette, and blew herself straight to the next world.

EXCERPT FROM THE DEPOSITION OF
EARL LOVICK, FORMER LIBBY MINE
SUPERINTENDENT, OCTOBER 27, 1998

Q: And you knew at least by 1962 that your men were being diseased, correct?

A: Yes, sir.

Q: It wasn't at risk of disease, they were in fact being diseased, correct?

A: Some of them, yes, sir.

Q: And they were in fact dying, correct?

A: Some of them, yes, sir.

Q: You had absolute proof that these men had been diseased up there at the mill by 1966 at the latest? Is that true?

A: Yes, sir, that would be true.

Q: And none of the records you had on that were shared with the men. Is that true?

A: Yes, sir.

Q: And so at this point it wasn't just a matter of men being exposed to something that might injure or kill them, these men were already injured and dying, and they were continuing to be exposed every day, is that true?

A: Yes, sir.

Q: And is it fair to say that since you knew that workers were going home with asbestos dust on them, that they were taking home toxic dust?

A: Yes.

• • •

Alan Stringer is in a bind. Stringer, fifty-seven, is an engineer of mines, after all, not an engineer of facts, and it turns out that it was an easier job to run an operation that exposed a town to hazard, as Stringer did in Libby from 1981 until the mine shut down, than it is to deal with the emotional, medical, and political fallout. But Stringer is a loyal man, a company man, and when W.R. Grace called on him to be its stand-up guy in Libby once again—dealing with flak from the press and the EPA and the community—he opened an office on Mineral Avenue, downtown, just down the block from the EPA, a few blocks farther from the Center for Asbestos-Related Disease.

"There's no question, it's a sad story," he says. Sadder, too, because W.R. Grace was an excellent record keeper, which only makes Stringer's job of defending the company tougher. A detailed paper trail demonstrates the company's awareness, even before it purchased Zonolite in 1963, of the asbestos problem in Libby. How to respond to a 1956 report by an inspector for Montana's Division of Disease Control noting that "the asbestos dust in the air is of considerable toxicity"? Or to an internal company memo, from 1967, that refers to "a potentially large group of employees who may already have the beginnings of [asbestosis]"? Or to a 1969 company briefing, marked CONFIDENTIAL and given the subject heading "Vermiculite Report for Mr. Grace," that concludes with the sentence "Tremolite asbestos is a definite health hazard at both the Libby operation and at the expanding plants using the ore"? Well, for Alan Stringer, the response is, "It was another time, another understanding."

Indeed, when times were good in Libby, no one—not workers, nor union representatives, nor politicians in a community in which W.R. Grace was the largest taxpayer—felt pressed to inquire too deeply into the health of miners. Among town doctors, silence was the rule. While the mine was active, W.R. Grace always occupied a seat on the board of the local hospital. As Black remembers, "If you'd have brought up this topic for discussion, you'd have been run out of town as a rabid environmentalist." The company was a pillar of the community. When civic groups were raising funds, the company was there. When the ball field needed new bleachers, the company was there.

But the company also failed to share the results of its own medical-screening program with its employees, even when, in 1969, those tests showed that 92 percent of longtime mineworkers were diseased. It would not, it seems, have been cost-effective to acknowledge that working at the mine could make a man terribly sick. A 1968 memo from high-ranking W.R. Grace executive Peter Kostic suggested that thirty-two diseased miners be shifted to less-strenuous work so that "we may be able to keep them on the job until they retire, thus precluding the high cost of total disability."

The company failed, as well, to provide workers with on-site showers, an amenity that might have reduced the amount of toxic material miners brought home with them. Another company memo, from 1983—when Stringer was mine superintendent—considered the $373,000 cost of installing such showers in forbidding tones, concluding, "I recommend that no action be taken at this time."

W.R. Grace says that the company complied with ever-changing regulations limiting asbestos exposure, which became more stringent during the 1970s and '80s, and that, alarmed by high rates of lung disease in its workers, it did take steps to reduce dust at the Libby mine. Only in retrospect, the company says, did it become clear that workers and residents had been exposed to harmful levels of tremolite asbestos. Still, the company's files are filled with material that has given Stringer a serious public relations headache.

But slick PR doesn't seem to be a strength at W.R. Grace, which was notably vilified in the book and movie *A Civil Action* for allegedly dumping cancer-causing chemicals in the drinking water of Woburn, Massachusetts. The company's image wasn't burnished any in Libby when, this past April, W.R. Grace filed for bankruptcy under Chapter 11, citing its need for protection from some 325,000 personal-injury claims that had been made against its asbestos-containing products, especially a fire-retardant spray-on insulator called Monokote. By its own account, the pared-down company, which began spinning off its assets in 1995, when it had revenues of $6 billion, did only $1.6 billion in business in 2000, while it forecasts asbestos-related liabilities of $878 million. "Grace cannot defend itself against unmeritorious claims," said Paul J. Norris, the company's chairman, president, and CEO, in announcing the bankruptcy.

Two days after the announcement, I meet with Roger Sullivan, a lawyer in Kalispell, Montana, ninety miles away. About fifteen years ago, a handful of diseased miners in Libby started suing the company, receiving small settlements—generally said to be less than $100,000 each—and agreeing to remain silent about the details of their suits. By the time Sullivan began advocating on behalf of clients in Libby in 1995, settlements had begun to creep up into the middle six figures—still barely enough to cover long-term medical costs. "In the course of developing a few early cases," he tells me, "the circle of victims just kept getting bigger and bigger." Sullivan and his partners, Jon Heberling and Allan McGarvey, have since settled thirty cases against W.R. Grace, have won three trials—including that of Les Skramstad—in front of juries, and have eighty suits pending, representing two hundred individuals.

Of course, these suits have been put on indefinite hold by W.R. Grace's bankruptcy filing, and according to Sullivan, his clients are "frustrated and confused by the chasm between the law and justice." Those with claims pending against W.R. Grace, and those who only recently learned of the harm done to them by the company, now stand a better chance of getting a payoff from gaming machines in local casinos.

> "It ought to scare the hell out of the whole town, but it don't. The town looks at us like we're the villains. Like this was a nice little town and we come along and upset the apple cart. A lot of people think we're dreaming this up and taking it out on this poor company. Well, if I strangled a single person—and that's what it amounts to if you've got asbestosis, you suffocate—I'd be in the penitentiary. And yet they do it to families, they do it to kids, and they get away with it."

> —LES SKRAMSTAD

•　　•　　•

Every weekday morning at ten, a group of men, mostly middle-aged or older, meet for coffee and conversation at a grimy little Mexican restaurant in downtown Libby called La Casa de Amigos. The restaurant doesn't open for business until eleven, which suits the members of the coffee klatch just fine. Although they would deny it, their meetings are not open to the public, but are instead the preserve of Libby's dilapidated power elite. Among the regulars who gather beneath faded piñatas and walls hung with threadbare serapes are an assortment of bankers, lawyers, and businessmen, as well as Alan Stringer, the mayor, and a representative to the state legislature. They take wagers on who will pay for their seventy-cent cups of coffee, and they trade gripes about the stigma that has blotted their town. "We're in dire straits," says Mike Munro, who runs a bar and restaurant called Treasure Mountain Casino, "and we've got no way of turning it around. The EPA has brought a different kind of cancer to this town." The men are scornful of the claims of those affected by asbestos-related disease. "There are people in town who are disappointed they haven't been diagnosed," one of them tells me. Another adds, "They thought they'd hit the lottery with this asbestos thing."

Since the EPA arrived in 1999, the town has fractured into a collection of outraged tribes. If Libby was, at one time, divided between blue-collar workers and managers—they lived in different neighborhoods, drank at different bars, prayed at different churches—now it is health, not wealth, that turns neighbors against one another.

Some, like the men in La Casa de Amigos, think the health hazards have been overblown by shiftless residents looking to cash in at the expense of W.R. Grace. Many others have refused to be examined for asbestosis, not wanting to condone the hysteria. Businessmen worry about the local economy: Tales have circulated about out-of-towners calling the Chamber of Commerce to ask if it is safe to drive through Libby, even with the windows rolled up. And there are those who want nothing more from W.R. Grace than acknowledgment in the form of an apology, which has not been forthcoming.

Then there are Libby's sick, who believe they are being persecuted for staining the town's reputation and ruining its economy. According to Laura Sedler, Libby's sole clinical social worker, who runs support groups for people with asbestos-related diseases, "There's an old-fashioned term for what happened to victims in this community: *shunning*." In 1997, when Les Skramstad took W.R. Grace to court, his suit didn't receive a word of coverage in the local newspapers. The county courtroom was empty of spectators, except for a few widows who wanted to find out what had happened to their husbands. More recently, a woman whose husband had just died of asbestosis stood in the checkout line at the supermarket and listened to the clerk gripe, "I'm sick of hearing about asbestos. We won't be done with this until they all just die off."

But residents in Libby are not only coming to terms with the realization that they have been liberally sprinkled with toxic dust; they also seem to be experiencing a childlike sense of abandonment. In the past decade, a prosperous silver mine shut down, and the timber mill that was the largest local employer scaled back its operations by 80 percent. Two thousand jobs have been lost, prompting an exodus of young, able-bodied, and motivated residents. Libby is the seat of what is now the second-poorest county in the second-poorest state in the country. A quarter of the town's population lives below the poverty line; another quarter isn't doing much better.

It's hard not to wonder whether the remoteness of Libby, and the complacency and lack of wealth and lack of influence of its residents—compared, in particular, with that of a onetime Fortune 500 company that donated $764,618 to political campaigns during the 1990s—might have allowed the disaster to occur in the first place. Several hundred sick poor people don't make for much of a political constituency.

Still, the week after W.R. Grace filed for Chapter 11, about two hundred residents air their grievances to a U.S. senator, Max Baucus. Baucus embraces the role of crusader for Libby's wounded. Facing the crowd at a local theater, he takes off his jacket, rolls up his sleeves, radiates Clintonesque empathy, and tells the audience, "What happened here is an outrage. We've got to get you justice. Grace can buy all the fancy lawyers they want, but I'm going to make sure you will be made whole." He listens to pleas for health-care facilities, pleas for criminal action against W.R. Grace, and, toward the end of the meeting, a plea from a young man, just diagnosed with scarring on his lungs, for Little League ball fields to replace the contaminated old diamonds. Then, just as suddenly as he arrived in Libby, Baucus is gone.

I mingle with the crowd after the meeting breaks up. I nod at Alan Stringer, who sat forlornly through the event in the back corner of the auditorium with his windbreaker zipped up. I spot Don Kaeding, with his oxygen tank, and Les Skramstad, in his loudest western shirt. Diane Keck is there, coughing dryly, and a few feet away stands Mike Powers, speaking vehemently about the need for aggressive cleanup of private homes. And I exchange a word or two with Jimmy Racicot, who has asbestosis and is a relative of the former governor. Or, as he tells me, in a joking and contemptuous tone, "He's related to me."

When I turn to leave the auditorium, I spot a plaque above the theater entrance, listing the donors who funded its renovation, and I read the familiar name W.R. Grace.

EXCERPT FROM THE DEPOSITION OF
LES SKRAMSTAD, JANUARY 13, 1997

Q: I understand you have had some psychological problems?
A: Yes.

Q: Tell me about those.

A: I have a little problem once in a while justifying my existence on this planet.

Q: Since you were diagnosed with asbestosis, have you experienced an increase in the frequency of bouts of depression?

A: Somewhat, yes.

Q: And what do you think it is attributable to?

A: Lack of air.

· · ·

The day before I am to leave Libby, I give myself a tour of the haunted landscape. I start at the base of Rainey Creek Road, the dirt road that miners took up Zonolite Mountain for sixty-seven years. Chris Weis, of the EPA, told me he will no longer drive up the road without wearing respiratory equipment. Yet it remains open to the public. A few days earlier, I saw a young man motor up Rainey Creek on a dirt bike, kicking up a storm of dust. Barely a mile up the road, I pass a clearing littered with beer bottles—and littered, according to recent tests, with asbestos—where teenagers party. Farther up lies a pond, rimmed with high grasses and cattails. Geese float on it. The pond was constructed to capture and neutralize waste from the mine. A hawk glides overhead. Cottonwoods are reflected in the surface of the water. The day is thoroughly still.

Rising above the pond is a reddish-brown world of loose rock, hundreds of feet high, striped with late-season snow. This is the waste mountain: millions of tons of discarded ore—slag—brimming with some five billion pounds of asbestos. The state of Montana once gave W.R. Grace an award for reclaiming the mountain, for planting yellow sweet clover and seeding the tailings with grass and speckling it with pine saplings. But as far as I can tell, nothing is growing there.

I drive back down the road, past the site where, for years, ore was sifted into bins and moved across the Kootenai River on open conveyor belts, and then dumped into boxcars of the Burlington Northern Railroad and spread across the country. Then I drive back to town, past the oval track at Libby High School, home of the Libby Loggers. A lone pole-vaulter practices his stride. I continue my drive past W.R. Grace's old expansion plant downtown, where the ore once popped like popcorn. The storage shed is still standing. It looks like the weathered plank barn in an Old West theme park. Part of a rope dangles from a rafter.

If Libby were a fallow kingdom in some obscure myth, a hero would appear to restore the landscape and its people. Libby, being real, has no such luck. When the EPA decides it has scraped W.R. Grace's old facilities clean, it will leave town. But being clean is not the same as being healthy. W.R. Grace says it will cover the medical costs of residents with asbestos-related diseases in perpetuity, but given its bankruptcy proceedings, its word is no longer considered good in this town.

Justice for Libby is a fantasy beneath the western sky. Senator Baucus vows to do his best to convene a Congressional inquiry into what happened in Libby and whether anyone at W.R. Grace should be held criminally accountable; perhaps he'll succeed. There is a legal precedent: In 1993, three managers at Film Recovery Systems, a silver-extraction company in Chicago, pleaded guilty to manslaughter charges after a worker died of cyanide poisoning in 1983. But no one in Libby is counting on it. Late this past May, thirty-two townspeople, realizing their efforts to get legal redress against W.R. Grace were futile, filed suit against the state of Montana, saying the state had "conspired with Grace to conceal the results of . . . studies and correspondence" related to the mine. The suit is the stuff of symbolism, which is not in short supply in Libby, and which will have to do for the moment.

Driving out of town the next day, I see a local named Richard

Weeks standing on the side of the road, and I stop to say good-bye. Weeks claims to be a prophet—or, more specifically, as he tells me, "the seventh spirit of Moses." He refers me to the texts in the Bible that prove his visionary powers, and that establish Bob Dylan as the prophet Ezekiel. Weeks lives in a red-white-and-blue van parked by the river. He has half a mustache and half a beard, which may be the right look for a town as divided as Libby. "I've been thinking about this asbestos thing," he says. "Dylan has a song about a great flood that will rise up and wash away sin. The flood begins on the Day of Reckoning, which is coming anytime. Look," he says, pointing to the sky, "it's beginning to rain."

Indeed it is. I drive off and leave Weeks standing in the rain, waiting for a cleansing tide to find its way to Libby. I roll down my window and let the rain wash in. It feels good. And the air, the mountain air, tastes good, full of spring. I leave town and take a deep breath and hold it in my lungs. Breathe out. Breathe again.

Harper's Magazine

WINNER, REVIEWS
AND CRITICISM

The Second Coming of Richard Yates

Lee Siegel's reviews on the state of American letters are models of original thinking and passionate writing. He energizes readers with his powers of description, his ability to amuse and surprise and his singular evocation of the dramatic stakes of high literary ambition. His tough-minded yet generous criticism is prose of uncommon power—work that dazzles readers by drawing them into the play of ideas and the enjoyment of lively, committed debate.

Lee Siegel

The Second
Coming of
Richard Yates

Neo-naturalism and
the inescapable past

The Culture of Retrieval is inescapable today. There are the ubiquitous memoirists retrieving their early lives, and the songs barely a decade old being remixed, and the children of famous writers and directors and entertainers taking up their parents' occupations (and drawing on their parents' professional connections). We have had *Jane Eyre* the musical, recently on Broadway, a stage revival of *The Producers*, also on Broadway, and a revival of *Hair* (can you imagine?) off-Broadway. There's *The Golden Bowl* on film, a rewrite (if it successfully makes its way through litigation) of *Gone with the Wind*, and at least three small publishers bravely dedicated to reprinting forgotten works by forgotten authors. Americans disrespect the past? Yes and no. We adore the past so intensely that we refuse to let it die, but in fact our indiscriminate homage to it can be a form of disrespect. We are caught in a cycle more inane than vicious. Weakly stimulated by the present, we compulsively return to the past, which has the effect of eclipsing the present, which makes us return to the past.

The inescapability of the past was a thematic obsession of the novelist and short-story writer Richard Yates, and so the publication of his collected short stories—along with the republication of *Revolutionary Road* and *The Easter Parade*—fits nicely into all this relentless retrospection. It was Yates, in fact, who introduced into American fiction the theme of inertia as catalyst. Portraying characters arrested by their personal histories, mired in memory and thus destined for the most irrationally self-defeating action, he shifted fiction from the Hemingway track back to the Frank Norris track, from realism back to naturalism. That is to say, he brought American fiction from the drama of free will back to the crisis of determining circumstances. In Yates's fiction, childhood and adult memories of what parents wrought exert the same power over the characters' destinies that economic forces did in Norris's *McTeague* or Theodore Dreiser's *Sister Carrie*.

Strangely, you won't ever hear Yates mentioned in connection with the American naturalists. He has most often been compared with Hemingway, the great American realist. And he is an acknowledged influence on the style and sensibility of an entire line of writers—from Raymond Carver through Ann Beattie, Andre Dubus, Tobias Wolff, Richard Russo, Richard Ford, and Jayne Anne Phillips—who consider themselves to have been fathered by Hemingway and, as it were, brought up by Yates. These writers have long and eloquently regretted the latter's lapsed reputation and the unavailability (until now) of his work, pointing to his plain, unobtrusive prose and to his bleak take on life (traits that can be traced, in their view, to Hemingway's lapidary sentences and to his Lost Generation pessimism). The present decision—on the part of three separate publishers—to bring Yates back into print can probably be traced to the noble efforts of these writers on his behalf. In 1999, in *Boston Review*, the Yates champion Stewart O'Nan predicted that:

> Eventually the books will make it back in print, just as Faulkner's and Fitzgerald's did, and Yates will take his place in the American canon. How this will come about it's impossible to say. Writers and editors are keenly aware of his situation, so perhaps his Malcolm Cowley is just moving up through the ranks at Norton or Doubleday.

Happily, Yates's books are indeed passing back into print. Inevitably, the response will be less a reconsideration than an uncritical celebration, since everybody loves a comeback, and since it is hard to resist an opportunity to redeem a writer whose work was often neglected during his lifetime. But if Yates was a writer of enormous talent, he had no less enormous limitations. By sentimentally ignoring those limitations, we miss the chance to see which of them occur as the necessary outgrowth of his gifts and which occur when his gifts falter.

·   ·   ·

First, there is Yates's style.

His prose is so easy and natural and transparent that it suggests a profound humility before life's inscrutable sadness. Almost ego-less, it recalls Kafka's remark that writing is a form of prayer. And Yates's language bestows upon his men and women, tortured and silenced by life as they are, what might be called a clemency of accurate observation. At times he writes less like an artist than like a witness. His cool humble chronicling of his characters' slow doom (and his characters are almost uniformly doomed) can read like a redemptive freedom in an afterlife of art, as in the following passage from *The Easter Parade*, a novel that follows the long, unhappy lives of two sisters, Emily and Sarah Grimes:

> It took only a couple of days for Howard to move his belongings out of the apartment. He was very apologetic about everything. Only once, when he flicked the heavy silken rope of his neckties out of the closet, was there any kind of scene, and that turned into such a dreadful, squalid scene—it ended with her falling on her knees to embrace his legs and begging him, begging him to stay—that Emily did the best she could to put it out of her mind.

The casually cruel flicking of the heavy silken ties is wonderful: Howard is leaving Emily for a younger woman, one who better satisfies his vanity. The repetition of "begging him," representing an abandonment of stylistic neutrality, is the only slightly false aesthetic note in the passage. Here, Yates's art—the art of the unaverted eye—briefly stumbles on his compassion. This is one of those fascinating moments when literary style becomes a moral, even a philosophical dilemma, no less than the question of whether a photojournalist should intervene on behalf of an innocent subject.

Such a style can be emotionally consoling in the way that it calmly reflects back to us an image of familiar pain, relieving our suffering with the sense that we do not suffer alone, but it is not always spiritually satisfying. Yates's style is very closely tied to the feelings it evokes. Hemingway's, by contrast, evokes an emotion of which he simultaneously makes intellectual sense. His style is no less unobtrusive to the eye, but it is a poeticized plainness, which rubs his characters against the reader's mind until the shape of each individual approaches the originality of a new idea. The reason we remember Hemingway's characters is that we've never seen them before; the reason we are moved so powerfully by Yates's characters, who then pass from our minds so quickly, is that we know them so well. Of course, Hemingway was a stoic, and stoicism is an idea that rules the emotions. Yates was a pessimist, and pessimism is a feeling that fends off thought.

.   .   .

In "The B.A.R. Man," now reprinted in *The Collected Stories*, Yates imagines with exquisite pacing and nuance the slow deterioration of an embittered and frustrated ex-soldier, John Fallon. But Fallon's eventual detonation flows from his predictable personality, and it conforms to the feeling that this near stereotype arouses in us. Fallon's fate is, typically, pronounced a certainty from the very first sentence: "Until he got his name on the police blotter, and in the papers, nobody had ever thought much of John Fallon."

The Collected Stories contains seven heretofore unpublished pieces, along with two that appeared in *Ploughshares* in the seventies, but the bulk, and heart, of the book consists of Yates's two story collections, *Eleven Kinds of Loneliness* (arguably his best-known work) and *Liars in Love*. The short form, with its special intensity, throws Yates's virtues and his deficiencies into stark relief. His truly magical storytelling whisks the attention from sentence to sentence, and not a word is wasted. Yet the stories often depend for their unfettered momentum on characterization that verges on stereotype. (Ralph and Gracie in "The Best of Everything" at times seem to be walking and talking on the set of *The Honeymooners*: "Whaddya—crazy?")

Yates's admirable sympathy for the plight of "ordinary people"—secretaries, cabdrivers, office clerks—is often dampened
by a narrow emphasis on their ordinariness. The defensively
arrogant young writer who narrates "Builders," from *Eleven
Kinds of Loneliness*, might take himself to task for regarding
Bernie—the cabdriver who has entangled him in his literary fantasies—as a vulgar, obnoxious, intellectually limited "Philistine,"
imprisoned "in the pathetic delusions of a taxicab driver." But at
the end of the story, Bernie is still a pathetic Philistine while the
narrator has become a minor hero simply by virtue of his realization that he has been a minor shit. There is something mildly
vindictive about Yates's vindications of ordinary people, a streak
of schadenfreude running through his horror at their ordeal.
Even Yates's famous unflinching depiction of life's cruelty has its
flawed underside. His honesty can be less like an artist's truthful-
ness than like a psychiatrist's candor. Each tale in *Eleven Kinds of
Loneliness* is like a deeply affecting icon expressing a variation on
a brute existential fact of life. Yet it is as if the loneliness had been
gouged raw and bleeding from the body of life, and then
processed into art by Yates's systematic pessimism. We are left
with the powerful reiteration of an experience rather than its
transformation. We are left, like analysands, alone with the harsh
illumination of isolated facts.

• • •

Call Yates's outlook, and that of his epigones, neo-naturalism.
For him, it was the family, rather than the mine, or the factory, or
the stockyards, that pulled destiny's strings. Pascal said that people could avoid all the trouble in their lives if they simply stayed
in their own rooms. In Yates's world, people can't leave their
childhood rooms, no matter how widely they travel the world as

adults. This is not their trouble; rather, their trouble is a *fait accompli*, which it is their fictional duty to live out.

The short story "A Glutton for Punishment" is representative in this regard. It tells the tale of a man who as a boy so loved to feign death when playing cops and robbers with other children that he courts and welcomes failure all his life. The internal process driving Yates's characters is frequently so simple that it recalls that old desk gadget with the row of metal balls hanging on strings; by lifting the ball on one end and sending it swinging into the other; the ball at the far end is propelled into the air without moving the ones in between. Indeed, Yates's fictional circumstances are just like those motionless, intermediary balls. They have no weight, no meaning in themselves, except to serve as the kinetic conduit between cause and effect, between past and present, or future, events. Between the first sentence and the last.

The Easter Parade carries this forced march to an extreme. The novel's first sentence is, "Neither of the Grimes sisters would have a happy life, and looking back it always seemed that the trouble began with their parents' divorce." One reads the novel waiting for this judgment—seemingly so cynical as to be naive— to be surprised by some kind of irony or extenuation, but what one encounters instead is a straightforward fictional syllogism that inexorably bears out its premise. Two girls are born to a transient alcoholic mother who is unable to maintain a relationship after the end of her marriage. Sarah Grimes marries an abusive husband and dies an alcoholic; Emily Grimes moves from apartment to apartment, and from job to job, unable to maintain an emotional relationship. *The Easter Parade* boasts what must be the only first sentence in the history of the novel that is also a sentencing.

Such a stranglehold of the personal past is a romanticism in retreat, and Yates stands out among postwar American writers for the breadth of his disappointed romanticism and the distance of his retreat. Bellow, Ellison, Updike, Salinger, Cheever, Malamud, Mailer, Roth, et al., all searched everyday life for a different form of heroism, for a quotidian stoicism, for grace under new kinds of pressure. Yates gave up on everyday life.

• • •

When did disappointment become a dominant theme in literature? We cannot say that Dante is disappointed with his life as he wanders through that dark wood. It would be absurd to call Don Quixote disappointed by his futile search for Dulcinea, or Faust disappointed in his quest for absolute happiness and power. Defining events happen in those fictional worlds, and disappointment becomes a describable issue in a world where nothing defining happens. Disappointment attracted literature's attention when the modern world became ordered beyond the individual's comprehension, and when inner life—middle-class, bourgeois life—began to compensate for the lack of outer efficacy. As a response without recourse, an aborted action converted into a mood, disappointment has no outlet, only a terminus. That's why the first and greatest novel of disappointment, *Madame Bovary*, ends with the heroine's suicide.

Since disappointment is a purely mental state, it is one of the more unexpected developments in literature that disappointment should also be one of the great themes of realist fiction. Unmoored as it is from the external world, the mood of disappointment required a new technique. Flaubert invented one. First, he set *Madame Bovary* in the suburbs (back then, they called them "the provinces"), thus providing a reality more easily correlated to a static interior mood than the city could be. Then, in *Madame Bovary's* celebrated Agricultural Fair scene, he introduced the essentially theatrical device of the ironic contrast into the novel. By juxtaposing the high-flown romantic sentiments that Rodolphe, the adulterous Emma's lover, declares to her, against a local provincial official's pompous speech, and putting alongside this the smell of cow manure, Flaubert incorporated outer reality into the mood of disappointment. He invented a dynamic environment in which to portray the arrest of personal motion.

Yates called *Madame Bovary* one of his two favorite novels (*The Great Gatsby* was the other), and *Revolutionary Road* is a distinct echo of it. Published in 1961, at the height of the postwar exodus from the cities, *Revolutionary Road* was part of a flood of fictions chronicling life in the suburbs that were quickly expanding around New York City. Like Flaubert's work, most of these novels and short stories identified the suburbs with the extinction of human vitality. I can't think of any novel, though, that presents life in the suburbs with as black a monotone as *Revolutionary Road*, the story of Frank and April, a young couple whose dreams founder on their illusions. Of course, novelists instinctively disdain the suburbs for the simple reason that the novel was born in the modern city and the suburbs offer a far more limited field of operations. If it's true, as Irving Howe once wrote, that the troubles of life are the convenience of literature, then the convenience of the suburbs puts a definite crimp in subject matter.

Then, too, in postwar America, the suburbs held out the very same *promesse de bonheur* that romantic novels once dangled before Emma Bovary. If art's job is to puncture deceit with illusion, any writer who takes on the suburbs as an end in itself rather than as a fictional means to incalculable ends will turn out one hostile Ironic Contrast after another. In fact, writers like Updike and Cheever used the suburbs the way Hemingway used the battlefield: not simply as a place but as a place of unfolding. Even Roth's *Goodbye, Columbus*, corrosive satire that it is, allows its characters to do what they would—or what they could—with their environment. Yates portrays the suburbs as an enveloping condition:

> The Revolutionary Hill Estates had not been designed to accommodate a tragedy. Even at night, as if on purpose, the development held no looming shadows and no gaunt silhouettes. It was invincibly cheerful, a toyland of white and pastel houses whose bright, uncurtained windows winked blandly through a dappling of green and yellow leaves. Proud floodlights were trained on some of the lawns, on some of the neat front doors and on the hips of some of the berthed, ice-cream colored automobiles.
> A man running down these streets in desperate grief was indecently out of place.

In other words, if their histories don't get Yates's characters, their environment will. Frank, like his father, dies spiritually in a soulless job; April, like her father, dies by her own hand; and all this happens in their house on Revolutionary Road, where America's revolutionary promise withers and dies in the coarse, materialistic suburbs.

Such an unyielding machinery of pessimism eventually shades into caricature, in much the way that Yates's characters themselves often shade into stereotype. Sometimes it seems that all it would take to bring a liberating light into Yates's world is the sudden appearance of a therapist, or a landscape architect.

•   •   •

Yates is a virtuoso craftsman, and his mature style is enviable. We are fortunate to have him back in print. But the quality of his moral outlook will determine his place in American letters. The best place to begin puzzling out the ethic of Yates's aesthetic is

The Easter Parade, in which Yates suppresses the bloated poeti-cizing of *Revolutionary Road*, allowing his themes to arise effort-lessly from the final pages of the novel.

After a life of unrelieved disappointment, Emily Grimes arrives at the New England home of her nephew, Peter. A newly ordained minister who has recently married and fathered a daughter, Peter is the only person in the Grimes family who seems to have come through. He has escaped his own abusive father and alcoholic mother and made a separate life for himself in a small college town. Sensing that his "Aunt Emmy" has reached the end of her rope, he invites her to stay with his family for an indefinite period of time.

The great naturalist heroines, Zola's Thérèse Raquin, Stephen Crane's Maggie, Dreiser's Carrie, went down swinging. Desire leads Thérèse to murder, and the passionate decay of desire into hatred leads her to suicide; Maggie desperately turns to crime and prostitution to survive; Carrie is borne up by the destruction of the men who seduce her. Even ill-fated Emma Bovary, whom "Aunt Emmy" is meant to put us in mind of, took a willful solace in her illusions—then, too, she summons her own destruction by plunging headlong into her chosen escape. Emily Grimes, on the other hand, has to be the most passive heroine in the history of literature. She does not, in the course of the entire novel, express a single desire of her own, except, pathetically, the desire not to be hurt or disappointed.

Emily is a saint in a world without a God, and so her saintliness has no dignity and her suffering holds no meaning. One wonders whether Yates is pulling the rug out from under the religious impulse itself. The novel, after all, takes its title from the idea of resurrection. Yates, however, offers us a parody of resurrection: a beautiful, hopeful photograph of Emily's sister, Sarah, and her future husband, Tony, taken on Easter Day at the time of their courtship, reappears toward the end of the novel, after the revelation of Tony's wife-beating and Sarah's inherited masochism and alcoholism. It's as if Yates had replaced the idea of resurrection with the concept of the return of the repressed.

The fate of Emily seems, on the surface, more ambiguous. On the brink of a nervous collapse, she tries to turn back from Peter's house and hospitality at the last minute. Peter comes down his driveway after her, and Emily hears "a jingle of pocketed coins or keys." An instant later, when Peter suddenly realizes the extent of her distress, he asks her if she's tired and then stands "looking at her in a detached, speculative way now, more like an alert young psychiatrist than a priest."

> "Yes, I'm tired," she said. "And do you know a funny thing? I'm almost fifty years old and I've never understood anything in my whole life."
>
> "All right," he said quietly. "All right, Aunt Emmy. Now. Would you like to come in and meet the family?"

Considering that the Grimes sisters' "trouble began with their parents' divorce," Peter's invitation to enter yet another family romance could be read—indeed, almost demands to be read—as the bitterest of ironies. But since he seems happily married, with his family intact, perhaps Emily does stand, if unsteadily, at the threshold of redemption. Yet is it the redemption of religious grace of the promise of "alert" psychoanalytic "understanding" that offers no love or sympathy? Are those the jingling keys to heaven's gate (as Peter's name suggests), or are they the coins of selfishness and greed? It hardly seems to matter. The expectation of grace in a world without God and mere psychiatric understanding in a world without grace are like two sides of an obscene joke. That is Yates's zero-degree ethos.

Such unsparing sobriety makes up the solidity of Yates's

achievement. Yates knew how to rivet the reader's attention on the quiet desperation of unacknowledged lives. His unpardonable failure (and perhaps his secret satisfaction) was never to give his implausibly ordinary men and women the freedom to respond.

Sports Illustrated

'Ring Tossed

Most of us will never drive a car at 200 kilometers per hour. Most of us would never want to. Yet in his article " 'Ring Tossed," Steve Rushin seduces the reader into joining him as he tests one of the world's fastest cars on one of the world's most famous racecourses. Rushin's white-knuckle tale plunks us all down in the passenger seat and rewards our nerve with images that linger long after the race is over.

Steve Rushin

'Ring Tossed

A visit to the Nürburgring—once the world's most treacherous racetrack, now a pedal-to-the-metal public playground—provides a crash course in German automania.

T he most unsettling thing about driving 142 mph on the German autobahn in James Bond's convertible with the top dropped is not the sudden realization that your head juts above the windshield, so that any airborne object—a pebble, a lug nut, the shedding payload of a flatbed truck—will forever be embedded in your coconut, like the coins and keys you sometimes see in the hot asphalt of city streets. Nor is it the banana-yellow Porsche GT3 that draws even with you in the passing lane, lingering off your left flank for 30 seconds, as if attempting the in-flight-refueling of a Stealth bomber, while its leering driver hand gestures you to drag-race him. (That terror passes quickly enough when the pilot of the Porsche loses patience and leaves you in his vapor trail at one fifth of Mach 1.) No. What makes a man vow to change his life, to say nothing of his underpants, should he survive such a journey is this: The journey hasn't even begun.

For you have come to test your driving skills not on the speed limit-less autobahn but on the Nürburgring, the ribbon of road that Germans drive when they find the autobahn too tame; the ribbon of road that racing legend Jackie Stewart called, without hyperbole, "the Green Hell"; the ribbon of road that a 24-year-old German named Mika Hahn told me, with furrowed brow, "is very, *very* dangerous"—far too dangerous for *him* to drive on, and he's a likely future world champion of speedway motorcycle racing.

The Nürburgring has long been too harrowing for Formula One racing. Since 1927 the picturesque Grand Prix track has lain, like a gold necklace on a rumpled bedspread, in the Eifel Mountains of western Germany. But over the decades, as cars became faster, the 14-mile, 170-turn course became deadlier: It closed forever to F/1 racing in 1976, after Austrian star Niki Lauda was famously set alight there when he crashed on the approach to a turn known as Bergwerk. By 1983 the 'Ring prudently had been closed to nearly every form of professional racing. Yet—and here's the rub—the Nürburgring remains open, as it ever has been, for the general public to drive on as fast as it pleases for as long as it pleases in whatever it pleases: race cars, jalopies or crotch-rocket motorcycles, many of which have become sarcophagi for their drivers.

Why on earth would anybody want to race there? "If you studied piano all your life and had a chance to play Carnegie Hall on a

Steinway, you would want to do that," says Dan Tackett, 42, a financial services manager from San Diego who has made 11 trips to the Nürburgring in the past 16 years. "This is the most difficult, challenging and rewarding racetrack in the world. For serious drivers, it remains the Holy Grail."

It is Everest in asphalt—"the single greatest piece of motor racing architecture in the world," says *Motor Sport* magazine of England—and it demands equipment that is up to the task. Which is how it is that I'm heading for the Nürburgring in a cherry-red BMW Z8, the model driven by 007 in *The World Is Not Enough* but piloted at this moment by English photographer Bob Martin, who is not licensed to kill and is, truth be told, barely licensed to drive.

We retrieved this astonishing feat of automotive engineering at the world headquarters of the Bayerische Motoren Werke in Munich. The company's skyscraper is a kind of architectural pun, constructed of four cylinders. Directly across the street is the 1972 Olympic athletes' village. The site where 11 Israelis were taken hostage at the Summer Games is now the world's most poignant apartment complex. Mesmerized by the view, I absent-mindedly signed a three-page document in German that rendered me legally responsible for returning, scratch-free, the $125,000, 400-horse-power, eight-cylinder, zero-to-60-in-4.5-seconds dream car that Bob was soon driving off the lot in the giddily overmatched manner of someone who has been given the keys to the space shuttle.

Or rather Bob, a giant of a man, was not so much driving the two-seater as he was wearing it. He looked like a man in a kayak. A very happy man: As we negotiated the streets of Munich, Bob began speaking in tongues about the "Zed 8" and its "bloody *brute*" of an engine, its "stop-on-a-sixpence" brakes and, "oooh!—all the beautiful bulgy bits" on its chassis. By the time we entered the autobahn and were swept away like a raft on rapids, all of *Bob*'s bulgy bits were aflame with excitement. He was fearless in his phallic chariot. "BMW!" Bob cackled, merging into traffic, throwing down the hummer, the wind whining in our ears. "Bob Martin's Wheels!"

"BMW," I muttered darkly, not liking the looks of this at all. "Bob Martin's *Willy*."

But he didn't respond. So, with an ever-deepening sense of disquiet, I shut up and rode shotgun toward a 'Ring of Hell unlike any imagined by Dante.

•   •   •

We overnight in the Alps and discover, in the morning, that our five-hour route to the 'Ring will take us roughly from Ulm to Bonn—from the birthplace of Einstein to the birthplace of Beethoven—in a vehicle that weds science and art. Construction of Ulm's Münster cathedral began in 1377. Its 536-foot steeple remains the tallest in the world. Mankind, alas, no longer builds such wonders. Or do we? "I think that cars today are almost the exact equivalent of the great Gothic cathedrals," French social critic Roland Barthes wrote of postwar Western civilization. "I mean the supreme creation of an era, conceived with passion by unknown artists, and consumed in image if not in usage by a whole population which appropriates them as a purely magical object."

Nowhere is the automobile more talismanic than in Germany, the country that gave us the concept of wanderlust, the word *fahrvergnügen* ("joy of driving"), the world's top driver (F/1 king Michael Schumacher) and high-performance automakers Mercedes-Benz, BMW, Porsche and Audi (as well as mid-performance automakers Opel and Volkswagen, and nonperformance automaker Trabant). Americans think of themselves as car crazy, but they don't know the half of it. "Germany is a car culture," says Tackett, the American 'Ring veteran. "America is a drive-through culture of convenience."

"In America cars are appliances," adds U.S. Air Force captain Todd Fry, 26, a motorcycle-riding F-16 pilot based at Spangdahlem Air Force base, an hour's ride from the Nürburgring. "Here, cars are the objects of passion."

So Bob and I continue hammering toward the village of Nürburg. Two hours south of the Green Hell, when we cross the Rhine at Karlsruhe, a black Mercedes SL 500 convertible with full body kit and mag tires appears suddenly in our rearview. Bob takes little notice, for he is dozing, an alarming prospect given that he is—at the same time—driving 100 mph with the top down.

In our cramped cockpit (we will later discover) Bob's right leg is mashed against a button that activates his electronic seat warmer. It is 95° on this afternoon, and Bob is being bumtoasted by red-hot coils hidden beneath the black leather upholstery of his seat. He is being lulled into a coma by heatstroke and highway hypnosis when the Benz—headlights strobing madly—gets on our back bumper like one of those KEEP HONKING, I'M RELOADING stickers so popular in the U.S.

We are both nodding like junkies when the horn sounds behind us. Bob snaps to attention. In a panic, he reflexively jerks the wheel. We career into the right lane, and the Benz passes. But as soon as it does, the middle-aged maniac in the driver's seat (Bob is now calling him a "plonker") maneuvers the Merc into the right lane, decelerates and begins to ride our *front* bumper. After 200 yards of this mouse-and-cat game, he exits the autobahn slowly, so that we can see him pointing at the exit sign as we pass. The man is laughing through his elaborate mustache. (The men—and not a few women—of this German region all have mustaches like the CBS golf announcer Gary McCord.) The plonker keeps pointing at the exit sign—a sign, we now see, for the Daimler-Benz complex in Wörth. The man in the Merc, evidently in the employ of that automaker, grins as if he's just won something. Perhaps he has.

Still we're 150 miles from the Green Hell. If drivers on the autobahn are hypercompetitive and brand-loyal, what kind of psychotics await us at the Nürburgring? "They are people who enjoy the sheer pleasure of driving," says BMW event manager Werner Briel when we pitch up at the 'Ring's parking lot. "They are concerned not only with velocity but with . . . *style*." Then, holding on to his homburg, he leans over and strokes his sweatered pet dachshund, Katya.

The Nürburgring drivers, in turn, attract an audience of rubber-neckers almost as interesting as the motorists themselves. "They come to see the cars, they come to see the crashes," says Reinhard H. Queckenberg, whose name sounds like that of a Groucho Marx character but in fact belongs to the owner of a small racetrack not far from the Nürburgring. "It is living theater."

·   ·   ·

The elevation changes 1,000 feet along the track's 14 miles. The road rolls out, like a rucked red carpet, over hill and dale and through primeval forest. Three towns and a 12th-century castle are contained within the Nürburgring's infield. But then you have already, no doubt, seen the circuit: Countless car commercials are filmed on it, the kind that carry the disclaimer, PROFESSIONAL DRIVER ON A CLOSED TRACK. DO NOT TRY THIS YOURSELF.

Yet, every year, thousands of drivers *do* try it. Each of them pays 21 deutsche marks—about $9.50—per lap and joins the 100-plus vehicles that are allowed on the loop at any one time. For most of its length, the road is little more than two lanes wide. Unlike modern F/1 circuits, the Nürburgring doesn't have a thousand yards of run-off area beyond its shoulders. Rather, it has no run-off area. If you leave the road, you collide with a tree or a cyclone fence or steel guardrails. Crash through the guardrails, and you, or your estate, must pay to have it replaced.

One ambulance and one flatbed wrecker truck are forever on

standby at the 'Ring's starting line. Drivers sign no waiver and are given no warnings. "This could never happen in the States," says Roger Scilley of Laguna Beach, Calif., whom we meet 10 minutes after arriving. "Lawyers wouldn't allow it. But over here, you're responsible for your own actions."

Which isn't to say that there are no warnings whatsoever at the Nürburgring. No, all along the perimeter of the track are signs that shriek, LEBENSGEFAHR! (Mortal Danger!), but those are for the *spectators*—and the ones behind the fencing, at that. There are no words for those race fans, like the four teenagers we'll encounter on our second day at the track, who watch the festivities, with a cooler full of beverages, from *inside* the guardrails. Imagine enjoying the Indy 500 while standing against the wall of Turn 2. Now imagine doing so when all the drivers are *amateurs*.

But then Germans are, generally speaking, better drivers than Americans. "In Germany," says Louis Goldsman, a 57-year-old retiree from Mission Viejo, Calif., on pilgrimage at the 'Ring, "you're required to attend a driving academy for four months before you can get a license. It costs the equivalent of $2,500 to obtain a license, and you can't get one until you're 18. Insurance is more expensive. All this makes for more serious drivers. The average 18-year-old German girl can outdrive the typical testosterone-polluted American male any day."

Goldsman has come to the Nürburgring with a group from the BMW Club of America. At 10 a.m. Eastern time on Monday, March 6, many of the club's 55,000 members called a toll-free number in hopes of getting one of the 72 available spots on the trip. Richard George speed-dialed the number 240 times from Dallas before securing one of the berths, which sold out in three hours. The trip cost each driver $2,500, plus airfare, and required him (or her) to have attended at least three high-performance driving schools. "We're freaks," says a woman who underscores the point by giving her name as Robyn McNutt. *"Freaks."*

The club has rented the track for three days. The first two days were devoted to learning the line of the course, mile by mile. Bob and I stumble upon these people on the final day, as they are grimly preparing to put the pedal to the metal and make their "graded lap" of the Nürburgring, at full speed, as expert judges stationed about the circuit make notations on their clipboards.

"We will be graded on a scale of one to 10, one being good and 10 being what the Germans call *totalkaos*," says Tackett, the club's best driver and de facto leader, in a pre-lap speech to his fellow motorists. "Now, you've all had some hot laps in practice, maybe even incurred the need for some laundry attention. You might want to slow it down a little this time: I have pictures of a car that rolled here to show you that this is serious business."

"Two years ago," whispers Dan Chrisman, a 53-year-old from Austin, "one driver on this trip took out 30 feet of fencing and wound up on his top in a BMW 328."

The driver of that car suffered nothing more than a cut, and his passenger walked away uninjured, but not all cars are that safe. Thirteen kilometers into the clockwise course is an infamous hairpin turn called the Karussell. It is a concrete former drainage ditch that drivers plunge into, leaving the track looming above them, like a paved wave threatening to break through the right-hand windows. "I have seen families in camper vans out on the course," says Chrisman, a three-time veteran of the circuit. "I've gone into the Karussell and looked above me to see a double-decker tour bus with little old ladies on the upper level looking down at me through their cameras."

There will be two hours of public racing after the BMW club completes its graded laps on this Friday evening, and already some heavy artillery is massing in the parking lot: Lancias, Porsches, Mercs, Ferraris, Vipers, a Lamborghini Diablo, a rare Dutch Donkervoort, a Fiat Uno with valve springs popping through the bonnet. Many cars have but a single seat, with a racing harness. There are racing motorcycles of every description, their leathered riders doing push-ups in the parking lot. "Those bikes," points out Mike Valente, a veteran English motor-sports photographer, "will be going 180 miles an hour on the final straightaway. On two wheels. Each wheel has a footprint the size of your shoe."

I am told to expect madness when the track opens to the public. "The Germans who live locally," says Tom Doherty, 41, an Indianapolis native who has attended every Indy 500 since 1966, "are all driving souped-up BMW M3s"—modified racing cars— "and they drive *blindingly* fast out here."

But before the public can have a go, Tackett has agreed to take me as a passenger on his graded lap. Everyone tells me that I'm lucky, that Tackett is the best American driver on site. But bad juju is confronting us everywhere as I hop into Tackett's BMW 523i sedan and we make our way to the starting chute.

Before Tackett and I set out, BMW of America Club member McNutt points to a spot on her map of the Nürburgring. "That's where Niki Lauda," she volunteers brightly, "had his barbecue."

Fritz-Jürgen Hahn, a 59-year-old member of an auto club in Düsseldorf, fondly recalls for me the first time he raced on the Nürburgring. "It was in 1963, in a Porsche Spyder," he says. That is the car James Dean died in.

"The track was built in 1927 as the German equivalent of a WPA project," Tackett says, attempting to soothe my nerves with conversation as we wait for a starting flag. "There are 170 turns, and I'm going to alert you to every one of them in advance, not to bore you, but to protect the interior of my car." With that, a flag drops and Tackett accelerates and the world goes by in a blur. I find myself riding a rail-free roller coaster at 125 mph, and I won't have a single coherent recollection—apart from removing my bucket hat and holding it over my mouth—of that first circuit.

"It's just a red fookin' mist out there, innit?" says Tom Thompson, an English motorcyclist we shall meet in a moment. "It is brain out, brick in."

. . .

Tackett takes me for two more laps when the course opens to the public. Though he follows the line expertly, the ride is sickening. For most of it I stick my head out the window like a black Lab. Ahead of us Bob Martin rides in the backseat of a convertible, facing backward through 170 turns at up to 140 mph, gamely taking pictures of the cars behind him. His shirt is pulled up over his mouth: At these speeds—and I am as serious as a heart attack here—a shower of vomit on a car windshield may prove fatal to the showeree. Bob had the Wiener schnitzel for lunch.

Bikes and cars flash past on either flank. The Nürburgring is exactly like a Grand Prix video game sprung to life, only instead of getting a GAME OVER message after crashing, you die.

Drivers must exit the circuit after each lap. Following my second shotgun lap with Tackett, one hour into public racing, cars are suddenly forbidden to go out again. The P.A. announcement in German states that the track is being cleared. The ambulance and the flatbed wrecker are dispatched, sirens wailing. Vague reports come back from the last drivers to cross the finish line that a yellow car spun out somewhere in the red fookin' mist. The wrecker truck will take 15 minutes to reach the far side of the track, seven miles away. After 10 minutes, a second ambulance sets out from the starter's chute, followed by a police car. The silence is hideous.

Twenty minutes later, a black Opel GTE crosses the finish line, its driver ashen-faced, evidently having lingered at the site of the accident. He drives through the parking lot and off into the dusk without telling any of us what he witnessed.

Many drivers at the Nürburgring mount video cameras in their cars. A young German who has just recorded his ride cues up the video for a crowd in the parking lot. About halfway through the circuit, as a diabolical turn comes into view, a spot of yellow begins to take shape on the shoulder. We view the tape in super-slow motion until three Zapruder-like frames reveal everything: a yellow Lancia marooned askew on the outside shoulder, its rear left wheel jammed all the way up into its well, the car's driver and passenger standing next to it, miraculously unharmed. The flatbed does not take the wreckage through the main gate, where all the drivers are parked waiting for the track to reopen. The driver of the Lancia is also spirited out some side gate. An announcement is made that the Nürburgring is closed for the night, but it will reopen on Sunday for 10 hours of public racing.

Tonight's public racing lasted 62 minutes before a near-catastrophe occurred. But we will be back on Sunday. We want to see the cars. We want to see the crashes. Reinhard H. Queckenberg was right. It *is* living theater.

· · ·

A modern F/1 track has been constructed next door to the Nürburgring, and on Saturday it hosts an extraordinarily dangerous event: vintage motorcycle-and-sidecar racing. The sidecars are really just square metal platforms bolted to the bikes. Sidecar passengers, called monkeys, ride a foot off the pavement at 135 mph, sometimes prone, sometimes supine, their helmeted heads an inch off the track when leaning into turns. "Last year at this race, there was a bad accident," says Mika Hahn, a sometime monkey. "Four sidecars went into a turn together, two touched and over-rolled. One person was totally killed and had to be—how you say?—reanimated. He survived."

"The perfect sidecar passenger should weigh six stone [84 pounds] and have a pointed nose for aerodynamics," says a 6' 7" 40-year-old biker whom I meet in the pits, "but I got this one: six-foot-seven and built like a brick s---house." He hooks a thumb at his towering 17-year-old son, who wears a black leather jumpsuit with his nickname stitched to the back: TINY.

"At least," says Tiny, "I got the nose."

Tom and Tiny Thompson are from Bulkington, England. Cheryl Thompson—Tom's wife, Tiny's mother—is a petite woman with painted nails who also wears full leathers. She too is a monkey. When her husband was 28, she explains, he rode his 1938 Triumph 250 everywhere. "He's so tall, he looked ridiculous on it," says Cheryl, a former sales executive with Prudential in London. "Like an elephant on a matchstick." She told him he needed an "outfit"— a sidecar—for aesthetic balance. "Get an outfit and I'll ride it," she promised, though she had no intention of doing any such thing. "Blimey if two weeks later he doesn't come home with a sidecar," says Cheryl. "I thought, *Crikey*." The couple painted THOMPSON TWINS on the Triumph. "The Thompson Twins," she says sheepishly of the new-romantic '80s band, "were popular at the time."

Cheryl sighs and says of Tiny, her only child. "He could ride a bike before he could walk." In 1983, Tom rigged a remote-control accelerator to his bike, tied a rope to its frame and let Tiny ride in a circle around him. Says Tom, "He was nine months old at the time."

"The other mothers in the park went mad," says Cheryl. "They said, 'Look at him, with no helmet!' I said, '*You* try finding a helmet for a nine-month-old!'"

Tiny was allowed to drop out of school at 14—"They didn't want me back," he explains—and now spends the summer traveling from race to race with his parents, living in the back of a rented van. He loves his parents, and they clearly love him. How many 17-year-olds would be willing to spend the summer with their parents, sharing a single mattress? Tiny may have quit school, but the Germans have a phrase that fits him well: *Reisen bildet*. "Travel educates."

The Thompsons are protective not only of each other but of their fellow amateur racers as well. "We take calculated risks," says Cheryl. "The last thing you need is some barmy git out there who's trying to kill people. But you do get them. At [England's] Mallory [Park speedway], on a hairpin, someone tried to push us out—to take a hole that wasn't there—and he smashed into my right hand. I could have killed him. Afterward, he looked at my hand and said to me, 'At least you can still peel the potatoes, luv.' I wanted to punch him out.

"We took a nasty bump at the gooseneck bend on [England's] Cadwell Circuit," Cheryl says with classic British understatement. "This chap was going full out, and his stupid idiot passenger rolled onto the track, and it was either hit the passenger and kill him or go into the wall. So we hit the tire wall at 90 miles an hour." Cheryl says she was "black from top to toe" for two months. Tom was catapulted over the tire wall and lay motionless for 30 seconds with a ruptured kidney and three broken ribs. He slowly returned to consciousness and shouted, "I'm alive!" He wiggled his toes: "My legs work!" He wiggled his fingers: "My arms work!" Then, after a pause, he wailed to his wife, "Oh, my God, I'm blind!"

"There was mud in his helmet," says Cheryl, rolling her eyes.

The point is, they risked their lives to save a monkey, and that says something hopeful about human nature. "We are all ever so close," Cheryl says of the amateur vintage sidecar community, "no matter what nationality. At the start of every race, we all look at each other and cross our fingers—we get sorta jinxy-like. Solo riders aren't like that. But sidecar racers have camaraderie."

The Thompsons' enthusiasm for amateur racing renews my desire to get behind the wheel on the 'Ring of Hell the next day. I am—how you say?—reanimated. Before leaving the vintage bike rally, I buy a Red Baron helmet and goggles from a Swiss trafficker in old-time driving gear. (His business card says, somewhat salaciously, that he also purveys "accessories in leather.") Cheryl kindly cuts a piece of fabric from the Triumph's tarpaulin, creating a white scarf that will billow behind me as I whip the Zed 8 'round the Nürburgring on a public-racing Sunday.

"I would never ride over there," Tiny says as Bob and I prepare to take our leave. "They say one a week goes over there." By *goes* he means *dies*. Then Tiny bids us a cheery farewell.

• • •

On Sunday I see it all: a man doing 110 with his dry-cleaning hanging in a back window; an Opel Kadett hammering into an S-turn while its gas cap flaps against the rear quarter panel; a guy getting airborne at Kilometer 4, his children's dolls looking impassively out the rear windshield; three teenage girls smoking in an Opel Swing hatchback, the driver applying lipstick in the rearview while idling in the starting chute; and a man in a drop-top whose hat flies off at the Flugplatz. Happily, the hat doesn't suction itself to the face of a biker behind him. Heaven knows it could.

Todd Fry, the young Air Force captain, likes to race his Honda CBR 900 RR Fireblade around the Nürburgring. "I'm not one of these guys who's an adrenaline junkie," says Fry, of Pompton Plains, N.J., roasting in his red-white-and-blue leather jumpsuit. "I've scared myself more often on the motorcycle than in an F-16. But fear is a good thing to have. Fear is life insurance out here."

If so, I am well insured. As Fry and I speak, an Opel Esona race-prepared road car blazes by on the track. A dozen Lotus Elises go into the starting chute together. A pink-and-white tour bus full of seniors from Kaiserslautern enters the raceway, hazard lights blinking absurdly. A ding-a-ling in a camper van survives two passes around the 'Ring, both times plunging into the Karussell turn. "Just pass him," advises Fry. "Everyone has a right to be out there. For the most part, you're just racing the road anyway."

Tell that to the driver of the Porsche GT2, an earlier, *more aggressive* version of the car whose driver wanted to drag-race Bob and me on our first day in the Alps. Tell that to the pilot of the Nissan Skyline GT-R, a Japanese-only supercar that was probably towed over here from England, street-illegal as it is. Tell that to the nutter in the purple Lamborghini Diablo. Tell that to all the mustachioed Germans doing 160 on their Italian-made Aprilia racing bikes.

"The biggest rush is when you're fully leaned over into a turn and you're scraping your knees on the track," says Mike Leong,

24, an Air Force lieutenant from Cincinnati who rides a Yamaha YZF-R1 racing bike. "When you take a turn right, you have 440 pounds and 150 horsepower and all those G's acting on you." He shows me the deep scuffing in the plastic guards sewn over the knees of his leathers. "That," he says, "is how you know you've made a good turn."

"The military isn't crazy about us doing this," says Fry, unnecessarily.

"My parents don't know I ride," says Leong, "but my brother gets SPORTS ILLUSTRATED, so I guess they'll find out. Oh, well."

The Zed 8 beckons from the parking lot. I have been reluctant to drive it even on the rural highways around the Nürburgring, which attract almost as many racing bikers as the raceway. Everywhere on those roads are signs that say RACEN IST OUT! (Racing Is Out!) above a silhouette of a biker sliding off his cycle into oblivion. "You know it's a good road," says Leong, without a trace of false machismo, "when you see those signs."

Leong and Fry have the Right Stuff for the Nürburgring. Michael Schumacher, who was winning the Canadian Grand Prix in Montreal on this Sunday afternoon, has the Right Stuff. Eighteen-year-old girls in Opel Swing hatchbacks have the Right Stuff. James Bond has the Right Stuff, and I have his car. But the question remains: Do *I* have the Right Stuff?

I came to the Nürburgring to test my driving skills—which is to say nerve—on the most difficult roadway in the world, the San Diego Freeway on acid. Of course, I really came to learn deeper truths about my courage under extreme duress. From afar, it seemed as if it would be good for a laugh. But this is what I've learned: I will not drive 125 mph on an automotive minefield in a borrowed car costing more than I'm worth, solely for the momentary diversion of a magazine editor back in New York City. Now I know. *Reisen bildet.* Travel educates.

I call that courage. You call me a wuss. Fine. But you'll have to say the same to Tiny, and trust me, you don't want to do that.

Harper's Magazine

FINALIST, PROFILE WRITING

Dr. Daedalus

Tackling a subject whose ideas are as radical as they are controversial, Lauren Slater's disturbing profile depicts a brilliant plastic surgeon who happens to believe that human beings will—and should—sprout wings and acquire fins. Slater resists oversimplifying this hyperbolic, contradictory personality, delivering a piece that rests on excellent reporting and soars on her perspicacity, her fluent writing and her willingness to reexamine her own assumptions about what it is, exactly, that makes us human.

Lauren Slater

Dr. Daedalus

A radical plastic surgeon wants to give you wings.

Part I: Beautiful People

Joe Rosen, plastic surgeon at the renowned Dartmouth-Hitchcock Medical Center, and by any account an odd man, has a cold. But then again, he isn't sure it's a cold. "It could be anthrax," he says as he hurries to the car, beeper beeping, sleet sleeting, for it's a freezing New England midwinter day when all the world is white. Joe Rosen's nose is running, his throat is raw, and he's being called into the ER because some guy made meat out of his forefinger and a beautiful teenager split her fine forehead open on the windshield of her SUV. It seems unfair, he says, all these calls coming in on a Sunday, especially because he's sick and he isn't sure whether it's the flu or the first subtle signs of a biological attack. "Are you serious?" I say to him. Joe Rosen is smart. He graduated cum laude from Cornell and got a medical degree from Stanford in 1978. And we're in his car now, speeding toward the hospital where he reconstructs faces, appends limbs, puffs and preens the female form. "You really wonder," I say, "if your cold is a sign of a terrorist attack?"

Joe Rosen, a respected and controversial plastic surgeon, wonders a lot of things, some of them directly related to his field, others not. Joe Rosen wonders, for instance, whether Osama bin Laden introduced the West Nile virus to this country. Joe Rosen wonders how much bandwidth it would take to make virtual-reality contact lenses available for all. Joe Rosen wonders why both his ex-wife and his current wife are artists, and what that says about his deeper interests. Joe Rosen also wonders why we insist on the kinds of conservative medical restraints that prevent him from deploying some of his most creative visions: wings for human beings; cochlear implants to enhance hearing, beefing up our boring ears and giving us the range of an owl; super-duper delicate rods to jazz up our vision—binocular, beautiful—so that we could see for many miles and into depths as well. Joe Rosen has ideas: implants for this, implants for that, gadgets, gears, discs, buttons, sculpting soft cartilage that would enable us, as humans, to cross the frontiers of our own flesh and emerge as something altogether . . . what? Something other.

And we're in the car now, speeding on slick roads toward the hospital, beeper beeping, sleet sleeting, passing cute country houses with gingerbread trim, dollops of smoke hanging above bright brick chimneys; his New Hampshire town looks so sweet. We pull into the medical center. Even this has a slight country flair to it, with gingham curtains hanging in the rows of windows. We skid. Rosen says, "One time I was in my Ford Explorer with my daughter, Sam. We rolled, and the next thing I knew we were on the side of the highway, hanging upside down like bats." He laughs.

We go in. I am excited, nervous, running by his bulky side with my tape recorder to his mouth. A resident in paper boots comes up to us. He eyes the tape recorder, and Rosen beams.

Rosen is a man who enjoys attention, credentials. A few days ago he boasted to me, "You shouldn't have any trouble with the PR people in this hospital. I've had three documentaries made of me here already."

"Can I see them?" I asked.

"I don't know," Rosen answered, suddenly scratching his nose very fast. "I guess I'm not sure where I put them," and something about his voice, or his nose, made me wonder whether the documentaries were just a tall tale.

Now the resident rushes up to us, peers at the tape recorder, peers at me. "They're doing a story on me," Rosen says. "For *Harper's.*"

"Joe is a crazy man, a nutcase," the resident announces, but there's affection in his voice.

"Why the beeps?" Rosen asks.

"This guy, he was working in his shop, got his finger caught in an electric planer . . . The finger's hamburger," the resident says. "It's just hamburger."

We go to the carpenter's cubicle. He's a man with a burly beard and sawdust-caked boots. He lies too big for the ER bed, his dripping finger held high in the air and splinted. It does look like hamburger.

I watch Rosen approach the bed, the wound. Rosen is a largish man, with a curly head of hair, wearing a Nordstrom wool coat and a cashmere scarf. As a plastic surgeon, he thinks grand thoughts but traffics mostly in the mundane. He has had over thirty papers published, most of them with titles like "Reconstructive Flap Surgery" or "Rhinoplasty for the Adolescent." He is known among his colleagues only secondarily for his epic ideas; his respect in the field is rooted largely in his impeccable surgical skill with all the toughest cases: shotgunned faces, smashed hands.

"How ya doin'?" Rosen says now to the carpenter. The carpenter doesn't answer. He just stares at his mashed finger, held high in the splint.

Rosen speaks softly, gently. He puts his hand on the wood-worker's dusty shoulder. "Looks bad," he says, and he says this with a kind of simplicity—or is it empathy?—that makes me listen. The patient nods. "I need my finger," he says, and his voice sounds tight with tears. "I need it for the work I do."

Rosen nods. His tipsiness, his grandiosity, seem to just go away. He stands close to the man. "Look," he says, "I'm not going to do anything fancy right now, okay? I'll just have my guys sew it up, and we'll try to let nature take its course. I think that's the best thing, right now. To let nature take its course."

The carpenter nods. Rosen has said nothing really reassuring, but his tone is soothing, his voice rhythmic, a series of stitches that promises to knit the broken together.

We leave the carpenter. Down the hall, the teenage beauty lies in still more serious condition, the rent in her forehead so deep we can see, it seems, the barest haze of her brain.

"God," whispers Rosen as we enter the room. "I dislike foreheads. They get infected so easily."

He touches the girl. "You'll be fine," he says. "We're not going to do anything fancy here. Just sew you up and let nature take its course."

I think these are odd, certainly unexpected words coming from a man who seems so relentlessly anti-nature, so visionary and futuristic in his interests. But then again, Rosen himself is odd, a series of swerves, a topsy-turvy, upside-down, smoke-and-mirrors sort of surgeon, hanging in his curious cave, a black bat.

"I like this hospital," Rosen announces to me as we leave the girl's room. "I like its MRI machines." He pauses.

"I should show you a real marvel," he suddenly says. He looks around him. A nurse rushes by, little dots of blood on her snowy smock. "Come," Rosen says.

We ride the elevator up. The doors whisper open. Outside, the sleet has turned to snow, falling fast and furious. The floor we're on is ominously quiet, as though there are no patients here, or as though we're in a morgue. Rosen is ghoulish and I am suddenly scared. I don't know him really. I met him at a medical-ethics convention at which he discussed teaching *Frankenstein* to his residents and elaborated, with a little light in his eye, on the inherent beauty in hybrids and chimeras, if only we could learn to see them that way. "Why do we only value the average?" he'd asked the audience. "Why are plastic surgeons dedicated only to restoring our current notions of the conventional, as opposed to letting people explore, if they want, what the possibilities are?"

Rosen went on to explain other things at that conference. It was hard for me to follow his train of thought. He vacillates between speaking clearly, almost epically, to mumbling and zigzagging and scratching his nose. At this conference he kangaroo-leapt from subject to subject: the army, biowarfare, chefs with motorized fingers that could whip eggs, noses that doubled as flashlights, soldiers with sonar, the ocean, the monsters, the marvels. He is a man of breadth but not necessarily depth. "According to medieval man," Rosen said to the convention, finally coming clear, "a monster is someone born with congenital deformities. A marvel," he explained, "is a person with animal parts—say, a tail or wings." He went on to show us pictures, a turn-of-the-century newborn hand with syphilitic sores all over it, the fingers webbed in a way that might have been beautiful but not to me, the pearly skin stretched to nylon netting in the crotch of each crooked digit.

And the floor we're on now is ominously quiet, except for a hiss somewhere, maybe some snake somewhere, with a human head. We walk for what seems a long time. My tape recorder sucks up the silence.

Rosen turns, suddenly, and with a flourish parts the curtains of a cubicle. Before me, standing as though he were waiting for our arrival, is a man, a real man, with a face beyond description. "Sweeny,"* Rosen says, gesturing toward the man, "has cancer of

Not his real name.

the face. It ate through his sinus cavities, so I scraped off his face, took off his tummy fat, and made a kind of, well, a new face for him out of the stomach. Sweeny, you look good!" Rosen says.

Sweeny, his new face, or his old stomach, oozing and swollen from this recent, radical surgery, nods. He looks miserable. The belly-face sags, the lips wizened and puckered like an anus, the eyes in their hills of fat darting fast and frightened.

"What about my nose?" Sweeny says, and then I notice: Sweeny has no nose. The cancer ate that along with the cheeks, etc. This is just awful. "That comes next. We'll use what's left of your forehead." A minute later, Rosen turns to me and observes that pretty soon women will be able to use their buttocks for breast implants. "Where there's fat," Rosen says, "there are possibilities."

•   •   •

The coffee is hot and good. We drink it in the hospital cafeteria while we wait for the weather to clear. "You know," Rosen says, "I'm really proud of that face. I didn't follow any protocol. There's no textbook to tell you how to fashion a face eaten away by cancer. Plastic surgery is the intersection of art and science. It's the intersection of the surgeon's imagination with human flesh. And human flesh," Rosen says, "is infinitely malleable. People say cosmetic surgery is frivolous—boobs and noses. But it's so much more than that! The body is a conduit for the soul, at least historically speaking. When you change what you look like, you change who you are."

I nod. The coffee, actually, is too damn hot. The delicate lining of skin inside my mouth starts to shred. The burn-pain distracts me. I have temporarily altered my body, and thus my mind. For just one moment, I am a burned-girl, not a writer-girl. Rosen may be correct. With my tongue I flick the loose skin, picture it, pink and silky, on fire.

•   •   •

No, plastic surgery is not just boobs and noses. Its textbooks
are tomes—thick, dusty, or slick, no matter—that all open up to
images of striated muscle excised from its moorings, bones—
white, calcium-rich—elongated by the doctor's finest tools. Plastic surgery, as a medical specialty, is very confusing. It aims, on
the one hand, to restore deformities and, on the other hand, to
alter the normal. Therefore, the patients are a motley crew. There
is the gorgeous blonde with the high sprayed helmet of hair who
wants a little tummy tuck, even though she's thin, and then there
is the Apert Syndrome child, the jaw so foreshortened the teeth
cannot root in their sockets. Plastic surgery—like Rosen, its pre-
mier practitioner—is flexible, high-minded, and wide-ranging,
managing to be at once utterly necessary and ridiculously frivolous, all in the same breath, all in the same scalpel.

According to the American Society of Plastic Surgeons, last year
more than 1.3 million people had cosmetic surgery performed by
board-certified plastic surgeons, an increase of 227 percent since
1992. (These numbers do not include medically necessary or reconstructive surgeries.) The five most popular procedures were liposuction (229,588), breast augmentation (187,755), eyelid surgery
(172,244), the just available Botox injections (118,452), and face lifts
(70,882). Most cosmetic surgeries are performed on women, but
men are catching up: the number of men receiving nose jobs—their
most popular procedure—has increased 141 percent since 1997.
The vast majority of patients are white, but not necessarily wealthy.
A 1994 study found that 65 percent of cosmetic-surgery patients
had a family income of less than $50,000, even though neither state
nor private health insurance covers the cost of cosmetic surgeries.
These figures alone point to the tremendous popularity and increasing acceptance of body alteration, and suggest that the slippery
slope from something as bizarre as eyelid tucks to something still
more bizarre, like wings, may be shorter than we think.

This medical specialty is ancient, dating back to 800 B.C., when hieroglyphics describe crude skin grafts. Rosen once explained to me that plastic surgery started as a means to blur racial differences. "A long time ago," he'd said, "Jewish slaves had clefts in their ears. And some of the first plastic-surgery operations were to remove those signs of stigma."

One history book mentions the story of a doctor named Joseph Dieffenbach and a man with grave facial problems. This man had the sunken nose of syphilis, a disease widely associated with immorality. Dieffenbach, one of the fathers of plastic surgery, so the story goes, devised a gold rhinoplasty bridge for this marginal man, thus giving him, literally, a Midas nose and proving, indeed, that medicine can make criminals kings.

As a field, plastic surgery is troubled, insecure. It is a lot like psychiatry, or dentistry, in its inferior status as a subspecialty of medicine. In fact, the first plastic-surgery association, started in 1921, was an offshoot of oral practitioners. Read: teeth people. Not to digress, but the other day I woke up with a terrible toothache and rushed in to see a dentist. I said to him, just to be friendly, "What sort of training do you need for your profession?" He said, "You need A LOT of training, believe me. I trained with the same guys who cure your cancer, but I don't get the same respect."

I wonder if Rosen ever feels like my dentist, and if that's why he's so grandiose, like the little boy who is a bully. Sander Gilman, a cultural critic of plastic surgery, writes that, in this group of doctors, there are a lot of big words thrown around in an effort to cover up the sneaking suspicion that their interventions are not important. One is not ever supposed to say "nose job"; it's called rhinoplasty. Gilman writes, "The lower the perceived status of a field . . . the more complex and 'scientific' the discourse of the field becomes."

Of course, I rarely meet a doctor who doesn't like jargon and doesn't like power. Rosen may be different only in intensity. "I'm not a cosmetic surgeon," Rosen keeps repeating to me.

He says, "Really, there's no such thing as just cosmetic surgery. The skin and the soul are one." On paper, maybe, this comment seems a little overblown, but delivered orally, in a New England town when all the world is white, it has its lyrical appeal.

When Rosen cries out that he's not "just a cosmetic surgeon," he's put his finger on a real conflict in his field. Where does necessary reconstruction end and frivolous interventions begin? Are those interventions really frivolous, or are they emblematic of the huge and sometimes majestic human desire to alter, to transcend? If medicine is predicated upon the notion of making the sick well, and a plastic surgeon operates on someone who is not sick, then can the patient truly be called a patient, and the doctor a doctor? Who pays for this stuff, when, where, and how? These are the swirling questions. Over a hundred years ago Jacques Joseph, another of plastic surgery's founding fathers, wrote that beauty was a medical necessity because a person's looks can create social and economic barriers. Repairing the deformity, therefore, allows the man to function in a fully healthy way in society. Voilà. Function and form, utilitarianism and aestheticism, joined at the hip, grafted together: skin tight.

•   •   •

Perhaps we can accept Joseph's formulation. Okay, we say. Calm down. We say this to all the hopping, hooting cosmetic surgeons who want to stake out their significance. Okay, we respect you. I'd like to say this to Rosen, but I can't. Rosen's ideas and aspirations, not to mention his anthrax concerns, go beyond what I am comfortable with, though I can't quite unearth the architecture of my concerns. After all, he doesn't want to hurt anyone. Maybe it's because Rosen isn't just talking about everyday beauty and its utilitarian aspects. He is talking EXTREMES. When Rosen thinks of beauty, he thinks of the human form stretched on the red-hot rack of his imagination, which is mired in medieval texts and books on trumpeter swans. At its outermost limits, beauty becomes fantastical, perhaps absurd. Here is where Rosen rests. He dreams of making wings for human beings. He has shown me blueprints, sketches of the scalpel scissoring into skin, stretching flaps of torso fat to fashion gliders piped with rib bone. When the arm stretches, the gliders unfold, and human floats on currents of air. Is he serious? At least partially. He gives lectures to medical students on the meaning of wings from an engineering perspective, a surgeon's perspective, and a patient's perspective. He has also thought of cochlear implants to enhance normal hearing, fins to make us fishlike, and echolocation devices so that we can better navigate the night. He does not understand the limits we place on hands. He once met a Vietnamese man with two thumbs on one hand. This man was a waiter, and his two thumbs made him highly skilled at his job. "Now," says Rosen, "if that man came to me and said, 'I want you to take off my extra thumb,' I'd be allowed, but I wouldn't be allowed to put an extra thumb on a person, and that's not fair."

We can call Rosen ridiculous, a madman, a monster, a marvel. We could dismiss him as a techno geek or a fool or just plain immature. But then there are the facts. First of all, Rosen is an influential man, an associate professor of surgery at Dartmouth Medical School and the director of the Plastic Surgery Residency Program at the medical center. He was senior fellow at the C. Everett Koop Institute from 1997 to 1998, and he has also served on advisory panels for the navy and for NASA's Medical Care for the Mission to Mars, 2018. Rosen consults for the American Academy of Sciences committee on the role of virtual-reality technology, and he is the former director of the Department of Defense's Emerging Technology Threats workforce. In other words, this is a man taken seriously by some serious higher-ups. "Echolocation devices," Rosen explains, "implanted in a soldier's head, could do a lot to enhance our military capacity." And this isn't just about the army's fantasies of the perfect soldier. Rosen travels worldwide (he gave over a dozen presentations last year) and has had substantial impact not only scalpeling skin but influencing his colleagues' ethics in a myriad of ways. "He has been essential in helping me to conceptualize medicine outside of the box," says Charles Lucey, MD, a former colleague of Rosen's at the Dartmouth Medical School. John Harris, a medical-ethics specialist in Manchester, England, writes in *Wonderwoman and Superman* that "in the absence of an argument or the ability to point to some specific harm that might be involved in crossing species boundaries, we should regard the objections *per se* to such practices . . . as mere and gratuitous prejudice." Rosen himself says, "Believe me. Wings are not way off. It is not a bad idea. Who would have thought we'd ever agree to hold expensive, potentially dangerous radioactive devices up to our ears for hours on end, day after day, just so we could gossip. That's cell phones for you," he says. And smiles.

Rosen has a nice smile. It's, to be sure, a little boyish, but it's charming. Sometimes Rosen is shy. "I mumble a lot," he acknowledges. "I don't really like people. I don't really like the present. I am a man who lives in the past and in the future only."

Now we leave the emergency room. The snow has stopped. The roads are membraned with ice. The sun is setting in the New Hampshire sky, causing the hills to sparkle as though they're full of little lights and other electric things. We drive back to his house, slowly. The emergencies are over, the patients soothed or suffering, he has done what can be done in a day, and still his nose runs. He coughs into his fist. "Truth be told," he says to me, "I didn't start out wanting to be a surgeon, even though I always, ALWAYS, had big ideas. In kindergarten, when the other kids were making these little ditsy arts-and-crafts projects, I was building a room-size Seventh Fleet ship." He goes on. As a child he wanted to be an artist. In high school he became obsessed with Picasso's *Guernica* and spent months trying to replicate it in the style of Van Gogh. As a freshman at Cornell, he made a robotic hand that could crack his lobster for him, and from then on it was hands, fingers, knees, and toes. His interests in the technical aspects of the body drew him away from the arts and eventually into medical school, which was, in his mind, somewhere between selling out and moving on.

We pull into his driveway. Rosen lives in a sprawling ranch-style house. He has a pet hen, who waits for us in the evergreen tree. His second wife, Stina Kohnke, is young and, yes, attractive. I'm afraid to ask how old she is; he looks to be at least fifty-three and she looks twenty-three, though maybe that's beside the point. Nevertheless, it all gets thrown into my mental stew: grandiose man, military man, medicine man, wants to make wings, young thing for a mate. Rooster and hen. Maybe there is no story here. Maybe there's just parody. All breadth, no depth. Except for this. Everyone I tell about Rosen and his wings, his *fin de siècle* mind, widens his or her eyes, leans forward, and says, "You're kidding." People want to hear more. I want to hear more. His ideas of altering the human form are repugnant and delicious, and that's a potent combination to unravel. And who among us has not had flying dreams, lifted high, dramatically free, a throat-catching fluidity in our otherwise aching form, above the ocean, all green, like moving marble?

•   •   •

Rosen and his wife have invited me for dinner. I accept. Stina is an artist. Her work is excellent. "Joe is an inspiration for me," she says. "He brings home pictures of his patients, and I sculpt their limbs from bronze." In her studio, she has a riot of red-bronze deformed hands clutching, reaching, in an agony of stiffness. She has fashioned drawer pulls from gold-plated ears. You go to open the breadbox, the medicine cabinet, the desk drawer, and you have to touch these things. It's at once creepy and very beautiful.

We sit at their stone dining-room table. Behind us is a seventy-gallon aquarium full of fish. Cacti, pink and penile, thrust their way into the odd air. Stina, homesick for her native California, has adorned the living room with paper palm trees and tiny live parakeets. We talk. Stina says, "Joe and I got married because we found in each other the same aesthetic and many moral equivalents. We found two people who could see and sculpt the potential in what others found just ugly."

"How did you two meet?" I ask.

"Oh, I knew Stina's sister, who was an art professor . . . That sort of thing," mumbles Rosen.

"I kissed him first," says Stina. She reaches across the table, picks up Rosen's hand, and wreathes her fingers through his. She holds on tightly, as if she's scared. I study Stina. She is conventionally pretty. She has a perfect Protestant nose and a lithe form, and a single black bra strap slips provocatively from beneath her blouse. Rosen, a man who claims to love the unusual, has picked a very usual beauty.

"Look!" Stina suddenly shouts. I jump, startled. "Look at her ears!" she says to Rosen.

Before I know it they are both leaning forward, peering at my ears. "Oh, my God," says Stina, "you have the most unusual ears."

Now, this is not news to me. I have bat ears, plain and simple. They stick out stupidly. In the fifth grade, I used to fasten them to the sides of my skull with pink styling tape in the hope of altering their shape. I have always disliked my ears.

Rosen uncurls his index finger and touches my left ear. He runs his finger along the bumpy, malformed rim. "You're missing the *scapha*," he says. "It's a birth defect."

"I have a birth defect?" I say. I practically shout this, being someone who desires deeply not to be defective. That's why I take Prozac every day.

"Joe," says Stina, "are those not the most amazing ears. They would be so perfect to sculpt."

"They're just a perfect example," Rosen echoes, "of the incredible, delectable proliferation of life-forms. We claim most life-forms gravitate toward the mean, but that's not true. Lots of valid life exists at the margins of the bell curve. You have beautiful ears," he says to me.

"I have nice ears?" I say. "Really?"

This is just one reason why I won't dismiss Rosen out of hand. Suddenly, I see my ears a little differently. They have a marvelous undulating ridge and an intricately whorled entrance, and they do not stick out so much as jauntily jut; they are ears with an attitude. Rosen has shifted my vision without even touching my eyes. He is, at the very least, a challenger of paradigms; he calls on your conservatism, pushes hard.

That night, I do not dream of wings. I dream of Sweeny and his oozing face. I dream he comes so close to me that I smell him. Then I wake up. Sweeny is very sick. He is going to die soon. Earlier in the day, I asked Rosen when, and Rosen said, "Oh, soon," but he said it as if he didn't really care. Death does not seem to interest Rosen. Beauty, I think, can be cold.

Part II: Monster and Marvels

Today, Rosen and I are attending a conference together in Montreal. Here, everyone speaks French and eats baguettes. The conference room is old-fashioned, wainscoted with rich mahogany, ornate carvings of creatures and angels studding the ceiling, where a single light hangs in a cream-colored orb. Around the table sit doctors, philosophers, graduate students: this is a medical-ethics meeting, and Rosen is presenting his ideas. On the white board, in bold black lines, he sketches out his wings, and then the discussion turns to a patient whose single deepest desire was to look like a lizard. He wanted a doctor to split his tongue and scale his skin, and then put horns on his head. "You wouldn't do that, would you?" a bespectacled doctor asks. "Once," says Rosen, dodging in a fashion typical of him, "there was a lady in need of breast reconstruction who wanted blue areolas. What's wrong with blue areolas? Furthermore, rhinoplasty has not reached its real potential. Why just change the nose? Why not change the gene for the nose, so that subsequent generations will benefit from the surgery. Plastic surgery, in the future, can be about more than the literal body. It can be about sculpting the genotype as well."

The bespectacled doctor raises his hand. "Would you make that man into a lizard?" the doctor asks again. "What I want to know is, if a patient came to you and said, 'I want you to give me wings,' or, 'Split my tongue,' would you actually do it?"

"Look," says Rosen, "we genetically engineer food. That's an issue."

"You're not answering my question," the doctor says, growing angry. Other people are growing angry, too. "Do you see any ethical dilemmas in making people into pigs, or birds?" another attendee yells out. This attendee is eating a Yodel, peeling off the chocolate bark and biting into a swirl of cream.

Rosen darts and dodges. "There is such a thing as liberty," he says.

"Yes," someone says, "but there's such a thing as the Hippocratic oath too."

This goes on and on. At last a professor of anthropology says, "Just tell us, clearly, please. Would you give a human being wings, if the medical-ethics board allowed it?"

Rosen puts down his black marker. He rubs his eyes. "Yes," he says, "I would. I can certainly see why we don't devote research money to it. I can see why the NIH would fund work on breast

cancer over this, but I don't have any problem with altering the human form. We do it all the time. It is only our Judeo-Christian conservatism that makes us think this is wrong. Who here," he says, "doesn't try to send their children to the best schools, in the hopes of altering them? Who here objects to a Palm Pilot, a thing we clasp to our bodies, with which we receive rapid electronic signals? Who here doesn't surround themselves with a metal shell and travel at death-defying speeds? We have always altered ourselves, for beauty or for power, and so long as we are not causing harm what makes us think we should stop?"

For a group of intelligent people everyone looks baffled. What Rosen has said is very right and very wrong, but no one can quite articulate the core conflicts. After all, we seem to think it's okay to use education as a way of neuronally altering the brain, but not surgery. We take Prozac, even Ritalin, to help transform ourselves, but recoil when it comes to wings. Maybe we're not recoiling. Maybe wings are just a dumb idea. No one in his right mind would subject himself to such a superfluous and strenuous operation. Yet socialite Jocelyne Wildenstein has dedicated much of her life to turning herself into a cat, via plastic surgery. She has had her lips enlarged and her face pulled back at the eyes to simulate a feline appearance. An even more well-known case is Michael Jackson, who has whitened himself, slimmed his nose, and undergone multiple other aesthetic procedures. The essential question here is whether these people are, and forever will be, outliers, or whether they represent the cutting edge of an ever more popular trend. Carl Elliott, a bioethicist and associate professor at the University of Minnesota, recently wrote in *The Atlantic* about a strange new "trend" of perfectly healthy folks who desire nothing more than to have a limb amputated, and about the British doctor who has undertaken this surgery, believing that if he doesn't amputate the patients will do it themselves, which could lead to gangrene. Elliott wonders whether amputation obsession will morph into another psychiatric diagnosis, whether, like hysteria, it will "catch on." The metaphor of contagion is an interesting one. Multiple-personality disorder "caught on"; hysteria caught on. Why then might not an unquenchable desire for wings or fins catch on, too? In any case, we use medical/viral metaphors to explain trends, and, in the case of plastic surgery, we then use medical means to achieve the trend's demands.

Rosen himself now repeats to the conferees, "We have always altered ourselves for beauty or for power. The chieftains in a certain African tribe remove their left ears, without Novocain. Other tribes put their bodies through intense scarification processes for the sake of style. In our own culture, we risk our bodies daily to achieve status, whether it's because we're bulimic or because we let some surgeon suck fat from us, with liposuction. Wings will be here," Rosen says. "Mark my words."

He suddenly seems so confident, so clear. We should do this; beauty is marvelous and monstrous. Beauty is difference, and yet, to his patients in the ER just two weeks back, he kept saying, "Let nature take its course." Perhaps he is more ambivalent than he lets on.

·   ·   ·

Later that evening, over dinner, conferees gossip about Rosen. "He's a creep," someone says. "A megalomaniac," someone else adds. For a creep or a megalomaniac, though, he's certainly commanding a lot of attention. Clearly, his notions are provocative. "The problem with wings," says someone, "is that only rich people would have them, would be able to afford them. Our society might begin to see rich people as more godly than ever."

I order a glass of wine. The waitress sets it on the table, where it blazes in its goblet, bright as a tulip. With this wine, I will tweak not only my mind but all its neuronal projections as well. My reflexes will slow down and my inhibitions will lift, making it possible for me to sound either very stupid or very smart. Is this wine an ethical problem? I ask the group that.

"Wine is reversible," someone says. "Wings aren't."

"Well, suppose they *were* reversible," someone says. "Supposing a surgeon could make wings that were removable. Then would we be reacting this way?"

"It's a question of degree," a philosopher pipes up. He is bald and skinny, with bulging eyes. "Rosen is going to the nth degree. It's not fair to lump that in with necessary alterations, or even questionably necessary alterations. Without doubt, it is very clear, diagnostically, that wings are not necessary."

I think about this. I think about what Rosen might say to this. I can imagine that his answer might have something to do with the fluidity of the concept of necessary. Four years ago, cell phones weren't necessary. Now they seem to be. Furthermore, he might say, if a person wants wings, if wings won't hurt a person, if they will help a person enjoy life and feel more beautiful, and if, in turn, the winged woman or man helps us to see beauty in what was before unacceptable, as we adjust and then come to love the sight of her spreading and soaring, then isn't this excellent? Later on, in my hotel room, I stand in front of the mirror, naked. My body contains eons. Once, we were single cells, then fish, then birds, then mammals, and the genes for all these forms lie dormant on their cones of chromosomes. We are pastiches at the cellular, genetic level. This may be why I fear open spaces, blank pages, why I often dream my house opens up into endless rooms I never knew were there, and I float through them with a kind of terror. It is so easy to seep, to be boundless. We clutch our cloaks of skin.

Back in Boston, I try to ascertain clearly, logically, what so bothers people about Rosen's ideas. At first glance, it might seem fairly obvious. I mean, wings. That's playing God. We should not play God. We should not reach for the stars. Myth after myth has shown us the dangers of doing so—Icarus, the Tower of Babel; absolute power corrupts absolutely. Bill Joy, chief scientist at Sun Microsystems, says, as our technological capabilities expand, "a sequence of small, individually sensible advances leads to an accumulation of great power and, concomitantly, great danger." Rosen's response to this: "So are we supposed to stop advancing? And who says it's bad to play God? We already alter the course of God's 'will' in hundreds of ways. When we use antibiotics to combat the flu, when we figure out a way to wipe smallpox off the very face of the earth, surely we're altering the natural course of things. Who says the natural course of things is even right? Maybe God isn't good."

The second objection might have to do with our notions of categorical imperatives. Mary Douglas wrote in her influential anthropological study *Purity and Danger* that human beings have a natural aversion to crossing categories, and that when we do transgress we see it as deeply dirty. In other words, shoes in themselves are not dirty, but when you place them on the dining-room table they are. When you talk about crossing species, either at the genetic or the anatomical level, you are mucking about in long-cherished categories that reflect our fundamental sense of cleanliness and aesthetics. Rosen's response to this, when I lob it at him in our next meeting: "Who says taboos are anything but prejudice at rock bottom? Just because it feels wrong doesn't mean it is. To a lot of people, racial intermingling and miscegenation feel wrong, but to me they're fine. I'm not a racist, and I'm not a conservative."

The third objection I can come up with has to do with the idea of proteanism. Proteus, a minor mythological figure, could shape-shift at will, being alternately a tiger, a lizard, a fire, a flood. Robert Lifton, one of, I think, the truly deep thinkers of the last century, has explored in his volumes how Proteus has become a symbol for human beings in our time. Lacking traditions, supportive institutions, a set of historically rooted symbols, we have lost any sense of coherence and connection. Today it is not uncommon for a human being to shift belief systems several times in a lifetime, and with relatively little psychological discomfort. We are Catholics, Buddhists, reborn, unborn, artists, and dot-commers until the dot drops out of the com and it all comes crashing down. We move on. We remarry. Our protean abilities clearly have their upsides. We are flexible and creative. But the downside is, there is no psychic stability, no substantive self, nothing really meaty and authentic. We sense this about ourselves. We know we are superficial, all breadth and no depth. Rosen's work embodies this tendency, literally. He desires to make incarnate the identity diffusion so common to our culture. Rosen is in our face making us face up to the fact that the inner and outer connections have crumbled. In our ability to be everything, are we also nothing?

For me, this hits the nail on the head. I do not object to Rosen on the basis of concerns about power, or of Mary Douglas's cross-category pollution theory. After all, who, really, would wings reasonably benefit but the window washers among us? And as for the pollution issue, protean person that I am, I could probably adjust to a little chimerical color. Rosen's ideas and aspirations are frightening to me because they are such vivid, visceral examples of a certain postmodern or perhaps, more precisely put, post-authentic sensibility we embrace and fear as we pop our Prozacs and Ritalins and decide to be Jewish and then Episcopalian and then chant with the monks on some high Himalayan mountain via a cheap plane ticket we purchased in between jobs and just before we sold our condo in a market rising so fast that when it falls it will sound like all of the precious china plates crashing down from the cabinet—a mess. What a mess!

Over and over again, from the Middle Ages on, when the theologian Pico wrote, in a direct and influential challenge to the Platonic idea of essential forms—"We have given you, Adam, no visage proper to yourself, nor endowment properly your own . . . trace for yourself the lineaments of your own nature . . . in order that you, as the free and proud shaper of your own being, fashion yourself in the form you may prefer. . . . [W]ho then will not look with awe upon this our chameleon . . ."—over and over, since those words at least, we as human beings have fretted about the question of whether there is anything fixed at our core, any set of unalterable traits that make us who we were and are and always will be. Postmodernism, by which I mean the idea of multiplicity, the celebration of the pastiche, and the rejection of logical positivism and absolutism as viable stances, will never die out, despite its waning popularity in academia. Its roots are too deep and ancient. And there has been, perhaps, no field like modern medicine, with all its possibilities and technological wizardry, to bring questions of authenticity to the burning forefront of our culture. At what point, in altering ourselves, would we lose our essential humanity? Are there any traits that make us essentially human? When might we become monsters or marvels, or are we already there? I vividly remember reading a book by a woman named Martha Beck. She had given birth to a Down syndrome child and she wrote in a few chilling sentences that because of one tiny chromosome, her child, Adam, is "as dissimilar from me as a mule is from a donkey. He is, in ways both obvious and subtle, a different beast." Is it really that simple, that small? One tiny chromosome severs us from the human species? One little wing and we're gone?

As for me, I am an obsessive. I like my categories. I check to make sure the stove is off three times before I go to bed. I have all sorts of other little rituals. At the same time, I know I am deeply disrooted. I left my family at the age of fourteen, never to return. I do not know my family tree. Like so many of us, I have no real religion, which is of course partly a good thing but partly a bad thing. In any case, last year, in some sort of desperate mood, I decided to convert from Judaism to Episcopalianism, but when it came time to put that blood and body in my mouth I couldn't go through with it. Was this because at bottom I just AM a Jew and this amness has profundity? Or was this because I don't like French bread, which is what they were using at the conversion ceremony? In any case, at the crucial moment of incorporation, I fled the church like the proverbial bride who cannot make the commitment.

I want to believe there is something essential and authentic about me, even if it's just my ears. And although my feelings of diffusion may be extreme, I am certainly not the only one who's felt she's flying too fast. Lifton writes, "Until relatively recently, no more than a single major ideological shift was likely to occur in a lifetime, and that one would be long remembered for its conflict and soul searching. But today it is not unusual for several such shifts to take place within a year or even a month, whether in the realm of politics, religion, aesthetic values, personal relationships. . . . Quite rare is the man or woman who has gone through life holding firmly to a single ideological vision. More usual is a tendency toward ideological fragments, bits and pieces of belief systems that allow for shifts, revisions, and recombinations."

What Lifton has observed in the psyche Rosen wants to make manifest in the body. I ask Rosen, "So, do you believe we are just in essence protean, that there is nothing fundamental, or core, to being human?"

He says, "Lauren, I am a scientist. My original interests were in nerves. I helped develop, in the 1980s, one of the first computer-grown nerve chips. The answer to your question may lie in how our nervous systems operate."

Part III: The Protean Brain

First, a lesson. In the 1930s, researchers, working on the brains of apes, found that the gray matter contained neural representations of all the afferent body parts. Ape ears, feet, skin, hands, were all richly represented in the ape brain in a series of neural etchings, like a map. Researchers also realized that when a person loses a limb—say, the right arm—this portion of the neural map fades away. Sometimes even stranger things happen. Sometimes amputees claimed they could feel their missing arm when, for instance, someone touched their cheek. This was because the arm map had not faded so much as morphed, joined up its circuitry with the cheek map, so it was all confused.

It was then discovered, not surprisingly, that human beings also have limb maps in their brains. Neurologists conceptualized this limb map as "a homunculus," or little man. Despite my feminist leanings, I am enchanted by the idea of a little man hunched in my head, troll-like, banging a drum, grinning from ear to ear. Of course the homunculus is not actually shaped like a human; it is, rather, a kind of human blueprint, like the drawing of the house in all its minute specificity. Touch the side of your skull. Press in. Buried, somewhere near there, is a beautiful etching of your complex human hand, rich in neural web-work and delicate, axonal tendrils designed to accommodate all the sensory possibilities of this prehensile object. Move your hand upward, press the now sealed soft spot, and you will be touching your toe map. Your eye map is somewhere in your forehead and your navel map is somewhere in your cerebellum, a creased, enfolded series of cells that recall, I imagine, ancient blue connections, a primitive love.

Today, Rosen is giving a lecture. I have come up to New Hampshire to hear him, and, unlike on the last visit, the day is beautiful and bright. Rosen explains how brains are truly plastic, which comes from the Greek root meaning to mold, to shape. When we lose a limb, the brain absorbs its map or rewires it to some other center. Similarly, Rosen explains, when we gain a limb, the brain almost immediately senses it and goes about hooking it up via neural representation. "If I were to attach a sonographically powered arm to your body," Rosen explains, "your brain would map it. If I were to attach a third thumb, your brain would map it, absolutely. Our bodies change our brains, and our brains are infinitely moldable. If I were to give you wings, you would develop, literally, a winged brain. If I were to give you an echolocation device, you would develop in part a bat-brain."

Although the idea of a brain able to incorporate changes so completely may sound strange, many neurological experiments have borne out the fact that our gray matter does reorganize according to the form and function of our appendages. Because no one has yet appended animal forms to the human body, however, no studies have been done that explore what the brain's response to what might be termed an "evolutionary insult" would be. Assuming, probably wrongly but assuming nevertheless, that human beings represent some higher form of species adaptation, at least in terms of frontal-lobe intelligence, the brain might find it odd to be rewiring itself to presumably more primitive structures, structures we shed a long time ago when we waded out of the swamps and shed our scales and feathers. Rosen's desire to meld human and animal forms, and the incarnation of this desire in people like the cat-woman and the lizard-man, raise some interesting questions about the intersection of technology and primitivism. Although we usually assume technology is somehow deepening the rift between nature and culture, it also can do the opposite. In other words, technology can be, and often is, extremely primitive, not only because it allows people a sort of id-like, limbic-driven power (i.e., nuclear weaponry) but also because it can provide the means to toggle us down the evolutionary ladder, to alter our brains, stuck in their rigid humanness, so that we become what we once were phylogenetically: tailed, winged, at last no longer landlocked.

All this is fascinating and, of course, unsettling to me. Our brains are essentially indiscriminate, able to morph—like the sea god Proteus himself—into fire, a flood, a dragon, a swan. I touch my brain and feel it flap. Now I understand more deeply what

Rosen meant when he said, "Plastic surgery changes the soul." To the extent that we believe our souls are a part of our brains, Rosen is right. And, all social conflict about its place in the medical hierarchy aside, plastic surgery is really neurosurgery, because it clearly happens, at its most essential level, north of the neck. When a surgeon modifies your body, he modifies your oh-so-willing, bendable brain.

I get a little depressed, hearing this lecture. It seems to me proof at the neuronal level that we have the capacity to be, in fact, everything, and thus in some sense nothing. It confirms my fear that I, along with the rest of the human species, could slip-slide through life without any specificity, or "specieficity." Last year, I had my first child. I wonder what I will teach her, what beliefs about the body and the brain and the soul I really hold. I think, "I will show her pictures of her ancestors," but the truth is, I don't have any pictures. I think, "I will teach her my morals," but I don't know exactly what my morals are, or where they came from. I know I am not alone. Like Rosen, perhaps, I am just extreme. Now I feel a kind of kinship with him. We are both self-invented, winging our way through.

Rosen comes up to me. He is finished with his talk. "So do you understand what I mean," he asks, "about the limitlessness of the brain?"

"Does it ever make you sad?" I say. "Does it ever just plain and simple make you scared?"

Rosen and I look at each other for a long time. He does seem sad. I recall him telling me once that when he envisions the future fifty years out, he hopes he is gone, because, he said, "While I like it here, I don't like it that much." I have the sense, now, that he struggles with things he won't tell me. His eyes appear tired, his face drained. I wonder if he wakes in the middle of the night, frightened by his own perceptions. Strange or not, there is something constant in Rosen, and that's his intelligence, his uncanny ability to defend seemingly untenable positions with power and occasional grace. In just three weeks he will travel to a remote part of Asia to participate in a group called Interplast, made up of doctors and nurses who donate their time to help children with cleft lips and palates. I think it's important to mention this—not only Bin Laden, bandwidth, anthrax, and wings but his competing desire to minister. The way, at the dinner table, he tousles his children's hair. His avid dislike of George W. Bush. His love of plants and greenery. Call him multifaceted or simply slippery, I don't know. All I do know is that right now, when I look at his face, I think I can see the boy he once was, the Seventh Fleet ship, the wonder, all that wonder.

"Do you and Stina want to go out for dinner? We could go somewhere really fancy, to thank you," I say, "for all your time."

"Sure," says Rosen. "Give me a minute. I'll meet you in the hospital lobby," and then he zips off to who knows where, and I am alone with my singular stretched self on the third floor of the Dartmouth-Hitchcock Medical Center. I wander down the long hallways. Behind the curtained cubicles there is unspeakable suffering. Surely that cannot be changed, not ever. Behind one of these cubicles sits Sweeny, and even if we learn to see him as beautiful, the bottom-line truth is that he still suffers. Now I want to touch Sweeny's dying face. I want to put my hand right on the center of pain. I want to touch Rosen's difficult face, and my baby daughter's face as well, but she is far from me, in some home we will, migrants that our family is, move on from sometime soon. I once read that a fetus does not scar. Fetal skin repairs itself seamlessly, evidence of damage sinking back into blackness. Plastic surgery, for all its incredible advances, has not yet been able to figure out how to replicate this mysterious fetal ability in the full-born human. Plastic surgery can give us wings and maybe even let us sing like loons, but it cannot stop scarring. This is oddly comforting to me. I pause to sit on a padded bench.

A very ill woman pushing an IV pole walks by. I lift up my pant leg and study the scar I got a long time ago, when I fell off a childhood bike. The scar is pink and raised and shaped like an *o*, like a hole maybe, but also like a letter, like a language, like a little piece of land that, for now, we cannot cross over.

Samantha Power

Bystanders to Genocide

Why the United States Let the Rwandan Tragedy Happen

The author's exclusive interviews with scores of participants in the decision-making, together with her analysis of a cache of newly declassified documents, yield a chilling narrative of self-serving caution and flaccid will—and countless missed opportunities to mitigate a colossal crime.

I. People Sitting in Offices

In the course of a hundred days in 1994 the Hutu government
of Rwanda and its extremist allies very nearly succeeded in exterminating the country's Tutsi minority. Using firearms, machetes,
and a variety of garden implements, Hutu militiamen, soldiers,
and ordinary citizens murdered some 800,000 Tutsi and politically moderate Hutu. It was the fastest, most efficient killing
spree of the twentieth century.

A few years later, in a series in *The New Yorker,* Philip Gourevitch recounted in horrific detail the story of the genocide and the
world's failure to stop it. President Bill Clinton, a famously avid
reader, expressed shock. He sent copies of Gourevitch's articles to
his second-term national-security adviser, Sandy Berger. The
articles bore confused, angry, searching queries in the margins. "Is
what he's saying true?" Clinton wrote with a thick black felt-tip
pen beside heavily underlined paragraphs. "How did this happen?" he asked, adding, "I want to get to the bottom of this." The
President's urgency and outrage were oddly timed. As the terror
in Rwanda had unfolded, Clinton had shown virtually no interest
in stopping the genocide, and his Administration had stood by as
the death toll rose into the hundreds of thousands.

Why did the United States not do more for the Rwandans at
the time of the killings? Did the President really not know about
the genocide, as his marginalia suggested? Who were the people
in his Administration who made the life-and-death decisions
that dictated U.S. policy? Why did they decide (or decide not to
decide) as they did? Were any voices inside or outside the U.S.
government demanding that the United States do more? If so,
why weren't they heeded? And most crucial, what could the
United States have done to save lives?

So far people have explained the U.S. failure to respond to the
Rwandan genocide by claiming that the United States didn't
know what was happening, that it knew but didn't care, or that

regardless of what it knew there was nothing useful to be done. The account that follows is based on a three-year investigation involving sixty interviews with senior, mid-level, and junior State Department, Defense Department, and National Security Council officials who helped to shape or inform U.S. policy. It also reflects dozens of interviews with Rwandan, European, and United Nations officials and with peacekeepers, journalists, and nongovernmental workers in Rwanda. Thanks to the National Security Archive (www.nsarchive.org), a nonprofit organization that uses the Freedom of Information Act to secure the release of classified U.S. documents, this account also draws on hundreds of pages of newly available government records. This material provides a clearer picture than was previously possible of the interplay among people, motives, and events. It reveals that the U.S. government knew enough about the genocide early on to save lives, but passed up countless opportunities to intervene.

In March of 1998, on a visit to Rwanda, President Clinton issued what would later be known as the "Clinton apology," which was actually a carefully hedged acknowledgment. He spoke to the crowd assembled on the tarmac at Kigali Airport: "We come here today partly in recognition of the fact that we in the United States and the world community did not do as much as we could have and should have done to try to limit what occurred" in Rwanda.

This implied that the United States had done a good deal but not quite enough. In reality the United States did much more than fail to send troops. It led a successful effort to remove most of the UN peacekeepers who were already in Rwanda. It aggressively worked to block the subsequent authorization of UN reinforcements. It refused to use its technology to jam radio broadcasts that were a crucial instrument in the coordination and perpetuation of the genocide. And even as, on average, 8,000 Rwandans were being butchered each day, U.S. officials shunned the term "genocide," for fear of being obliged to act. The United

States in fact did virtually nothing "to try to limit what occurred." Indeed, staying out of Rwanda was an explicit U.S. policy objective.

With the grace of one grown practiced at public remorse, the President gripped the lectern with both hands and looked across the dais at the Rwandan officials and survivors who surrounded him. Making eye contact and shaking his head, he explained, "It may seem strange to you here, especially the many of you who lost members of your family; but all over the world there were people like me sitting in offices, day after day after day, who *did not fully appreciate* [pause] the depth [pause] and the speed [pause] with which you were being engulfed by this *unimaginable* terror."

Clinton chose his words with characteristic care. It was true that although top U.S. officials could not help knowing the basic facts—thousands of Rwandans were dying every day—that were being reported in the morning papers, many did not "fully appreciate" the meaning. In the first three weeks of the genocide the most influential American policymakers portrayed (and, they insist, perceived) the deaths not as atrocities or the components and symptoms of genocide but as wartime "casualties"—the deaths of combatants or those caught between them in a civil war.

Yet this formulation avoids the critical issue of whether Clinton and his close advisers might reasonably have been expected to "fully appreciate" the true dimensions and nature of the massacres. During the first three days of the killings U.S. diplomats in Rwanda reported back to Washington that well-armed extremists were intent on eliminating the Tutsi. And the American press spoke of the door-to-door hunting of unarmed civilians. By the end of the second week informed nongovernmental groups had already begun to call on the Administration to use the term "genocide," causing diplomats and lawyers at the State Department to begin debating the word's applicability soon thereafter. In order not to appreciate that genocide or something close to it was under way, U.S. officials had to ignore public reports and internal intelligence and debate.

The story of U.S. policy during the genocide in Rwanda is not a story of willful complicity with evil. U.S. officials did not sit around and conspire to allow genocide to happen. But whatever their convictions about "never again," many of them did sit around, and they most certainly did allow genocide to happen. In examining how and why the United States failed Rwanda, we see that without strong leadership the system will incline toward risk-averse policy choices. We also see that with the possibility of deploying U.S. troops to Rwanda taken off the table early on— and with crises elsewhere in the world unfolding—the slaughter never received the top-level attention it deserved. Domestic political forces that might have pressed for action were absent. And most U.S. officials opposed to American involvement in Rwanda were firmly convinced that they were doing all they could—and, most important, all they *should*—in light of competing American interests and a highly circumscribed understanding of what was "possible" for the United States to do.

One of the most thoughtful analyses of how the American system can remain predicated on the noblest of values while allowing the vilest of crimes was offered in 1971 by a brilliant and earnest young foreign-service officer who had just resigned from the National Security Council to protest the 1970 U.S. invasion of Cambodia. In an article in *Foreign Policy,* "The Human Reality of Realpolitik," he and a colleague analyzed the process whereby American policymakers with moral sensibilities could have waged a war of such immoral consequence as the one in Vietnam. They wrote,

> The answer to that question begins with a basic intellectual approach which views foreign policy as a lifeless, bloodless set of abstractions. "Nations," "interests," "influence," "prestige"—all are disembodied and dehumanized terms which encourage easy inattention to the real people whose lives our decisions affect or even end.

Policy analysis excluded discussion of human consequences. "It simply is not *done*," the authors wrote. "Policy—good, steady policy—is made by the 'tough-minded.' To talk of suffering is to lose 'effectiveness,' almost to lose one's grip. It is seen as a sign that one's 'rational' arguments are weak."

In 1994, fifty years after the Holocaust and twenty years after America's retreat from Vietnam, it was possible to believe that the system had changed and that talk of human consequences had become admissible. Indeed, when the machetes were raised in Central Africa, the White House official primarily responsible for the shaping of U.S. foreign policy was one of the authors of that 1971 critique: Anthony Lake, President Clinton's first-term national-security adviser. The genocide in Rwanda presented Lake and the rest of the Clinton team with an opportunity to prove that "good, steady policy" could be made in the interest of saving lives.

II. The Peacekeepers

Rwanda was a test for another man as well: Romeo Dallaire, then a major general in the Canadian army who at the time of the genocide was the commander of the UN Assistance Mission in Rwanda. If ever there was a peacekeeper who believed wholeheartedly in the promise of humanitarian action, it was Dallaire. A broad-shouldered French-Canadian with deep-set sky-blue eyes, Dallaire has the thick, calloused hands of one brought up in a culture that prizes soldiering, service, and sacrifice. He saw the United Nations as the embodiment of all three.

Before his posting to Rwanda Dallaire had served as the commandant of an army brigade that sent peacekeeping battalions to Cambodia and Bosnia, but he had never seen actual combat himself. "I was like a fireman who has never been to a fire, but has dreamed for years about how he would fare when the fire came," the fifty-five-year-old Dallaire recalls. When, in the summer of 1993, he received the phone call from UN headquarters offering him the Rwanda posting, he was ecstatic. "It was answering the aim of my life," he says. "It's *all* you've been waiting for."

Dallaire was sent to command a UN force that would help to keep the peace in Rwanda, a nation the size of Vermont, which was known as "the land of a thousand hills" for its rolling terrain. Before Rwanda achieved independence from Belgium, in 1962, the Tutsi, who made up 15 percent of the populace, had enjoyed a privileged status. But independence ushered in three decades of Hutu rule, under which Tutsi were systematically discriminated against and periodically subjected to waves of killing and ethnic cleansing. In 1990 a group of armed exiles, mainly Tutsi, who had been clustered on the Ugandan border, invaded Rwanda. Over the next several years the rebels, known as the Rwandan Patriotic Front, gained ground against Hutu government forces. In 1993 Tanzania brokered peace talks, which resulted in a power-sharing agreement known as the Arusha Accords. Under its terms the Rwandan government agreed to share power with Hutu opposition parties and the Tutsi minority. UN peacekeepers would be deployed to patrol a cease-fire and assist in demilitarization and demobilization as well as to help provide a secure environment, so that exiled Tutsi could return. The hope among moderate Rwandans and Western observers was that Hutu and Tutsi would at last be able to coexist in harmony.

Hutu extremists rejected these terms and set out to terrorize Tutsi and also those Hutu politicians supportive of the peace process. In 1993 several thousand Rwandans were killed, and some 9,000 were detained. Guns, grenades, and machetes began arriving by the planeload. A pair of international commissions—one sent by the United Nations, the other by an independent collection of human-rights organizations—warned explicitly of a possible genocide.

But Dallaire knew nothing of the precariousness of the Arusha Accords. When he made a preliminary reconnaissance trip to Rwanda, in August of 1993, he was told that the country was committed to peace and that a UN presence was essential. A visit with extremists, who preferred to eradicate Tutsi rather than cede power, was not on Dallaire's itinerary. Remarkably, no UN officials in New York thought to give Dallaire copies of the alarming reports from the international investigators.

The sum total of Dallaire's intelligence data before that first trip to Rwanda consisted of one encyclopedia's summary of Rwandan history, which Major Brent Beardsley, Dallaire's executive assistant, had snatched at the last minute from his local public library. Beardsley says, "We flew to Rwanda with a Michelin road map, a copy of the Arusha agreement, and that was it. We were under the impression that the situation was quite straightforward: there was one cohesive government side and one cohesive rebel side, and they had come together to sign the peace agreement and had then requested that we come in to help them implement it."

Though Dallaire gravely underestimated the tensions brewing in Rwanda, he still felt that he would need a force of 5,000 to help the parties implement the terms of the Arusha Accords. But when his superiors warned him that the United States would never agree to pay for such a large deployment, Dallaire reluctantly trimmed his written request to 2,500. He remembers, "I was told, 'Don't ask for a brigade, because it ain't there.'"

Once he was actually posted to Rwanda, in October of 1993, Dallaire lacked not merely intelligence data and manpower but also institutional support. The small Department of Peacekeeping Operations in New York, run by the Ghanaian diplomat Kofi Annan, now the UN secretary general, was overwhelmed. Madeleine Albright, then the U.S. ambassador to the UN, recalls, "The global nine-one-one was always either busy or nobody was there." At the time of the Rwanda deployment, with a staff of a few hundred, the UN was posting 70,000 peacekeepers on seventeen missions around the world. Amid these widespread crises and logistical headaches the Rwanda mission had a very low status.

Life was not made easier for Dallaire or the UN peacekeeping office by the fact that American patience for peacekeeping was thinning. Congress owed half a billion dollars in UN dues and peacekeeping costs. It had tired of its obligation to foot a third of the bill for what had come to feel like an insatiable global appetite for mischief and an equally insatiable UN appetite for missions. The Clinton Administration had taken office better disposed toward peacekeeping than any other Administration in U.S. history. But it felt that the Department of Peacekeeping Operations needed fixing and demanded that the UN "learn to say no" to chancy or costly missions.

Every aspect of the UN Assistance Mission in Rwanda was run on a shoestring. UNAMIR (the acronym by which it was known) was equipped with hand-me-down vehicles from the UN's Cambodia mission, and only eighty of the 300 that turned up were usable. When the medical supplies ran out, in March of 1994, New York said there was no cash for resupply. Very little could be procured locally, given that Rwanda was one of Africa's poorest nations. Replacement spare parts, batteries, and even ammunition could rarely be found. Dallaire spent some 70 percent of his time battling UN logistics.

Dallaire had major problems with his personnel, as well. He commanded troops, military observers, and civilian personnel from twenty-six countries. Though multinationality is meant to be a virtue of UN missions, the diversity yielded grave discrepancies in resources. Whereas Belgian troops turned up well armed and ready to perform the tasks assigned to them, the poorer contingents showed up "bare-assed," in Dallaire's words, and demanded that the United Nations suit them up. "Since nobody else was offering to send troops, we had to take what we could get," he says. When Dallaire expressed concern, he was instructed by a senior UN official to lower his expectations. He recalls, "I was told, 'Listen, General, you are NATO-trained. This is not NATO.'" Although some 2,500 UNAMIR personnel had arrived by early April of 1994, few of the soldiers had the kit they needed to perform even basic tasks.

The signs of militarization in Rwanda were so widespread that even without much of an intelligence-gathering capacity, Dallaire was able to learn of the extremists' sinister intentions. In January of 1994 an anonymous Hutu informant, said to be high up in the inner circles of the Rwandan government, had come forward to describe the rapid arming and training of local militias. In what is now referred to as the "Dallaire fax," Dallaire relayed to New York the informant's claim that Hutu extremists "had been ordered to register all the Tutsi in Kigali." "He suspects it is for their extermination," Dallaire wrote. "Example he gave was that in 20 minutes his personnel could kill up to 1000 Tutsis." "Jean-Pierre," as the informant became known, had said that the militia planned first to provoke and murder a number of Belgian peacekeepers, to "thus guarantee Belgian withdrawal from Rwanda." When Dallaire notified Kofi Annan's office that UNAMIR was poised to raid Hutu arms caches, Annan's deputy forbade him to do so. Instead Dallaire was instructed to notify the Rwandan President, Juvénal Habyarimana, and the Western ambassadors of the informant's claims. Though Dallaire battled by phone with New York, and confirmed the reliability of the informant, his political masters told him plainly and consistently that the United States in particular would not support aggressive peacekeeping. (A request by the Belgians for reinforcements was also turned down.) In Washington, Dallaire's alarm was discounted. Lieutenant Colonel Tony Marley, the U.S. military liaison to the Arusha process, respected Dallaire but knew he was operating in Africa for the first time. "I thought that the neophyte meant well, but I questioned whether he knew what he was talking about," Marley recalls.

III. The Early Killings

On the evening of April 6, 1994, Romeo Dallaire was sitting on the couch in his bungalow residence in Kigali, watching CNN with Brent Beardsley. Beardsley was preparing plans for a national Sports Day that would match Tutsi rebel soldiers against Hutu government soldiers in a soccer game. Dallaire said, "You know, Brent, if the shit ever hit the fan here, none of this stuff would really matter, would it?" The next instant the phone rang. Rwandan President Habyarimana's Mystère Falcon jet, a gift from French President François Mitterrand, had just been shot down, with Habyarimana and Burundian President Cyprien Ntaryamira aboard. Dallaire and Beardsley raced in their UN jeep to Rwandan army headquarters, where a crisis meeting was under way.

Back in Washington, Kevin Aiston, the Rwanda desk officer, knocked on the door of Deputy Assistant Secretary of State Prudence Bushnell and told her that the Presidents of Rwanda and Burundi had gone down in a plane crash. "Oh, shit," she said. "Are you sure?" In fact nobody was sure at first, but Dallaire's forces supplied confirmation within the hour. The Rwandan authorities quickly announced a curfew, and Hutu militias and government soldiers erected roadblocks around the capital.

Bushnell drafted an urgent memo to Secretary of State Warren Christopher. She was concerned about a probable outbreak of killing in both Rwanda and its neighbor Burundi. The memo read,

> If, as it appears, both Presidents have been killed, there is a strong likelihood that widespread violence could break out in either or both countries, particularly if it is confirmed that the plane was shot down. Our strategy is to appeal for calm in both countries, both through public statements and in other ways.

A few public statements proved to be virtually the only strategy that Washington would muster in the weeks ahead.

Lieutenant General Wesley Clark, who later commanded the NATO air war in Kosovo, was the director of strategic plans and policy for the Joint Chiefs of Staff at the Pentagon. On learning of the crash, Clark remembers, staff officers asked, "Is it Hutu and Tutsi or Tutu and Hutsi?" He frantically called for insight into the ethnic dimension of events in Rwanda. Unfortunately, Rwanda had never been of more than marginal concern to Washington's most influential planners.

America's best-informed Rwanda observer was not a government official but a private citizen, Alison Des Forges, a historian and a board member of Human Rights Watch, who lived in Buffalo, New York. Des Forges had been visiting Rwanda since 1963. She had received a Ph.D. from Yale in African history, specializing in Rwanda, and she could speak the Rwandan language, Kinyarwanda. Half an hour after the plane crash Des Forges got a phone call from a close friend in Kigali, the human-rights activist Monique Mujawamariya. Des Forges had been worried about Mujawamariya for weeks, because the Hutu extremist radio station, Radio Mille Collines, had branded her "a bad patriot who deserves to die." Mujawamariya had sent Human Rights Watch a chilling warning a week earlier: "For the last two weeks, all of Kigali has lived under the threat of an instantaneous, carefully prepared operation to eliminate all those who give trouble to President Habyarimana."

Now Habyarimana was dead, and Mujawamariya knew instantly that the hard-line Hutu would use the crash as a pretext to begin mass killing. "This is it," she told Des Forges on the phone. For the next twenty-four hours Des Forges called her friend's home every half hour. With each conversation Des Forges could hear the gunfire grow louder as the militia drew closer. Finally the gunmen entered Mujawamariya's home. "I don't want you to hear this," Mujawamariya said softly. "Take care of my children." She hung up the phone.

Mujawamariya's instincts were correct. Within hours of the plane crash Hutu militiamen took command of the streets of Kigali. Dallaire quickly grasped that supporters of the Arusha peace process were being targeted. His phone at UNAMIR headquarters rang constantly as Rwandans around the capital pleaded for help. Dallaire was especially concerned about Prime Minister Agathe Uwilingiyimana, a reformer who with the President's death had become the titular head of state. Just after dawn on April 7 five Ghanaian and ten Belgian peacekeepers arrived at the Prime Minister's home in order to deliver her to Radio Rwanda, so that she could broadcast an emergency appeal for calm.

Joyce Leader, the second-in-command at the U.S. embassy, lived next door to Uwilingiyimana. She spent the early hours of the morning behind the steel-barred gates of her embassy-owned house as Hutu killers hunted and dispatched their first victims. Leader's phone rang. Uwilingiyimana was on the other end. "Please hide me," she begged.

Minutes after the phone call a UN peacekeeper attempted to hike the Prime Minister over the wall separating their compounds. When Leader heard shots fired, she urged the peacekeeper to abandon the effort. "They can see you!" she shouted. Uwilingiyimana managed to slip with her husband and children into another compound, which was occupied by the UN Development Program. But the militiamen hunted them down in the yard, where the couple surrendered. There were more shots. Leader recalls, "We heard her screaming and then, suddenly, after the gunfire the screaming stopped, and we heard people cheering." Hutu gunmen in the Presidential Guard that day systematically tracked down and eliminated Rwanda's moderate leadership.

The raid on Uwilingiyimana's compound not only cost Rwanda a prominent supporter of the Arusha Accords; it also triggered the collapse of Dallaire's mission. In keeping with the plan to target the Belgians which the informant Jean-Pierre had relayed to UNAMIR in January, Hutu soldiers rounded up the peacekeepers at Uwilingiyimana's home, took them to a military camp, led the Ghanaians to safety, and then killed and savagely mutilated the ten Belgians. In Belgium the cry for either expanding UNAMIR's mandate or immediately withdrawing was prompt and loud.

In response to the initial killings by the Hutu government, Tutsi rebels of the Rwandan Patriotic Front—stationed in Kigali under the terms of the Arusha Accords—surged out of their barracks and resumed their civil war against the Hutu regime. But under the cover of that war were early and strong indications that systematic genocide was taking place. From April 7 onward the Hutu-controlled army, the gendarmerie, and the militias worked together to wipe out Rwanda's Tutsi. Many of the early Tutsi victims found themselves specifically, not spontaneously, pursued: lists of targets had been prepared in advance, and Radio Mille Collines broadcast names, addresses, and even license-plate numbers. Killers often carried a machete in one hand and a transistor radio in the other. Tens of thousands of Tutsi fled their homes in panic and were snared and butchered at checkpoints. Little care was given to their disposal. Some were shoveled into landfills. Human flesh rotted in the sunshine. In churches bodies mingled with scattered hosts. If the killers had taken the time to tend to sanitation, it would have slowed their "sanitization" campaign.

IV. The "Last War"

The two tracks of events in Rwanda—simultaneous war and genocide—confused policymakers who had scant prior understanding of the country. Atrocities are often carried out in places that are not commonly visited, where outside expertise is limited. When country-specific knowledge is lacking, foreign governments become all the more likely to employ faulty analogies and to "fight the last war." The analogy employed by many of those who confronted the outbreak of killing in Rwanda was a peacekeeping intervention that had gone horribly wrong in Somalia.

On October 3, 1993, ten months after President Bush had sent U.S. troops to Somalia as part of what had seemed a low-risk humanitarian mission, U.S. Army Rangers and Delta special forces in Somalia attempted to seize several top advisers to the warlord Mohammed Farah Aideed. Aideed's faction had ambushed and killed two dozen Pakistani peacekeepers, and the United States was striking back. But in the firefight that ensued the Somali militia killed eighteen Americans, wounded seventy-three, and captured one Black Hawk helicopter pilot. Somali television broadcast both a video interview with the trembling, disoriented pilot and a gory procession in which the corpse of a U.S. Ranger was dragged through a Mogadishu street.

On receiving word of these events, President Clinton cut short a trip to California and convened an urgent crisis-management meeting at the White House. When an aide began recapping the situation, an angry President interrupted him. "Cut the bullshit," Clinton snapped. "Let's work this out." "Work it out" meant walk out. Republican Congressional pressure was intense. Clinton appeared on American television the next day, called off the manhunt for Aideed, temporarily reinforced the troop presence, and announced that all U.S. forces would be home within six months. The Pentagon leadership concluded that peacekeeping in Africa meant trouble and that neither the White House nor Congress would stand by it when the chips were down.

Even before the deadly blowup in Somalia the United States had resisted deploying a UN mission to Rwanda. "Anytime you mentioned peacekeeping in Africa," one U.S. official remembers, "the crucifixes and garlic would come up on every door." Having lost much of its early enthusiasm for peacekeeping and for the United Nations itself, Washington was nervous that the Rwanda mission would sour like so many others. But President Habyarimana had traveled to Washington in 1993 to offer assurances that his government was committed to carrying out the terms of the Arusha Accords. In the end, after strenuous lobbying by France (Rwanda's chief diplomatic and military patron), U.S. officials accepted the proposition that UNAMIR could be the rare "UN winner." On October 5, 1993, two days after the Somalia firefight, the United States reluctantly voted in the Security Council to authorize Dallaire's mission. Even so, U.S. officials made it clear that Washington would give no consideration to sending U.S. troops to Rwanda. Somalia and another recent embarrassment in Haiti indicated that multilateral initiatives for humanitarian purposes would likely bring the United States all loss and no gain.

Against this backdrop, and under the leadership of Anthony Lake, the national-security adviser, the Clinton Administration accelerated the development of a formal U.S. peacekeeping doctrine. The job was given to Richard Clarke, of the National Security Council, a special assistant to the President who was known as one of the most effective bureaucrats in Washington. In an interagency process that lasted more than a year, Clarke managed the production of a presidential decision directive, PDD-25, which listed sixteen factors that policymakers needed to consider when deciding whether to support peacekeeping activities: seven factors if the United States was to vote in the UN Security Council on peace operations carried out by non-American soldiers, six additional and more stringent factors if U.S. forces were to participate in UN peacekeeping missions, and three final factors if U.S. troops were likely to engage in actual combat. In the words of Representative David Obey, of Wisconsin, the restrictive checklist tried to satisfy the

American desire for "zero degree of involvement, and zero degree of risk, and zero degree of pain and confusion." The architects of the doctrine remain its strongest defenders. "Many say PDD-25 was some evil thing designed to kill peacekeeping, when in fact it was there to save peacekeeping," Clarke says. "Peacekeeping was almost dead. There was no support for it in the U.S. government, and the peacekeepers were not effective in the field." Although the directive was not publicly released until May 3, 1994, a month into the genocide, the considerations encapsulated in the doctrine and the Administration's frustration with peacekeeping greatly influenced the thinking of U.S. officials involved in shaping Rwanda policy.

V. The Peace Processors

Each of the American actors dealing with Rwanda brought particular institutional interests and biases to his or her handling of the crisis. Secretary of State Warren Christopher knew little about Africa. At one meeting with his top advisers, several weeks after the plane crash, he pulled an atlas off his shelf to help him locate the country. Belgian Foreign Minister Willie Claes recalls trying to discuss Rwanda with his American counterpart and being told, "I have other responsibilities." Officials in the State Department's Africa Bureau were, of course, better informed. Prudence Bushnell, the deputy assistant secretary, was one of them. The daughter of a diplomat, Bushnell had joined the foreign service in 1981, at the age of thirty-five. With her agile mind and sharp tongue, she had earned the attention of George Moose when she served under him at the U.S. embassy in Senegal. When Moose was named the assistant secretary of state for African affairs, in 1993, he made Bushnell his deputy. Just two weeks before the plane crash the State Department had dispatched Bushnell and a colleague to Rwanda in an effort to contain the escalating violence and to spur the stalled peace process.

Unfortunately, for all the concern of the Americans familiar with Rwanda, their diplomacy suffered from three weaknesses. First, ahead of the plane crash diplomats had repeatedly threatened to pull out UN peacekeepers in retaliation for the parties' failure to implement Arusha. These threats were of course counterproductive, because the very Hutu who opposed power-sharing wanted nothing more than a UN withdrawal. One senior U.S. official remembers, "The first response to trouble is 'Let's yank the peacekeepers.' But that is like believing that when children are misbehaving, the proper response is 'Let's send the baby-sitter home.'"

Second, before and during the massacres U.S. diplomacy revealed its natural bias toward states and toward negotiations. Because most official contact occurs between representatives of states, U.S. officials were predisposed to trust the assurances of Rwandan officials, several of whom were plotting genocide behind the scenes. Those in the U.S. government who knew Rwanda best viewed the escalating violence with a diplomatic prejudice that left them both institutionally oriented toward the Rwandan government and reluctant to do anything to disrupt the peace process. An examination of the cable traffic from the U.S. embassy in Kigali to Washington between the signing of the Arusha agreement and the downing of the presidential plane reveals that setbacks were perceived as "dangers to the peace process" more than as "dangers to Rwandans." American criticisms were deliberately and steadfastly leveled at "both sides," though Hutu government and militia forces were usually responsible.

The U.S. ambassador in Kigali, David Rawson, proved especially vulnerable to such bias. Rawson had grown up in Burundi, where his father, an American missionary, had set up a Quaker hospital. He entered the foreign service in 1971. When, in 1993, at age fifty-two, he was given the embassy in Rwanda, his first, he could not have been more intimate with the region, the culture, or the peril. He spoke the local language—almost unprecedented for an ambassador in Central Africa. But Rawson found it difficult to imagine the Rwandans who surrounded the President as conspirators in genocide. He issued pro forma demarches over Habyarimana's obstruction of power-sharing, but the cable traffic shows that he accepted the President's assurances that he was doing all he could. The U.S. investment in the peace process gave rise to a wishful tendency to see peace "around the corner." Rawson remembers, "We were naive policy optimists, I suppose. The fact that negotiations can't work is almost not one of the options open to people who care about peace. We were looking for the hopeful signs, not the dark signs. In fact, we were looking away from the dark signs . . . One of the things I learned and should have already known is that once you launch a process, it takes on its own momentum. I had said, 'Let's try this, and then if it doesn't work, we can back away.' But bureaucracies don't allow that. Once the Washington side buys into a process, it gets pursued, almost blindly." Even after the Hutu government began exterminating Tutsi, U.S. diplomats focused most of their efforts on "re-establishing a cease-fire" and "getting Arusha back on track."

The third problematic feature of U.S. diplomacy before and during the genocide was a tendency toward blindness bred by familiarity: the few people in Washington who were paying attention to Rwanda before Habyarimana's plane was shot down were those who had been tracking Rwanda for some time and had thus come to expect a certain level of ethnic violence from the region. And because the U.S. government had done little when some 40,000 people had been killed in Hutu-Tutsi violence in Burundi in October of 1993, these officials also knew that Washington was prepared to tolerate substantial bloodshed. When the massacres began in April, some U.S. regional specialists initially suspected that Rwanda was undergoing "another flare-up" that would involve another "acceptable" (if tragic) round of ethnic murder.

Rawson had read up on genocide before his posting to Rwanda, surveying what had become a relatively extensive scholarly literature on its causes. But although he expected internecine killing, he did not anticipate the scale at which it occurred. "Nothing in Rwandan culture or history could have led a person to that forecast," he says. "Most of us thought that if a war broke out, it would be quick, that these poor people didn't have the resources, the means, to fight a sophisticated war. I couldn't have known that they would do each other in with the most economic means." George Moose agrees: "We were psychologically and imaginatively too limited."

VI. Foreigners First

David Rawson was sitting with his wife in their residence watching a taped broadcast of *The MacNeil/Lehrer NewsHour* when he heard the back-to-back explosions that signaled the destruction of President Habyarimana's plane. As the American ambassador, he was concerned primarily for American citizens, who, he feared, could be killed or injured in any outbreak of fighting. The United States made the decision to withdraw its personnel and nationals on April 7. Penned into his house, Rawson did not feel that his presence was of any use. Looking back, he says, "Did we have a moral responsibility to stay there? Would it have made a difference? I don't know, but the killings were taking place in broad daylight while we were there. I didn't feel that we were achieving much."

Still, about 300 Rwandans from the neighborhood had gathered at Rawson's residence seeking refuge, and when the Americans cleared out, the local people were left to their fates. Rawson recalls, "I told the people who were there that we were leaving and the flag was coming down, and they would have to make their own choice about what to do . . . Nobody really asked us to take them with us."

Rawson says he could not help even those who worked closest to him. His chief steward, who served dinner and washed dishes at the house, called the ambassador from his home and pleaded, "We're in terrible danger. Please come and get us." Rawson says, "I had to tell him, 'We can't move. We can't come.'" The steward and his wife were killed.

Assistant Secretary Moose was away from Washington, so Prudence Bushnell, the acting assistant secretary, was made the director of the task force that managed the Rwanda evacuation. Her focus, like Rawson's, was on the fate of U.S. citizens. "I felt very strongly that my first obligation was to the Americans," she recalls. "I was sorry about the Rwandans, of course, but my job was to get our folks out . . . Then again, people didn't know that it was a genocide. What I was told was 'Look, Pru, these people do this from time to time.' We thought we'd be right back."

At a State Department press conference on April 8 Bushnell made an appearance and spoke gravely about the mounting violence in Rwanda and the status of Americans there. After she left the podium, Michael McCurry, the department spokesman, took her place and criticized foreign governments for preventing the screening of the Steven Spielberg film *Schindler's List*. "This film movingly portrays . . . the twentieth century's most horrible catastrophe," he said. "And it shows that even in the midst of genocide, one individual can make a difference." No one made any connection between Bushnell's remarks and McCurry's. Neither journalists nor officials in the United States were focused on the Tutsi.

On April 9 and 10, in five different convoys, Ambassador Rawson and 250 Americans were evacuated from Kigali and other points. "When we left, the cars were stopped and searched," Rawson says. "It would have been impossible to get Tutsi through." All told, thirty-five local employees of the embassy were killed in the genocide.

Warren Christopher appeared on the NBC news program

Meet the Press the morning the evacuation was completed. "In the great tradition, the ambassador was in the last car," Christopher said proudly. "So that evacuation has gone very well." Christopher stressed that although U.S. Marines had been dispatched to Burundi, there were no plans to send them into Rwanda to restore order: they were in the region as a safety net, in case they were needed to assist in the evacuation. "It's always a sad moment when the Americans have to leave," he said, "but it was the prudent thing to do." The Republican Senate minority leader, Bob Dole, a spirited defender of Bosnia's besieged Muslims at the time, agreed. "I don't think we have any national interest there," Dole said on April 10. "The Americans are out, and as far as I'm concerned, in Rwanda, that ought to be the end of it."

Dallaire, too, had been ordered to make the evacuation of foreigners his priority. The UN Department of Peacekeeping Operations, which had rejected the field commander's proposed raid on arms caches in January, sent an explicit cable: "You should make every effort not to compromise your impartiality or to act beyond your mandate, but [you] may exercise your discretion to do [so] should this be essential for the evacuation of foreign nationals. This should not, repeat not, extend to participating in possible combat except in self-defense." Neutrality was essential. Avoiding combat was paramount, but Dallaire could make an exception for non-Rwandans.

While the United States evacuated overland without an American military escort, the Europeans sent troops to Rwanda so that their personnel could exit by air. On April 9 Dallaire watched covetously as just over a thousand French, Belgian, and Italian soldiers descended on Kigali Airport to begin evacuating their expatriates. These commandos were clean-shaven, well fed, and heavily armed, in marked contrast to Dallaire's exhausted, hungry, ragtag peacekeeping force. Within three days of the plane crash estimates of the number of dead in the capital already exceeded 10,000.

If the soldiers ferried in for the evacuation had teamed up with UNAMIR, Dallaire would have had a sizable deterrent force. At that point he commanded 440 Belgians, 942 Bangladeshis, 843 Ghanaians, 60 Tunisians, and 255 others from twenty countries. He could also call on a reserve of 800 Belgians in Nairobi. If the major powers had reconfigured the thousand-man European evacuation force and the U.S. Marines on standby in Burundi—who numbered 300—and contributed them to his mission, he would finally have had the numbers on his side. "Mass slaughter was happening, and suddenly there in Kigali we had the forces we needed to contain it, and maybe even to stop it," he recalls. "Yet they picked up their people and turned and walked away."

The consequences of the exclusive attention to foreigners were felt immediately. In the days after the plane crash some 2,000 Rwandans, including 400 children, had grouped at the Ecole Technique Officielle, under the protection of about ninety Belgian soldiers. Many of them were already suffering from machete wounds. They gathered in the classrooms and on the playing field outside the school. Rwandan government and militia forces lay in wait nearby, drinking beer and chanting, *"Pawa, pawa,"* for "Hutu power." On April 11 the Belgians were ordered to regroup at the airport to aid the evacuation of European civilians. Knowing they were trapped, several Rwandans pursued the jeeps, shouting, "Do not abandon us!" The UN soldiers shooed them away from their vehicles and fired warning shots over their heads. When the peacekeepers had gone out through one gate, Hutu militiamen entered through another, firing machine guns and throwing grenades. Most of the 2,000 gathered there were killed.

In the three days during which some 4,000 foreigners were evacuated, about 20,000 Rwandans were killed. After the American evacuees were safely out and the U.S. embassy had been closed, Bill and Hillary Clinton visited the people who had manned the emergency-operations room at the State Department and offered congratulations on a "job well done."

VII. Genocide? What Genocide?

Just when did Washington know of the sinister Hutu designs on Rwanda's Tutsi? Writing in *Foreign Affairs* last year, Alan Kuperman argued that President Clinton "could not have known that a nationwide genocide was under way" until about two weeks into the killing. It is true that the precise nature and extent of the slaughter was obscured by the civil war, the withdrawal of U.S. diplomatic sources, some confused press reporting, and the lies of the Rwandan government. Nonetheless, both the testimony of U.S. officials who worked the issue day to day and the declassified documents indicate that plenty was known about the killers' intentions.

A determination of genocide turns not on the numbers killed, which is always difficult to ascertain at a time of crisis, but on the perpetrators' intent: Were Hutu forces attempting to destroy Rwanda's Tutsi? The answer to this question was available early on. "By eight A.M. the morning after the plane crash we knew what was happening, that there was systematic killing of Tutsi," Joyce Leader recalls. "People were calling me and telling me who was getting killed. I knew they were going door to door." Back at the State Department she explained to her colleagues that three kinds of killing were going on: war, politically motivated murder, and genocide. Dallaire's early cables to New York likewise described the armed conflict that had resumed between rebels and government forces, and also stated plainly that savage "ethnic cleansing" of Tutsi was occurring. U.S. analysts warned that mass killings would increase. In an April 11 memo prepared for Frank Wisner, the undersecretary of defense for policy, in advance of a dinner with Henry Kissinger, a key talking point was "Unless both sides can be convinced to return to the peace process, a massive (hundreds of thousands of deaths) bloodbath will ensue."

Whatever the inevitable imperfections of U.S. intelligence early on, the reports from Rwanda were severe enough to distinguish Hutu killers from ordinary combatants in civil war. And they certainly warranted directing additional U.S. intelligence assets toward the region—to snap satellite photos of large gatherings of Rwandan civilians or of mass graves, to intercept military communications, or to infiltrate the country in person. Though there is no evidence that senior policymakers deployed such assets, routine intelligence continued to pour in. On April 26 an unattributed intelligence memo titled "Responsibility for Massacres in Rwanda" reported that the ringleaders of the genocide, Colonel Théoneste Bagosora and his crisis committee, were determined to liquidate their opposition and exterminate the Tutsi populace. A May 9 Defense Intelligence Agency report stated plainly that the Rwandan violence was not spontaneous but was directed by the government, with lists of victims prepared well in advance. The DIA observed that an "organized parallel effort of *genocide* [was] being implemented by the army to destroy the leadership of the Tutsi community."

From April 8 onward media coverage featured eyewitness accounts describing the widespread targeting of Tutsi and the corpses piling up on Kigali's streets. American reporters relayed stories of missionaries and embassy officials who had been unable to save their Rwandan friends and neighbors from death. On April 9 a front-page *Washington Post* story quoted reports that the Rwandan employees of the major international relief agencies had been executed "in front of horrified expatriate staffers." On April 10 a *New York Times* front-page article quoted the Red Cross claim that "tens of thousands" were dead, 8,000 in Kigali alone, and that corpses were "in the houses, in the streets, everywhere." The *Post* the same day led its front-page story with a description of "a pile of corpses six feet high" outside the main hospital. On April 14 *The New York Times* reported the shooting and hacking to death of nearly 1,200 men, women, and children in the church where they had sought refuge. On April 19 Human

Rights Watch, which had excellent sources on the ground in Rwanda, estimated the number of dead at 100,000 and called for use of the term "genocide." The 100,000 figure (which proved to be a gross underestimate) was picked up immediately by the Western media, endorsed by the Red Cross, and featured on the front page of *The Washington Post*. On April 24 the *Post* reported how "the heads and limbs of victims were sorted and piled neatly, a bone-chilling order in the midst of chaos that harked back to the Holocaust." President Clinton certainly could have known that a genocide was under way, if he had wanted to know.

Even after the reality of genocide in Rwanda had become irrefutable, when bodies were shown choking the Kagera River on the nightly news, the brute fact of the slaughter failed to influence U.S. policy except in a negative way. American officials, for a variety of reasons, shunned the use of what became known as "the g-word." They felt that using it would have obliged the United States to act, under the terms of the 1948 Genocide Convention. They also believed, understandably, that it would harm U.S. credibility to name the crime and then do nothing to stop it. A discussion paper on Rwanda, prepared by an official in the Office of the Secretary of Defense and dated May 1, testifies to the nature of official thinking. Regarding issues that might be brought up at the next interagency working group, it stated,

1. Genocide Investigation: Language that calls for an international investigation of human rights abuses and possible violations of the genocide convention. *Be Careful. Legal at State was worried about this yesterday—Genocide finding could commit [the U.S. government] to actually "do something"* [Emphasis added.]

At an interagency teleconference in late April, Susan Rice, a rising star on the NSC who worked under Richard Clarke, stunned a few of the officials present when she asked, "If we use the word 'genocide' and are seen as doing nothing, what will be the effect on the November [congressional] election?" Lieutenant Colonel Tony Marley remembers the incredulity of his colleagues at the State Department. "We could believe that people would wonder that," he says, "but not that they would actually voice it." Rice does not recall the incident but concedes, "If I said it, it was completely inappropriate, as well as irrelevant."

The genocide debate in U.S. government circles began the last week of April, but it was not until May 21, six weeks after the killing began, that Secretary Christopher gave his diplomats permission to use the term "genocide"—sort of. The UN Human Rights Commission was about to meet in special session, and the U.S. representative, Geraldine Ferraro, needed guidance on whether to join a resolution stating that genocide had occurred. The stubborn U.S. stand had become untenable internationally.

The case for a label of genocide was straightforward, according to a May 18 confidential analysis prepared by the State Department's assistant secretary for intelligence and research, Toby Gati: lists of Tutsi victims' names and addresses had reportedly been prepared; Rwandan government troops and Hutu militia and youth squads were the main perpetrators; massacres were reported all over the country; humanitarian agencies were now "claiming from 200,000 to 500,000 lives" lost. Gati offered the intelligence bureau's view: "We believe 500,000 may be an exaggerated estimate, but no accurate figures are available. Systematic killings began within hours of Habyarimana's death. Most of those killed have been Tutsi civilians, including women and children." The terms of the Genocide Convention had been met. "We weren't quibbling about these numbers," Gati says. "We can never know precise figures, but our analysts had been reporting huge numbers of deaths for weeks. We were basically saying, 'A rose by any other name . . .'"

Despite this straightforward assessment, Christopher remained reluctant to speak the obvious truth. When he issued his guidance, on May 21, fully a month after Human Rights Watch had put a name to the tragedy, Christopher's instructions were hopelessly muddied.

> The delegation is authorized to agree to a resolution that states that "acts of genocide" have occurred in Rwanda or that "genocide has occurred in Rwanda." Other formulations that suggest that some, but not all of the killings in Rwanda are genocide . . . e.g. "genocide is taking place in Rwanda"—are authorized. Delegation is not authorized to agree to the characterization of any specific incident as genocide or to agree to any formulation that indicates that all killings in Rwanda are genocide.

Notably, Christopher confined permission to acknowledge full-fledged genocide to the upcoming session of the Human Rights Commission. Outside that venue State Department officials were authorized to state publicly only that *acts* of genocide had occurred.

Christine Shelly, a State Department spokesperson, had long been charged with publicly articulating the U.S. position on whether events in Rwanda counted as genocide. For two months she had avoided the term, and as her June 10 exchange with the Reuters correspondent Alan Elsner reveals, her semantic dance continued.

Elsner: How would you describe the events taking place in Rwanda?

Shelly: Based on the evidence we have seen from observations on the ground, we have every reason to believe that acts of genocide have occurred in Rwanda.

Elsner: What's the difference between "acts of genocide" and "genocide"?

Shelly: Well, I think the—as you know, there's a legal definition of this . . . clearly not all of the killings that have
taken place in Rwanda are killings to which you
might apply that label . . . But as to the distinctions
between the words, we're trying to call what we have
seen so far as best as we can; and based, again, on the
evidence, we have every reason to believe that acts of
genocide have occurred.

Elsner: How many acts of genocide does it take to make
genocide?

Shelly: Alan, that's just not a question that I'm in a position
to answer.

The same day, in Istanbul, Warren Christopher, by then under
severe internal and external pressure, relented: "If there is any
particular magic in calling it genocide, I have no hesitancy in
saying that."

VIII. "Not Even a Sideshow"

Once the Americans had been evacuated, Rwanda largely
dropped off the radar of most senior Clinton Administration
officials. In the situation room on the seventh floor of the State
Department a map of Rwanda had been hurriedly pinned to the
wall in the aftermath of the plane crash, and eight banks of
phones had rung off the hook. Now, with U.S. citizens safely
home, the State Department chaired a daily interagency meeting,
often by teleconference, designed to coordinate mid-level diplomatic and humanitarian responses. Cabinet-level officials
focused on crises elsewhere. Anthony Lake recalls, "I was obsessed
with Haiti and Bosnia during that period, so Rwanda was, in
William Shawcross's words, a 'sideshow,' but not even a
sideshow—a no-show." At the NSC the person who managed

Rwanda policy was not Lake, the national-security adviser, who happened to know Africa, but Richard Clarke, who oversaw peacekeeping policy, and for whom the news from Rwanda only confirmed a deep skepticism about the viability of UN deployments. Clarke believed that another UN failure could doom relations between Congress and the United Nations. He also sought to shield the President from congressional and public criticism. Donald Steinberg managed the Africa portfolio at the NSC and tried to look out for the dying Rwandans, but he was not an experienced infighter and, colleagues say, he "never won a single argument" with Clarke.

The Americans who wanted the United States to do the most were those who knew Rwanda best. Joyce Leader, Rawson's deputy in Rwanda, had been the one to close and lock the doors to the U.S. embassy. When she returned to Washington, she was given a small room in a back office and told to prepare the State Department's daily Rwanda summaries, drawing on press and U.S. intelligence reports. Incredibly, despite her expertise and her contacts in Rwanda, she was rarely consulted and was instructed not to deal directly with her sources in Kigali. Once, an NSC staffer did call to ask, "Short of sending in the troops, what is to be done?" Leader's response, unwelcome, was "Send in the troops." Throughout the U.S. government Africa specialists had the least clout of all regional specialists and the smallest chance of effecting policy outcomes. In contrast, those with the most pull in the bureaucracy had never visited Rwanda or met any Rwandans. They spoke analytically of "national interests" or even "humanitarian consequences" without appearing gripped by the unfolding human tragedy. The dearth of country or regional expertise in the senior circles of government not only reduces the capacity of officers to assess the "news." It also increases the likelihood—a dynamic identified by Lake in his 1971 *Foreign Policy* article— that killings will become abstractions. "Ethnic bloodshed" in Africa was thought to be regrettable but not particularly unusual.

As it happened, when the crisis began, President Clinton himself had a coincidental and personal connection with the country. At a coffee at the White House in December of 1993 Clinton had met Monique Mujawamariya, the Rwandan human-rights activist. He had been struck by the courage of a woman who still bore facial scars from an automobile accident that had been arranged to curb her activities. Clinton had singled her out, saying, "Your courage is an inspiration to all of us." On April 8, two days after the onset of the killing, *The Washington Post* published a letter that Alison Des Forges had sent to Human Rights Watch after Mujawamariya had hung up the phone to face her fate. "I believe Monique was killed at 6:30 this morning," Des Forges had written. "I have virtually no hope that she is still alive, but will continue to try for more information. In the meantime . . . please inform everyone who will care." Word of Mujawamariya's disappearance got the President's attention, and he inquired about her whereabouts repeatedly. "I can't tell you how much time we spent trying to find Monique," one U.S. official remembers. "Sometimes it felt as though she was the only Rwandan in danger." Miraculously, Mujawamariya had not been killed—she had hidden in the rafters of her home after hanging up with Des Forges, and eventually managed to talk and bribe her way to safety. She was evacuated to Belgium, and on April 18 she joined Des Forges in the United States, where the pair began lobbying the Clinton Administration on behalf of those left behind. With Mujawamariya's rescue, reported in detail in the *Post* and *The New York Times,* the President apparently lost his personal interest in events in Rwanda.

During the entire three months of the genocide Clinton never assembled his top policy advisers to discuss the killings. Anthony Lake likewise never gathered the "principals"—the Cabinet-level members of the foreign-policy team. Rwanda was never thought to warrant its own top-level meeting. When the subject came up, it did so along with, and subordinate to, discussions of Somalia,

Haiti, and Bosnia. Whereas these crises involved U.S. personnel and stirred some public interest, Rwanda generated no sense of urgency and could safely be avoided by Clinton at no political cost. The editorial boards of the major American newspapers discouraged U.S. intervention during the genocide. They, like the Administration, lamented the killings but believed, in the words of an April 17 *Washington Post* editorial, "The United States has no recognizable national interest in taking a role, certainly not a leading role." Capitol Hill was quiet. Some in Congress were glad to be free of the expense of another flawed UN mission. Others, including a few members of the Africa subcommittees and the Congressional Black Caucus, eventually appealed tamely for the United States to play a role in ending the violence—but again, they did not dare urge U.S. involvement on the ground, and they did not kick up a public fuss. Members of Congress weren't hearing from their constituents. Pat Schroeder, of Colorado, said on April 30, "There are some groups terribly concerned about the gorillas . . . But—it sounds terrible—people just don't know what can be done about the people." Randall Robinson, of the nongovernmental organization TransAfrica, was preoccupied, staging a hunger strike to protest the U.S. repatriation of Haitian refugees. Human Rights Watch supplied exemplary intelligence and established important one-on-one contacts in the Administration, but the organization lacks a grassroots base from which to mobilize a broader segment of American society.

IX. The UN Withdrawal

When the killing began, Romeo Dallaire expected and appealed for reinforcements. Within hours of the plane crash he had cabled UN headquarters in New York: "Give me the means and I can do more." He was sending peacekeepers on rescue missions around the city, and he felt it was essential to increase the size and improve the quality of the UN's presence. But the United States opposed the idea of sending reinforcements, no matter where they were from. The fear, articulated mainly at the Pentagon but felt throughout the bureaucracy, was that what would start as a small engagement by foreign troops would end as a large and costly one by Americans. This was the lesson of Somalia, where U.S. troops had gotten into trouble in an effort to bail out the beleaguered Pakistanis. The logical outgrowth of this fear was an effort to steer clear of Rwanda entirely and be sure others did the same. Only by yanking Dallaire's entire peace-keeping force could the United States protect itself from involvement down the road.

One senior U.S. official remembers, "When the reports of the deaths of the ten Belgians came in, it was clear that it was Somalia redux, and the sense was that there would be an expectation everywhere that the U.S. would get involved. We thought leaving the peacekeepers in Rwanda and having them confront the violence would take us where we'd been before. It was a foregone conclusion that the United States wouldn't intervene and that the concept of UN peacekeeping could not be sacrificed again."

A foregone conclusion. What is most remarkable about the American response to the Rwandan genocide is not so much the absence of U.S. military action as that during the entire genocide the possibility of U.S. military intervention was never even debated. Indeed, the United States resisted intervention of any kind.

The bodies of the slain Belgian soldiers were returned to Brussels on April 14. One of the pivotal conversations in the course of the genocide took place around that time, when Willie Claes, the Belgian Foreign Minister, called the State Department to request "cover." "We are pulling out, but we don't want to be seen to be doing it alone," Claes said, asking the Americans to support a full UN withdrawal. Dallaire had not anticipated that Belgium would extract its soldiers, removing the backbone of his mission and stranding Rwandans in their hour of greatest need. "I expected the ex-colonial white countries would stick it out even if they took casualties," he remembers. "I thought their pride would have led them to stay to try to sort the place out. The Belgian decision caught me totally off guard. I was truly stunned."

Belgium did not want to leave ignominiously, by itself. Warren Christopher agreed to back Belgian requests for a full UN exit. Policy over the next month or so can be described simply: no U.S. military intervention, robust demands for a withdrawal of all of Dallaire's forces, and no support for a new UN mission that would challenge the killers. Belgium had the cover it needed.

On April 15 Christopher sent one of the most forceful documents to be produced in the entire three months of the genocide to Madeleine Albright at the UN—a cable instructing her to demand a full UN withdrawal. The cable, which was heavily influenced by Richard Clarke at the NSC, and which bypassed Donald Steinberg and was never seen by Anthony Lake, was unequivocal about the next steps. Saying that he had "fully" taken into account the "humanitarian reasons put forth for retention of UNAMIR elements in Rwanda," Christopher wrote that there was "insufficient justification" to retain a UN presence.

> The international community must give highest priority to full, orderly withdrawal of all UNAMIR personnel as soon as possible . . . We will oppose any effort at this time to preserve a UNAMIR presence in Rwanda . . . Our opposition to retaining a UNAMIR presence in Rwanda is firm. It is based on our conviction that the Security Council has an obligation to ensure that peacekeeping operations are viable, that they are capable of fulfilling their mandates, and that UN peacekeeping personnel are not placed or retained, knowingly, in an untenable situation.

"Once we knew the Belgians were leaving, we were left with a rump mission incapable of doing anything to help people," Clarke remembers. "They were doing nothing to stop the killings."

But Clarke underestimated the deterrent effect that Dallaire's very few peacekeepers were having. Although some soldiers hunkered down, terrified, others scoured Kigali, rescuing Tutsi, and later established defensive positions in the city, opening their doors to the fortunate Tutsi who made it through roadblocks to reach them. One Senegalese captain saved a hundred or so lives single-handedly. Some 25,000 Rwandans eventually assembled at positions manned by UNAMIR personnel. The Hutu were generally reluctant to massacre large groups of Tutsi if foreigners (armed or unarmed) were present. It did not take many UN soldiers to dissuade the Hutu from attacking. At the Hotel des Mille Collines ten peacekeepers and four UN military observers helped to protect the several hundred civilians sheltered there for the duration of the crisis. About 10,000 Rwandans gathered at the Amohoro Stadium under light UN cover. Brent Beardsley, Dallaire's executive assistant, remembers, "If there was any determined resistance at close quarters, the government guys tended to back off." Kevin Aiston, the Rwanda desk officer at the State Department, was keeping track of Rwandan civilians under UN protection. When Prudence Bushnell told him of the U.S. decision to demand a UNAMIR withdrawal, he turned pale. "We can't," he said. Bushnell replied, "The train has already left the station."

On April 19 the Belgian Colonel Luc Marchal delivered his final salute and departed with the last of his soldiers. The Belgian withdrawal reduced Dallaire's troop strength to 2,100. More crucially, he lost his best troops. Command and control among Dallaire's remaining forces became tenuous. Dallaire soon lost every line of communication to the countryside. He had only a single satellite phone link to the outside world.

The UN Security Council now made a decision that sealed the Tutsi's fate and signaled the militia that it would have free rein. The U.S. demand for a full UN withdrawal had been opposed by some African nations, and even by Madeleine Albright; so the United States lobbied instead for a dramatic drawdown in troop strength. On April 21, amid press reports of some 100,000 dead in Rwanda, the Security Council voted to slash UNAMIR's forces to 270 men. Albright went along, publicly declaring that a "small, skeletal" operation would be left in Kigali to "show the will of the international community."

After the UN vote Clarke sent a memorandum to Lake reporting that language about "the safety and security of Rwandans under UN protection had been inserted by US/UN at the end of the day to prevent an otherwise unanimous UNSC from walking away from the at-risk Rwandans under UN protection as the peacekeepers drew down to 270." In other words, the memorandum suggested that the United States was *leading* efforts to ensure that the Rwandans under UN protection were not abandoned. The opposite was true.

Most of Dallaire's troops were evacuated by April 25. Though he was supposed to reduce the size of his force to 270, he ended up keeping 503 peacekeepers. By this time Dallaire was trying to deal with a bloody frenzy. "My force was standing knee-deep in mutilated bodies, surrounded by the guttural moans of dying people, looking into the eyes of children bleeding to death with their wounds burning in the sun and being invaded by maggots and flies," he later wrote. "I found myself walking through villages where the only sign of life was a goat, or a chicken, or a songbird, as all the people were dead, their bodies being eaten by voracious packs of wild dogs."

Dallaire had to work within narrow limits. He attempted simply to keep the positions he held and to protect the 25,000 Rwandans under UN supervision while hoping that the member states on the Security Council would change their minds and send him some help while it still mattered.

By coincidence Rwanda held one of the rotating seats on the Security Council at the time of the genocide. Neither the United States nor any other UN member state ever suggested that the representative of the genocidal government be expelled from the council. Nor did any Security Council country offer to provide safe haven to Rwandan refugees who escaped the carnage. In one instance Dallaire's forces succeeded in evacuating a group of Rwandans by plane to Kenya. The Nairobi authorities allowed the plane to land, sequestered it in a hangar, and, echoing the American decision to turn back the *S.S. St. Louis* during the Holocaust, then forced the plane to return to Rwanda. The fate of the passengers is unknown.

Throughout this period the Clinton Administration was largely silent. The closest it came to a public denunciation of the Rwandan government occurred after personal lobbying by Human Rights Watch, when Anthony Lake issued a statement calling on Rwandan military leaders by name to "do everything in their power to end the violence immediately." When I spoke with Lake six years later, and informed him that human-rights groups and U.S. officials point to this statement as the sum total of official public attempts to shame the Rwandan government in this period, he seemed stunned. "You're kidding," he said. "That's truly pathetic."

At the State Department the diplomacy was conducted privately, by telephone. Prudence Bushnell regularly set her alarm for 2:00 A.M. and phoned Rwandan government officials. She spoke several times with Augustin Bizimungu, the Rwandan military chief of staff. "These were the most bizarre phone calls," she says. "He spoke in perfectly charming French. 'Oh, it's so nice to hear from you,' he said. I told him, 'I am calling to tell you President Clinton is going to hold you accountable for the killings.' He said, 'Oh, how nice it is that your President is thinking of me.'"

X. The Pentagon "Chop"

The daily meeting of the Rwanda interagency working group was attended, either in person or by teleconference, by representatives from the various State Department bureaus, the Pentagon, the National Security Council, and the intelligence community. Any proposal that originated in the working group had to survive the Pentagon "chop." "Hard intervention," meaning U.S. military action, was obviously out of the question. But Pentagon officials routinely stymied initiatives for "soft intervention" as well.

The Pentagon discussion paper on Rwanda, referred to earlier, ran down a list of the working group's six short-term policy objectives and carped at most of them. The fear of a slippery slope was persuasive. Next to the seemingly innocuous suggestion that the United States "support the UN and others in attempts to achieve a cease-fire" the Pentagon official responded, "Need to change 'attempts' to 'political efforts'—without 'political' there is a danger of signing up to troop contributions."

The one policy move the Defense Department supported was a U.S. effort to achieve an arms embargo. But the same discussion paper acknowledged the ineffectiveness of this step: "We do not envision it will have a significant impact on the killings because machetes, knives and other hand implements have been the most common weapons."

Dallaire never spoke to Bushnell or to Tony Marley, the U.S. military liaison to the Arusha process, during the genocide, but they all reached the same conclusions. Seeing that no troops were forthcoming, they turned their attention to measures short of full-scale deployment which might alleviate the suffering. Dallaire pleaded with New York, and Bushnell and her team recommended in Washington, that something be done to "neutralize" Radio Mille Collines.

The country best equipped to prevent the genocide planners from broadcasting murderous instructions directly to the population was the United States. Marley offered three possibilities. The United States could destroy the antenna. It could transmit "counter-broadcasts" urging perpetrators to stop the genocide. Or it could jam the hate radio station's broadcasts. This could have been done from an airborne platform such as the Air Force's Commando Solo airplane. Anthony Lake raised the matter with Secretary of Defense William Perry at the end of April. Pentagon officials considered all the proposals non-starters. On May 5 Frank Wisner, the undersecretary of defense for policy, prepared a memo for Sandy Berger, then the deputy national-security adviser. Wisner's memo testifies to the unwillingness of the U.S. government to make even financial sacrifices to diminish the killing.

> We have looked at options to stop the broadcasts within the Pentagon, discussed them interagency and concluded jamming is an ineffective and expensive mechanism that will not accomplish the objective the NSC Advisor seeks.
>
> International legal conventions complicate airborne or ground based jamming and the mountainous terrain reduces the effectiveness of either option. Commando Solo, an Air National Guard asset, is the only suitable DOD jamming platform. It costs approximately $8500 per flight hour and requires a semi-secure area of operations due to its vulnerability and limited self-protection.
>
> I believe it would be wiser to use air to assist in Rwanda in the [food] relief effort . . .

The plane would have needed to remain in Rwandan airspace while it waited for radio transmissions to begin. "First we would have had to figure out whether it made sense to use Commando Solo," Wisner recalls. "Then we had to get it from where it was already and be sure it could be moved. Then we would have needed flight clearance from all the countries nearby. And then we would need the political go-ahead. By the time we got all this, weeks would have passed. And it was not going to solve the fundamental problem, which was one that needed to be addressed militarily." Pentagon planners understood that stopping the genocide required a military solution. Neither they nor the White House wanted any part in a military solution. Yet instead of undertaking other forms of intervention that might have at least saved some lives, they justified inaction by arguing that a military solution was required.

Whatever the limitations of radio jamming, which clearly would have been no panacea, most of the delays Wisner cites could have been avoided if senior Administration officials had followed through. But Rwanda was not their problem. Instead justifications for standing by abounded. In early May the State Department Legal Advisor's Office issued a finding against radio jamming, citing international broadcasting agreements and the American commitment to free speech. When Bushnell raised radio jamming yet again at a meeting, one Pentagon official chided her for naiveté: "Pru, radios don't kill people. *People* kill people!"

The Defense Department was disdainful both of the policy ideas being circulated at the working-group meetings and, memos indicate, of the people circulating them. A memo by one Defense Department aide observed that the State Department's Africa bureau had received a phone call from a Kigali hotel owner who said that his hotel and the civilians inside were about to be attacked. The memo snidely reported that the Africa bureau's proposed "solution" was "Pru Bushnell will call the [Rwandan] military and tell them we will hold them personally responsible if anything happens (!)." (In fact the hotel owner, who survived the genocide, later acknowledged that phone calls from Washington played a key role in dissuading the killers from massacring the inhabitants of the hotel.)

However significant and obstructionist the role of the Pentagon in April and May, Defense Department officials were stepping into a vacuum. As one U.S. official put it, "Look, nobody senior was paying any attention to this mess. And in the absence of any political leadership from the top, when you have one group that feels pretty strongly about what *shouldn't* be done, it is extremely likely they are going to end up shaping U.S. policy." Lieutenant General Wesley Clark looked to the White House for leadership. "The Pentagon is always going to be the last to want to intervene," he says. "It is up to the civilians to tell us they want to do something and we'll figure out how to do it."

But with no powerful personalities or high-ranking officials arguing forcefully for meaningful action, mid-level Pentagon officials held sway, vetoing or stalling on hesitant proposals put forward by mid-level State Department or NSC officials. If Pentagon objections were to be overcome, the President, Secretary Christopher, Secretary Perry, or Anthony Lake would have to step forward to "own" the problem, which did not happen.

The deck was stacked against Rwandans who were hiding wherever they could and praying for rescue. The American public expressed no interest in Rwanda, and the crisis was treated as a civil war requiring a cease-fire or as a "peacekeeping problem" requiring a UN withdrawal. It was not treated as a genocide demanding instant action. The top policymakers trusted that their subordinates were doing all they could do, while the subordinates worked with an extremely narrow understanding of what the United States *would* do.

XI. PDD-25 in Action

No sooner had most of Dallaire's forces been withdrawn, in late April, than a handful of nonpermanent members of the Security Council, aghast at the scale of the slaughter, pressed the major powers to send a new, beefed-up force (UNAMIR II) to Rwanda.

When Dallaire's troops had first arrived, in the fall of 1993, they had done so under a fairly traditional peacekeeping mandate known as a Chapter VI deployment—a mission that assumes a cease-fire and a desire on both sides to comply with a peace accord. The Security Council now had to decide whether it was prepared to move from peacekeeping to peace *enforcement*—that is, to a Chapter VII mission in a hostile environment. This would demand more peacekeepers with far greater resources, more-aggressive rules of engagement, and an explicit recognition that the UN soldiers were there to protect civilians.

Two proposals emerged. Dallaire submitted a plan that called for joining his remaining peacekeepers with about 5,000 well-armed soldiers he hoped could be gathered quickly by the Security Council. He wanted to secure Kigali and then fan outward to create safe havens for Rwandans who had gathered in large numbers at churches and schools and on hillsides around the country. The United States was one of the few countries that could supply the rapid airlift and logistic support needed to move reinforcements to the region. In a meeting with UN Secretary General Boutros Boutros-Ghali on May 10, Vice President Al Gore pledged U.S. help with transport.

Richard Clarke, at the NSC, and representatives of the Joint Chiefs challenged Dallaire's plan. "How do you plan to take control of the airport in Kigali so that the reinforcements will be able to land?" Clarke asked. He argued instead for an "outside-in" strategy, as opposed to Dallaire's "inside-out" approach. The U.S. proposal would have created protected zones for refugees at Rwanda's borders. It would have kept any U.S. pilots involved in airlifting the peacekeepers safely out of Rwanda. "Our proposal was the most feasible, doable thing that could have been done in the short term," Clarke insists. Dallaire's proposal, in contrast, "could not be done in the short term and could not attract peacekeepers." The U.S. plan—which was modeled on Operation Provide Comfort, for the Kurds of northern Iraq—seemed to assume that the people in need were refugees fleeing to the border, but most endangered Tutsi could not make it to the border. The most vulnerable Rwandans were those clustered together, awaiting salvation, deep inside Rwanda. Dallaire's plan would have had UN soldiers move to the Tutsi in hiding. The U.S. plan would have required civilians to move to the safe zones, negotiating murderous roadblocks on the way. "The two plans had very different objectives," Dallaire says. "My mission was to save Rwandans. Their mission was to put on a show at no risk."

America's new peacekeeping doctrine, of which Clarke was the primary architect, was unveiled on May 3, and U.S. officials applied its criteria zealously. PDD-25 did not merely circumscribe U.S. participation in UN missions; it also limited U.S. support for other states that hoped to carry out UN missions. Before such missions could garner U.S. approval, policymakers had to answer certain questions: Were U.S. interests at stake? Was there a threat to world peace? A clear mission goal? Acceptable costs? Congressional, public, and allied support? A working cease-fire? A clear command-and-control arrangement? And, finally, what was the exit strategy?

The United States haggled at the Security Council and with the UN Department of Peacekeeping Operations for the first two weeks of May. U.S. officials pointed to the flaws in Dallaire's proposal without offering the resources that would have helped him to overcome them. On May 13 Deputy Secretary of State Strobe Talbott sent Madeleine Albright instructions on how the United States should respond to Dallaire's plan. Noting the logistic hazards of airlifting troops into the capital, Talbott wrote, "The U.S. is not prepared at this point to lift heavy equipment and troops into Kigali." The "more manageable" operation would be to create the protected zones at the border, secure humanitarian-aid deliveries, and "promot[e] restoration of a ceasefire and return to the Arusha Peace Process." Talbott acknowledged that even the minimalist American proposal contained "many unanswered questions":

> Where will the needed forces come from; how will they be
> transported . . . where precisely should these safe zones be
> created; . . . would UN forces be authorized to move out of
> the zones to assist affected populations not in the zones . . .
> will the fighting parties in Rwanda agree to this arrange-
> ment . . . what conditions would need to obtain for the
> operation to end successfully?

Nonetheless, Talbott concluded, "We would urge the UN to
explore and refine this alternative and present the Council with a
menu of at least two options in a formal report from the [Secre-
tary General] along with cost estimates before the Security
Council votes on changing UNAMIR's mandate." U.S. policymakers were asking valid questions. Dallaire's plan certainly
would have required the intervening troops to take risks in an
effort to reach the targeted Rwandan or to confront the Hutu
militia and government forces. But the business-as-usual tone of
the American inquiry did not seem appropriate to the unprecedented and utterly unconventional crisis that was under way.

On May 17, by which time most of the Tutsi victims of the
genocide were already dead, the United States finally acceded to a
version of Dallaire's plan. However, few African countries
stepped forward to offer troops. Even if troops had been immediately available, the lethargy of the major powers would have
hindered their use. Though the Administration had committed
the United States to provide armored support if the African
nations provided soldiers, Pentagon stalling resumed. On May
19 the UN formally requested fifty American armored personnel
carriers. On May 31 the United States agreed to send the APCs
from Germany to Entebbe, Uganda. But squabbles between the
Pentagon and UN planners arose. Who would pay for the vehicles? Should the vehicles be tracked or wheeled? Would the UN
buy them or simply lease them? And who would pay the ship-
ping costs? Compounding the disputes was the fact that Depart-

ment of Defense regulations prevented the U.S. Army from preparing the vehicles for transport until contracts had been signed. The Defense Department demanded that it be reimbursed $15 million for shipping spare parts and equipment to and from Rwanda. In mid-June the White House finally intervened. On June 19, a month after the UN request, the United States began transporting the APCs, but they were missing the radios and heavy machine guns that would be needed if UN troops came under fire. By the time the APCs arrived, the genocide was over—halted by Rwandan Patriotic Front forces under the command of the Tutsi leader, Paul Kagame.

XII. The Stories We Tell

It is not hard to conceive of how the United States might have done things differently. Ahead of the plane crash, as violence escalated, it could have agreed to Belgian pleas for UN reinforcements. Once the killing of thousands of Rwandans a day had begun, the President could have deployed U.S. troops to Rwanda. The United States could have joined Dallaire's beleaguered UNAMIR forces or, if it feared associating with shoddy UN peacekeeping, it could have intervened unilaterally with the Security Council's backing, as France eventually did in late June. The United States could also have acted without the UN's blessing, as it did five years later in Kosovo. Securing congressional support for U.S. intervention would have been extremely difficult, but by the second week of the killing Clinton could have made the case that something approximating genocide was under way, that a supreme American value was imperiled by its occurrence, and that U.S. contingents at relatively low risk could stop the extermination of a people.

Alan Kuperman wrote in *Foreign Affairs* that President Clinton was in the dark for two weeks; by the time a large U.S. force could deploy, it would not have saved "even half of the ultimate victims." The evidence indicates that the killers' intentions were known by mid-level officials and knowable by their bosses within a week of the plane crash. Any failure to fully appreciate the genocide stemmed from political, moral, and imaginative weaknesses, not informational ones. As for what force could have accomplished, Kuperman's claims are purely speculative. We cannot know how the announcement of a robust or even a limited U.S. deployment would have affected the perpetrators' behavior. It is worth noting that even Kuperman concedes that belated intervention would have saved 75,000 to 125,000—no small achievement. A more serious challenge comes from the U.S. officials who argue that no amount of leadership from the White House would have overcome congressional opposition to sending U.S. troops to Africa. But even if that highly debatable point was true, the United States still had a variety of options. Instead of leaving it to mid-level officials to communicate with the Rwandan leadership behind the scenes, senior officials in the Administration could have taken control of the process. They could have publicly and frequently denounced the slaughter. They could have branded the crimes "genocide" at a far earlier stage. They could have called for the expulsion of the Rwandan delegation from the Security Council. On the telephone, at the UN, and on the Voice of America they could have threatened to prosecute those complicit in the genocide, naming names when possible. They could have deployed Pentagon assets to jam— even temporarily—the crucial, deadly radio broadcasts.

Instead of demanding a UN withdrawal, quibbling over costs, and coming forward (belatedly) with a plan better suited to caring for refugees than to stopping massacres, U.S. officials could have worked to make UNAMIR a force to contend with. They could have urged their Belgian allies to stay and protect Rwandan civilians. If the Belgians insisted on withdrawing, the White House could have done everything within its power to make sure that Dallaire was immediately reinforced. Senior officials could have spent U.S. political capital rallying troops from other nations and could have supplied strategic airlift and logistic support to a coalition that it had helped to create. In short, the United States could have led the world.

Why did none of these things happen? One reason is that all possible sources of pressure—U.S. allies, Congress, editorial boards, and the American people—were mute when it mattered for Rwanda. American leaders have a circular and deliberate relationship to public opinion. It is circular because public opinion is rarely if ever aroused by foreign crises, even genocidal ones, in the absence of political leadership, and yet at the same time, American leaders continually cite the absence of public support as grounds for inaction. The relationship is deliberate because American leadership is not absent in such circumstances: it was present regarding Rwanda, but devoted mainly to suppressing public outrage and thwarting UN initiatives so as to avoid acting.

Strikingly, most officials involved in shaping U.S. policy were able to define the decision not to stop genocide as ethical and moral. The Administration employed several devices to keep down enthusiasm for action and to preserve the public's sense—and, more important, its own—that U.S. policy choices were not merely politically astute but also morally acceptable. First, Administration officials exaggerated the extremity of the possible responses. Time and again U.S. leaders posed the choice as between staying out of Rwanda and "getting involved everywhere." In addition, they often presented the choice as one between doing nothing and sending in the Marines. On May 25, at the Naval Academy graduation ceremony, Clinton described America's relationship to ethnic trouble spots: "We cannot turn away from them, but our interests are not sufficiently at stake in so many of them to justify a commitment of our folks."

Second, Administration policymakers appealed to notions of

the greater good. They did not simply frame U.S. policy as one contrived in order to advance the national interest or avoid U.S. casualties. Rather, they often argued against intervention from the standpoint of people committed to protecting human life. Owing to recent failures in UN peacekeeping, many humanitarian interventionists in the U.S. government were concerned about the future of America's relationship with the United Nations generally and peacekeeping specifically. They believed that the UN and humanitarianism could not afford another Somalia. Many internalized the belief that the UN had more to lose by sending reinforcements and failing than by allowing the killings to proceed. Their chief priority, after the evacuation of the Americans, was looking after UN peacekeepers, and they justified the withdrawal of the peacekeepers on the grounds that it would ensure a future for humanitarian intervention. In other words, Dallaire's peacekeeping mission in Rwanda had to be destroyed so that peacekeeping might be saved for use elsewhere.

A third feature of the response that helped to console U.S. officials at the time was the sheer flurry of Rwanda-related activity. U.S. officials with a special concern for Rwanda took their solace from mini-victories—working on behalf of specific individuals or groups (Monique Mujawamariya; the Rwandans gathered at the hotel). Government officials involved in policy met constantly and remained "seized of the matter"; they neither appeared nor felt indifferent. Although little in the way of effective intervention emerged from mid-level meetings in Washington or New York, an abundance of memoranda and other documents did.

Finally, the almost willful delusion that what was happening in Rwanda did not amount to genocide created a nurturing ethical framework for inaction. "War" was "tragic" but created no moral imperative.

What is most frightening about this story is that it testifies to a system that in effect worked. President Clinton and his advisers had several aims. First, they wanted to avoid engagement in a conflict that posed little threat to American interests, narrowly defined. Second, they sought to appease a restless Congress by showing that they were cautious in their approach to peacekeeping. And third, they hoped to contain the political costs and avoid the moral stigma associated with allowing genocide. By and large, they achieved all three objectives. The normal operations of the foreign-policy bureaucracy and the international community permitted an illusion of continual deliberation, complex activity, and intense concern, even as Rwandans were left to die.

One U.S. official kept a journal during the crisis. In late May, exasperated by the obstructionism pervading the bureaucracy, the official dashed off this lament:

A military that wants to go nowhere to do anything—or let go of their toys so someone else can do it. A White House cowed by the brass (and we are to give lessons on how the armed forces take orders from civilians?). An NSC that does peacekeeping by the book—the accounting book, that is. And an assistance program that prefers whites (Europe) to blacks. When it comes to human rights we have no problem drawing the line in the sand of the dark continent (just don't ask us to *do* anything—agonizing is our specialty), but not China or anyplace else business looks good.

We have a foreign policy based on our amoral economic interests run by amateurs who want to stand for something—hence the agony—but ultimately don't want to exercise any leadership that has a cost.

They say there may be as many as a million massacred in Rwanda. The militias continue to slay the innocent and the educated . . . Has it really cost the United States nothing?

XIII. A Continuum of Guilt

Because this is a story of nondecisions and bureaucratic business as usual, few Americans are haunted by the memory of what they did in response to genocide in Rwanda. Most senior officials remember only fleeting encounters with the topic while the killings were taking place. The more reflective among them puzzle occasionally over how developments that cast the darkest shadow over the Clinton Administration's foreign-policy record could have barely registered at the time. But most say they have not talked in any detail among themselves about the events or about the system's weaknesses (and perverse strengths). Requests for a congressional investigation have gone ignored.

According to several advisers, toward the end of his term of office Clinton himself snapped at members of his foreign-policy team, angry with them for not steering him toward a moral course. He is said to have convinced himself that if he had known more, he would have done more. In his 1998 remarks in Kigali he pledged to "strengthen our ability to prevent, and if necessary to stop, genocide." "Never again," he declared, "must we be shy in the face of evidence." But the incentive structures within the U.S. government have not changed. Officials will still suffer no sanction if they do nothing to curb atrocities. The national interest remains narrowly constructed to exclude stopping genocide. Indeed, George W. Bush has been open about his intention to keep U.S. troops away from any future Rwandas. "I don't like genocide," Bush said in January of 2000. "But I would not commit our troops." Officials in the Bush Administration say the United States is as unprepared and unwilling to stop genocide today as it was seven years ago. "Genocide could happen again tomorrow," one said, "and we wouldn't respond any differently."

Anthony Lake, who used to call himself "the national-security adviser to the free world," today teaches international relations at Georgetown University. He wonders, as he should, how he and his colleagues could have done so little at the time of the Rwandan genocide. Much of Lake's identity remains entwined with the ideas in his 1971 *Foreign Policy* article. He cannot quite understand how a White House that, he insists, was finally sensitive to the "human reality of realpolitik" could have stood by during one of the gravest crimes of the twentieth century. "One scenario is that I knew what was going on and I blocked it out in order to not deal with the human consequences," he says. "Here I'm absolutely convinced that I didn't do that, but maybe I did and it was so deep that I didn't realize it. Another scenario is that I didn't give it enough time because I didn't give a damn about Africa, which I don't believe because I know I do. My sin must have been in a third scenario. I didn't own it because I was busy with Bosnia and Haiti, or because I thought we were doing all we could . . ."

Lake is further confounded by his slow processing of the moral stakes of the genocide. After the Rwandan Patriotic Front seized control, in July, several million Hutu refugees, including many of those responsible for the genocide, fled to Zaire and Tanzania. With a humanitarian crisis looming, Lake took control, spearheading a multilateral aid effort. "There are people dying," his colleagues remember his saying. "The President wants to do this, and we don't care what it takes." In December of 1994 Lake visited putrid mass graves in Rwanda. He does not understand how, after 800,000 people were killed, he could have felt angry but not at all responsible. "What's so strange is that this didn't become a 'how did we screw this up?' issue until a couple years later," he says. "The humanitarian-aid mission did not feel like a guilt mission."

Since senior officials in the U.S. government hadn't felt responsible when the killings were actually happening, it should not be altogether surprising that most didn't feel responsible after the fact. With the potential for an American military presence dismissed out of hand, Rwanda policy was formulated and debated heatedly by U.S. officials further down the chain. Because Lake never took control of the policy, the sense of responsibility he eventually acquired, although genuine, seems superimposed. He has an academic understanding that under the principle of command responsibility, those at the top must answer even for policies they do not remember consciously crafting. But lurking at the margins of Lake's consciousness seems to be an awareness that in light of press coverage at the time, he must have simply chosen to look away. And as disengaged as he was from the policy, he probably qualifies as the most engaged U.S. official in the Clinton Cabinet. "I'm not going to wallow," he says, "because if you blew it you should not wallow or ask for public forgiveness. But in a way I'm as guilty as anybody else, because to the degree that I didn't care about Africa, it would be understandable, but since I was more inclined to care, I don't know why I didn't."

Lake's guilt is of a second order—guilt over an absence of guilt. What about the other officials involved in Washington's Rwanda policy—how do they view their performance in retrospect? Today they have three main options.

They can defend the U.S. policy. This is the position of Richard Clarke, who believes, all things considered, that he and his colleagues did everything they could and should have done. "Would I have done the same thing again?" Clarke asks. "Absolutely. What we offered was a peacekeeping force that would have been effective. What [the UN] offered was exactly what we said it would be—a force that would take months to get there. If the UN had adopted the U.S. [outside-in] proposal, we might have saved some lives . . . The U.S. record, as compared to everyone else's record, is not something we should run away from. I don't think we should be embarrassed. I think everyone else should be embarrassed by what they did, or did not do."

Another position holds that no matter what any one person did at the time, there were larger forces at work: genocide would have consumed Rwanda no matter what, and American decision-makers in the White House or on Capitol Hill would never have countenanced the risks required to make a real difference. Radio jamming and other technical fixes were merely palliatives aimed at soothing guilty consciences. This is the view adopted by many Pentagon officials who worked on the issue day-to-day.

The least-inviting option leaves those involved questioning their performances and wondering what they should have done differently: Saved even one life by pushing harder? Chosen a telling moment for a high-profile resignation? "Maybe the only way to draw attention to this was to run naked through the building," Prudence Bushnell says. "I'm not sure anybody would have noticed, but I wish I had tried."

Africa specialists are the ones most affected by the Rwandan genocide. David Rawson, the former ambassador to Rwanda, retired in 1999. He lives with his wife in Michigan and has begun to write about his experiences. He still believes that efforts to pursue a cease-fire were worthwhile, and that "both sides" have a lot to answer for. But he acknowledges, "In retrospect, perhaps we were—as diplomats always are, I suppose—so focused on trying to find some agreement that we didn't look hard enough at the darker side." Predisposed toward state actors, trusting of negotiation and diplomacy, and courtly toward his interlocutors, Rawson, the diplomat, was outmatched.

Donald Steinberg, the NSC staffer who managed the NSC's Africa directorate, felt a deep emotional attachment to the continent. He had tacked the photos of two six-year-old African girls he had sponsored above his desk at the White House. But when he began seeing the bodies clogging the Kagera River, he had to take the photos down, unable to bear the reminder of innocent lives being extinguished every minute. The directorate, which was tiny, had little influence on policy. It was, in the parlance, "rolled" by Richard Clarke. "Dick was a thinker," one colleague says. "Don was a feeler. They represented the duality of Bill Clinton and his presidency, which was torn between the thinkers, who looked out for interests, and the feelers, who were moved by values. As we all know, in the end it was always going to be the thinkers who won out." After the genocide, according to friends and colleagues, Steinberg threw himself into the humanitarian relief effort, where at last he might make a difference. But eventually he plummeted into depression. He asked himself again and again, if only he had been at the White House longer . . . if only he had known how to pull the right levers at the right time . . . if only he had . . . ? Now deputy director of policy planning at the State Department, Steinberg has told friends that his work from here on out is "repayment for a very large bill that I owe."

Susan Rice, Clarke's co-worker on peacekeeping at the NSC, also feels that she has a debt to repay. "There was such a huge disconnect between the logic of each of the decisions we took along the way during the genocide and the moral consequences of the decisions taken collectively," Rice says. "I swore to myself that if I ever faced such a crisis again, I would come down on the side of dramatic action, going down in flames if that was required." Rice was subsequently appointed NSC Africa director and, later, assistant secretary of state for African affairs; she visited Rwanda several times and helped to launch a small program geared to train selected African armies so that they might be available to respond to the continent's next genocide. The American appetite for troop deployments in Africa had not improved.

Prudence Bushnell will carry Rwanda with her permanently. During the genocide, when she went walking in the woods near her home in Reston, Virginia, she would see Rwandan mothers cowering with their children behind the trees, or stacked in neat piles along the bike path. After the genocide, when the new President of Rwanda visited Washington and met Bushnell and others, he leaned across the table toward her, eyes blazing, and said, "You, madame, are partially responsible for the genocide, because we told you what was going to happen and you did nothing." Haunted by these memories and admonitions, when Bushnell was later appointed ambassador to Kenya and saw that her embassy was insecure, she was much more assertive, and pleaded repeatedly with Washington for security to be upgraded—requests that were, notoriously, ignored. The bombing of the U.S. embassy in Kenya will forever be encapsulated in American minds by the image of a bloodied Bushnell staggering away from the explosion with a towel pressed to her wounds.

Currently serving as ambassador to Guatemala, Bushnell can muster a black humor about the way death and killing keep hounding her. Like Steinberg, she is trying to make peace with her inability to have secured even the tamest commitments from her colleagues in the bureaucracy. "For a long time I couldn't live with it, but now I think I can look back and say, 'I knew what was happening, I tried to stop what was happening, and I failed.' That is not a source of guilt, but it is a tremendous source of shame and sadness."

And then, finally, there is Romeo Dallaire. It is both paradoxical and natural that the man who probably did the most to save Rwandans feels the worst. When he returned to Canada, in August of 1994, he behaved initially as if he had just completed a routine mission. As the days passed, though, he began to show signs of distress. He carried a machete around and lectured cadets on post-traumatic stress disorder; he slept sparingly; and he found himself nearly retching in the supermarket, transported back to Rwandan markets and the bodies strewn within them. When the international war-crimes tribunal called him to testify, he plunged back into the memories and his mental health worsened. Dallaire was told by his superiors that he would have to choose between leaving the "Rwanda business" behind him or leaving his beloved armed forces. For Dallaire only one answer was possible: "I told them I would never give up Rwanda," he says. "I was the force commander and I would complete my duty, testifying and doing whatever it takes to bring these guys to justice." In April of 2000 Dallaire was forced out of the Canadian armed services and given a medical discharge.

Dallaire had always said, "The day I take my uniform off will be the day that I will also respond to my soul." But since becoming a civilian he has realized that his soul is not readily retrievable. "My soul is in Rwanda," he says. "It has never, ever come back, and I'm not sure it ever will." He carries the guilt of the genocide with him, and he feels that the eyes and the spirits of those killed are constantly watching him. He says he can barely stand living and has attempted suicide.

In June of last year a brief Canadian news-wire story reported that Dallaire had been found unconscious on a park bench in Hull, Quebec, drunk and alone. He had consumed a bottle of scotch on top of his daily dose of pills for post-traumatic stress disorder. He was on a death mission. Dallaire sent a letter to the Canadian Broadcast Corporation thanking them for their sensitive coverage of this episode. On July 3, 2000, the letter was read on the air.

Thank you for the very kind thoughts and wishes.

There are times when the best medication and therapist simply can't help a soldier suffering from this new generation of peacekeeping injury. The anger, the rage, the hurt, and the cold loneliness that separates you from your family, friends, and society's normal daily routine are so powerful that the option of destroying yourself is both real and attractive. That is what happened last Monday night. It appears, it grows, it invades, and it overpowers you.

In my current state of therapy, which continues to show very positive results, control mechanisms have not yet matured to always be on top of this battle. My doctors and I are still [working to] establish the level of serenity and productivity that I yearn so much for. The therapists agree that the battle I waged that night was a solid example of the human trying to come out from behind the military leader's ethos of "My mission first, my personnel, then myself." Obviously the venue I used last Monday night left a lot to be desired and will be the subject of a lot of work over the next while.

Dallaire remained a true believer in Canada, in peacekeeping, in human rights. The letter went on:

This nation, without any hesitation nor doubt, is capable and even expected by the less fortunate of this globe to lead the developed countries beyond self-interest, strategic advantages, and isolationism, and raise their sights to the realm of the pre-eminence of humanism and freedom . . . Where humanitarianism is being destroyed and the innocent are being literally trampled into the ground . . . the soldiers, sailors, and airpersons . . . supported by fellow countrymen who recognize the cost in human sacrifice and in resources will forge in concert with our politicians . . . a most unique and exemplary place for Canada in the league of nations, united under the United Nations Charter.

I hope this is okay.

Thanks for the opportunity.

Warmest regards,

Dallaire

New York Magazine

Sullivan's Travels

Provocative, intelligent, and artfully written, Michael Wolff's columns in New York *Magazine accomplish a difficult feat: proffering shrewd judgments about some of the most influential characters in the media business while also charting changes in the broader cultural landscape.*

Michael Wolff

Sullivan's Travels

**Ambitious and
self-absorbed, ex-pat
Andrew Sullivan
has made a career
out of his personal
and political
contradictions—
and pissing people off.**

I am gamely casting about for someone to compare Andrew
Sullivan to.

"Orwell," he offers, as his pancakes, eggs, and a milk-
shake are set on the table. We're having breakfast at the Diner—a
place he describes as "un-Washington"—near his house in
Adams-Morgan.

Now, it isn't that Orwell is completely out of context. Sullivan's public airing and working out of his conservatism, Catholicism, and homosexuality (although not necessarily in that order)
seems to me in the tradition of a generation of English journal-

ists who used the personal essay as social criticism—Malcolm Muggeridge, Cyril Connolly, and Arthur Koestler, for instance. It's just that Orwell is the greatest of all such essayists—few writers have ever become so much the conscience of their time.

"Not that *I* would compare myself to Orwell," Sullivan adds, sensing that I might be nonplussed.

Not that he shouldn't, I reassure him; Sullivan is certainly *trying* to be the conscience of his generation; and in a way, you could argue that Sullivan is often at odds with the official gay community the way Orwell was at odds with the Stalinist-leaning left (Sullivan treats the official gay community as well as a portion of liberal Democrats as the moral equivalent of Stalinists).

But to get a glimpse of how ambitious someone is, to get a sneak peek at how large he sees himself, to have a person come right out with his fantasy (and not *as* fantasy) is always a surprise.

.   .   .

Ambition itself is in fact one of Sullivan's personal dilemmas. On the one hand, there is the "fame thing"—which for him includes regretting the Gap ad he did and his ambivalence about notoriety and its value in the gay community. ("We're the one subculture where fame reduces your ability to get laid—if someone comes up to me in a bar and says *I saw you on television,* that's it, I have no interest in having sex with that person.") On the other hand, there's his overwhelming desire not just to succeed but to represent, to epitomize, to suffer for his generation.

Certainly, he sees himself as an important entity; he believes that he is the most significant gay public intellectual in America today—and he may well be. He sees himself, too, as among the most important conservative thinkers and Catholic thinkers as well, and, to the extent that he is publicly wrestling with the meaning of these things—while so many other people are not—he may well be.

At the same time, the legions of people whom he has antagonized, or who are jealous of him, or who have unhappily worked with him, would hurry to point out that he doesn't really represent any of these philosophies or identities. It's a canard, a media put-up job, that he has become the spokesperson for gay life, or the new conservatism (if such a thing even exists), or contemporary Catholicism; in each instance, instead, he's an extreme anomaly.

In fact, that he should have become such a representative figure drives a lot of people crazy. America is filled with openly gay writers, and yet the stand-out one is beset with conflicted positions that, other gay advocates believe, render his gayness, at best, a little perverse (he is most often accused of expressing "self-loathing" instead of a requisite gay pride). You can only imagine how the conservatives and Catholics feel about him.

· · ·

Of course, this is another of his contradictions and dilemmas: He wants to represent, but he doesn't want to represent (if he had a sense of humor, which he doesn't, he might well see himself more as Philip Roth than as George Orwell).

He believes so much in his own virtue that it makes absolute sense to him that he should be the representative man, the model—the world would be a better place if all gays were conservative and all Catholics were gay and all liberals Catholic. But he knows too the value of his own uniqueness. Sullivan has become famous by not being representative at all. He gets airtime for being an oxymoron. We love this stuff: a gay Catholic, a black conservative, a pregnant lesbian, etc.

There are, naturally, those who believe that what Sullivan is doing is largely shtick. Conflict is drama. Sullivan, it sometimes seems, gets into the straitjacket just to fight it—as a gay person in Washington, as a conservative at *The New Republic,* as a Catholic in a leather bar.

For instance, living and making his career in Washington seems like an especially stubborn and contrary thing to do. Why would a writer deeply concerned with personal issues, with the expression of emotional conflicts, live in the one place in America that eschews anything personal? Why would a gay writer consciously choose a closeted community? ("My social and professional lives," he says fatefully, "are hermetically sealed." Conversely, he says, "If I wasn't gay, I'd suffocate in this town," meaning, I take it, that being gay is a way to escape dull, ungay Washington.)

One answer might be that he is a throwback. The modern media sexual culture has moved forward, and Andrew Sullivan is trying to move himself backward, to re-create some kind of fifties life for himself, some restraints to chafe under, some moral imperative to defend, when it was possible not to cut your conscience to fit today's fashions. (His book *Virtually Normal* argues that homosexuality is the paramount battleground in the culture of our time.)

Another answer is that he saw a great career opportunity. While it would be hard to get traction as a gay writer in New York, a gay writer in Washington can break the bonds of Puritanism and convention all over again. (While he is tight with polite society in Washington, he is also well known, he says, in every bar in town.)

The third answer is that there are quite clearly multiple countries, or parallel countries, in America, and while you or I might comfortably live in one or the other, only Andrew Sullivan is struggling to live in them all.

• • •

Then again, in some ways, his struggles are not especially American. To be a gay Brit is to fight battles fought here a generation ago; to be a British conservative—a Thatcherite—is about class rebellion; and to be Catholic in the U.K. involves age-old identity issues that no American could imagine or, likely, would want to bother trying to.

Still, it's an attractive package. As a young, gay, Reaganaut-Thatcherite-Catholic-pro-Israel Brit, president of the Oxford Union, would-be politician, he gets a Harvard fellowship, then applies for internships at *The New Republic, The National Review,* and *The New York Times.* He lands the *New Republic* job through the Marty Peretz-Harvard connection. Sullivan and Jacob Weisberg are the *New Republic* interns of the mid-eighties; Michael Kinsley is editor and mentor. All the ingredients mix: Kinsley is proto-British; the traditionally liberal *New Republic* is becoming more conservative; Sullivan and the magazine are rabidly pro-Israel; and Marty Peretz likes overly verbal, Harvard-educated, Israel-supporting young men. In 1991, following in *The New Republic*'s tradition of appointing someone bright and inexperienced as editor, Sullivan gets the job.

His tenure is marked by three things. He is gay—which instantly becomes Jackie Robinson sort of big news in Washington. He learns in 1993 that he is HIV-positive—which turns the polemical to the potentially tragic. And he is a ghastly manager—the magazine is riven by internecine warfare; during his tenure, he famously fights with Leon Wieseltier, the magazine's powerful literary editor, and even, grandly, tries to raise money to "relaunch" the 86-year-old magazine. (Although the magazine is, under his editorship, arguably the most interesting it has ever been—Sullivan is for *The New Republic* what Tina Brown was for *The New Yorker.*)

• • •

He is forced out of the *New Republic* job in 1996 to await, he believes, his imminent death. Then, when he grows healthy again, he sets about becoming the media face of the remission era (although Sullivan, a mumbler in a plaid shirt, is not, despite his myriad appearances, very good on television). He fancies himself the voice of a new and chastened world—a world that he believes should come to a certain moral attention. (The ultimate symbol for moral sloth is, for him, Bill Clinton.)

He is hired by *The New York Times Magazine* to write a column and a steady stream of features, provoking more fulmination—Sullivan becomes another piece of evidence in the complex history of the *Times* and the gay community. In fact, the oddness, or out-of-placeness, or look-at-me emphasis of a voice like Sullivan's in *The New York Times Magazine* makes him seem like something of a house gay. A kind of Joyce Maynard for his generation. The gay nongays love. A show thing. But it is the solipsism of this voice from such a public platform that most angers many people. When he speaks of the nineties—his generation—as the great transforming epoch of the gay experience, it leaves many other less-self-involved people to point out that the seventies and eighties were hardly chopped liver, and that, in part, Sullivan's high profile stems from the fact that so many of his elders are dead.

And then there is the weirdness, the eccentricness of his myriad positions—or it may be just the fact that he has so many opinions—that makes people crazy. His beat encompasses, but is hardly limited to, animal welfare, gender research, an array of para-sciences (for instance, his famous piece in the *Times* on testosterone), a steady pummeling of one-two punches against Bill Clinton, and, more recently, a big embrace of George Bush ("He's kicking ass"). There may not be a day that goes by that Sullivan does not propound a contrary opinion—in the *Times;* in his weekly column in the Sunday *Times* of London; in the *TRB* column, which he writes each week in *The New Republic;* through his pundit duties across the cable spectrum; and on his andrewsullivan.com Website, a daily labor of love that he is sure advertisers will soon flock to. Indeed, it may be this media narcissism, this constant claim on everyone's attention, that most infuriates people.

•   •   •

In America, we tend to leave the social arguments to partisans and windbags like Bill Bennett. We invariably regard someone with relentless (or annoying) opinions as an agent of a cause or agenda. The argument as a form rather than a position is not, in this cryptic age, a popular notion.

Nobody likes a know-it-all. Talking for the sake of talking is not a virtue (and yet, why not?).

It is in this vacuum of everyone standing around, refusing to offer an opinion, mostly indifferent in their allegiances, trying to be politic and please all their future bosses, that you get Andrew Sullivan. The man likes to hear himself talk; he thrives on the conniptions of people listening to him; he revels in his provocations.

I think the critics who charge him with self-loathing have it all wrong.

The New Yorker

WINNER, PROFILE WRITING

The Lost Tycoon

To profile someone as well-known as Ted Turner is its own particular challenge. In "The Lost Tycoon," Ken Auletta does more than elicit fresh insights from friend, foe, and subject alike. By cutting through the clutter of legend with meticulous reporting and research, he also creates the definitive portrait of a maverick media genius at a personal turning point.

Ken Auletta

The Lost Tycoon

Now he has no wife, no job, and no empire, but Ted Turner may just save the world.

Early last year, Ted Turner seemed invincible. He was the largest shareholder in AOL Time Warner, owning around four per cent of the soon-to-be-merged companies; his celebrated name was on the door of a major division, Turner Broadcasting System; and his dimpled chin, gap-toothed smile, and pencil-thin Gable-esque mustache were recognizable everywhere. His life is documented by the framed magazine covers that crowd the walls of his Atlanta office: Turner in 1976, launching the first "Superstation," by transforming a weak local television signal into a robust cable network; Turner in 1977, skippering his boat, Courageous, to victory in the America's Cup; Turner pioneering the purchase of professional sports teams as cheap and reliable programming; Turner inventing the twenty-four-hour Cable News Network; Turner buying Hollywood film libraries to create new cable-television networks; Turner as *Time*'s Man of the Year.

Ted Turner's business successes didn't end when, in 1996, Turner Broadcasting merged with Time Warner. His influence at the world's largest media company was pervasive; he played the role of crazy-uncle-in-the-basement whose large appetite for cost-cutting has to be appeased, and in the process he helped revive the company's stock. But when, in January of 2000, Time Warner and Turner agreed to join with the Internet company America Online, Turner was not invited to participate in the talks about how the merged company would function.

Less than four months later, Ted Turner was fired. The news, Turner says, was delivered during a telephone call from Gerald Levin, the C.E.O. of Time Warner, who told Turner what Turner had often told others: the company was going to reorganize. Turner Broadcasting would no longer report to Turner but, rather, to Robert Pittman, the chief operating officer of AOL. "You can't report to Pittman, so you have to have a more senior role," Levin remembers telling Turner. As Turner recalls, Levin went on to say, "Sorry, Ted, but you lose your vice-chairman title as well." According to Levin, Turner offered to give up his vice-chairmanship in order to keep running the Turner Broadcasting division, which included CNN, TNT, Turner Classic Movies, the TBS Superstation, the Cartoon Network, the New Line Cinema studio, the Atlanta Braves baseball team, the Atlanta Hawks basketball team, the Atlanta Thrashers hockey team, and Time Warner's HBO. "I didn't fire Ted," Levin insists today. "I said, 'This is the way we need to run the company.'"

Turner protested, in a series of calls first to Levin, then to Steve Case, the C.E.O. of AOL, who was to be the chairman of the new company, demanding that he not be deprived of supervision of CNN and the other cable networks that he had started. He thought that he would prevail, and in early May—perhaps because he, like Levin, hates confrontation, or perhaps because making speeches has become his accustomed mode of communication and he had now spoken—Turner got on his plane and headed for New Mexico, where he owns a five-hundred-and-eighty-thousand-acre ranch, and where he had invited some friends to join him. Turner is America's largest individual landowner, with nearly two million acres, or the rough equivalent of the land area of Delaware and Rhode Island combined. He owns twenty-two properties, in nine states and Argentina, and he spends about half his time at one or another of them.

Turner didn't see that his travels often slowed decision-making at Turner Broadcasting. Although he entrusted most matters to a deputy, Terence F. McGuirk, he expected to approve major projects himself. AOL and Time Warner executives, however, were impatient with the peripatetic Turner. He is sixty-two, and even his friends wanted him to slow down. Jane Fonda, his former wife, thinks that she knows why he is so restless: "I say this with all the love in the world. . . . He has been severely, hauntingly traumatized. He always thinks something is about to be pulled out from him. He has no belief in permanency and stability. It's one reason why I'm not with him. Older age is about slowing down and growing vertically, not horizontally. That's not Ted."

Something was "pulled out" from Turner while he was in New Mexico, as he learned from a five-page fax that he received there. The fax, a press release issued by AOL Time Warner, announced a new management team for the company, awarding Turner one of two vice-chairmanships and "the additional title of Senior Advisor." The fax did not say that he had lost much of his authority, or that his five-year contract to manage Turner Broadcasting had been abrogated a year early. John Malone, the chairman of Liberty Media and an old friend of Turner's, who was a guest at the ranch, recalls that when the fax arrived "Ted went white. He was very upset. He thought it was extremely bad behavior for them to do it that way." Malone told Turner, "You can sue, but you won't get your job back. You'll just get money."

Turner's bosses tried to defuse the publicity with praise. At a press luncheon for CNN's twentieth anniversary, four weeks after the announcement, Case told reporters, "Ted Turner has been a hero of mine for twenty-five years, and he and I are basically going to be joined at the hip." Turner can be seduced with kind words, with pleas to work for the good of the team, but he wasn't this time. " 'Vice-chairman' is usually a title you give to somebody you can't figure out what else to do with," he says. He likened himself to a monarch.

Turner says that last year was one of the most miserable of his life. His marriage to Fonda ended, after eight years, and this, too, was announced in January. In addition, he smashed his foot in a skiing accident; his beloved black Labrador, Chief, contracted coonhound disease and was temporarily paralyzed; his back hurt and he thought that he needed surgery; and two of his grandchildren were diagnosed with Hurler's syndrome, a rare and sometimes lethal enzyme deficiency. Most adults have the support of a spouse and family, friends, and a job; Turner didn't have a spouse, had never had intimate friends, and no longer ran his own company. "I felt like Job," Turner told me, adding, not for the first time, that he had felt "suicidal."

·   ·   ·

Yet Turner has, in the past several years, been commanding more attention outside his company, making a new identity for himself as a philanthropist—"I want to be Jiminy Cricket for America," he has said. In 1997, before it was fashionable for billionaires to make such gifts, he pledged a billion dollars to the United Nations. The Turner Foundation, which he controls, awarded fifty million dollars last year to environmental causes. (Turner is a devoted environmentalist—he can name every species of bird and animal on his ranches—and during the oil embargo of 1973 he sold his Cadillac and switched to more fuel-efficient cars; recently, he exchanged his Ford Taurus for a hybrid electric-and-gas Toyota Prius, which averages about fifty miles a gallon.) Last year, Turner started a foundation, the Nuclear Threat Initiative, whose goal is to curb the proliferation of nuclear, chemical, and biological weapons, and he has pledged two hundred and fifty million dollars over the next five years. In December, to solve a long-running dispute between what the United States owed the United Nations and what Congress was willing to pay, Turner joined Richard C. Holbrooke, then the Ambassador to the U.N., to shape an extraordinary compromise: Turner would contribute the thirty-four-million-dollar differ-ence, and the U.N. would adjust its future dues formula.

Turner calls himself "a do-gooder." He says so in a loud voice, and it gets louder as he gets excited. Turner is uninhibited, and is usually blissfully unaware of others; for one thing, he is hard of hearing and is too vain to use a hearing aid. "Half the people alive today are already living in what we would consider intolera-ble conditions," he declares. "One-sixth don't have access to clean drinking water; one-fifth live on less than a dollar a day; half the women in the world don't have equal rights with men; the forests are shrinking; the temperature's rising, and the oceans are rising, because of the melting of the ice cap." He sounds like a billion-aire Jeremiah. In a hundred years, he believes, New York will be under water and it will be "so hot the trees are going to die." He continues, "It will be the biggest catastrophe the world has ever seen—unless we have nuclear war." He is outraged that the United States and others don't do more to alleviate these horrors and to combat the defense and foreign policies of George W. Bush. "The new Administration attempts to make enemies out of the Russians, the North Koreans, and the Chinese to justify the gigantic military buildup it wants to make in peacetime," he says. "The economy of North Korea is smaller than the economy of Detroit!" And he is disturbed by the world's exploding popula-tion; although he has five children, he once declared, "If I was doing it over again, I wouldn't have had that many, but I can't shoot them now that they're here."

Turner's contradictions are as clear as his views. He successfully opposed unionization at his company, yet he rails against élites. He has called himself "a socialist at heart" and a fiscal "conservative." Turner speaks out on behalf of the rights of women but refuses to denounce Islamic states that suppress women's rights. He has compared Rupert Murdoch, who owns the Fox network, to Hitler, yet when he is asked if he thinks Saddam Hussein is evil he says, "I'm not sure that I know enough to be able to answer that question." And though he preaches tolerance, he has uttered some intolerant words; for example, on Ash Wednesday, seeing the black smudge on the foreheads of some CNN staff members, he asked them whether they were "Jesus freaks." As he frequently does when he says something unwise, Turner apologized, blithely assuming that the furor would pass. It did. A week later, Turner told me, "That's the downside of speaking spontaneously."

Turner has two offices, in New York and Atlanta, and they seem to capture the odd mixture of his views: in his New York office, which is nearly bare, a bust of Alexander the Great peers from a shelf, while the Atlanta office, which is vast and crammed with trophies and artifacts, features busts of Martin Luther King, Jr., and Gandhi. "I've gone from a man of war to a man of peace," Turner explains. He offers the Turner principle of world diplomacy: "Just about everybody will be friendly toward us if we are friendly with them."

Despite Turner's success, people who meet him often think that he is peculiar. They hear his piercing laugh and the long "Ahhhhhhhhh's he utters as he pauses between words or thoughts, which veer off in surprising directions, and they have no other explanation. A former director of Turner Broadcasting's board who counts himself a friend and a fan describes Turner as a fascinating amalgam of opposites: "He's a mixture of a genius and a jackass. I think Ted could have run for President of the United States—if there were not the jackass side."

The "jackass side" of Turner appears because, he himself says, "I don't have any idea what I'm going to say. I say what comes to my mind." Gerald Levin puts this in the best light: "Ted is by far the most interesting person I've ever met—how he reacts to things. It's as if a child were speaking, without any social inhibitions. You don't say in business, 'I got fired.' He'll just speak out loud what may be going through someone's mind, and he'll say it to everybody. I think that's a beautiful characteristic. He's angelic. The whole world is socially constrained. I love and respect this about Ted, but for other people it may be very difficult."

In November of 1996, for instance, the Friars Foundation honored Turner at a lifetime-achievement black-tie dinner. After he received his award and made a short speech, the lights dimmed, and then, as various entertainers, including the comedian Alan King, prepared to roast him, Turner, who insists on getting to bed early, grabbed Fonda's arm and departed, leaving the crowd gasping and King bellowing, "Rupert Murdoch was right—you are nuts."

On other occasions, humor redeems the situation. In January of 1999, Turner was invited to address the American Chamber of Commerce in Berlin. Eason Jordan, who oversaw international coverage for CNN, had briefed Turner on what he shouldn't say to his audience, made up largely of Germans. Nevertheless, Jordan recalls, the CNN staff was nervous, because Turner had said, "I'll wing it." And he did.

"You know, you Germans had a bad century," Turner declared. "You were on the wrong side of two wars. You were the losers." He continued, "I know what that's like. When I bought the Atlanta Braves, we couldn't win, either. You guys can turn it around. You can start making the right choices. If the Atlanta Braves could do it, then Germany can do it." The audience laughed with Turner, not at him. He left the podium to a standing ovation.

Turner likens himself to Zorba the Greek: "I lose my self-restraint and . . . just get up and dance sometimes." Gail Evans, a senior executive at Turner Broadcasting, says that Turner is always "winking," and she recalls the time he asked her to take the oceanographer Jacques Cousteau to lunch: "Go buy Mr. Cousteau a tuna-fish sandwich!" Today, associates are not laughing; they speak of Turner in the past tense, offering epitaphs. "He's the last of the revolutionary and creative minds in our business," CNN's chief international correspondent, Christiane Amanpour, who joined the company in 1983, says. "The idea of twenty-four-hour news and global news is his creation. That's changed the world. It's changed people's relations with their governments. It's meant that governments can no longer crack down with impunity on protests. And Ted's business also had a human face and a moral face and a social face. It wasn't just about making money and building an empire." She adds, sadly, "He's been shunted aside."

Even Turner talks about himself in a retrospective cadence: "My business side is coming to a close. It's time for me to move on, anyway." Last May, after AOL and Time Warner announced the new management structure, Robert Pittman tried to debunk press speculation that Turner was unhappy, saying, "I think Ted's going to have more influence than he had before." Now Pittman, who was born in Mississippi and has spent weekends hunting with Turner, says, "For me, Ted has a very big role. I don't make major decisions about Turner Broadcasting without talking to Ted." This is not what Turner thinks. "They tell me I have moral authority, and that's great," he says. He looks down at his tie, which is decorated with orange bison, and goes on to say, wistfully, "I'm very busy. Over the last three to four years, I've created another life for myself, and even if they had offered me the chairmanship of the company I probably wouldn't have taken it. It would require all my time, and I'd have to move to New York and I don't want that. I've got this other stuff that I think is in many ways more important."

In March, Turner's business influence was further diminished when the parent company announced that his top lieutenants at Turner Broadcasting—Terence McGuirk, the chairman and C.E.O., and Steven J. Heyer, the president—would be replaced by Jamie Kellner, the chief executive and founder of the WB broadcast network. To achieve more of the company's much touted synergies, Turner Broadcasting would be folded into a combined broadcast-and-cable-television division, which would be run by Kellner; Kellner would move to Atlanta from Hollywood. In a press release, Turner applauded Kellner's promotion. He was pleased that the separate fiefdoms in his old company and Time Warner would be joined—he blames Levin for wanting "to keep everybody weak, so he could be stronger"—but sorry that AOL Time Warner was practicing what he thinks of as management by the numbers.

Since Turner's dismissal, his offices, at the CNN Center, in Atlanta, and at Time Warner's headquarters, at 75 Rockefeller Plaza, have been largely idle. Friends notice that his shoulders slope more, that his hair has turned white, that his hearing is worse, that he complains about pain in his back and his foot, that he is self-conscious about his age. His energy level has decreased, along with his business authority. He is a member of the company's official executive committee, but it meets just once a month; the core corporate executive committee meets for lunch every Monday without him.

Still, the needy side of Turner compels him to want to please. Before an Advertising Council dinner at the Waldorf-Astoria last November in honor of Turner and Levin, Turner stood awkwardly beside Levin in a receiving line. As they turned to enter the ballroom, Turner pointed to me and told Levin that I was writing about him. Levin said he knew, and that prompted Turner to reassure him: "I checked first with corporate communications. I would not have done this unless I had approval." Such behavior does not surprise Jane Fonda. Turner is insecure,

she says, noting that the man who thinks of himself as Rhett Butler is really the more vulnerable character in his favorite movie:
"He loves 'Gone with the Wind' for lots of reasons, and one of
them is that he identifies with Scarlett O'Hara."

Rick Kaplan, who was fired as president of CNN/U.S. last September, recalls being taken to lunch by Turner at a Southern-
kitchen restaurant, where "you thought you were walking in with
Babe Ruth to Yankee Stadium." For the first time, Kaplan
noticed, Turner talked mostly about the past: "Whenever I had
spent any time with him, he'd always talk about the future. All of
a sudden, gone from his conversation were dreams for the future.
And he was supposed to be there to make me feel better. Instead,
I left feeling worse for him. I spent more time telling him positive, uplifting things, telling him the truth—that people revere
him and it doesn't matter what his title is and it doesn't matter
what anyone says his responsibilities are. Ted could sell all his
stock, divest himself of every nickel he's got, and if he walked
into the CNN newsroom the place would stand at attention."

Perhaps, but in the new world of AOL Time Warner it is probably not premature to write Ted Turner's business obituary.

●   ●   ●

The first word that Robert Edward Turner III uttered was not
"mama" or "dada" but "pretty." It was an odd choice, since he also
remembers that, growing up in the shadow of the Second World
War, he yearned first to be a fighter pilot with the R.A.F., and then
to conquer the world, like his first hero, Alexander the Great.
Turner was born in 1938 in Cincinnati; a sister, Mary Jane, was
born three years later. His father, Robert Edward (Ed) Turner, Jr.,
ran a successful outdoor-advertising company. Ted's mother was
a dutiful wife, who tried to obey her husband's wishes. Ed Turner
was a charming, gifted salesman who was on the road or at work

far more than he was at home. He was propelled by the memory of his own father, a cotton farmer in Mississippi, who lost his farm in the Depression and, refusing to declare bankruptcy, became a sharecropper instead. Often, Ed Turner would warn his son that Franklin D. Roosevelt and Harry Truman were Communists and that the Communists would take over America and execute anyone with more than fifty dollars in his pocket. For years, Ted never carried around more than forty-nine dollars.

Ted was obstreperous. He pulled ornaments off the Christmas tree, and smeared mud on a neighbor's sheets that were hanging out to dry. His father instructed him to read two books each week, and to eat every vegetable on his plate. Ed was often drunk, and would fly into a rage when Ted disobeyed; he frequently beat him, sometimes with a wire coat hanger. He would untwist it until it was straight, like a whip, and then hit his son, exclaiming, "This hurts me more than it does you." When this didn't seem to tame Ted, he reversed the punishment, pulling down his pants, lying down, and ordering his son to administer the lashings. With tears streaming down his cheeks, Ted obeyed. "It was the most painful thing I ever did in my entire life," he recalls, giving his father credit for understanding that "that would be a more effective punishment than him beating me."

Apparently, it was not effective enough; when Ed Turner joined the Navy, during the Second World War, and was assigned to the Gulf Coast, the family joined him—except for young Ted, who stayed with his grandmother and was eventually sent to boarding school in Cincinnati. Ted was miserable; he was impossible to control, and was suspended. When he was about ten, the family moved to Savannah, Georgia. Intent on teaching his son obedience, Ed Turner became more formal, no longer hugging him but greeting him with a handshake. He sent Ted off to the Georgia Military Academy, outside Atlanta, and then to the military program at the McCallie School, in Chattanooga.

Ted read non-stop, committing poems and military history to memory, but he hated boarding school. "I was hurt," he told me. "I didn't want to go off so young. It was like a prison. You couldn't leave the campus. There was a bell when you got out of bed in the morning and a bell to go to meals, and a bell to go to bed at night." And, he added, "there were no parents there—no mom, no dad." Yet Turner defends and even romanticizes his harsh father, saying that he deliberately instilled insecurity: "He thought that people who were insecure worked harder, and I think that's probably true. I don't think I ever met a super-achiever who wasn't insecure to some degree. A superachiever is somebody that's never satisfied."

By the time he was a teenager, Ted knew that he did not want to join his father's business. He was religious, and he decided that he was going to be a missionary. Then his sister became ill. He was fifteen when Mary Jane, who was twelve, contracted systemic lupus erythematosus, a disease in which the immune system attacks the body's tissue. She was racked with pain and constantly vomiting, and her screams filled the house. Ted regularly came home and held her hand, trying to comfort her. He prayed for her recovery; she prayed to die. After years of misery, she succumbed. Ted lost his faith. "I was taught that God was love and God was powerful," he says, "and I couldn't understand how someone so innocent should be made or allowed to suffer so."

The experience transformed Turner. "I decided I wanted to be a success," he says. Though he wasn't much of an athlete, he became a good boxer; the same tenacity that enabled him to resist his father helped him in boxing, because, he recalls, "I could take punishment." To impress his father, he took up debating and excelled at it; as a senior, he won the state high-school debating championship. He also became an accomplished sailor.

Ed Turner was constantly giving his son instructions: where he should work during the summers, whom he should date, how he had to save to pay his college tuition. When Ted was at home, his father even charged him room and board. Expecting his son to attend Harvard, he was displeased when a rejection letter arrived. Ted was accepted at Brown, and that mollified his father, but not for long. According to a detailed account of Ted's Brown years in Robert and Gerald Jay Goldberg's "Citizen Turner," he wasn't much of a student. He gambled. He got into noisy arguments, defending the South, defending war as a means of ridding the planet of the weak, defending nationalism. He delighted in irritating liberal sensibilities. He kept a rifle in his room, and sometimes poked it out the dormitory window and fired off a round or two. He partied and drank too much. He talked about dates as if he were describing military conquests. But Ted could be charming and funny, and, as is still the case, he was hard to miss. He joined the Brown sailing team, and was named the best freshman sailor in New England.

His father, who had divorced Ted's mother in 1957 and was now remarried, tried, in his son's word, to "micromanage" his life, to treat college as preparation for a business career. When Ted chose to major in classics, his father wrote angrily:

> I am appalled, even horrified, that you have adopted Classics as a Major. As a matter of fact, I almost puked on the way home today. . . . I am a practical man, and for the life of me I cannot possibly understand why you should wish to speak Greek. With whom will you communicate in Greek? I have read, in recent years, the deliberations of Plato and Aristotle, and was interested to learn that the old bastards had minds which worked very similarly to the way our minds work today. I was amazed that they had so much time for deliberating and thinking and was interested in the kind of civilization that would permit such useless deliberation. . . . I suppose everybody has to be a snob of some sort, and I suppose you will feel that you are distinguishing yourself from the herd by becoming a Clas-

sical snob. I can see you drifting into a bar, belting down a few, turning around to a guy on the stool next to you—a contemporary billboard baron from Podunk, Iowa—and saying, "Well, what do you think about old Leonidas?"... It isn't really important what I think. It's important what you wish to do with the rest of your life. I just wish I could feel that the influence of those odd-ball professors and the ivory towers were developing you into the kind of man we can both be proud of.... I think you are rapidly becoming a jackass, and the sooner you get out of that filthy atmosphere, the better it will suit me.

Agitated by the letter, Ted brought it to the Brown student newspaper, the *Daily Herald*, and, as Porter Bibb says in his biography "Ted Turner: It Ain't As Easy As It Looks," the paper published it anonymously.

• • •

In his junior year, Ted was expelled for smuggling a coed into his room. In fact, it was just the last straw, and, if Ed Turner was unhappy with his son's behavior, he was glad to have him come home and enter the billboard business. Despite their feuds, Ted now rarely questioned that he would work for his father. "I liked the advertising business," he said. Father and son were similar in many ways. Both were persuasive and headstrong. Both viewed seduction as a game of conquest. Both were self-centered. Both were political conservatives. Both liked whiskey. Both battled moments of depression. And both had unsuccessful marriages.

In 1960, after a brief stint in the Coast Guard, Ted married Julia (Judy) Gale Nye, the daughter of a prominent sailor from Chicago, and they moved to Macon. A year later, when she gave birth to Laura Lee, Ted, intent on winning the America's Cup, was off sailing. Marriage did not stop him from carousing, and he often returned home late at night, as if in a *Playboy* cartoon, with lipstick on his collar and alcohol on his breath. Two years after they were married, Judy filed for divorce. Then she discovered that she was pregnant again, and the couple reconciled. In May of 1963, Robert Edward Turner IV was born. Ted soon returned to his earlier habits, and finally, after a sailing competition in which he rammed his wife's boat in order to win, Judy decided that the marriage was finished.

Turner was a Barry Goldwater supporter, and he met his second wife, Jane Smith, who was a stewardess based in Atlanta, at a campaign rally. They married in June of 1964, and had three children in short order—Rhett, Beauregard, and Jennie. In 1967, Ted also got custody of the two children from his first marriage. The Turners lived in Atlanta, and Ted was not much better as a father than he was as a husband. He was "a dictator," Laura, who is now close to her father, recalls. Because of the sailing season, he was rarely home for Christmas, and because of work the family took few vacations together. In the summer, because Turner refused to install air-conditioning, the family baked. But, Ted says, recalling his own father, "I treated my children entirely differently than he did. I let them make a lot of their decisions for themselves." Yet he had sudden mood changes, and his temper frightened the children. They were expected to be in bed by 8 P.M. and at breakfast before eight. Good manners were required at the table. Television was limited. If they wanted soda or candy on the weekend, they collected empty bottles to earn the money.

While Ted Turner concentrated on mastering the outdoor-advertising business, his father was trying to escape depression; he drank, smoked three packs of cigarettes a day, and took a huge assortment of pills. In 1961, Ed Turner had sought treatment, and he spent a summer at the Silver Hill psychiatric hospital, in New Canaan, Connecticut. A year after he left Silver Hill, Ed Turner made the boldest business decision of his career, paying four million dollars for the Atlanta, Richmond, and Roanoke divisions of General Outdoor Advertising. Instantly, Turner Advertising was the foremost outdoor-advertising company in the South.

Ted was convinced that they had scored a coup. His father, though, was strangely morose, worrying that he lacked the resources to absorb such a large company. He returned to Silver Hill, and from there placed a panicky call to a friend in the outdoor-advertising business and pressed him to buy the new divisions for the amount they had cost him. The friend, not wanting to take advantage, threw in a fifty-thousand-dollar bonus. Ed Turner still could not shake his depression. "I don't want to hurt anybody. I just feel like I've lost my guts," he wrote to his wife. On March 5, 1963, Ed Turner had break-fast with his wife, went upstairs, placed a .38-calibre silver pistol in his mouth, and pulled the trigger. He was fifty-three.

His son later told Christian Williams, who wrote an early biography of him, that he and his father "had terrible, terrible fights. It was after one of those fights—we disagreed about how the business should be run—that he blew his brains out." The message was clear: Ed Turner abandoned his dreams of business glory because he felt inadequate, and because his son wasn't up to the task, either. The son, who was twenty-four, had to face another message: perhaps he was responsible. For all that, Ted Turner says that he lost his "best friend."

· · ·

In the weeks and months after his father's suicide, Turner was distraught yet surprisingly focussed. He told his father's advisers and bankers that Ed Turner had not known what he was doing when he resold the company divisions he had just bought; that he, Ted, would sue if necessary to reclaim them; and that, in any case, he was prepared to run the entire enterprise. His ferocity and his mastery of the numbers were impressive. The bankers came through with the loans, and his father's friend sold back the divisions he had bought.

Soon after that, Turner began to dream of going beyond the billboard business, of building a media empire. His first venture came five years after his father's suicide, in 1968, when he bought a Chattanooga radio station, WAPO. Within a year, he had also acquired radio stations in Jacksonville and Charleston. In 1970, he acquired his first television property, Channel 17 in Atlanta, a money-losing UHF station. He borrowed heavily to make the purchase, and the consensus was that he had been outsmarted; although he changed the station's call letters from WJRJ to WTCG, it looked as if he would lose everything. "Working in UHF television at that time was like being in the French Foreign Legion," recalls Terry McGuirk, who was hired by Turner the summer after his junior year at Middlebury College, and who became Turner's protégé. The staff consisted of about thirty employees; for many, the pay was thirty dollars a week and all you could eat. The finances became even more dire when Turner acquired a second TV station, in Charlotte. McGuirk, who was dispatched to sell ads, says that the new station was costing Turner fifty thousand dollars a month. And a good deal of the time Turner was away sailing, a hobby that commanded nearly as much of his attention as business did. But he managed to motivate his tiny staff, just as he did his sailing crew.

Turner charmed and wheedled to get ads, and he introduced inexpensive programming. News was alien to the man who would become identified with CNN—too negative, Turner complained—and at first it was aired only in the early-morning hours. Turner programmed "The Mickey Mouse Club" and Three Stooges movies and every sports event he could find. Although profits were slim, he became obsessed with broadcasting. He wanted a national network, and, since he couldn't afford a broadcast network (there were none for sale, anyway), he discovered a way to get one on the cheap. In 1975, Gerald Levin, of Home Box Office, which was then a regional cable service, owned by Time Inc., that offered movies to subscribers, decided that he could transform HBO into a national pay-TV network by distributing it over the newly launched RCA satellite: all he had to do was get cable operators to invest a hundred thousand dollars in a thirty-foot dish. At the time, broadcast-TV stations like Turner's Channel 17 relied on microwave signals that bounced off transmission towers. Turner, however, had a tower that was twice the height of most other such towers, and his station already reached beyond its broadcast range, of forty miles, to five states. But a network of towers was expensive, and the signals were impeded by tall buildings and deteriorated over long distances.

Cable had other advantages: unlike broadcasting, which produced revenue solely from advertising, it had monthly subscription charges. But cable in those days had little programming of its own; it had started as a way to improve TV reception, and then became a way to extend television to rural communities that didn't get broadcast signals. Turner saw an opportunity. With satellites, as HBO had demonstrated, signals could be sent across the nation, and so Channel 17 could become a cable network. He renamed the new network TBS—Turner Broadcasting System.

Turner was taking not only a huge business risk—he borrowed heavily—but a political risk, too, since he needed approval from the Federal Communications Commission. The broadcast networks and the local TV stations were implacably opposed. They were joined by the Hollywood studios, which complained that Turner would be paying a local price for their movies and exhibiting them nationally, and by professional sports teams, which said that Turner was stealing their product.

Turner and others in the cable industry saw the broadcast networks and their allies as a cartel that had induced the government to impose regulations crippling cable's ability to compete.

Cable conventions at that time were like revival meetings, with speaker after speaker fervently denouncing this satan. As a master salesman, Turner knew that Congress had long been concerned about the pervasive power of Hollywood and the three big New York-based broadcast networks, and he assured congressional leaders that he, a broadcaster, was trying to help the nascent cable industry provide consumers with more choices—and better choices, too, since his station would not, he vowed, program violent, sexually explicit movies, like Martin Scorsese's "Taxi Driver." Of course, viewers would not be receiving first-class alternative fare, since Turner was offering movies and sports in the evening and "Lassie," "The Munsters," and "The Flintstones," among other programs, during the day. Nevertheless, the F.C.C. allowed tiny Channel 17 to become the Superstation, an overnight rival to the networks.

·   ·   ·

Cable was starved for programming, and TBS and HBO became its building blocks. To insure continuous baseball coverage that could not be taken off his Superstation, Turner, in 1976, bought the Atlanta Braves; although he paid a bargain price of ten million dollars, he went into debt to do it. He attended most Braves home games: he ran out onto the field to lead the fans in "Take Me Out to the Ballgame"; sitting behind the Braves dugout, he'd spit Red Man tobacco juice into a cup and swill beer, in hot weather peeling off his shirt; when a Brave hit a home run, he'd jump over the railing and rush to the plate to greet him; he played cards with his players and insisted that they call him Ted. Ralph Roberts, the founder of Comcast Communications, which is now the nation's third-largest cable company, says of TBS, "We thought it was the greatest thing in the world." Roberts was charmed by Turner; others were not. Turner would drop to the floor, histrionically, to beg for business; once, telling a roomful of Southern ladies how to woo advertisers, he explained, "My daddy said, 'If advertisers want a blow job, you get down on your knees.'"

He became Captain Outrageous. Celebrating his victory in the 1977 America's Cup, he swigged almost a whole bottle of aquavit that had been given to him by the Swedish team, and then, drinking champagne, pulled his shirt up to his neck and yelled at some nearby women, "Show me your tits!" Earlier that same year, his second as a team owner, the baseball commissioner, Bowie Kuhn, suspended him for the season, accusing him of tampering when he tried to sign a player who was under contract to another team.

Turner tales became legendary. While racing in Newport, Rhode Island, in 1978, Turner coaxed the French-born Frédérique D'arragon—then, as now, a girlfriend—to wait until their boat came to the reviewing stand and then jump naked into the water. Jimmy Carter remembers that when he became President, in 1977, he invited his fellow-Georgian to state dinners. "He was very raucous," Carter said. "He was loud, and he interrupted sedate proceedings." Carter was amused by Turner. Dick Cavett, on the other hand, was not. During a taping of his television show, Cavett pressed him: "You are a colorful, boisterous, sometimes inebriated playboy type. Maybe it's an act or it's created by the press, but that is your image. You wouldn't deny that, would you?"

"I have heard that you are a little twinkle-toed TV announcer," Turner responded. "Would you deny that?"

By the late seventies, Turner was rich, and although he still behaved in unconventional ways, he had become more serious. He had great respect for Jimmy Carter, and no doubt Carter's more liberal views affected Turner's own politics. He began to liken himself to "an ambassador for good will." He saw himself as a rabbit—"a rabbit that's small and fast. All my big competitors were like a pack of wolves, and they were all chasing me, but I was fast enough to be out in front of them." The emblem of the rabbit was Turner's brand-new Cable News Network.

Reese Schonfeld, a creative and prickly executive, had discussed the cable-news-channel idea with Turner in 1978, and he served as CNN's first president. Turner, who was generous with his money but cheap in sharing credit with Schonfeld, told cable operators that CNN would do for the cable industry what Edward R. Murrow and Huntley-Brinkley had done for network news. CNN would make news the star, not overpaid anchors, and it would not be clotted with ads. Schonfeld travelled the country to sign up cable operators. And at most cable conventions there was Ted Turner, to make a speech and inspire his cable army.

The new cable network, based in Atlanta, made its official début on June 1, 1980, with three military bands striking up music and a nervous Ted Turner standing at a lectern in a blue blazer. Sporting Elvis sideburns, he began by reciting "a little poem that was written by Ed Kessler," and that reflected CNN's mission: "To act upon one's convictions while others wait, to create a positive force in a world where cynics abound, to provide information to people when it wasn't available before." A band played "The Star-Spangled Banner," and when it ended Turner whooped "Awww-riiight!" and CNN went live.

CNN's production values were initially amateurish—"video wallpaper," or "talking heads," network news executives sneered—and ratings were poor. Most of the work of building a staff, imposing news values, and winning clearance from local cable operators was taken on by Schonfeld. But Turner was the galvanizer, the risk-taker. He practically lived in his office, hurrying through the newsroom and rarely spending more than thirty seconds with anyone. Nick Charles, a sports reporter who was one of the first people to be hired at CNN, recalls that most of the staff worked six or seven days a week and relied on portable toilets outside, and that employees would show up in the morning and see Ted, wearing a robe or wrapped in a towel, wandering out of his office, where he slept on a Murphy bed, to retrieve coffee from the newsroom. Once, Steve Heyer remembers, he walked into Turner's office and the great man was sitting at his desk stark naked. "Don't get up!" someone exclaimed. Nick Charles recalls, "He was much more than a cheerleader. He was the kind of guy you'd want to run through a wall for."

At first, many CNN employees were dubious. Daniel Schorr, a former CBS correspondent, who was hired early on, was worried every time he heard Turner extoll the importance of good news, as if what he wanted were more happy news. Worry spread when, in 1982, Turner, frustrated by Schonfeld's close-to-the-vest management style and ownerlike ego, abruptly fired him. Lou Dobbs, another CNN pioneer, who was a business-news anchor, remembered Turner as a drunken sailor and thought that he might not be "the right fellow to lead the effort." Dobbs was afraid that Turner was more an "eccentric" than a "visionary"—until he got to know him. "He is a natural-born leader," Dobbs says. "I once asked him his definition of a leader. He said, 'A leader has the ability to create infectious enthusiasm.'"

CNN started as an all-day, mostly live, and mostly domestic news service. But it strayed to cover Cuba's 1981 May Day parade and a speech by Fidel Castro, and that led to an invitation for Turner to visit the island. Turner, who had never been to a Communist country, and whose politics continued to soften, was curious about it, and the next year he accepted the invitation. For the better part of four days, the Cuban communist and the Southern conservative hung out, smoking cigars, attending a baseball game, duck hunting, visiting schools, discussing politics, and night-clubbing. To an associate, Turner said, "Fidel ain't a Communist. He's a dictator, just like me." He learned that Castro watched CNN's signal from southern Florida; ever the salesman, he persuaded Castro to tape a promotional spot. Castro, in turn, urged Turner to take his news service worldwide. "Ted came back fired up," Eason Jordan remembers.

International news quickly expanded—CNN sent its first signal to Asia in late 1982 and to Europe in 1985. Jordan was twenty-eight when he started running CNN's foreign-news coverage.

In the beginning, the broadcast networks refused to include CNN in their pooled coverage of White House events. Turner filed a federal lawsuit in Atlanta against the "cartel" and the Reagan Administration, claiming violations of the antitrust laws and of CNN's rights under the First Amendment. To build support for CNN in Congress, Turner spent thirteen thousand dollars to install a satellite dish for the House and cabled the office of each member of Congress. Because CNN had twenty-four hours of news to fill, a congressman had a much better chance of being seen there. Ted Turner would win the battle for public support; more important, in a landmark ruling in the spring of 1982, the Atlanta court declared in CNN's favor, and by the mid-eighties CNN's triumph was apparent.

·   ·   ·

One reason for Turner's success—with CNN, with the Super-station, with buying sports teams to supply cable programming—is identified by Bob Wright, the president and C.E.O. of NBC. "He sees the obvious before most people do," Wright says. "We all look at the same picture, but Ted sees what you don't see. And after he sees it, it becomes obvious to everyone." As the networks shrank their overseas bureaus, CNN expanded. It invested in "flyaway" portable satellite dishes, costing about two hundred and fifty thousand dollars each, that could be carried in a suitcase and used anywhere in the world to "uplink" to a satellite. Turner wanted to grow bigger still. Although Turner Broadcasting had a mere two hundred and eighty-two million dollars in revenue in 1984, and the New York banks spurned his request for credit, in 1985 Turner got junk-bond financing that enabled him to make a $5.4-billion offer for a broadcast network: CBS.

Knowing that he was an underdog, Turner sought political support from Senator Jesse Helms, of North Carolina. Helms had mounted a campaign against CBS's "liberal bias," and he encouraged Turner to meet with a group called Fairness in Media, which had sent letters to a million conservatives begging them to buy CBS stock and "become Dan Rather's boss." Up North, many in the media expressed horror at the prospect of Turner, whom they regarded as an unsophisticated Southerner—a redneck—owning "the Tiffany network." Thomas Wyman, who was the C.E.O. of CBS, questioned Turner's moral fitness to run a network and accused him of being in bed with ideological groups, although he didn't name any. Wyman and CBS, hoping to block Turner, welcomed the "white knight" financing of Laurence Tisch, of the Loews Corporation, and Tisch stealthily gained control of CBS.

By the mid-eighties, however, Turner was not the provincial portrayed by CBS. As he sought to build CNN overseas, he became much more of an internationalist; he was more concerned with saving the environment, eradicating poverty, and ending the Cold War. He met and became friends with Jacques Cousteau, the primatologist Jane Goodall, the civil-rights leader Andrew Young, and the environmentalist Russell Peterson. "I was hanging around with people who cared about the future of the planet, both of the human race and of the environment," he says. "And they had an impact on me." Although he had once been a smoker, he now refused to hire anyone who smoked. "I figured any young person who's dumb enough to smoke is too dumb to work at CNN or TBS," he says. In 1985, he established the Better World Society, whose purpose was to subsidize documentaries on the dangers of environmental pollution, nuclear weapons, and the population explosion. He also began to proselytize for an end to the Cold War. After the United States boycotted the 1980 Summer Olympics, following the Soviet Union's invasion of Afghanistan, and the Soviet Union withdrew from the 1984 Los Angeles Games, Turner financed and launched the Goodwill Games to foster athletic competition between the United States and the U.S.S.R. During this time, Turner even thought of running for President.

But to those who didn't know him—and even to some members of his board, who did—Turner was still often seen as Captain Outrageous. They were tired of hearing that he was going to own a network or a Hollywood studio, that he was going to make movies like "Gone with the Wind." So when, in August of 1985, Turner, without fully consulting his board, bought, for a billion and a half dollars, the M-G-M film studio, its Culver City lot, and its library of more than thirty-five hundred motion pictures the consensus was that he had overpaid. The financing for his impulsive decision was arranged by Drexel Burnham's junk-bond king, Michael Milken, who was representing both Turner and the owner of M-G-M, Kirk Kerkorian. Milken reduced the amount of cash Turner needed by persuading Kerkorian to accept stock in Turner Broadcasting. The difficulty was that Turner found himself with two billion dollars' worth of debt; within three months, he was forced to sell the studio and other parts of M-G-M back to Kerkorian, for three hundred million dollars.

He kept the film library, however, and he brilliantly exploited this asset. The movies became a source of cheap television programming, and Turner created new cable networks—such as TNT (Turner Network Television), launched in 1988, and TCM (Turner Classic Movies), in 1994—to showcase them. Looking back, he is pleased with himself for having done this "right under the networks' noses" and for having managed to grow "from one-thousandth the size of the networks to two and a half times bigger." He says, "They laughed at me when I started with CBS. They laughed at me when I started CNN. They laughed at me when I bought the Braves. They laughed at me when I bought the Hawks. They laughed at me when I bought M-G-M. I spent a lot of time thinking, and I did not fear, because of my classical background. When Alexander the Great took control when his dad died, he was twenty years old. He took the Macedonian Army, which was the best army in the world at the time, and conquered Greece, got the Greeks to all join with him, and then marched across the Hellespont and invaded Asia. They didn't even know where the world ended at that time. And he was dead at thirty-three, thirteen years later. He kept marching. He hardly ever stopped. And he never lost a battle."

·　　·　　·

Turner did lose battles, even if they were within the company. Kerkorian, it was revealed, had a stipulation that if Turner did not reduce his debt within six months he would have to pay Kerkorian in TBS stock, and Turner worried that Kerkorian could soon gain control of his company. On top of this, companies like Rupert Murdoch's were turning a raptor's eye on the debt-ridden Turner empire. To avoid losing everything, Turner, in 1987, looked to a consortium of thirty-one cable companies— in particular, T.C.I. and Time Inc.'s cable subsidiary—for a bailout. In return for more than five hundred million dollars in cash, Turner ceded more than one-third ownership to them; he also granted the cable executives seven of fifteen board seats and an effective veto over any expenditure exceeding two million dollars. "In hindsight, you could say that Ted lost his company," Terry McGuirk says. "But, at the time, it was in many ways Nirvana, because Ted partnered with his best customers." Turner, however, wanted to expand, and his new partners did not. They wanted to protect Turner's programming assets for the cable industry and keep them away from broadcast rivals. Or they wanted the assets for themselves.

Turner had watched as, in 1985 and 1986, Murdoch formed the

Fox network, and CBS, NBC, and ABC got new owners. Increasingly frustrated, he began to spend even more time away from Atlanta. Whenever he wanted to do something bold—buy a studio or a network, for example—he confronted a veto from his board. Decisions about acquisitions were made by committee. One of the few acquisitions that the board approved, in 1991, and only after Turner wore board members down, was of Hanna-Barbera, whose animation library included more than a third of all the animated cartoons ever made in this country; with this library, Turner was able to create the now thriving Cartoon Network.

When it came to programming decisions, Turner remained in charge. Brad Siegel, the president of Turner's Entertainment Networks, remembers that when, in 1993, he was hired to run TNT Turner involved himself in such questions as what programs provided the proper lead-ins for 8 P.M. adult dramas. "One of the great things about Ted is that he watches everything," Siegel says. "Everything we make on the entertainment side—the pilots, the movies, the specials—Ted watches everything on tape. You always got a call." And when the ratings were poor but the program was good—as when TNT aired a "David Copperfield" movie—Turner congratulated Siegel.

Turner's most visible success came ten years after CNN went on the air—with its coverage of the Gulf War. Unlike the other networks, CNN made a financial commitment to cover any potential war from ground zero, Baghdad. Eason Jordan figured that the Iraqi communications system would be taken out in any allied air raid, so he recommended that CNN invest in a suitcase version of a satellite phone; this expenditure, of fifty-two thousand dollars, would be added to the extra millions that CNN was committed to spend to cover what might be the first live war. Tom Johnson, a former Los Angeles *Times* publisher, had taken over as president of CNN on August 1, 1990; the Iraqi invasion of Kuwait came on his second day at work. Johnson recalls going to Turner with various spending plans for war coverage. He asked Turner, "What am I authorized to spend?"

"You spend whatever you think it takes, pal," Turner said. Johnson was amazed, especially because, he recalls, "I'm not even sure he remembered my name."

Johnson posted people around the clock in Baghdad and Amman and Saudi Arabia and Israel and the White House and the Pentagon and the State Department. CNN, he says, spent twenty-two million dollars covering the war. CNN got permission from the Iraqi government to circumvent the Al Rashid Hotel switchboard and set up a four-wire telephone transmission from Baghdad to Amman, and then to Atlanta. When the United States destroyed the telephone system in Baghdad, only CNN had a telephone. When the Bush Administration urged the broadcast networks to pull their crews out of Iraq, they complied. Tom Johnson tells how he received calls from President Bush and other government officials, urging him to leave Baghdad, and how vexing this was. When he met with Turner and told him about these calls, and about two bureau chiefs who had been killed when he was at the Los Angeles *Times*, Turner was unmoved. He told Johnson, "I will take on myself the responsibility for anybody who is killed. I'll take it off of you if it's on your conscience." Johnson adds, "I, frankly, was about to order them back to Amman. I thought they'd all get killed."

No one got killed. And Turner was acclaimed as a different kind of businessman, one who thought about more than profit margins. When he commissioned a CNN documentary series, of more than twenty hours, on the Cold War, Rick Kaplan says, "his attitude was, if we break even on 'The Cold War' it would still be an enormous success." Turner understood, in a way that many corporate leaders do not, that building a brand can be expensive.

·   ·   ·

In the late eighties, Turner's personal life became happier. Jimmy Carter remembers that he was hunting and fishing with Turner at Avalon, Turner's estate in Tallahassee, Florida, when Turner read that Jane Fonda was planning to divorce Tom Hayden, the sixties activist. Turner told Carter that he had always admired Fonda, as an actor and as an outspoken liberal. "I think I'm going to ask her for a date," he said. When he called, Fonda put him off. She was not yet ready to date, she told Turner, although she was soon photographed at St. Bart's cavorting with an Italian soccer player.

Turner's second marriage had ended in 1988, after twenty-four years, three children, and many dalliances. His dating patterns conformed to his travel schedule; he took up with, among others, a Playboy bunny and the female pilot of his private plane. Turner was persistent with Fonda, and finally, in late 1989, they had their first date. It was followed by many others, including an Academy Awards ceremony, a White House dinner, a Kremlin dinner with Mikhail Gorbachev. They went horseback riding at Turner's Montana ranches; later, Turner, with Fonda by his side, would point out a cabin to visitors and announce that this was where they first made love. Both were famous, opinionated, rich, and attractive. Both loved the outdoors. Both had endured difficult childhoods under severe fathers. Neither finished college. And both felt profound guilt after the suicide of a parent; Fonda's mother had slashed her own throat at the age of forty-two. "She is fiercely focussed and full of idealism and, like all of us, full of insecurities, too. And so is he," the former Colorado senator Tim Wirth, who is a friend of both, says. "She reinforced all the best qualities in him. And she said to me the sweetest thing. She said, 'You know, Ted is the only person who's apologized more than I have.' They are really good, vulnerable people."

The couple held hands on Larry King's CNN program. They kissed in public. Turner brought her to CNN executive meetings and they sent mash notes to each other. She got him to drink less and diet more, to spruce up his wardrobe and buy art for his houses. Turner's mood swings became less pronounced; he yelled less, and he stopped taking lithium, which he had been on for about three years because, he says, "a quack" psychiatrist misdiagnosed him as "manic."

Turner and Fonda married in December of 1991 at his Florida estate, where bride and groom wore white and were surrounded by their children; they dined on fresh quail that Fonda had shot herself, candied yams, collard greens, and corn bread. Turner hates being alone, so Fonda moved to Atlanta. For much of the next decade, she was at his side. In Montana, Turner announced that he was getting rid of his cattle and sheep and returning the land to bison, the animals that grazed there two centuries ago. Fonda became an enthusiastic hunter. Gerald Levin, who says that he is "constitutionally opposed to killing animals," remembers how, on a visit to one of Turner's properties, he learned that Fonda had shot a deer and loaded it into a pickup truck. "I was appalled," Levin says. "It was Bambi in the back of the truck!"

In Atlanta, Turner did not live in a grand style. He poked a hole in the roof of the CNN Center building and put in a spiral staircase to connect the office to what has been called a penthouse but is really a seven-hundred-square-foot efficiency apartment, with a cramped bedroom. (One wall of the bedroom is a two-hundred-gallon saltwater fish tank, on the other side of which is the living room.) The most striking features of the apartment are a terrace, largely unused, with sweeping views of downtown (for a long while, Turner says, he "was the only downtown resident—except homeless people!"), and a photograph— one of the few on display—of Ed Turner looking up adoringly at his son. Turner had slept in his old office for a decade; this apartment allowed him to walk to work and to order room service from the Omni Hotel. To accommodate Fonda, he converted the bedroom closet into a windowless office for her—"a storage closet," Fonda called it.

"I learned a lot from Jane," Turner says. Laura Seydel, his eld-est daughter, explains that her father only reluctantly celebrated Christmas and, until he married Fonda, did not invest time in planning family gatherings. Soon Fonda and Turner and his five children and their families had reunions twice a year, and swapped Christmas presents, and attended church christenings. Laura and her husband, Rutherford Seydel II, live in Atlanta with three young children and are active in charitable activities; Sey-del works as a lawyer for Turner. He and Laura think of Turner as a great man, but he was not always a great family man. After he married Fonda, however, Grandpa Turner was around more.

Turner was surprised but not displeased that Fonda attracted more attention than he did when they travelled. Fonda says that Turner was never jealous of the notice she received. "He doesn't have that kind of ego," she says. "He put me on a pedestal. He loved my successes." Although he is not an introspective or patient man, Turner probably opened up more to Fonda than he ever had to anyone else, male or female. By most accounts, the marriage was a good one, and Turner's friends and family came to adore Fonda. Laura says, "She's grandma to our kids. She filmed our firstborn." Embraced by senior female executives at Turner Broadcasting, she went on three-day all-"girls" trips. "Her influence was profound," Jimmy Carter told me. Carter smiled as he talked about Turner. "Ted has always been very hyper, in that he's constantly having visions of grandiose things. He was very restless . . . always dreaming. Ted told us he was taking sedation to calm himself. . . . When he and Jane got together, Ted became much more relaxed."

. . .

In the early nineties, Turner began worrying once more that his company was too small. The networks had persuaded the government to relax the rules that prohibited them from owning and syndicating TV programs, which is where television fortunes are made. Turner didn't own a studio, and he feared that the studios would reserve their best programs for their networks, starving Turner Broadcasting. Nor could he match the resources of NBC, now owned by G.E., in bidding for world rights to televise the Olympics, or ABC, owned by Disney, in bidding for Monday Night Football. Turner Broadcasting got smaller compared with its competitors. The usual edge of an entrepreneur like Turner— the rabbit's advantage—seemed less vital than size.

"You need to control everything," Turner said one day recently in his New York office, his foot up against an empty coffee table. "You need to be like Rockefeller with Standard Oil. He had the oil fields, and he had the filling stations, and he had the pipelines and the trucks and everything to get the gas to the stations. And they broke him up as a monopoly. You want to control everything. You want to have a hospital and a funeral home, so when the people die in the hospital you move them right over to the funeral home next door. When they're born, you got 'em. When they're sick, you got 'em. When they die, you got 'em." He smiled and added, "The game's over when they break you up. But in the meantime you play to win. And you know you've won when the government stops you."

Turner set his sights once more on buying a studio or a TV network, or arranging a business partnership with one. With John Malone, he tried to buy Paramount. When Viacom won that competition, Turner and Malone explored purchasing ABC and then entered what Turner thought were serious negotiations to acquire NBC; again, some of the cable owners on his board opposed him. Turner says that Gerald Levin, of Time Warner (Time Inc. had merged with Warner Communications in 1990), which owned nineteen per cent of Turner's company, used that position to veto the five-billion-dollar purchase. Levin was straightforward; he said that the interests of separate companies often diverge. If Turner wanted a network, so did Levin, who was planning to launch his own network, WB.

"Everyone wanted to merge with Ted," Malone told me. "No one wanted to turn control over to Ted." This was true of Rupert Murdoch, who had once gone skiing with Turner. "He is one of the most charming people you'd ever meet," Turner says. "He told me he loved CNN the way it was and if we merged with him he wouldn't change a thing." Turner, who detests Murdoch, says that he didn't believe him. (Murdoch declined to comment.) There was a brief courtship by Bill Gates, of Microsoft; Gates thought that the power of CNN's brand could be transformed into an instantly successful online-news site. Turner thought that Microsoft's deep pockets could be used to help finance a bid for CBS. But the talks went nowhere. (Not long after this, Microsoft became a partner in MSNBC.) Meanwhile, Time Warner was determined that, if anyone was going to take over CNN and Turner's assets, it was going to be Time Warner.

When Turner is agitated, the people close to him try to prevent him from talking to reporters or giving a speech. Around this time, however, he was scheduled to speak at a National Press Club luncheon in Washington. Jane Fonda says that she was aware of the "fragility" of the relationship between Turner and Time Warner. "One false move and it would fall apart. I didn't sleep that night. Ted slept like a baby." When Turner rose to speak, he startled the audience by mentioning a story on clitorectomies that CNN had aired. Suddenly, he started comparing the mutilation of women to what Gerald Levin was doing to him. He cried out, "You talk about barbaric mutilation. Well, I'm in an angry mood. I'm angry at that, too. I'm being clitorized by Time Warner!"

"I slid under my seat," Fonda says. Levin, more diplomatically, says, "Ted is Ted. He not only says what he thinks; he gives the most amazing speeches. While I think his analogy is a little stretched, he was peeved at the time. He actually called me up, and we talked about it. It wasn't a problem."

It was a problem. Turner felt fenced in, as he does when he is handed a speech to read or when he's told that he can't do something. "My inner dream is to go to the place," he starts to explain—and suddenly breaks into the old Roy Rogers theme song—"where the West commences, gaze at the moon till I lose my senses. . . . Don't fence me in." Fences loom large in Turner's mind; he hates them, and that is one reason that his land-holdings are so vast. "I'm happiest when I'm on a horse on my ranch," he says. At the same time, he can't stand to be alone.

This much is clear: by 1995, after thirty-two years in business, Turner no longer felt like a nimble rabbit. In the spring and early summer of that year, Terry McGuirk, representing Turner, tried to extricate Turner Broadcasting from Time Warner. "I spent about six months negotiating an exit from Time Warner and doing a deal with John Malone," McGuirk recalls. But, much as Turner admired Malone, he feared placing CNN in the hands of such a committed conservative. He was also concerned about Malone's business partnerships with Murdoch. Turner's own biases clearly infected CNN. It was an international network that slavishly covered the United Nations, from whose vocabulary, by Turner's dictate, the term "foreign news" was banished, that aired documentaries on subjects Turner cared about. People at CNN undoubtedly knew what the boss wanted. But CNN was not used to punishing Turner's foes, as Murdoch's newspapers sometimes did to Murdoch's foes. Turner "never once had me pull a story," Tom Johnson says. Nor, says Gail Evans, the CNN executive vice-president in charge of booking guests, did he ever order executives to help a friend. "In my twenty years here, Ted has never once asked me to book a guest," she says.

Meanwhile, Gerald Levin had concluded that his company was not big enough; he saw CNN as "the jewel" that he could link with Time Warner's magazines. Levin also knew that he had to move fast, before Turner was bought by a competitor. After talking it over with only two members of his team—Richard Parsons, the president, and Richard Bressler, the chief financial officer—Levin phoned Turner and asked if he could fly to Montana to discuss an "important" matter.

This was in August of 1995, and by then, Turner says, "I knew I was selling the company. And there was another reason I did it, too. I was a little bit tired." He was tired of his cable partners. Whatever differences he had with Levin, however, Turner knew that Levin cared deeply about journalism, for he was a proud defender of his magazines' independence. Turner also knew that a merger would connect Turner Broadcasting to a Hollywood studio, a giant music company, the country's largest magazine-publishing enterprise, and its foremost cable system.

When Levin's plane landed that morning, Jane Fonda picked him up. Although Turner had weekend house guests—including his neighbors Meredith and Tom Brokaw—he and Levin went out on the porch alone and Levin consulted ten or so points he had jotted down on a piece of paper about why Turner and Time Warner were a perfect fit. Turner Broadcasting, he said, "would be the pivot point in the center of the company," and Ted Turner would be a partner, not an employee. When he and Levin walked back into the house and Turner saw Brokaw, who had just arrived, he shouted, "Hey, buddy. We just made a deal. We're going to merge." Brokaw remembers that Levin looked startled when Turner revealed their secret.

Turner had traded a silent boss for a real one. But he still owned almost eleven per cent of the merged company, and he was not timid. He pressed Levin to sell off company airplanes and expensive American art and to curb costs at the Hollywood studio. He stepped in to stop a fifty-million-dollar sale of Warner Bros. movies to CBS, insisting that the Warner films should be offered first to its own cable networks. He won control of all new international channels, preventing Warner Bros. from spending millions to build a staff that would duplicate Turner Broadcasting's. He pushed for across-the-board budget reductions, and, as the *Wall Street Journal* reported, he even fired his own son, Robert E. (Teddy) Turner IV, who was a promotions manager for Turner Home Entertainment, bluntly warning him over a family dinner, "You're toast."

Whether by design or by accident, Levin began to use Turner for his own purposes. "The edict from Gerry Levin was 'Let Ted be Ted,'" a Levin confidant recalls. "Time Warner was buttoned up and bureaucratic. Ted was a breath of fresh air, and Gerry used that to the advantage of the company." When they met with employees, he remembers, "Ted would get up and say, 'I've got one suit. I don't spend my money on suits. I own ten per cent of the company and each dollar you waste, ten cents comes from me.'" Levin remembers that he was "very comfortable" with Ted's saying whatever he wanted, and had no illusions that it could be any other way. Levin and many other Time Warner executives were pleasantly surprised that Turner was a team player. Within the Turner Broadcasting group, Gail Evans says, Turner didn't change the way he worked, except to occasionally say, "I have to check with the boss."

· · ·

No matter how many times Turner checked, however, he and Levin never grew close. They didn't communicate regularly. Turner was hurt that Levin, who is intensely private, never invited him to his home for dinner. They had business differences—Turner, for example, wanted Levin to fold the Warner Bros. television operations into Turner Broadcasting. He still resented Levin's veto of his potential purchase of NBC, believing that if he had succeeded he never would have sold his company and, he laments, "I'd have bought Time Warner instead of going the other way." Levin, who then wore a thick mustache chopped at the ends, as if he'd got tired of shaving, was reclusive and weighed his words carefully; the six-foot-one Turner towered over him and was impulsive. Levin was a schemer; Turner could become so focussed on the moment that sometimes when he got off his horse he dropped the reins and the horse galloped away, leaving him stranded. "There are probably not two more different individuals that I've ever worked with," Terry McGuirk says.

Inevitably, perhaps, after the Time Warner merger Turner and Murdoch declared war on each other. Turner said that Murdoch had to be stopped before he took over the media and used them as a weapon to advance his conservative agenda and his business interests. Turner asserts that men of good will can resolve differences between, say, Arabs and Israelis, yet he does not believe that it is possible to play Chamberlain to Murdoch's Hitler. "How do you make peace with a mega-maniac?" Turner said to me in a November, 1996, interview. "Chamberlain tried to make peace. When you've got somebody like that, I don't think there's a spark of human decency in him—except he likes his family." Turner said that Murdoch's Fox News network would do in America what Murdoch had done in China, where he removed the BBC from his satellite system in order to gain favor with the government. Murdoch's New York *Post* taunted Turner, describing him as a doormat for foreign dictators, suggesting that he was wacky, and portraying Fonda as Hanoi Jane. The battle became so ferocious that executives in both camps grew concerned; after all, Fox wanted television shows from Warner Bros. and Warner Bros. needed Murdoch's satellites. Fox would need Time Warner cable systems to carry its new cable news service. In the end, business interests outweighed principles, a truce was arranged, and, though Turner has never altered his view of Murdoch, he began to focus on other things.

With McGuirk running Turner Broadcasting day to day, Turner had more time. And, with Time Warner's stock price soaring, he also had more money. In September of 1997, he was to be honored by the United Nations Association-USA, and he had the idea of giving a billion dollars—then a third of his wealth—to the United Nations. The Turners were flying to New York when Turner told his wife what he planned. "I was extremely moved," Jane Fonda says, adding that she told her husband, "Don't you think you should talk to your lawyers first?" He did, and learned that he could not make the gift directly to the U.N.

The next day, as U.N. Secretary-General Kofi Annan recalls, Turner walked into Annan's office and blurted, "Hi, Kofi. I'm going to give you a billion dollars."

"I thought it was a joke," Annan says, shaking his head in wonderment.

That night, Turner announced that he would give a hundred million dollars a year for ten years to support such U.N. programs as the elimination of land mines, providing medicine for children, and easing the plight of refugees. He hired Tim Wirth, who eventually recruited a staff of thirty-two, to oversee the effort. Turner's only condition was that his money be used only minimally for administrative overhead. Annan remembers that Turner also said, "All of you billionaires out there, watch out. I'm coming after you."

Turner has written his own version of the Ten Commandments, which he keeps on typed cards in his wallet. Without prompting, he will read from a list that includes these vows: " 'I promise to care for planet earth and all living things thereon'; 'I promise to treat all persons everywhere with dignity, respect, and friendliness'; 'I promise to have no more than one or two children'; 'I reject the use of force'; 'I support the United Nations.'" Along with his manifest generosity, Turner remains enough of a ham to seek a fitting reward: a Nobel Prize. "I've thought about it a little bit," Turner said when I asked him. "Of course I've thought of it."

Turner is easily moved to tears. He sobbed openly when Princess Diana was killed. On a trip to China in October of 1999, with Fonda reading and CNN's Eason Jordan working, Turner put on his headphones and popped in the videotape of a popular Warner Bros. cartoon movie, "The Iron Giant," the story of the friendship between a young boy and a metallic being from outer space who sacrifices himself for the sake of the planet. Jordan remembers looking over at his boss. "Tears were streaming down his face," he says. "I never saw anybody cry like that in my life." As the credits rolled, Turner called out, "That's the saddest thing I've ever seen!"

America and Russia still have some seven thousand nuclear weapons targeted at each other, and Turner is terrified that these— along with chemical and biological weapons—could fall into the wrong hands. He dismisses the Bush Administration's effort to build an anti-missile defense system as madness; the technology won't work, he says, and, in any case, it won't prevent weapons of mass destruction from being delivered by car, by ship, or in a suit-case. All these dangers are "off the radar screen," he says. "We have a huge job. Probably ninety-five per cent of the U.S. population doesn't know about it." Thus Turner's Nuclear Threat Initiative. To lead it, he has recruited former Senator Sam Nunn, who once chaired the Armed Services Committee, and who signed on only after Turner agreed to allow him a free hand. "When he gets behind something, people know it's serious, and it's going to have the energy and resources," Nunn says. Most days, Turner is a fan of the cautious Nunn; some days, he worries that Nunn is fencing him in.

•   •   •

Turner's miserable last year actually began a few years ago, when Fonda began spending more time in Atlanta and less time with him. She wanted to be with her daughter Vanessa Vadim, who had moved to Atlanta and was raising a child on her own. Fonda's daughter Lulu, whose father was a Black Panther, and whom Jane took in when she and Tom Hayden ran a California camp for troubled kids, had also moved to Atlanta. In addition, Fonda had started the Georgia Campaign for Adolescent Pregnancy Prevention, and had taken up the cause of nurturing teen mothers. During this time (according to an E! biography of Fonda that aired last fall), Fonda started attending services at the Providence Missionary Baptist Church. Turner, who alternately describes himself as an atheist and an agnostic, told me his reaction: "I had absolutely no warning about it. She didn't tell me she was thinking about doing it. She just came home and said, 'I've become a Christian.' Before that, she was not a religious person. That's a pretty big change for your wife of many years to tell you. That's a shock. I mean, normally that's the kind of thing your wife or husband would discuss with you before they did it or while they were thinking about it. . . . Obviously, we weren't communicating very well at that time."

"My becoming a Christian upset him very much—for good reason," Fonda says. "He's my husband and I chose not to discuss it with him—because he would have talked me out of it. He's a debating champion. He saw it as writing on the wall. And it was about other things. He knew my daughter was having a baby and it would take me away from him. He needs someone to be there one hundred per cent of the time. He thinks that's love. It is not love. It's babysitting. I didn't want to tell you this. We went in different directions. I grew up." Turner's daughter Laura doesn't think religion per se was the real basis of their disagreement. She says, "It was another male"—Jesus. "It took time away from him."

There were other differences, friends of both say, including Turner's libido and his insecurities. "My problem is I love every woman I meet," Turner has said. He and Fonda visited marriage counsellors and psychiatrists, to no avail. On January 4, 2000, they announced an official separation; before the announcement, Frédérique D'arragon, who is fifty-one, and has been in and out of Turner's life for more than thirty years, came back into it. She is almost a foot shorter than Turner, and prefers jeans to designer dresses. Fonda and D'arragon had lunch recently in Atlanta, and Fonda makes it clear that D'arragon will be available for Ted in ways she no longer can be: "He needs to be taken care of. She has no children. And she's loved him a long time." But travelling with Ted has taken its toll on D'arragon, just as it did on Fonda. Turner admits that the persistent travel is "driving her nuts."

A close friend says that Turner is burdened by three things: an insecurity that can be traced back to his abusive father; a manic, restless nature; and lust. "Each one of these is a great huge bear," the friend says. "Turner must wrestle with three bears, and they sometimes overwhelm him." Fonda puts it another way: "Why this guy didn't go under psychologically at age five, I don't know. It scarred him for life. It colors everything—his relationships, his anxieties . . ."

Fonda and Turner insist that they still love each other; in fact, the best I have ever seen Turner look—his white hair washed and carefully combed, his thin white mustache trimmed, a chocolate-brown sports jacket nicely contrasting with pressed gray slacks, a burgundy tie, and brown Gucci loafers—was a December day in Atlanta when he and Fonda had a lunch date. Both friends and family are distressed by their split. But Fonda, despite her own notoriety as an actor and as a political activist, had lived in the shadow of three dominant husbands. By leaving Turner, she also announced her own liberation.

Turner was despondent, and his sense of abandonment was heightened by the announcement, around the same time, that Time Warner was merging with AOL—more accurately, AOL was acquiring Time Warner. The price, based on the stock values of the companies on the day of the announcement, was pegged at a hundred and sixty-five billion dollars, the largest corporate marriage ever. Although Turner had been alerted to the merger discussions, he had not been invited by Gerald Levin to participate.

"Ted was not a strategic partner," a senior executive at Time Warner who is close to Turner told me. "Gerry is a sole practitioner. He keeps things to himself. Ted was not in the loop. Yet Ted did not hesitate to endorse the deal." It was, after all, a growth strategy. Nor, according to an AOL strategist who was a party to the negotiations, was Turner's future role even a minor part of these discussions. What was talked about much more, he continued, was what a great fit CNN and AOL would be. "You can AOL-ize CNN and do cross-promotions," the executives said enthusiastically. CNN, in fact, was desperately in need of promotion, for its ratings had plunged and its promotion budget had been cut.

Turner would own four per cent (now just over three and a half per cent) of the new company and remain on the board, and he had won a vice-chairman title. But, while executives at the two companies respected Turner's many successes and his "vision," they also found him unfathomable. One senior AOL executive who was working with Turner for the first time says, "In meetings I've been in with him, he just sits there and in a piercing voice—louder than you would expect someone to talk—he interrupts or conveys a sense of 'Hurry up! Why am I here?' He gives off a feeling that he's in a rush, even if he's not doing anything."

Over the next several months, as the two companies tried to get their executives working together and achieve the synergies they had touted, Turner was in Atlanta or New York no more than four or five days a month. He was not involved in budget details, as Terry McGuirk was, and soon McGuirk, an original Turner loyalist, signalled that he "wanted out from under Ted," a senior member of the AOL Time Warner team explains. McGuirk admired Turner, but, if he was to be held responsible, then he wanted the authority, too.

There was one other difficulty. In the reorganized company, Steve Case was going to be the chairman and Levin the C.E.O., and the idea was to divide the company into separate spheres, each reporting to one of two presidents. Time Warner's Richard Parsons would oversee movies, music, publishing, legal affairs, and human resources. AOL's Robert Pittman would oversee AOL, cable, the magazines, television (including HBO, Turner Broadcasting, and the WB television network), and business development. "By a process of elimination, it made sense for Terry McGuirk to report to Bob and for Ted to take a strategic role," a senior AOL Time Warner strategist says.

Sometimes Turner made light of his diminished role. Lou Dobbs remembers being invited to Turner's Montana ranch for a weekend. While they were fishing, Dobbs, who left CNN in 1999 to start an Internet venture, Space.com—and who returned last week to, among other things, anchor "Moneyline News Hour"—said, "Ted, I outrank you. I'm C.E.O. and chairman."

"You're forgetting," Turner said. "I'm also chairman of the Turner Foundation."

"Ted, that's nonprofit!"

"What do you think Space.com is?" Turner retorted, laughing.

Dobbs laughs, too, when telling this story, but, like many of Turner's friends, he is angry. "He has not been treated with the respect due him," Dobbs says. Jane Fonda agrees. "The way it was handled was really shocking," she says. "It makes me mad. How dare they give him a phone call!" Surely Turner did not feel that he was treated properly when CNN cancelled a pet project of his—a multi-part documentary exploring the proliferation of nuclear weapons. He recruited a producer, George Crile, but, soon after Crile started work, Turner told him that he was encountering budget opposition at CNN. They would have to scale the project back to three hours. By October, 2000, it was down to a single hour. "There's a lot of pressure to make the budgets," Turner explained, disappointed. In fact, he is so agitated by the budgeting strictures at CNN that, in December, he told me, "I am going to produce, myself, ten hours on nuclear proliferation and chemical and biological warfare. I'll give first crack to CNN, and if they don't want it I'll give it to PBS." (By

March, CNN's founder had given up on CNN documentaries. Together with former associates like Pat Mitchell, who is the president of PBS, and Robert Wussler, who had been a top Turner Broadcasting executive, he plans to team up with Bill Moyers for a series of PBS documentaries on world issues; the Turner Foundation will provide half the financing. "Over the next few years I would hope we would do one hundred hours," Wussler says.)

When he cut the Crile project from three hours to one, Tom Johnson says, "Ted wasn't happy. I don't think he's happy with me. Ted knows I'm in a new world today." Turner was reminded of this "new world" when he invited me to sit in on a CNN executive-committee meeting on December 19th, and the invitation was rescinded. "He invited you to a meeting that is not his meeting," an AOL Time Warner executive explained.

Then, this past January, although Turner calls CNN "the most profitable news operation in the world"—it earned three hundred million dollars the previous year—its staff, of more than four thousand, was reduced by nearly ten per cent. Those who are gone include such Turner stalwarts as Elsa Klensch, Barbara Pyle, Nick Charles, Larry Woods, Gene Randall, and the Atlanta-based Turner Environment Division, with its show "People Count," which Fonda sometimes hosted. On CNN evening programs, talk replaced news reports—often the shouting-head format that CNN inaugurated with "Crossfire" and which Fox News and MSNBC had copied and extended. "Basically, the Fox prime-time schedule is just talk radio," Rick Kaplan, the former CNN/U.S. president, says.

Tom Johnson, who is worried about the future of CNN, says that Bob Pittman assured him that he and his colleagues in New York believed in CNN's mission. But Pittman's definition of CNN's mission may not match Johnson's or Turner's. Daily journalism is an inherently wasteful process: it involves waiting for calls to be returned, for airlines to fly, keeping forty-two bureaus functioning, chasing stories that don't pan out, and sometimes working for days on a single story. Will stockholders think this productive? As late as December, a longtime Turner executive predicted, "Ted will protect us."

Less than three months later, Turner was unable to protect two longtime lieutenants—Terry McGuirk and Steve Heyer. Turner says McGuirk and Heyer chafed at AOL Time Warner's demand that Turner Broadcasting's "operating profits" (EBITDA, which are earnings before interest, taxes, depreciation, and amortization) grow by thirty-nine per cent in 2001—which Turner says is nearly double the actual profit-growth average of the company over the past five years. "They were unhappy mainly that the financial goals they were given were unachievable without really hurting the company," Turner says.

AOL Time Warner executives insist that the true profit-growth target for the Turner Broadcasting division is half that, and that Turner's percentage does not reflect significant accounting changes. (Nonsense, senior executives at Turner Broadcasting say, claiming that their operating profits in 2000 were just under a billion dollars and that their company-imposed goal for 2001 is nearly $1.4 billion; the growth target that AOL Time Warner presented to Wall Street for the entire company in 2001 is thirty-one per cent.) Associates say Pittman is disturbed that CNN has lost market share to Fox News and MSNBC; CNN's prime-time ratings for the first quarter of 2001 were down five per cent from last year, while Fox News's climbed by a hundred and twenty-six per cent and MSNBC's by seventeen per cent. Turner is particularly worried about Fox News, which is in fewer homes but has talk-show hosts like the conservative Bill O'Reilly, who is now reaching a larger audience than Larry King, CNN's ratings champion.

Turner says that he is uncomfortable with what he believes are arbitrary budget goals—what he called the company's new preoccupation with "short-term fluctuations" in its stock price—

saying, "I never ran the company by the numbers." Pittman denies that the company is being run strictly by the numbers. "I think CNN is one of the great assets in the world," he says. "But it takes a long time to build a franchise based on reliability and trust. They got it. That's something you can't replace overnight. That's the core, the value." And, Pittman adds, "everyone agreed on" a growth-target number, including, he implies, McGuirk. McGuirk, asked about the growth target, refuses to comment. He does say, "The numbers are given to us, not negotiated."

•   •   •

Ted Turner today gets more notice outside his company than in it. When Fidel Castro came to New York last year for a three-day summit meeting at the U.N., he wanted to spend one night having dinner with Turner, who flew in from Montana for the occasion. The dinner stretched past midnight, and Castro was in the middle of a long-winded story when Turner raised his hand and exclaimed, "Fidel, this story is never going to end, is it? I got to go!" Castro laughed as Turner exited. Turner was the first Western businessman to have a private audience with Russia's new President, Vladimir Putin, who, Turner remembers, used to drive him when Turner visited St. Petersburg and Putin was a deputy to the city's mayor. "I learned the value of being nice to everyone," Turner says, jokingly. In a trip arranged by George Crile, last May, Turner was also among the few private citizens to visit a nuclear command center outside Moscow. General Vladimir Yakovlev, the commander of Russia's Strategic Rocket Forces, cautioned, "Don't touch any buttons!" There was a Pow-erPoint presentation, in English, delineating Russia's various nuclear forces. Turner learned that each of seven thousand warheads could obliterate everything within a one-to-two-mile radius before the radiation and the fires spread. Turner sat mute,

Eason Jordan recalls, for an hour and a half, transfixed by what he heard and saw. "It was the only time I ever saw him speechless," Jordan says.

Yakovlev and Putin, like Castro, watch CNN. "The Carter Center has programs in sixty-five different nations," Jimmy Carter says. "We deal with leaders of nations who have a human-rights problem or conflict. . . . We go to those countries, and they quite often do not have a U.S. embassy in them. Invariably, in the offices there will be a TV station tuned to CNN." They know about Turner, and they know, Carter adds, that Turner is a true citizen of the world, a man who speaks up for what he believes even when it offends his government. Carter describes Turner as a personal "hero." Kofi Annan sees this in Turner's appeal. "He and Castro have a similar quality," Annan says. "They are folk heroes of a sort. You can have one hundred heads of state here, and most people will gravitate toward Castro. You can have one hundred media heads here, and people will gravitate toward Ted."

In mid-March, Turner made a two-day visit to Harvard. An evening appearance at the Kennedy School of Government drew a large audience, and he was introduced by Alex S. Jones, the director of the Joan Shorenstein Center on the Press, Politics and Public Policy, who said, "Ted Turner changed America." Turner jumped up on the low platform, pumped Jones's hand, and started talking, with Jones still at his side. Turner used no notes. He wore a blue corduroy jacket and gray slacks. Perhaps it was the way he jumped up and, in his joltingly loud voice, started talking quickly, or the way he suddenly paused and drawled, "Ahhhhhhhhhh"; or perhaps it was the way he seemed to lapse into self-pity when he said, "I'm just trying to do the best I can," or the way he raced from subject to subject, sometimes letting thoughts collide—how he was rejected by Harvard when he applied, and how he'd given Jane Fonda a hundred million dollars, and how, just recently, she bestowed more than twelve million of that sum on Harvard's School of Education for the study of gender and education, and how he wasn't a journalist but had related to the species since he sold newspapers as a boy—perhaps it was these quirks that caused the audience, as often happens when Turner speaks, to giggle. Michael Baumgartner, a first-year graduate student, initially thought Turner sounded drunk. Watching Turner speak is like watching live TV, with the audience wondering what will happen next.

But although at first people seemed to be laughing at Turner, the feeling in the room soon changed. On being told that President Bush earlier that day had abandoned a campaign pledge to establish "mandatory reduction targets" for carbon-dioxide emissions by power plants, Turner was momentarily silenced. "That's heartbreaking news," he said finally. "I mean, I can't take any more bad news. I've lost my job and my wife this year!" Turner went on to talk about the environment, and about curbing nuclear weapons, and about his commitment to news. When he finished, students clamored to shake his hand.

That night, Turner was discreet about CNN. Asked about its future, he said, "Well, I hope it's a bright one." But, while Turner thinks CNN has programmed "too much" talk, he has no idea how to cure its ratings woes: "Quite frankly, I'm not sure I have the answers." Privately, he is concerned about a general dumbing down that is taking place in the media, putting "DiSiprio"—he means Leonardo DiCaprio—"on the cover of *Time*. Obviously, it should be on the cover of *People* or *Entertainment Weekly*!"

By the next morning, the man who confesses to a congenital inability to police a secret was no longer restrained. Turner did not criticize the recent round of cutbacks at CNN, but he did criticize the parent company's growth target. This was impossible to achieve, Turner said, without doing harm to CNN's journalism. "I always wanted CNN to be the New York *Times* of the television business," he said, a little sadly.

●　　　●　　　●

Although the AOL Time Warner merger took effect only in January, there have already been some successes. As the largest individual shareholder in the conglomerate, Turner is enthusiastic about a new emphasis on coordination and synergy. Of Gerald Levin's management over the past five years, Turner bluntly says, "The Time Warner divisions did not cooperate the way they should have. . . . I think he did a pretty marginal job of running the company." Now, with roughly forty per cent of Americans using AOL to reach the Internet, AOL is vital in promoting each division of the company. In the eight months ending January 31st, for example, Pittman told Wall Street analysts, AOL had sold eight hundred thousand new subscriptions to Time Inc.'s different magazines. The company is in various businesses, Levin said at a conference earlier this month, but one word united them: "subscriptions"—a total of a hundred and thirty million subscribers.

Turner, however, is afraid that when journalistic divisions like CNN shrink corporate executives may try to "avoid doing stories that are critical of the big companies, like the oil companies and the automobile companies. It's not easy to do stories that are critical of G.E.—you know, nuclear-power-plant stories. When was the last time you saw stories on TV critical of G.E. or DuPont? Better to stay away from the corporations—they're the sponsors. That's the danger." Turner, to be sure, does not talk about the embarrassments of his own tenure, including CNN's unceasing coverage of the O. J. Simpson murder case and trial.

At another of his Harvard appearances—a session in which he was questioned by Jones and several others for an hour and then stayed for an hour more as the six finalists for the Goldsmith Prize for Investigative Reporting discussed their stories—Turner said, "I've already been fired, and I probably will be again shortly." One of the Shorenstein Fellows rose and condescendingly suggested that Turner might follow the example of Henry Ford, who also left his job but who set up the Ford Foundation, which is "one of the most influential forces for the framing of issues in the country. You have a life and a future and can use your contacts—"

"I am," Turner interrupted, and he mentioned his gift to the U.N. Foundation. "No other individual in the world is giving as much to the poor world as I am. I'm spending fifty million dollars in the United States, mostly on environmental and family-planning causes. Ahhhhhhhh . . . I mean, family planning is under attack. You know, pro-lifers have got control of the White House. Roe v. Wade is hanging on by a thread. A woman's right to choose? They want to take that away. We're fighting global warming." He mentioned the Nuclear Threat Initiative and the dues payment to the U.N. "And let me tell you what else I'm doing. I'm very close to making an announcement of a personal partnership through our foundation with public broadcasting to fund important documentaries that Turner Broadcasting has dropped. . . . And I've been trying desperately to get my network. It won't be NBC, but it will start with an N—NTV. The good news? I'm gonna get my network. The bad news? It's in Russia! I'm gonna try and help freedom of the press. I mean, I am doing plenty, Bubba!"

It's not entirely clear whether Turner will own a network in Russia. In early April, he announced a plan to purchase part of the network founded by the Russian press baron Vladimir A. Gusinsky. This pleased independent Russian journalists like Masha Lipman, the deputy editor of the magazine *Itogi*, who says, "It will be much more difficult for the Russian authorities to play dirty jokes" on Turner. But the hard questions, she says, are two: Who will control the journalistic enterprise—Turner or the Russian authorities? And will Turner receive real guarantees of editorial freedom? Turner's longtime colleague Bob Wussler says that Gazprom, the state-dominated monopoly that has asserted control over the TV network, told him and Turner, "You go do a deal with Gusinsky and come back and we'll do a deal with you." And even though President Putin stopped short of offering what Wussler calls "a ringing endorsement" of press freedom when Turner asked for it, Wussler feels that "Putin is a politician and can say just so much. We took it as a good sign." Last week, however, Turner was struggling to invent a formula to satisfy Gusinsky, Gazprom, and the journalists themselves. On the surface, the deal is consistent with Turner's world-diplomacy principle—"Just about everybody will be friendly toward us if we are friendly with them." But it may also suggest a certain naïveté.

Turner's ability to give his money away has diminished as his principal stock holding—AOL Time Warner—has declined by more than thirty per cent since the merger announcment, reducing his net worth by about two billion dollars. It is possible, he tells me, that he will end his association with the company entirely. He hasn't quite accepted the idea that his business career is largely over, but he believes that his primary mission now is to help save the world, and perhaps himself.

"For some reason, he has a guilty conscience," Jane Fonda told me. "He went much further than his father thought he would. So what's left? To be a good guy. He knows he will go down in history. He won't go down as a greedy corporate mogul. Although he claims to be an atheist, at the end of every speech he says, 'God bless you.' He wants to get into Heaven." Fonda told me of a family outing in 1992 on the occasion of the five-hundredth anniversary of Columbus's discovery of America. They went to a matinée of a film about Columbus and in the darkened theatre someone screamed out a litany of Columbus's supposed sins. There was a silence, until Turner blurted, "I never did that!" Fonda reached over and soothed her husband by patting his knee and said, "It's O.K., honey. I know you didn't." She now says, "I did that a lot." Turner concedes, "I wish I didn't apologize as much as I do."

Over breakfast at the Charles Hotel, in Cambridge, I asked Turner why he felt so burdened. "It's the position you're in," he said. "Because I was at CNN, because I had commitments, because I did the Goodwill Games, because I was concerned, because I did all those documentaries, I developed a self-imposed sense of responsibility. If Gandhi and Martin Luther King could make the kind of sacrifices with their lives that they did, and that our parents did fighting in World War I and World War II, why couldn't I make sacrifices, too?" At that, Turner looked up from his hearty chipped-beef-and-biscuit breakfast, in the middle of the hotel dining room, and, as people at nearby tables leaned forward to listen, he performed from memory parts of Thomas Macaulay's "Horatius":

> And how can man die better
> Than facing fearful odds,
> For the ashes of his fathers,
> And the temples of his gods. . . .
>
> Haul down the bridge, Sir Consul
> With all the speed ye may;
> I, with two more to help me,
> Will hold the foe in play.
> In yon straight path a thousand
> May well be stopped by three.
> Now who will stand on either hand,
> And keep the bridge with me?

"Pretty cool, huh," Turner said, grinning; he had, in the longer version that he recited, got almost every word right. "If Horatius could do it, I can do it. He saved Rome. . . . He stopped the Etruscans." His smile widened, and he couldn't resist a final bow, with a loud "heh-heh-heh." Then he leaned over and whispered, as if to a co-conspirator, "I know *a lot*. My knowledge is my burden. If I didn't know so much, I could just go through life as a dilettante." He stood up and, watched by everyone in the room, walked briskly to the door.

The Atlantic Monthly

FINALIST, REVIEWS
AND CRITICISM

Confessions of a Prep School College Counselor

Caitlin Flanagan's writing flows with engaging humor and bracing common sense. Whether she's dissecting the grandiose vulgarity of the modern wedding, the temptingly lurid appeal of supermarket tabloids, or the Inquisition-like process of college admissions, Flanagan combines personal perspective with critical distance, constructing arguments that engage readers on a variety of levels. Hers is a truly fresh voice in the critical chorus.

Caitlin Flanagan

Confessions of a Prep School College Counselor

The author looks at books about college admissions—and at the unexamined prejudices fueling the "elite" college admissions frenzy.

Several years ago I was teaching *The Great Gatsby* to a class of eleventh-graders at Harvard-Westlake, a private school in Los Angeles. We began our discussion with a consideration of Tom and Daisy Buchanan. The students more or less understood Daisy. These were teenagers from Beverly Hills and Brentwood and Encino, kids for whom Daisy, with her particular collection of pleasures and discontents, her fluttering dress and her voice like money, was not entirely beyond the realm of experience. Tom was another matter.

"What's he like?" I asked. A hand shot up: "He's highly intelligent." I looked at the boy who said this with some puzzlement. He had just read the chapter in which Tom sputters out the theories—"scientific stuff"—that he has gleaned from a book called *The Rise of the Colored Empires,* among them that "it's up to us, who are the dominant race, to watch out or these other races will have control of things." This is not the sort of opinion with which children from Beverly Hills and Brentwood and Encino tend to be sympathetic.

"What makes you think he's so smart?" I asked. The boy replied, "Because he went to Yale." I burst out laughing and then gave the class a little lecture regarding the way that Ivy League schools have changed in the past several decades—about what a Yale degree suggested about someone fifty years ago as opposed to what it suggests today. That despite the current admissions crunch there are still plenty of nimrods collecting Yale diplomas was a life lesson I decided to let them learn out in the field.

.   .   .

A couple of years later, when I became a college counselor at the school, I was introduced to such odd and inexplicable notions about colleges that I felt nostalgic for the good old days of explaining that holding a Yale degree doesn't make Tom Buchanan a genius. I had assumed, naively, that the new job would be easy. By every objective measure our students were among the best-prepared for college in North America; in a typical year a quarter of the class attends either an Ivy League school or Stanford University. More impressive, the ones from the bitter bottom of the class were going off to colleges that most high school seniors can only dream about.

I had no idea what I was in for—no idea that the confident,

buoyant students for whom I'd had such great affection when I encountered them in the classroom would so often turn into complete neurotics the moment they crossed the threshold of the college-counseling office. Or that their parents, who had always been lovely and appreciative when I was teaching their children, would become irritable and demanding once I was helping them all select a college. Granted, every year there were families who impressed me with their good cheer and resource-fulness in the face of the thorny admissions climate. But invari-ably a core group seemed to be teetering on the brink of emo-tional collapse. What I was observing, I later discovered, was a common phenomenon among the families of college-bound students of a certain social class, one aptly described by the psy-chologist Michael Thompson in a justly famous 1990 essay titled "College Admission as a Failed Rite of Passage." College admis-sions, Thompson wrote, "can make normal people act nutty, and nutty people act quite crazy." Bingo. I had inherited a Rolodex full of useful phone numbers (the College Board, a helpful coun-selor in the UCLA admissions office), but the number I kept handing out was that of a family therapist. "Maybe he could help you a bit," I would say gently after yet another unexpectedly combustive family meeting. I could have understood the forceful nature of the families' emotions if the stakes had been higher. If the child had a single shot at a scholarship and a college educa-tion, and a letter of rejection meant that he or she would lead a fundamentally different life—that was a situation I could imag-ine being rife with heartache and regret. But when the sting of a Bowdoin rejection was lessened (the same day) by the salve of a Colby acceptance, when a rejection from Dartmouth meant the student would be off to Penn—where was the horror? If a family had the wherewithal to send a beloved and supremely well pre-pared child off to one of the hundred or so first-rate colleges in America, the resources to offer a semester abroad, the connec-tions necessary to facilitate a wonderful summer internship in

New York or Hollywood or Costa Rica, and the ability to bankroll, without blinking, all of graduate school, then what was the source of these unstoppable tears?

Each of the hot hundred colleges held a certain position in a vast and inscrutable cosmology that only the students and their parents seemed to understand. The very names of schools I had always considered excellent made many students shudder—Kenyon, for example. They would snap briskly to attention if I said "Williams" or "Amherst." So why not Kenyon?

On the other hand, schools that I had never considered particularly dazzling turned out to be white-hot centers of the universe. In vast, high-achieving droves, for example, these kids wanted to go to Duke. Fine, but here's where I couldn't figure them out: they were dying to go to Duke, but Chapel Hill left them cold. Why? They couldn't put it into words exactly; it was as inexplicable and irreducible as falling in love. They would do whatever it took to get themselves to Duke—enroll in as many AP classes as they could, stuff their heads full of Robert Lowell poems and differential equations and plein air paintings, invest untold, unrecoverable hours cramming for standardized tests that a growing number of admissions experts hope to abolish altogether.

•   •   •

Certainly, I understood why students who had worked so hard and done so well would want to go to schools like Harvard and Princeton, but many places seem to be prestigious simply because student fads and crazes have made them hard to get into. Brazenly capitalizing on the whims and passions of teenagers seems a questionable practice for institutions dedicated, in part, to the well-being of young people. Here's how Rachel Toor describes her former job as an admissions officer at Duke in her new book, *Admissions Confidential*:

I travel around the country whipping kids (and their parents) into a frenzy so that they will apply. I tell them how great a school Duke is academically and how much fun they will have socially. Then, come April, we reject most of them.

The university devotes a considerable amount of money and effort to recruiting BWRKs ("bright, well-rounded kids") only because denying them boosts the school's selectivity rating. Although Toor seems disillusioned by the task of pumping up application rates, she also seems to believe that some measure of a school's worth can be found in the number of students it rejects.

Although the books devoted to "elite" and "top" and "highly selective" college admissions currently make up a vast literature, the very notion of a how-to manual devoted to the secrets of blasting one's way into the Ivy League is, in fact, a relatively recent phenomenon. The 1961 book *The Ivy League Today*, for example, was much more concerned with "Ivy mores and conduct" than with test scores and personal essays. The first chapter, "The Couth and the Uncouth," approvingly described the Ivy Leaguer's "amused tolerance" of the nationwide craze for all things Ivy that had begun in the late fifties. Ivy fashion "became an absolute uniform among the college students of the nation," Frederic Birmingham, the book's author, wrote. "It was also adopted by nightclub comics, prizefighters, delivery boys, and gangsters appearing before Senate committees, although these usually muscular gentlemen emphasized a snugger fit at hips and thigh."

This newly heightened national interest in the Ivy League was probably the impetus for the publication of another 1961 book on the subject, this one a bit less insouciant in tone and nature: *How an Ivy League College Decides on Admissions*. It was the culmination of a year-long investigation of admissions practices at Yale, and was first published, in shorter form, as an essay in *The*

New Yorker (it may in fact be the ur-text for the sort of book of which *Admissions Confidential* is the most recent). Although the Yale depicted in the book seems to have given longer shrift to grades and scores than *The Ivy League Today* would have one believe, great care was taken not to admit a class composed entirely of "successful test-takers" and (to use the dean of admissions's telling term) "little twerps." Pushiness, overeagerness, any display of uncouthly aggressive behavior, was an unpardonable sin to the admissions office. One boy's future at Yale was grievously jeopardized by his zealous father, who used a chance encounter with an admissions officer to brandish a scrapbook of his son's accomplishments. The admissions officer on whom the scrapbook was foisted sadly remarked.

> "The pitiful thing is that the boy is a great kid. The whole incident, which will do him no good, will have to be brought out at the committee meeting. The parental strategy here gives a slight insight into the boy's home life and background."

This chilling use of the word "background" is more revealing of what did or did not constitute Ivy material than anything else in the book.

Two decades later the world had changed. By the 1980s being able to wear a pair of khakis with a certain casual elegance no longer greased the skids in an Ivy League admissions office, because suddenly numberless ruffians with all manner of more substantial accomplishments were gumming up the works. By the 1980s admissions guidebooks no longer took the form of sociological surveys; they had become utterly prescriptive in nature. The subtitle of the first chapter of *How to Get Into an Ivy League School* (1985) was "A Gate Crasher's Guide to the Ivy League," and the chapter described an admissions scene in which eagerness and grinding preparation were the very stuff of which an Ivy League admission was made. This was the beginning of the era in which Ivy League applicants needed almost ludicrously impressive bona fides if they were to be alive in the water. Even a girl who was "streamlined Ivy, prepped from the cradle," needed not only a high school visit to Israel to give her the stuff of a winning essay but a visit that happened to occur (some kids are just born lucky) "during the invasion of Lebanon."

Had the current admissions climate existed back then, of course, her trip wouldn't have clinched the deal unless her *destination* had been Lebanon. Nothing makes today's Ivy League admissions officer sit up and take notice more than a flak jacket and flying shrapnel—that is, as long as it's accompanied by a 5 on the AP physics exam and a combined SAT score of 1420 or better. For the most part, the current books on the subject of elite-college admissions share a numbing sameness, although I did find The Princeton Review's *College Admissions* remarkable for its rather caustic counsel: "Misspellings in your application can make you look like a moron," it advises, and "You probably should not attach a photograph to your application if you are very overweight." I'd like to have most of these books burned. They explain that if kids are to have any chance at a top college, they must pursue the most rigorous curriculum available to them, both within and without the walls of their secondary schools. That's true. It is also true that such a curriculum is going to crush a lot of kids. A regimen of brutal academic hazing may be appropriate in some disciplines, for medical students or Ph.D. candidates, but it is not appropriate for fifteen-year-olds.

A subcategory of this genre of books is composed of in-depth narrative accounts of the experiences of individual students applying to Ivy League colleges, their every emotional nuance dwelled on in luxuriant detail. It's a kind of admissions porn, which, like all pornography produced for a niche market, can seem simultaneously comical and befuddling to those outside the niche. Bill Paul's

Getting In (even the title is suggestive) describes the experiences of five Princeton applicants. Paul recounts his interviews with these teenagers in a style appropriate to, say, a Sue Grafton novel ("Lucy spoke with the hard, nasal accent of southern New Jersey as she held aloft a solitary French fry and pointed it at me"), adding to the impression that these kids are not merely applying to college but are in fact involved in a drama of almost life-and-death consequence. The teenagers described in such books have transferred the most profound and elemental of adolescent emotions—romantic attraction—onto the most unromantic of pursuits: college selection. *Getting Into Yale* is, according to its jacket copy, "the tale of Josh Berezin, who after only one visit, became obsessed with entering the hallowed halls and tree-lined yards of Yale." What happened during this visit to turn the poor boy into an obsessive? Well, he loved the Gothic architecture, and he had a good meal ("the best calzone *ever*") at a restaurant five minutes from campus, and an admissions person told him that Yale students like to argue vehemently and then go out and play Frisbee. (Were these arguments perhaps about whether or not to play Frisbee? Unclear.) Although its rather misleading subtitle—"How One Student Wrote *THIS* Book and Got Into the School of His Dreams"—suggests that Berezin's admission was the result of a stunt, in fact he had the goods, carrying a healthy number of APs (four in his junior year), scoring notably well on his boards (all but one of his scores were in the 700s), and participating on the varsity football and wrestling teams. He did the requisite bit of community service, including a stint with Habitat for Humanity ("the most exciting moment was when I got called a 'white bitch' by some kid on a bike"), and also endured an arduous Outward Bound program ("I'm talking *Deliverance* backwoods here"). The most revealing part of the book consists of diary entries, which clearly show just how hard high school students bound for elite colleges must work. The busy roster of extracurricular activities that Berezin pursued during the summer after his junior year was brutal enough ("For the past four days I've been running from football to the ghetto and back again"). But the demands of the coursework itself are what really command attention. Late one night in the midst of his studies he wonders.

> Where the hell did the time go? The only way I could finish all my homework would be to stay up till about 3 a.m., but if I do there's no way I'll be productive tomorrow. I suppose I probably should get used to it now if I plan to go to medical school.

. . .

Students who are up for this kind of rigor should consider doing several things. First, they should buy a single very useful guidebook: *A Is for Admission: The Insider's Guide to Getting Into the Ivy League and Other Top Colleges*, by Michele Hernández, a former assistant director of admissions at Dartmouth. In a roundabout way Hernández teaches upper-middle-class kids a lesson that refined mothers used to inculcate from the cradle onward. If you've got it don't flaunt it.

> If your father is the president and CEO of a big-name investment bank, the committee is going to be expecting quite an amazing applicant, one who has gone beyond his comfy lifestyle to make himself known. You might just write down "banker" for occupation. It's not a lie, but at the same time, it doesn't create such a high expectation in terms of wealth and privilege. Rather than saying "chief neurosurgeon," why not just M.D.? Rather than "chief partner in a major law firm," just put "lawyer."

The second thing applicants ought to consider seriously is that it's a great big PC world out there in Ivy-admissions land, and they can either get hip or go to State. Rachel Toor seems to think that her progressive social views—which she showcases to a curious degree in the book—put her in the minority among admissions people at elite colleges, but this was not my experience of these people as I came to know them during school visits and conventions. In my experience her viewpoint is the norm rather than the exception. In one sense the fact that such people dominate the field is a good thing. In the past twenty years the elite colleges have made an earnest and highly laudable effort to enroll and graduate significant numbers of black and Hispanic students, and this is the direct result of the hard work and relentless advocacy of people like Rachel Toor. But many of these people don't begin to acknowledge their *own* biases. Toor is to be congratulated, for example, for pointing out the greatly disturbing fact that many teachers' recommendations for female African-American students describe the students physically, with terms such as "beautiful," "striking," "elegant," and "statuesque." She is right to characterize this as "racial stereotyping," to acknowledge that these students have been "sexualized" in their teachers' descriptions of them. But Toor herself describes an applicant whom she has encountered in an interview thus: "She is exquisitely and expensively dressed in a pearl-pink linen sheath. Her shiny WASP-straight hair is pulled into an elegant bun, her makeup simple, emphasizing her natural beauty." As soon as I got to "WASP," I knew we were looking at a loser; and indeed, the girl turns out to be some clunker rich kid who, maddeningly, must be admitted because of Papa's dough—and who may therefore be "sexualized" with impunity. In evaluating students' extracurricular activities Toor is "personally most turned off by Junior Statesmen of America and by kids who started investment clubs at their schools." Pity the poor kid stuck out there in Louisville or Grand Rapids: he knows no better. Get a clue, kid! Dump the Statesmen! Join the Gay/Straight Student Alliance. Enroll in a women's-studies class—I don't care if you have to take two buses to get there. In fact, get to know the people on the bus and become incensed about their oppression (but not so incensed that you liberate the housekeeper while Mom's tied up in moot court).

The goal here is to raise your consciousness enough to attract the attention of an admissions officer at an elite college, but not so much that you find the very idea of an elite college objectionable. It's a fine line. As a PC naif, you might assume, for example, that it is constructive and worthwhile to read books reflective of cultures different from your own and to try to learn and grow from this experience. Not so fast! Toor is characteristically dismissive of white kids who are drawn to "novels of nonidentity" and write "gee-whiz essays about 'Native Son,' 'Invisible Man,' or any of a number of Toni Morrison books." Better to pick something by a dead white guy and explain what it taught you about the patriarchy. Try smacking the Hemingway piñata. Be creative. You might also enter into a brief, awareness-raising romance with someone of either a different race or the same sex or— Hello, New Haven!—both. Today's applicant to the elite colleges enters a game in which the opportunity for committing a faux pas is just as great as it was fifty years ago, only now the faux pas is on the order of joining the Junior Statesmen of America rather than of sporting ill-fitting khakis. The Junior Statesmen strike an infelicitous note in the elite-college admissions office in part because they are presumably not keenly sensitized to the tyranny of the patriarchy, but even more so because the very name is redolent of the kind of middle-middle-class earnestness that the elite colleges have always shunned. At the deep heart of the current college mania is something irrational and inexpressible, and it largely stems from that most irrational and inexpressible of American anxieties: class anxiety.

·   ·   ·

As a college counselor, I saw that even the parents of applicants, much as they talked about wanting their children to get a "good education," seemed to know that more was driving their family's mania for certain colleges than simply the quality of the academic fare on offer. Often one of the parents, usually the father, would tell me about the way he had chosen his own college, how it had been a painless and straightforward process. Often the choice had hinged on geography (many had gone to UCLA) or the recommendation of a guidance counselor or a parent. These remarks never concluded with a confession that "because of the indiscriminate nature of my college-selection process, I sit before you as dumb as a bunny rabbit." Nor should they have. The parents tended to be highly—sometimes stratospherically—successful. They ran studios, they were partners in huge law firms, surgeons with national reputations, CEOs, bankers. But they wanted something more than that for their children. What was it, exactly?

In a 1996 *New York* magazine article titled "Poor Little Smart Kids," a Manhattan mother is quoted as saying,

> "There's almost a fetishistic sense of power, being able to associate your child with one of these schools . . . especially at one of these East Side dinner parties . . . the women don't work, so all they talk about is school. It's like belonging to the same country club or something."

This is somewhat uncharitable. For the most part, I found that the parents I dealt with wanted what all good parents want: to give their children the very best. To a certain kind of parent— to me, for example—the very words "better" or "best" are often potent enough to preclude rational analysis of almost any given set of options.

Perhaps one might leave all the fads and fashions aside and

think sensibly, calmly, about what one wants from college. (Revealingly, although Berezin wrote a whole book about how he got into Yale, he never answered the most obvious question his book provokes: Why, precisely, did he want to go there so desperately? It clearly wasn't because he had a burning desire to study under Martin Shubik or David Brion Davis.)

Almost all the parents I dealt with believed that an elite college would give their children the best education, the best chance of success in their chosen fields (particularly in the most remunerative fields), and a set of incalculably valuable "connections" that would open doors (the phrase "the way the world really works" was often employed in this context) for the child long after the parents had gone on to their own reward. On at least one count they were perhaps misinformed. As James Fallows points out elsewhere in this issue (citing a study for the National Bureau of Economic Research), "the economic benefit of attending a more selective school [is] negligible."

Do the most highly selective colleges really offer a better education than less selective ones? This would be a much easier question to answer if the University of Chicago weren't such an unfashionable place among so many undergraduates. There it sits, with its dreamy Gothic architecture of the precise type that kids nowadays go in for, its bumper crop of Nobel laureates (the most in the nation), its hugely impressive student-faculty ratio, its demonstrably extraordinary programs and departments. But the kids don't really like it. Why? It's too intellectual. What, then, do they mean by the term "good education"? Good but not too good, I guess. It's the kind of education you can get at certain places but not others—at Georgetown but not at the University of Washington; at Duke but not at Chapel Hill. It's the kind of education you can get definitely at Stanford, less so at Berkeley, much less so at Michigan, hardly at all at Wisconsin, and not at all at the University of Illinois. That kind of thinking has always bewildered me.

Even though Rachel Toor has genuine respect for Duke, she finds herself unable to provide a rational explanation for the school's current enormous popularity with students eyeing elite colleges. During admissions presentations for the university she would, for example, dutifully conclude her remarks about the faculty by saying that "the best-known professors are teaching our youngest students." But other facts gave her pause. She writes,

> It's also the case that we have not one Nobel laureate on our faculty. We have fewer than two dozen members of the National Academy of Sciences . . . What we have are a lot of very competent—and a handful of excellent—academics.

And Duke is a place where many of Toor's friends on the faculty complained "that their students never challenged them, that the kids tended to imbibe information dully and without questioning"—a place that a politically active and aware Berkeley girl might find "oppressively politically apathetic."

The perception of what constitutes an "elite" school often has little to do with academic excellence. After all, one important measure of a university's quality is how many of its faculty members belong to the National Academy of Sciences, the National Academy of Engineering, and the Institute of Medicine. The ultra-selective Brown counts among its faculty sixteen who are members. Duke, the object of many a prep school student's swoon, has thirty-five. But the University of Washington has seventy-one, Wisconsin sixty-four. Michigan fifty-eight, Texas fifty-four, and Illinois fifty-three.

Part of my problem in getting on board the college frenzy was that I genuinely believed that any one of the colleges on our approved list of a hundred or so was capable of providing students with a good, even a great, education. The funny thing about teenagers is that very often the best of them, the most interesting and curious, are rather lousy high school students.

They have other things on their minds than geeking out every single point on the AP U.S. history exam. They are very often readers, and preparation for elite-college admission does not allow one to be a reader; it's far too time consuming. These "lousy" students were often among my favorites, and I never feared that they were going to lose a chance at a great education because they didn't have the stuff of an "elite" admission. They *themselves* were smart. They didn't need some Ferrari of a college nudging them along the path to a great education; they were going to get one wherever they went.

·   ·   ·

So, what we are left with is "the way the world really works." Here's the thinking: you go to Brown, wander through in a delighted haze of great classes and cool intellectual—but not too intellectual—discussions about *Un Chien Andalou*, and then, in an eleventh-hour spasm of professional ambition that strikes you in the middle of a killer game of ultimate Frisbee, you decide it would be fun to work in a museum. Wait a minute, your roommate says. That guy Joe Blow—isn't his mom on like the board or something at like the Met? You know Joe! You and Joe were in a semiotics seminar junior year! Somebody stubs out a joint and gets you the student directory (it's the spirit of camaraderie that really makes these places so wonderful). Badda-bing, badda-boom, Joe's mom makes a phone call. Before you know it, you, your best suit, and your soon-to-be-conferred Brown degree are hurtling toward the island of Manhattan, where the curator of works on paper eagerly awaits your thoughts on the Caprichos; if they're good enough, you'll be answering the works-on-paper telephone and enjoying an employee discount at the gift shop in no time flat. (Feel free, in the spirit of fairness, to imagine this scenario taking place at another elite college—Dartmouth, say—and then change the variables accordingly: *The Birth of a Nation* . . . the middle of Winter

Carnival . . . an internship at the International Monetary Fund . . . *Federalist Papers* seminar . . . sets down a Molson Golden Ale . . . and so forth.) Does this really happen? Sometimes. In some fields, particularly in the news and entertainment media and in the arts, an Ivy League degree and the host of "connections" that often accompany it are distinct advantages for first-time job seekers. (Of course, in just as many other fields an Ivy education doesn't pull much weight. The highest echelons of corporate America, for instance, contain remarkably few men and women who obtained bachelor's degrees from elite schools.) And even if Ivy-oriented jobs rarely blossom into full-blown careers (many of the most glamorous fields are full of dead-end jobs held by insanely well educated people), they can provide a very nice interlude between college and the pursuit of an M.B.A. or a law degree or whatever other kind of graduate degree is necessary for one of the really "good" jobs of the sort that young people who have endured the rigors and expectations of elite education tend to want for themselves.

Of course, connections aren't going to help when it comes time to apply to those supercompetitive law and business schools, at which point one will be up against not only straight-*A* students from Yale and Amherst but also ferociously smart applicants from "sub-elite" universities that are nonetheless home to supercompetitive graduate-level programs (for instance, the University of Michigan, whose law school, ranked by academics, judges, and lawyers as the seventh best in the country, is one of the places the Amherst and Yale grads will be clawing to get into). And winning a clerkship on the Court of Appeals or an offer from Goldman Sachs is going to depend on having done extraordinarily well in law or business school—not on where you spent your undergraduate years. And of course, whether or not you make partner at a tony law firm or investment bank will depend on stellar performance for seven years at those places. *That's* how the world really works in 2001. (By the way, a certain Boston-based, Brahmin-ish, highbrow magazine was edited from 1981 through 1999 by a graduate of the University of Oklahoma and is now edited by a University of New Hampshire grad. The man who preceded both of them never went to college. I have noticed that many organizations are well staffed by Ivy graduates but helmed by graduates of other schools—maybe the *true* "Admissions Confidential" is this: *Ivy Grads Face Glass Ceiling!*)

•   •   •

There is another way to go about all of this. If a student wants a great university, why on earth would Berkeley hold less cachet than Stanford—let alone than such places as Brown and Georgetown, whose admissions selectivity may not reflect a commensurate level of academic quality? If a demonstrably superior academic environment is important, again, why not the University of Chicago? If the atmosphere there is too relentlessly intellectual, what about the world-class University of Michigan or California; or the first-rate University of Texas, Washington, Wisconsin, North Carolina, Iowa, or Illinois; or the University of Pittsburgh or Carnegie Mellon? They boast extraordinary faculties and also offer students thriving social lives. And if the superachieving college applicant from, say, Montclair or Burlingame is really looking for a culturally enriching experience, he or she is far more likely to find it by spending the undergraduate years in flyover country than by spending them on the opposite coast. When it comes to excellent small colleges with reasonable admissions requirements, there are almost too many to list: Occidental, Kenyon, Bucknell, Carleton, Macalester, Reed, University of the South, Hobart and William Smith, New College, Davidson, Washington and Lee, Beloit, Lawrence, Gettysburg, Lewis & Clark, Lafayette, Hamilton, Whitman, Grinnell, Colgate. (Students and their parents might want to compare two columns in the *U.S. News & World Report* rankings: "Reputation"—that is, how college and university administrators regard a school—and "Acceptance rate." They'll find a number of schools that are easier to get into than their reputation would suggest, and vice versa.) There are also schools with relaxed admissions standards, such as Pitzer and the University of Massachusetts, that belong to consortiums in which students can take classes at some of the most "elite" and "selective" colleges in the country, such as Pomona and Amherst. Instead of getting so nutty, families might think deeply about what the student really wants to accomplish in college. *Making the Most of College* (2001), by Richard Light, is full of excellent suggestions and might help families to find useful and meaningful criteria for school selection.

Powerful emotions get mixed up in the college-admissions process. Michael Thompson wrote in "College Admission as a Failed Rite of Passage" that central to this experience is "the most important and most difficult transition in all of life: the end of childhood and the late-adolescent separation and individuation from parents." He continued,

> The frantic involvement of many parents in the process is, from my perspective, a cover for this profound parental anxiety: Did I do a good job with this child? Did I do everything I needed to do for this child? Is this child prepared? Is this child going to have a good life? Such fears about letting go of an unfinished child exist in all families. How can we let go of a child who is still so young in so many ways?

Surely he's right about this. Also lurking uncomfortably beneath the surface of these waters are class anxiety, the culture wars, and a whole set of unexamined prejudices about what does or does not constitute a "good" college. All this drama is nice for admissions offices that like to see applications stacked to the roof and supplicants spilling out into hallways as they wait nervously for information sessions to begin. None of it is good for seventeen-year-olds just taking their first tentative steps into adult life.

Los Angeles Magazine

FINALIST, PROFILE WRITING

Hollywood's Information Man

Nervous Peter. Condescending Peter. Mentor Peter. Evasive Peter. Pundit Peter. These are the many faces of Variety editor/über-hustler Peter Bart. Bart is as chimerical as Hollywood itself, but thanks to her dogged reporting, Amy Wallace manages to paint a clear portrait of this master of tall tales and reinvention. Despite his legal threats, playful cajoling, evasion, and outright lies, Wallace presents a profile that is entertaining and shocking, and one that resulted in Bart's temporary suspension from Variety.

Amy Wallace

Hollywood's Information Man

Peter Bart is on the phone, and he's threatening to sue. "I really take umbrage at the gotcha nature of your interrogation," he says. His voice is taut. I can't see his knees, but I'm sure at least one is twitching.

Bart, the editor-in-chief of Variety, the entertainment industry's dominant newspaper, is accustomed to being in charge.

Studio heads woo him; strivers kiss his ass. Everyone wants his insight and his wisdom—or prominent placement in Variety's big, glossy pages. In his weekly column, "The Back Lot," he alternately strokes and scolds moguls and movie stars, addressing them by their first names. When Bart telephones the powerful, he is put right through. Now he's calling me.

"I think to plunk documents out of context," he says, "on people whose lives are as busy as yours or mine is a little unfair. This is not consistent with the access and cooperation I have afforded you."

Over several months I have encountered a dizzying variety of Peters. I have spent many hours with Charming Peter, who is smart, funny, fierce. I have gotten to know Judgmental Peter, who *loves to size up others. I've met Crude Peter, Brilliant Peter, Hypo-critical Peter, Loyal Peter.*

Bart calls himself "Zelig-like." A setter of rules who hates to follow them, a lover of labels who resents being characterized, a seeker of the truth who doesn't always tell it, Bart believes he is immune to the conflicts that derail lesser men. It's one of the things that place him among the most despised and feared people in Hollywood. I listen to him speaking now. It's a Peter I've never met.

"When you're in public life, people attack you," Intimidating Peter, tells me. "But I'm taken aback by a bogus document suddenly being slammed on the desk. I'll send you a note saying I will sue you, which I sure as hell will."

. . .

If you are a doctor or a grocer or an airline pilot with no ties to the business that produces America's number-one export—entertainment—you probably have never heard of Peter Bart. But if you are among the 70,000 people in Los Angeles, New York, and around the world who can't start the day without knowing which big-name movie director just got a two-picture deal, Bart is an institution.

Over nearly four decades in Los Angeles he's been a reporter for *The New York Times,* an executive at three movie studios, an independent film producer, a screenwriter, and an author of both novels and nonfiction. For the past dozen years he has been the editor of and most influential columnist at *Daily Variety* and *Weekly Variety,* the sister publications whose zippy headlines, who's-in-who's-out reporting, and largely anonymous sources routinely make and break reputations. In clout-conscious Hollywood, that makes Bart not just an observer but a player.

There are two keys to success in Hollywood: relationships and information. Bart traffics in both. He lunches almost every day with a studio chief, a marketing executive, a top manager or talent agency head, an entertainment lawyer or lobbyist. In the course of just a few weeks earlier this year he dined with screenwriter William Goldman; Ron Meyer, president of Universal Studios; Lorenzo di Bonaventura, Warner Bros. president of worldwide production; Michael Ovitz, CEO of Artists Management Group; Mike De Luca, former New Line president of production (and now production chief at DreamWorks SKG); Mike Medavoy, chairman of Phoenix Pictures; Tom Sherak, partner at Revolution Studios; Rob Friedman, vice chairman at Paramount Pictures; John McLean, executive director of the Writers Guild of America; Don Marron, chairman of Paine Webber; and Skip Brittenham, a partner in the entertainment law firm Ziffren, Brittenham, Branca & Fischer.

These meals aren't interviews, according to Bart, but meetings between equals. After all, in his 17 years as an executive, most prominently at Paramount Pictures, Bart was one of them. He likes to think he still is. "Some people say I owe Joe Roth a lot," Bart says of the former Disney chief who now runs Revolution Studios. "But I don't. Joe Roth owes *me*. I gave him *his* first job." (While Bart was president of Lorimar Film Company, Roth produced the 1979 dud *Americathon*, but it was Roth's fourth film, not his first.)

"The same with John Calley," Bart says of the head of Sony Pictures. Bart has known Calley since the late 1960s, when Bart says Calley pitched him *Catch-22*. Bart calls Calley "the country gentleman"—a vaguely catty reference to Calley's decision to leave the world of moviemaking for 13 years, only to return in 1993 as president of MGM/United Artists. "I owe John Calley a lot? John Calley owes *me*," he says, asserting that a positive column he wrote made Calley a contender for the post. "I think I was very important in getting him his job at MGM."

In his weekly *Variety* column and in bimonthly pieces in *GQ*, Bart speaks as one who knows Hollywood and everyone in it. His vocabulary is a mix of the colloquial (he refers often to "the rules," "the game," "the fat cats," "the old farts," "the suits") and the arcane. Rare is the attractive woman whom Bart does not label "lissome."

Most notably, in a town infamous for air kisses and false praise, Bart often writes what he means. DreamWorks' Jeffrey Katzenberg is "hyperactive," while a conversation with Sandy Litvack, a former top executive at Disney, is "akin to poking one's head in an oven." Producer Brian Grazer and director Ron Howard "exude about as much charisma as Wal-Mart managers," while George Lucas is "simply so rich and mythologized that no one professes to be able to interact with [him] on a normal human level."

"Perhaps," Bart wrote last year in a column addressed to Robert Redford, "there's something in your . . . head that says 'I'm a star, I take up a lot of ego space; my movies should, too.' " He's made the same complaint to Warren Beatty, whom he calls the priapic prince. Bart has written several columns about Beatty's filmmaking and womanizing—even going so far as to describe the sounds the actor-director-writer-producer supposedly makes during "moments of sexual congress."

"You have to understand, if Peter is criticizing or praising you, the thing that's solid about it is this is a guy who knows our business," says Harvey Weinstein, Miramax's disheveled cofounder, whom Bart has called a slob more than once. "He said my shirt looked like I was a refugee from a food fight. He calls me roly-poly. But this guy put *The Godfather* into production! It's my favorite movie of all time. So even if I'm mad at him, I can't be mad at him."

Peter Guber, former chairman of Sony Pictures goes further. "Peter is riding in the general's car—*Variety* is the general's car. And you salute the general's car even when the general's not in it," Guber says. "I say to him, 'Never let go of this job, because the wolves will attack. People are kept at bay by your power.' It's a tremendous platform and weapon and people view it as such. So he's feared and respected—or respected and feared—depending on the person."

Besides, says Sherry Lansing, chair of Paramount Pictures. "Peter has the power to affect the way people think."

That power derives in large part from his position at *Variety*, the Industry's 96-year-old broadsheet that doesn't just cover entertainment news but helps make it. It is Hollywood's prime bulletin board—what one marketing consultant likens to "a high school newspaper that everyone has a tremendous need to see their names in." It's not just an ego thing. In a world built on illusions, being mentioned in *Variety* lends legitimacy. It makes you seem real. In Hollywood, seeming is believing.

When *Variety* reports that Leonardo DiCaprio is in talks to star in a film, for example, savvy readers know chances are good that someone is merely floating DiCaprio's name. Why? To turn up the heat on Matt Damon, say, or some other foot-dragging actor the movie studio *really* wants to sign. Agents and publicists often complain that *Variety* writes about deals before they're done. But those same people plant stories in *Variety* all the time in hopes of clinching a deal or killing someone else's.

Here, pecking order determines more than just who gets a table with an ocean view. The perception of who's on top determines which projects are produced, who will work on them, and how much money they'll make. More than any other entity, *Variety* reflects and informs Hollywood's collective consciousness. Readers don't just parse the information on its pages; they dissect what stories are where, who is quoted up high, who is relegated to beyond the jump. With its trademark "slanguage," *Variety* helps its subscribers keep score—an essential service in a town obsessed with rank. Whether you've "ankled" (quit) or been "upped" (promoted) at a "praisery" (public relations firm), a "diskery" (record company), or a "tenpercentery" (talent agency), if the story runs on *Variety*'s front, it means you matter. By extension, Bart matters to you.

In 1997 Emilio Estevez, the actor-director, was so distressed by Bart's dismissal of his film *The War at Home* that he fired off a two-page letter that was widely distributed around town. The letter was intended to diminish Bart, but its vitriol only confirmed Bart's central place in the Industry.

"In you, I see a failed movie producer, hiding behind the protective veil of your post. . . . It is sad and pathetic," Estevez wrote.

He urged Bart to "1. Simply not see my films. 2. Drop dead sometime soon. 3. Go fuck yourself." He signed off with this: "Enjoy life from your bully pulpit, little man."

Not for nothing did one top executive in town famously dub Bart "the most hated man in Hollywood." For not only does Bart control the Industry's bible, but by virtue of his station he always gets something that everyone—in and out of Hollywood—desperately wants: the last word.

．　　　．　　　．

"I have Peter Bart for you."

The silken voice of Bart's assistant could not be more different from his own, which is slightly nasal, rapid-fire. His accent is so hard to place and his delivery at times so oddly paced that some have speculated, half seriously, that he modeled it after Al Pacino's staccato in The Godfather.

This is Condescending Peter calling, as he often does, to talk trash about other journalists. "Did you read Patrick Goldstein's column today? What was he talking about? You know who's running out of ideas? Goldstein," he'll say, referring to the Los Angeles Times*'s movie columnist. When Charles Fleming, a former* Variety *reporter, writes an opinion piece in the* Times *about the ethical dilemmas of the Hollywood press corps, Bart sniffs, "This story epitomizes him. It's like a blur. A lot of undeveloped ideas."*

Today his target is Variety*'s archrival,* The Hollywood Reporter. *"Poor little George Christy," Bart says, referring to the* Reporter*'s gossip columnist. "I'm all for exposés, but George Christy? The level of small-time stuff he does, I mean, who cares?" Christy is being investigated for accepting expensive gifts and movie credits—which qualified him for Screen Actors Guild health benefits—from the people he writes about. When the* Reporter*'s own labor writer, David Robb, filed a piece on Christy, its publisher refused to run it. Robb and Anita M. Busch, the trade paper's editor, resigned in protest.*

Bart, however, sees the Christy affair as an indictment not so much of a journalist allegedly on the take but of the editor and the reporter who fought to reveal it. Both Robb and Busch once worked at Variety. *It's hard to tell whom he loathes more.*

"It's a fascinating implosion," Bart says gleefully. "It reminds me of when Robert Altman directed a picture—this was when he was drinking. At a certain point he would turn on his main characters and make them into hideous creatures. That's what Dave Robb and Anita Busch would have done here, too, but I wouldn't have it, and I fired them."

Actually, he did no such thing. Variety's *personnel department confirms Robb's and Busch's assertions that they both resigned.*

. . . .

It's Oscar Eve, and Peter Bart has just arrived at his third party in less than 24 hours. "I could use a drink," he tells his wife, as some of Hollywood's biggest movie stars preen before him: Julia, Russell, Kevin.

Owlish in round spectacles, with tufts of thinning black and gray hair, Bart is five feet nine inches tall and has the trim, tanned physique of a tennis player. He looks for a moment as if he is standing at the edge of a pool, weighing whether to get wet. Actors tend to bore him, so it's not the press of famous flesh that's making him thirsty. Bart, who is 69 years old, has a complicated relationship with the industry he covers. Never are his conflicts more glaring than during Hollywood's High Holy Days—Academy Awards time—when the movie business celebrates and contemplates itself.

Before Bart can order a vodka martini, however, he is spotted by Bill Maher, who steps up and gives him a nudge. "Well," the host of TV's *Politically Incorrect* says with gusto, "if it isn't Hollywood's top fucking information man!"

Having worn many hats during his long career, Bart delights

these days in wearing several at once. When he wants to attend a Writers Guild of America meeting that is closed to the press, he dusts off his screenwriter credentials. (He claims to be the only editor who is an active voting member of the WGA.) When he wants to cast a vote for Best Picture, he activates "the part of me that's an Academy voter." (His Academy membership is a holdover from his years as a producer.) When he wants to collect a speaking fee, he turns into a paid adviser, giving tips—to cite one recent example—to the film division of cable network HBO.

"I have lived a split-level life in Hollywood," he wrote in the introduction to his 1999 book, *The Gross: The Hits, the Flops— the Summer That Ate Hollywood.* But he will commit to neither one. His "dualities," as he calls them, are not liabilities but the keys to his success. "I enjoy the fact that my relationships with people have so many different colorations," Bart says. "I've never thought of myself as just a whatever I was. I always think it's fun to try and reinvent yourself."

On the weekend of the Academy Awards ceremony, Bart's many identities come out to play. Three days of self-congratulatory events unfold like so many garish, pungent flowers. Some on the A-list grumble about the chaos of Oscar-party fever—the long waits for valet parking, the glut of hors d'oeuvres—but those who are not invited are so mortified about what their omission implies that some leave town to save face.

Variety's top man doesn't have to worry. It all begins with Friday night's annual celebration at the Beverly Hills mansion of agent-to-the-stars Ed Limato. The dinner is a magnet for Oscar nominees as well as Limato's top drawer clients. The embossed invitations are hard to come by, and the media are, officially, not welcome. Bart is an exception. This year, as every year, he RSVP'd yes.

Saturday afternoon, literary agent Bob Bookman throws a garden party for screenwriters and agents at his Hancock Park home. Bart makes an appearance. Then he stops home, dons a cobalt blue dress shirt and black blazer—the dark-on-dark uniform of Hollywood's male elite—and heads back to Beverly Hills for Miramax's bash at the Regent Beverly Wilshire Hotel. The event is known for skits that spoof the Oscar contenders, and to gain entrance the media must agree to leave all spoofing off the record. For Bart the restriction is moot: He never carries a reporter's notebook.

He pushes through a ring of admirers who surround the night's host, Miramax's Harvey Weinstein. Barrel-shaped and garrulous, Weinstein is one of Bart's favorite sources. He is also a principal in Miramax/Talk Books, and he has bid to publish Bart's books. Bart and Weinstein shake hands, but there are others waiting, and Bart backs away. "There's something kind of primitive about him," Bart says. He means it as a compliment.

Bart scans the crowd and heads straight for movie producer David Brown, whose many films range from *Jaws* to last year's *Chocolat.* Brown contributed a blurb to the jacket of Bart's most recent book, calling it "must reading for all who care." Bart greets Brown warmly, then maneuvers toward producer-director Irwin Winkler. Their friendship dates to the 1970s, when Bart—then vice president of production at Paramount Pictures—set up Winkler's movie *The Gambler.* A quick hello, a pat on the shoulder, and Bart keeps moving. Near a buffet table piled with crab cakes and Peking duck, he makes a lunch date with Ted Field, a music and film mogul to whom Bart gave his first break in the movie business. It was the early '80s, and Bart was senior vice president of production at MGM.

"When I was at MGM I said to Ted, 'Why don't you get a picture going? Here's an idea. If you want it, it's yours,'" Bart says, explaining how he sold Field a treatment that he had written with his youngest daughter, Dilys. The treatment became the 1984 film *Revenge of the Nerds,* and the sale helped pay Dilys's way through Stanford University.

Completing his first lap around the room, Bart returns to his table, nods fondly at his wife, and finally takes a few sips of vodka. By the time Nigel Sinclair, cochairman of the British film company Intermedia, stops by to pay his respects, Bart is coiled less tightly. So, as he often does, he launches into a ribald tale from one of his past lives. In this one a panicky crew member calls Bart from the set of the 1972 movie *The Getaway* to say that the film's two stars are having an affair. What made this report especially juicy at the time: One of them, Ali MacGraw, was married to Bart's friend and then boss at Paramount, Robert Evans.

"I was the guy who got the phone call: Ali went into Steve McQueen's trailer 24 hours ago, and they haven't come out. What should we do?" Bart says, enjoying the story he has dined out on for 30 years. "I said, 'Take a hint from this.' And I hung up."

•   •   •

Mentor Peter is at Le Dome, telling me what to eat.

He's invited me to lunch at the frumpy power restaurant on the Sunset Strip. With a flourish he orders us each a chicken burger with mixed greens—the favorite meal, he says, of his own mentor, Robert Evans. "There's no bun so it's the Atkins diet," he tells me. "Not that you or I are in dire need of diets. You look like a jock."

Then he offers career advice. "I'd like to see you do books. You are a disciplined writer and for someone who can write and be disciplined about it, doing books and magazine articles is a wonderful thing. That's why I like writing for GQ every other month. I would love to see you do that sort of thing," he says, taking a bite. "The New Yorker is looking for someone. Everybody is."

For a moment I find myself basking in Mentor Peter's regard. Then Withholding Peter takes over, delivering a critique of the magazine for which I actually work. "The last issue—I really liked it, but I wonder if it's a little overdesigned. Where are the big stories you want to read? Having said that, I liked the energy. But even your last story was just . . . THERE. I wish you guys nothing but the best," he says, chewing slowly. "I just hope your magazine succeeds."

•   •   •

Bart's 17 years inside the moviemaking machine is the foundation on which he's built the rest of his career. His management style stems from it. His books and columns draw credibility from it. More than anything else, it confirmed his belief in a credo he'd had drummed into him since childhood: Self-invention is the route to power.

"I was raised with one adamant dictum: Don't allow yourself to be imprisoned in any socioeconomic category, religious category, ethnic category, whatever," Bart says one afternoon. We are sitting in the peach-colored living room of his home in Fremont Place, the Mid Wilshire enclave that was one of Los Angeles's first gated communities. The eight-bedroom house used to belong to Harry Cohn, the producer and movie-studio founder whom Bart likes to call "the mean-spirited czar of Columbia." Bart and his wife have refurbished Cohn's screening room to its original 1920s splendor, and he delights in referring to a separate alcove as "Harry's phone room." But there's another commonality that Bart does not wish to talk about. Cohn, like many of Hollywood's founding fathers, was Jewish. When I ask Bart about his own ethnicity, he turns elusive. It's peculiar, to say the least. Of all American industries, Hollywood has historically been a place where Jews have not only achieved acceptance but thrived. But following his parents' dictum, Bart keeps his ancestry a secret.

Here are a few things Bart would tell me about his upbringing: Peter Benton Bart was born in 1932 and raised on Manhattan's Upper West Side. His only brother is six years older. His parents were public-school teachers who had immigrated to the United States, though their son won't say from where. ("They were very Americanized," he says.) The elder Barts were fiercely irreligious and ferociously anticommunist. ("They told me if I was caught playing with a communist, they wouldn't feed me.") For reasons he never understood, they served Chinese food "morning, noon, and night." ("They weren't the kind of people you sat down with and said, 'Tell me the origins of this fetish.'") Although not wealthy, the family enjoyed some luxuries: a nanny, private schooling for the kids, and a vacation home in Martha's Vineyard.

Here are a few things Bart wouldn't tell me: Both his parents were born in Austria. His mother, whose maiden name was Clara Ginsberg, arrived at Ellis Island in 1914. Her passenger record includes this notation: "Ethnicity: Austria (Hebrew)." There is no record of a Max S. Bart entering the United States through Ellis Island. Bart's father may have traveled under another name. But there is a listing for a Moses Bart, which was the name of Bart's paternal grandfather. Moses came to America in 1913, when he was 57 years old. His ethnicity: "Austria, Hebrew."

Bart has kept even his closest friends confused about his past. "He was brought up a Quaker, wasn't he?" asks Evans. It's an honest mistake. You can't spend more than an hour with Bart without hearing about his attending Friends Seminary and Swarthmore College—both Quaker institutions.

"I don't want to talk about it," Bart says of his religious heritage, as one of his knees begins bouncing up and down. "I resent people's militancy on these issues. Everyone wants to peg everyone else because everyone is predictable. And I'm not."

Over several months he will volunteer that he has never once dated a Jewish girl, never attended a seder, and has been inside a synagogue only once, for the bar mitzvah of then-agent Michael Ovitz's son. ("I wanted to see what one was like.") "Listen, I got berated by the vice president in charge of business affairs at Paramount," he says, "because I did not take off Jewish holidays. And I was affronted. I basically told him to mind his own damned business."

At one point he tries to explain his discomfort by comparing himself to his longtime assistant, a light-skinned black woman: "She struggles with this, too. She feels she's a black person. But she's about as black as Felix [Bart's Siamese cat]. I feel she is a bit victimized by, again, that need to identify with some subculture that will help you.

"You talk to a lot of the better-educated, wealthy black people. You know, they're not very black. The big distinction is between the people they call 'niggers'—who are the ghetto blacks, who can't even speak, can't get a job, and bury themselves in black-itude—and those people who are better looking, better educated, smarter, and who own the world: the black middle class," he says. "A lot of people in Hollywood—let's say if they happen to be Jewish people who come from Brooklyn—they are most comfortable with those people. Which is fine. It just doesn't happen to describe me."

A few minutes later he asks, "Can you and I make a deal about this whole thing about religion? I would love it if we could dodge it in some way that you don't think is dishonest." He will repeat this request more than once.

·   ·   ·

Pundit Peter is in my living room, on television.

When network news shows need someone to speak for Holly-wood—on the impact of possible strikes, for example, or Washington's campaign against violent entertainment—they often turn to Bart. Tonight the man Bill Maher introduces as a "former big-time studio honcho prexy" is making his second appearance on Politically Incorrect.

The show is an ideal forum for Bart. He loves a good sword fight. Dapper in a black dress shirt and beige suit, Bart fences with Monica Crowley, a political commentator for Fox News, and actors Martin Short and Alec Baldwin. The topic: Richard Nixon. "Nixon was famous for being a self-made man who only admired self-made men," Maher says. "What do you think Nixon would have thought of George W. Bush?"

"He would have said he was a patrician nothing," Bart says. Then

Bart assesses his fellow panelists and proclaims, "I'm the only Republican here." Bart, too, prides himself on being self-made. He's also self-made-up. He's been a registered Democrat since 1994.

· · · ·

Bart describes his childhood as "annoyingly happy, except there was a definite imperative to perform. My parents never said. 'This report card isn't good enough.' But you weren't supposed to fuck up."

Bart attended the academically rigorous Swarthmore, where he succeeded upperclassman Victor Navasky, now the publisher of *The Nation,* as editor of the college newspaper. Bart majored in politics, did a brief stint as a copyboy at *The New York Times,* and then had a fellowship at the London School of Economics. He was hired by *The Wall Street Journal* in 1956. A few years later he returned to *The New York Times* as a reporter to cover advertising and the media.

He married a publicist named Dorothy Callman in 1961, and their first daughter, Colby, was born a year later. In 1964 Bart was made a national correspondent in Los Angeles. That's when he first met a former actor named Robert Evans. In 1966, a few months after Bart's second daughter, Dilys, was born, he wrote a profile of Evans for the *Times* that portrayed him as a tireless producer, an elegant operator. The very next day, on the basis of the article, Charles Bluhdorn, who had recently bought Paramount Pictures, hired Evans as a vice president; Evans had yet to make his first picture. In 1967, when Evans rose to become Paramount's youngest-ever production chief, he hired Bart as his number two. Together they decided what movies would get made.

They were an unlikely pair. Movie-star handsome, Evans was a wheeler-dealer with a passion for filmmaking and a seductive personal style. Bart was college educated, East Coast, intense. He trumped others with his command of the facts. Evans understood actors' fragile, self-absorbed psyches, but he didn't like to read. Bart read everything and wasn't afraid to say what he liked. Each man saw in the other something he did not see in himself.

More than three decades later Bart remains loyal to Evans, who has weathered a cocaine conviction, the murder of a business partner, and persistent money troubles. Although still widely considered an invaluable sounding board—for years Warren Beatty, Jack Nicholson, and Robert Towne have sought his advice—Evans, now 71, hasn't produced a hit film in more than 20 years. He spends much of his time rattling around his overgrown French Regency estate that was once Greta Garbo's Beverly Hills hideaway. Bart, though, still believes in him.

"Turn him loose on somebody and, I'll tell you, it's amazing," Bart will say today, admitting that part of him still longs for when he and Evans worked side by side. Alone neither enjoyed the same success. When Evans signed a new production deal with Paramount in 1991, Bart ran a banner headline on *Variety*'s front page along with a story about Evans's "comeback." But the comeback never materialized. Sometimes, Bart says, "I feel a little bit guilty. I feel like if we became a team again, we could get things done."

Evans says Bart has not changed at all since Paramount. "He was always frank," he says. "Always combative. He wasn't a fence straddler. He was a bit sarcastic. Biting. He always had an inner pleasure in ruffling feathers."

The film industry was in the toilet when the former actor and his journalist sidekick took over at the studio. They faced enormous pressure to turn things around. Bart knew little about movies, but he was well suited to the job. Whether as a child of demanding parents or as a reporter meeting daily deadlines, he had learned how to thrive under stress: Do your homework and stand your ground.

"The head of distribution comes in one day and sees me watching the dailies of *Paper Moon*. He says, 'This movie is in black and white?'" Bart recalls of the Depression-era story that would pair the father-daughter team of Ryan and Tatum O'Neal.

Bart had discovered the book on which the movie was based and had approved its being shot in black and white—not the usual recipe for commercial success. "I said. 'No, no, it's in color. I'm just watching dailies in black and white. Don't worry.' And we finished the movie. These are the lessons of selective deviousness."

Then as now, Bart was exacting. "In the go-go days of the '70s, when everybody was running around smoking a joint or trying to look like they were, Peter was a little more buttoned down," remembers Irwin Winkler. "He was thoughtful, well read—almost like a boarding school headmaster."

One day while driving to work with Evans, Bart championed a project so eccentric that it could have cost them their jobs. "We needed to get some hits going, and Peter was telling me about a script he'd read the previous night," Evans remembers. "He said, 'It's about an 18-year-old boy who falls in love with an 80-year-old woman.' I said. 'Stop the car. Are you crazy?' He says, 'When you get to your office, lock yourself in the bathroom and read the script. And if you think I'm wrong. I'm wrong.'" The script became the cult film *Harold and Maude.*

Evans and Bart (along with chief corporate officer Stanley Jaffe, president Frank Yablans, and others) presided over the resuscitation of Paramount. Marrying an extraordinary generation of young directors—Francis Ford Coppola, Roman Polanski, Peter Bogdanovich—with commercial topics, they helped change the very notion of the Hollywood film. As Peter Biskind writes in his book *Easy Riders, Raging Bulls,* the '70s were a golden age for moviemaking, "the last time Hollywood produced a body of risky, high-quality work—as opposed to the errant masterpiece—work that was character- rather than plot-driven, that defied traditional narrative conventions . . . that broke the taboos of language and behavior, that dared to end unhappily." Much of that work came out of Paramount: *Rosemary's Baby; Goodbye, Columbus; Love Story; The Godfather; Don't Look Now; Chinatown; The Godfather II; The Conversation.*

Bart had left journalism in his mid thirties because he was weary, he says, "of writing about people who were doing things. I wanted to try doing something myself." His timing was perfect. In those days a junior production executive could have impact. Evans says it was Bart who acquired *The Godfather* and who suggested that Coppola direct it; Bart would later convince a reluctant Coppola to make *The Godfather II*. "In the '60s and '70s, studio business was conducted in an offhand, even anarchic, style," Bart has written. "The mood of that era was to thumb your nose at the rules." He fit right in.

Bart was building relationships with Hollywood's future power players. Jeff Berg, now the head of International Creative Management, was a young agent when they met in 1970. Berg used to come over and read Bart's daughters bedtime stories. That bond has helped make peace on the countless occasions since then when the two have stopped speaking.

"He has a very bitter wit, which is an acquired taste," says Berg. "He is very quick to call his friends to task as well as his foes. When you get nailed in *Variety* you try to kiss it off, but it's part of the fossil record. Still, he never apologizes. What he'll do is say 'I haven't heard from you in a year or so. Why don't we have a drink?'"

Whether Bart's rough edges played a part in his departure from Paramount in 1974 is a matter of debate. There has been speculation that he was forced out when Barry Diller was installed as the studio's new chief. Bart denies this, and Evans also pooh-poohs it, saying Bart left to head up an independent film production company and finally make the kind of big money that had eluded him at Paramount. Whatever the truth, Bart likes to poke at Diller. At dinner parties and in his *Variety* column, he has told and retold a story (that both Evans and Diller have denied) about Charles Bluhdorn, the owner of Paramount Pictures, trying to marry off Diller so nobody would believe the persistent rumor that he was gay.

"Diller has always had one of the easiest rides with the press," Bart will say with a mixture of disdain and awe. "People will go up and ask him something, and he'll say 'That's a stupid question.' And their reaction is 'He's such a smart man.'" Bart has a different assessment: "He treats everyone like shit."

• • •

Evasive Peter is ducking the press.

He's flown to New York City to host "The Front Row," a business symposium that Variety *holds each year to make money and boost its profile. This year's lineup includes Diller, now CEO of USA Networks; News Corp. chairman Rupert Murdoch; Sony Corp. CEO Howard Stringer; and Viacom president Mel Karmazin, with Bill Clinton delivering the keynote. Bart is both point man and emcee.*

"I feel like I'm the producer of some B movie," he says. So when Credit Suisse First Boston, the investment bank cosponsoring the event, suddenly gets cold feet about being affiliated with Clinton (and removes all signage bearing its name from the conference venue), Bart does damage control. It's a good story—a prominent bank, active in the entertainment industry, distancing itself from the former president. But the story won't break in Variety. *Bart makes sure of that.*

"You feel like a shit, playing hide-and-seek with the press," Bart says on the eve of the symposium. He spends the day avoiding the few journalists who have gotten wind of the brouhaha. "It's hard when you can't be completely candid. But in this case, I think that's probably the best course."

• • •

On a Friday morning Bart sits in his window-lined office on the first floor of the *Variety* building on Wilshire Boulevard. A French-language poster of *Islands in the Stream,* a movie he produced in 1977, fills one wall, while another wall displays the grip-and-grin photos you see in the offices of politicians: Bart with director Steven Spielberg, lobbyist Jack Valenti, celebrity lawyer Robert Shapiro. On his desk there is no computer, just an electric typewriter. On a bookshelf sits one of those kitschy fake grenades mounted on a plaque. COMPLAINT DEPT., it reads. TAKE A NUMBER.

Bart motions executive editor Elizabeth Guider and managing editor Timothy M. Gray toward a circular table. It's time to talk headlines.

Variety's pun-filled headlines are famously deft and often hilarious—"Sticks Nix Hick Pix," from 1935, is considered the classic—and Bart understands they are central to the paper's appeal. A few weeks after he arrived at *Variety* in 1989, he got people talking by topping a story about a feud between playwright David Hare and *New York Times* theater critic Frank Rich with this bombshell: "Ruffled Hare Airs Rich Bitch." Nearly 12 years later, while he leaves much of the day-to-day editing of *Variety* to others, he still weighs in on front-page headlines.

Bart sometimes writes the heads himself as he did for a recent piece about teen movies' waning box office receipts: "No Pop in Zit Pix." But the soft-spoken Tim Gray is Bart's ace in the headline hole. It was Gray, for example, who wrote "Ovitz No Govitz at MCA" (for a story about the agent not becoming MCA's chairman). For the grossest of these ("Movies Get a Bad Case of the Runs") Bart has coined a term: "secretional headlines."

"We are now in the post-secretional period," Bart says, grinning. "It ended after we described some relationship as 'warm and runny.'"

Guider frowns. "It was awful," she says.

"It's a Britishism," protests Bart. "It's not lewd."

Today's challenge is a story about 20th Century Fox's decision to premiere director Baz Luhrmann's movie musical *Moulin Rouge* at the Cannes Film Festival. There are a lot of elements—the studio's gamble, the festival, the painter Toulouse-Lautrec—

and Gray has assembled a list of contenders that seek to hit them all: "The Thin 'Rouge' Line." "Schmooze and 'Rouge,'" "Cannes: Le Trek for Lautrec," and "Bed, Baz, and Beyond."

"Only someone truly demented would write 'Bed, Baz, and Beyond,'" Bart says approvingly, scanning the list. "But shouldn't we say something a little more explanatory?"

"Riviera's Risk with 'Rouge'?" Gray offers.

"Fox's Riviera Risk," Bart counters.

"'Moulin' Not Foolin' Around?" asks Gray.

Bart gets up and goes to his typewriter, pounds the keys, and rips out a page. He hands the sheet to Guider, who reads aloud: "Will Frogs Flog Fox on Riv?" Everybody laughs. By meeting's end the headline has been reworked ten times. "Fox Takes Risk on the Riviera," it says. " 'Rouge' schmooze cues renewed rapport between H'w'd, Cannes."

In meetings like these and as a public speaker, Bart is irresistible. He takes control of a room, interweaving economic analysis, authoritative opinions, and barbs. At this year's Festival of Books at UCLA, he appeared on a panel moderated by Kenneth Turan, the *Los Angeles Times*'s chief movie critic. When Turan asked Bart what he'd most like to change about Hollywood, Bart responded, "I think that film critics should dress better." Amid hoots of laughter from both the audience and the rumpled Turan, Bart then got serious.

"What the present moment in Hollywood history shows is that the system is not working either artistically or financially," he said, singling out two films as proof. "*Town & Country* just opened to a sterling $3 million, which is the price of the movie's catering bill. *Driven* is so lame, Stallone's likeness isn't even featured on the poster. This is corporate Hollywood. And I do have a certain fondness for that epoch when movies were made because of a director's passion, not because McDonald's or a toy company or German [financiers] were interested."

Bart gets Hollywood. Even those he's treated harshly say it's true. "He's knowledgeable enough about film to go right to the heart of the matter every time," says Dan Cox, a longtime *Variety* reporter whom Bart fired earlier this year. "That's what Peter is brilliant at."

As a teenager Bart dreamed of being Somerset Maugham, "traveling the world and writing short stories and novels about extraordinary people and situations." In many ways, *Variety* gave him his wish. As its editor—a job that pays him about $500,000 a year including bonuses, plus a green BMW convertible and a lavish expense account—he has become Hollywood's informal ambassador to the world. He travels frequently: to Australia for a speaking tour; to Italy, in part to research a *GQ* article about director Martin Scorsese; and almost every May, to France to attend the Cannes Film Festival. He is currently completing a book of short stories, one of which—"Dangerous Company: In Hollywood, Getting Laid Can Be a Career Breaker"—appeared in *GQ* this summer. His fourth nonfiction book, an anecdotal guide to the movie business written with his good friend, producer Peter Guber, will be published by Putnam in March.

For all Bart's past lives, this one most suits him. "Peter has the best job he's ever had, for Peter," says *Variety* publisher Charles Koones.

When *Variety* first came calling, Bart had returned to writing— the lowest rung in Hollywood. In the years since he left Paramount he'd gone back and forth between producing movies, writing novels and screenplays, and serving as an executive at Lorimar and MGM. In 1989 he completed *Fade Out: The Calamitous Final Days of MGM*. Lively and caustic, the book skewered many of Bart's colleagues and would become a best-seller. Around the same time, Reed Elsevier, a Dutch company that had bought *Variety*, was looking for a new editor. Its headhunter saw in Bart the perfect hybrid, while Bart—then 57, ancient by Hollywood standards—saw a chance to reinvent himself once again.

"They wanted someone with lots of experience in both journalism and the Industry," he says. "The headhunter gave them a list with only one name on it: mine." (Actually, there was another name on the list: Caroline Miller, now the editor-in-chief of *New York* magazine.)

• • •

Controlling Peter is checking up on me.

"I hear you're calling all sorts of strange people. I mean, Jerry Weintraub?" he asks. Weintraub, a movie producer and a former colleague at MGM, is not one of Bart's favorite people. "The last time I saw a movie with Jerry Weintraub," Bart wrote in a Variety column earlier this year, "he arrived with a bottle of Stolichnaya. 'How did you like the movie?' I asked him during final credits. 'What movie?' he replied."

Two months after that column appeared, I left a message for Weintraub. The next morning Weintraub called Bart, and now Bart is on the phone to me. "We have never gotten along," he says. "If you're trying to find a non-fan club, I think he would be it."

Bart predicts that Weintraub will not speak to me. Sure enough, Weintraub's publicist soon calls to say his client is much too busy to talk. That's odd, I say, since his client found time to call Bart.

A few hours later Weintraub's gravelly voice is in my ear. "I didn't want you to think I wouldn't call back," he says, adding that he has nothing to say. What, I ask, is Bart's reputation in the Industry?

"I have no idea," he replies. "I'm 63 years old. I've been doing this for 43 years. You think you're going to get me to talk about something I don't want to talk about?"

Why, then, did he call Bart?

"That's my business," he barks.

When told of this exchange, Bart sums up Weintraub this way: "He's definitely in the life-is-too-short category."

•   •   •

Bart was hired to run *Weekly Variety* out of New York in 1989. The publication was losing $3 million a year. Circulation had dropped from 52,000 in 1980 to less than 29,000. *The Hollywood Reporter* was competing both for scoops and for advertising dollars. Bart's impact was felt immediately. He upgraded from newsprint to glossy paper, changed the color of the logo, and set about dismantling the old staff and assembling the new. Nearly two years later Bart was put in charge of *Daily Variety* as well. He merged the staffs and returned to Los Angeles.

Bart absolutely refuses to call *Variety* a trade paper, even though it gets 90 percent of its ad revenue from the Industry. It is, he asserts, a newspaper—"a vivid chronicle of our pop culture." Bart has made *Variety* more global, more sophisticated, more fun to read. Today the paper embraces the full scope of the entertainment economy, from tech news to broadcasting and cable, from magazines to books, from movies to theater. Its critics—particularly Todd McCarthy, who reviews films—are well respected, and it has Washington correspondents, a London office, and writers stationed around the world.

Bart has become one of those people everyone loves to psychoanalyze, partly because he lives to be in the red-hot center and is so willing to offend. You can see it in his frequent, lecturing "Memo To" columns, in which he gives unsolicited advice to the likes of Robin Williams ("Robin—enough of the message stuff") and Leonardo DiCaprio ("Go to college, Leo"). You can see it, too, in the way he runs *Variety*.

Staffers praise him for hating all the right things: lawyers, committees, focus groups—anything that obstructs *Variety*'s (and his own) ability to act quickly, on instinct. But he also brings the imperious manner of a studio exec into *Variety*'s newsroom. He walks out of meetings in the middle, without explanation. He has nicknames—many of them unflattering— for everyone. Years ago Bart emptied a wastebasket on a reporter's head. ("That was very calculated," he says. "I knew it was the only way to get his attention.")

Max Alexander, a former editor for *Weekly Variety* in New York, moved to Los Angeles at Bart's behest, first to be managing editor and then executive editor. Alexander calls Bart "probably the smartest person I've ever worked for." But Bart was always restless. Alexander remembers visiting the Barts at their rented English Tudor house in Benedict Canyon—a low-slung hunting lodge of a place. "It was all furnished in chintz fabric," says Alexander, "with beautiful wraparound sofas that matched the drapes. There were hunting scenes and tapestries. It had a medieval feel to it." A year later the Barts moved to another house nearby, "a contemporary, Mies van der Rohe kind of house. Now it was Barcelona chairs, chrome, glass, swatches of color by painters who'd committed suicide. I asked, 'What happened to the tapestries?' Peter waved his hand and laughed and said, 'It was just time for a change,' and I realized this is the essence of this man. He likes to suddenly sweep the table clean."

Stephen West can attest to that. In 1991 Bart hired West away from the *Los Angeles Times,* where he was assistant business editor. After five years as *Daily Variety*'s executive editor, West was summoned without warning to Bart's office and told his job had been eliminated.

"There's the good Peter and there's the bad Peter," says West, now media editor at *Bloomberg News* in San Francisco. He still admires Bart, despite what he wryly calls his own "public execution." "Peter really is like Mao Tse-tung, in that he loves perpetual revolution. He's never satisfied. Even when things are running well, he wants to change it."

The scenario would be played out again and again. Bart, who is known to address his male staffers with the paternal "my boy," would eventually turn on nearly all of them. Paying homage to director Spike Lee's *Mo' Better Blues,* staffers coined a term for the inevitable moment when Bart would blow: "M'Boy Better Blues."

"If someone said, 'Peter would like to see you in his office,' you'd walk in not knowing if you were going to get your ass kissed, your head handed to you on a plate, or an invitation to dinner," says one former *Variety* writer. "It's a management technique—so when it's time to crack the whip, everybody is already ready to flinch."

Bart so relishes flouting political correctness that he lets loose on everyone: the French, Germans, blacks, Jews, lawyers, agents, actors, publicists, feminists, fat people. A gay man says that Bart asked him about his health during a job interview. Another former *Variety* reporter heard Bart say, "I'm not hiring any more fags, because they get sick and die." According to more than half a dozen people, he peppers meetings at *Variety* with derogatory terms: *fags, bitches, cunts, Nips.*

Yet Bart, as always, is confounding. In contrast to the comments people attribute to him—which he denies making—staffers say he has treated ailing gay employees well. During his tenure *Variety* has begun acknowledging longtime companions in obituaries of gay people. Bart has promoted women and tried, with limited success, to diversify *Variety*'s mostly white staff.

"Is Peter homophobic? Possibly. Racist? Possibly. Misogynistic? Possibly," says one former *Variety* employee who knows him well. "But most of the stuff that gets traced to him isn't about that. It's about his desperate need to draw fire and rile stuff up. He can't bear to be ignored even for a minute."

· · ·

Bart hates to take notes.

"I don't like to," he says. "I just find when you take out a notebook, it just changes the atmosphere." Nevertheless, in his column he frequently quotes conversations he has had with Hollywood fig-

ures. The quotes, which he also inserts in reporters' stories, are nearly always unattributed. He often dictates them off the top of his head, which may explain why some of Variety's anonymous sources sound a lot like Inventive Peter.

Bart favors the terms fat cats *and* suits. *So do a fair number of people who sound off in his columns. He loves to use* damned, *as in "You know damned well he intends to deliver for his clients." When run through Bart's typewriter, lots of people around town start cussing just like that, from "a senior marketing official at Paramount" to "one major agent" to "one of the town's top lawyers."*

Read enough of Bart's work and you begin to hear the echo. In his own voice he will write, "It's all about those statuettes, stupid," or "It's all about the waivers from SAG." A few months later he'll quote one "candid" CEO ("It's all about intimidation") or "the production chief of one major [studio]" ("It's all about money").

"I have," he says, "an incredible memory."

•   •   •

If Peter Bart has a motto, it is this: "I know now there is no one thing that is true. It is all true." The words are Hemingway's, from his novel *Islands in the Stream*. Once Bart quoted them in a column, adding, "Now there's a manifesto for you."

Everyone knows that in Hollywood people lie as a matter of course, exaggerating their accomplishments, minimizing their failures. They don't fret about it. Building up one's own buzz is part of doing business—a means to an end. Bart is notable, though, because he is editor of the Industry's most important publication, so his fibs, amplifications, and outright lies masquerade as candor.

"I have covered . . . wars," he recently asserted in a letter to the editor of the *Los Angeles Times*. When pressed, though, he admits he hasn't. He frequently refers to his time as "a young kid studio executive," even though he was 35 when he got his first studio job and 53 when he left his last one. One publicist recalls Bart calling her angrily after she asked for a correction to a *Variety* article. "I ran three studios," yelled the man who did no such thing, "and I will not be dictated to by a fucking flack!"

One former colleague says Bart had a term for the kind of embellishment he practices: "novelizing." Another who remains fond of Bart says, "His relationship to the truth is very plastic. I'd go on interviews with him and he'd write something and I'd think, 'Were we in the same room?' He's just a storyteller. The narrative needs are more immediate to his imagination than what actually happened."

Bart's philosophy permeates *Variety.* There's the way he praises friends, associates, and even his own movies without acknowledging his involvement. He'll call Richard Heller "a scrupulous New York practitioner" without noting that Heller has been his lawyer for 25 years. Ronda Gomez is "one of the town's veteran literary agents." She was also his assistant at Paramount Pictures. Michelle Manning, president of production at Paramount, is "one of the sharper young executives in town." A year before he wrote that, Manning also bought the movie rights to a Bart project, but he doesn't mention that. If a reporter or an editor at a major daily newspaper flaunted the basic rules of journalism the way Bart does, they'd be shown the door.

Most people in show business deceive to gain advantage—to downplay their cost overruns, say, or to boost their salaries. Bart, too, misrepresents for strategic advantage, but he also lies for no apparent reason. Consider what happened when we discussed the infamous *Patriot Games* incident of 1992, when *Variety* film critic Joe McBride wrote a blistering review of Paramount Pictures' Tom Clancy adaptation. The studio, apoplectic over the review's potential dampening of interest among overseas exhibitors, pulled its advertising from *Variety.* Bart got mad, but not at the studio. He decreed that McBride would no longer review Paramount films.

The New York Times wrote a story about the McBride dustup

that said *Variety* staffers were aghast that their boss would curry favor with Paramount. The article quoted from a private apology that Bart had sent to Martin S. Davis, the studio's then chairman and CEO. "Marty Davis and I have known each other for 25 years," Bart told the *Times*. "I simply dropped him a friendly note."

Nine years later, however, when I first ask Bart about the note, he insists it never existed. "I never wrote any," he says, adding that he disliked Davis intensely, so "the idea that I would contact these people was bizarre." How to explain the *Times* story, written by veteran reporter Bernard Weinraub? "It was a reminder to me about the nastiness of journalists toward each other," Bart says, shaking his head.

A few weeks later I obtained a copy of the letter. Bart's lie didn't make sense. Had he forgotten that it was typed by his own secretary on *Variety* stationary? (Bart's secretary at the time had a couple of well-known idiosyncrasies—using a double dash in phone numbers, spelling out fax with spaces between the letters—both of which are in evidence.) Did he really think that he could alter the "fossil record," to borrow Jeff Berg's phrase, and rewrite history?

When I presented a copy of the letter to Bart—the first of two occasions that he would later denounce as "gotcha"journalism—he declared it "blatantly bogus." He disputed the signature. He suggested the letterhead had been faked. "Editorial director, Variety Inc.?" he said, reading the words under his name. "I don't ever remember having that title." (*Variety*'s masthead from that period shows that, in fact, he did.) "I agree with the contents of the letter," he said after perusing it for a minute, "but I didn't write it."

Later he would call me to clarify. Even if he had written the letter, he said, "that incident is not relevant to me, only because it never recurred. I'd think it was interesting if it were a syndrome. But since it's a stand-alone . . ." It sounded like an acknowledgment, sort of. His voice trailed off.

What was more striking than Bart's dissembling, however, was a part of the letter that *The New York Times* hadn't seen fit to quote. In one paragraph, it captures how Bart perceives his place in Hollywood: "I know that you and Stanley [Jaffe] feel that *Variety* has developed an anti-Paramount tilt in its coverage. This distresses me—we go back together many years and I personally feel a keen sense of camaraderie. Clearly you feel, however, that the 'old comrades' aren't taking care of each other. If that's your feeling, you and Stanley deserve better and I intend to take personal charge of this situation to set it right."

"Taking care of each other"—that is Bart's defining editorial principle. That doesn't mean he rolls over, necessarily. If he thinks a top executive needs a kick in the pants, he's happy to administer it. But he's no adversary. He's more like a teammate, or even a coach. He may be editor-in-chief of *Variety*, but he is still one of them.

People who have worked with Bart say he would call his favorite sources—Guber, Ovitz, Weinstein, Evans, producer Arnon Milchan—and vet stories that mentioned them, letting them make adjustments. When confronted by the reporters whose bylines topped the altered stories, Bart would say he got better information after deadline. "This is my paper," one remembers him saying. "I'll do as I please."

Bart has internalized Hollywood's A-list mentality, mistaking the highest-placed source for the best source, even when the higher-up has much to gain by what they're leaking. When Milchan was negotiating to take his production company from Warner Bros. to 20th Century Fox, for example, the reporters working the story established that Warner Bros. had capped its offer at $100 million. Bart added another knowledgeable source, who put the number at $130 million. The source, the reporters were shocked to learn, was Milchan, whose bargaining position was sure to be strengthened by the $30 million boost.

"It might have been," Bart says, "that I just called him and asked him what the number was." But didn't that help Milchan?

"People like that, they don't need my help. They're doing fine. And let's be pragmatic. You can't use a newspaper to help your friends. You'll end up getting fired."

In almost the next breath, though, Bart says friendship does guide him. He recalls visiting Guber's office one day when Guber was chairman of Sony. "The purpose of my mission was to yell at him. You don't like to see a friend messing up," Bart says. "I was telling him among other things how badly he was handling the press and how he was not being confrontative enough with the problems at Sony. It had nothing to do with reporting. No notes were taken. It had nothing to do with journalism." Bart insists, however, that despite offering such counsel, he directed his reporters to grill Guber's regime as they would any other.

"Is Guber a friend of mine? Certainly. I have never denied that," Bart says. "Was he an effective president of Sony? No." Those who attended a gala tribute to Bart at the Beverly Hilton Hotel in 1997, meanwhile, remember that Guber began the roast with this joke: "Will everyone here who owes Peter a favor for having killed a negative story please remain seated?" The room—filled with Hollywood's heaviest hitters—erupted in laughter. Everybody stayed in their seats.

· · · ·

Nervous Peter has questions.

The magazine's fact checker has just spent the day going over the story with him, and he wants to discuss a few things with me. "When we entered into this thing, I said to you, 'When I write about people, I don't write about religious beliefs or sexual orienta-tion,'" he says. "I honestly felt you would respect that." I remind him that all along I have told him that the profile would take into account his history.

"What concerns me is if you are characterizing me as a runaway

Jew," he says. "It's not that I don't acknowledge it. I just don't talk about it. It's not a part of my life. Isn't this the equivalent of outing someone?" he asks.

I tell him I don't equate revealing a person's homosexuality with saying his parents were Austrian Jews.

He then changes course. "Do me one favor," he says. "To avoid me being blackballed, quote me saying, 'I have no problem saying my ethnicity is Jewish.' Otherwise you're going to get me into trouble with all these people."

When I tell him I can do that, but that I'm sure my editor will insist that we put the quote in context, making it clear that it came after a call from a fact checker, he snaps: "Is he some kind of professional Jew, too?"

•   •   •

It has long been rumored—but never proved—that the editor of *Variety* writes scripts on the side. Bart has always denied this, but people still whisper. Earlier this year *The Hollywood Reporter*'s David Robb, who has never hidden his antipathy for his former boss, wrote an article about it.

In March, after Bart attended a Writers Guild meeting that was closed to the press and then published a report on *Variety*'s front page, Robb investigated why Bart was still an active guild member. He discovered that to remain active, Bart had to have sold a script within the past four years. Robb thought he'd found what to Bart's enemies amounts to the Holy Grail: proof that Bart was engaging in journalism's most serious conflict of interest—profiting from those you cover.

Robb, however, never laid his hands on the offending script. If he had, he might have been disappointed. According to Bart, the script he sold within the last four years was *Nobody's Children,* a drama about a gang of gypsy thieves that he wrote in the early

'80s. Bart says the transaction that kept him active in the WGA was merely the extension of a preexisting option—one that was entered into long before he came to *Variety*.

"Dave has this fascination, trying to prove that I am still writing and selling scripts," Bart says, adding that these days the mere act of reading a script makes him physically ill. When it comes to screenplays, he says, his "entire oeuvre" was written before he got to *Variety*. "I'm not writing or selling scripts. I don't even want to write and sell scripts. But Dave is still trying to find another script."

For the record, *Variety* has a policy that prevents its reporters from being seduced by Hollywood while they are covering it. As Bart explained it to me, "You cannot shop a script while you're writing for us. Obviously it's different if you write a book or a novel and it sells to a movie studio. I have no problem with that, except I'm not going to write the script. I don't think the line is that blurry."

Things were about to get blurrier, though. One night I came home and found that a manila envelope had been forced through my mail slot. Inside was a 108-page script.

By this point I had heard many accounts of how Bart had earned people's enmity. Even if I took them all at face value, which I didn't, these stories never implied that Bart was a dimwit. In a town full of blowhards, where money is often a substitute for intelligence, Bart is considered supremely—if sometimes vengefully—bright. But, as I was about to discover, he was not bright enough to compensate for his Achilles' heel: his loyalty to his friend and mentor, Robert Evans.

In 1998 *Variety* reported that Michelle Manning at Paramount Pictures had acquired the rights to a novel written by Bart. The novel was called *Power Play*, and the plan was for Evans to develop it. It was set in Las Vegas and focused on a power struggle between established casino owners and Indian tribes. Bart had used a pseudonym, the article said, "to avoid any potential conflict of interest."

I'd read all of Bart's novels but had never heard of *Power Play*. When I first asked Bart about it, he said, "It's not a novel. It's a novella. It needs work. I never finished it." When I asked to read it, he told me he had no idea where it was. "I did it to try to help Bob out. And Bob never did anything with it," he said, referring to Evans.

So no script was ever written? "Not to my knowledge," he said. "In the old days I'd have swung into action, gotten a director assigned, gotten it off the ground. But I don't do that for a living anymore. And it's not what I should do."

Then the script arrived. It was called *Crossroaders,* but it was the same story as *Power Play*. Its title page read: "By Leslie Cox"—the maiden name of Bart's current wife—"Based on the novel by Peter Bart, September, 1996."

I call Bart and arrange for a final interview. Over several months I had come to know many Peters, but when he welcomes me to his office I don't know which one to expect. I tell Bart I have a copy of the 1996 script he wrote. "The script I wrote," he repeats, neither confirming nor denying. I look into the face of the man with the incredible memory. It is blank. But one knee starts jiggling, and he fiddles idly with the band of his watch.

"Boy, you got me. Did I write a script? Now I'm facing memory loss," he says, as I pull a copy of *Crossroaders* out of my bag. He looks it over. "Let's just say this is a script that has Leslie's name on it. What does that indicate? Therefore—therefore, what?"

I repeat that I know he wrote it. "I may have written this," he says. But, I counter, you said you hate writing scripts. "I do. Maybe this taught me never to do it again. I'd love to read this. Is it any good?"

Persuasive Peter, Argumentative Peter, Smooth Peter—they're all here, and they're taking turns. "You know something? In all honesty, I do not remember writing this," he says. "I guess it was written to work out the novel. That would be my answer."

Bart summons his assistant to look for the novella—the one he told me he couldn't locate. She beelines for a cabinet behind his chair and retrieves a slim bound volume with a navy blue cover. She hands it to him. The search takes less than 20 seconds.

"This is an 86-page novel," he says. "This was what was bought. It was the only thing that was ever submitted to Paramount." He admits that he probably spent a weekend transforming the *Crossroaders* script into the wisp of a novel he holds in his hand. I look at the novel's cover page, which displays not the pseudonym the *Variety* article had promised but the words "By Peter Bart." When I tell him the whole thing looks like an elaborate way of circumventing the rules, effectively selling a script by ginning up a novel, he objects.

"I don't think it looks that way," he says. "If you're saying therefore that I wrote and marketed the script, you can say it, but I would deny it. I contend to you that a novel was written of this, and that's what Bob bought. There's no rule that says you can't write a script that no one sees."

Except, of course, that Evans—the man developing the project—did see the script. "I'm sure Bob has," he says, "but I'll tell you about Bob." He laughs. "Bob having it is like the crypt."

As the interview winds up, Bart is almost playful. He jokes that I'm a "troublemaker" and "mean." "It's really scary," he says, "when you start remembering things about me that I don't remember."

·   ·   ·

The next morning Litigious Peter picks up the phone. He's still at home. His voice is tight and angry. He accuses me of using material stolen from his files. He feels betrayed that I gave him no warning. The details of why he wrote a screenplay as a warm-up for a novella are coming back to him, he says, though "vaguely." "I'm glad I did it that way," he says. "The book sure is lean.

"One thing I'm not is self-destructive," he says. "To break my own rules is just stupid. I was trying to get Bob's career going." He pauses. "I would appreciate it if you could tell me how you're going to handle this, so I can send to the magazine this legal document that will say I will sue you."

A week later Conflicted Peter calls.

"I haven't heard from my nemesis for a while. Have you given up on this project, I hope?" he says, his voice almost warm. "I must say, I'm still a little nettled."

Despite his better judgment, he has more to say. "It's always a favor that kills you. No one ever did see that fucking script. In retrospect, I shouldn't have done it. I will guarantee you that I will never do it again."

· · ·

In his *Crossroaders* script, Bart sets a key scene at a press conference in Las Vegas's most decadent gambling casino. The casino's owner takes a few questions from the assembled media, then invites them to do some gambling—on him. The offer prompts this ethical debate:

FIRST REPORTER (to a colleague): The son-of-a-bitch has no shame. I mean, he's prepared to buy out the entire press corps if necessary.

SECOND REPORTER: He's an asshole. (A pause.) On the other hand, since it's on the house, I don't think fifteen minutes at the Money Wheel will compromise my scruples.

As so often happens with Bart, there is a duality. Both reporters are him.

The New Yorker

WINNER, FICTION

A House on the Plains

The New Yorker *demonstrates time and again a masterly ability to publish layered, complex, and emotionally moving short fiction. This story—about a kindly widow with murder on her mind—has thoroughly developed characters and voices, and is rendered with lyrical precision and grace.*

E. L. Doctorow

A House on the Plains

Mama said I was thenceforth to be her nephew, and to call her Aunt Dora. She said our fortune depended on her not having a son as old as eighteen who looked more like twenty. Say Aunt Dora, she said. I said it. She was not satisfied. She made me say it several times. She said I must say it believing that she had taken me in since the death of her widowed brother Horace. I said, I didn't know you had a brother named Horace. Of course I don't, she said with an amused glance at me. But it must be a good story if I could fool his son with it.

I was not offended as I watched her primp in the mirror, touching her hair as women do although you can never see what afterward is different.

With the life insurance, she had bought us a farm fifty miles west of the city line. Who would be there to care if I was her flesh-and-blood son or not? But she had her plans and was looking ahead. I had no plans, I had never had plans, just the inkling of something, sometimes, I didn't know what. I hunched over and went down the stairs with the second trunk wrapped to my back with a rope. Outside, at the foot of the stoop, the children were waiting with their scraped knees and socks around their ankles. They sang their own dirty words to a nursery rhyme. I shooed them away and they scattered off for a minute, hooting and hollering, and then of course came back again as I went up the stairs for the rest of the things.

Mama was standing at the empty bay window. While there is your court of inquest on the one hand, she said, on the other is your court of neighbors. Out in the country, she said, there will be no one to jump to conclusions. You can leave the door open and the window shades up. Everything is clean and pure under the sun.

Well, I could understand that, but Chicago to my mind was the only place to be, with its grand hotels and its restaurants and paved avenues of trees and mansions. Of course, not all Chicago was like that. Our third-floor windows didn't look out on much besides the row of boarding houses across the street. And it is true that in the summer people of refinement could be overcome with the smell of the stockyards, although it didn't bother me. Winter was another complaint that wasn't mine. I never minded the cold. The wind in winter blowing off the lake went whipping the ladies' skirts like a demon dancing around their ankles. And winter or summer you could always ride the electric streetcars if you had nothing else to do. I above all liked the city because it was filled with people all a-bustle, and the clatter of hooves and carriages, and with delivery wagons and drays and peddlers and the boom and clank of freight trains. And when those black clouds came sailing in from the west, pouring thunderstorms upon us so that you couldn't hear the cries or curses of humankind, I liked that best of all. Chicago could stand up to the worst God had to offer. I understood why it was built—a place for trade, of course, with railroads and ships and so on, but mostly to give all of us a magnitude of defiance that is not provided by one house on the plains. And the plains is where those storms come from.

Besides, I would miss my friend Winifred Czerwinska, who stood now on her landing as I was going downstairs with the suitcases.

Come in a minute, she said, I want to give you something. I went in and she closed the door behind me. You can put those down, she said of the suitcases.

My heart always beat faster in Winifred's presence, I could feel it and she knew it too and it made her happy. She put her hand on my chest now and she stood on tiptoes to kiss me with her hand under my shirt feeling my heart pump.

Look at him, all turned out in a coat and tie. Oh, she said, with her eyes tearing up, what am I going to do without my Earle? But she was smiling.

Winifred was not a Mama type of woman. She was a slight, skinny thing, and when she went down the stairs it was like a bird hopping. She wore no powder or perfumery except, by accident, the confectionery sugar that she brought home on her from the bakery where she worked behind the counter. She had sweet cool lips, but one eyelid didn't come up all the way over the blue, which made her not as pretty as she might otherwise be. And of course she had no titties to speak of.

You can write me a letter and I will write back, I said.

What will you say in your letter?

I will think of something, I said.

She pulled me into the kitchen, where she spread her feet and put her forearms flat on a chair so that I could raise her frock and fuck into her in the way she preferred. It didn't take that long, but even so while Winifred wiggled and made her little cat sounds I could hear Mama calling from upstairs as to where I had gotten.

We had ordered a carriage to take us and the luggage at the same time rather than sending it off by the less expensive American Express and taking a horsecar to the station. That was not my idea, but how much money we had after Mama bought the house only she knew. She came down the steps under her broad-brim hat and widow's veil and held her skirts at her shoe tops as the driver helped her into the carriage.

We were making a grand exit in full daylight. This was pure

Mama as she lifted her veil and glanced with contempt at the neighbors looking out from their windows. As for the nasty children, they had gone quite quiet at our display of elegance. I swung up beside her and closed the door and at her instruction threw a handful of pennies on the sidewalk and I watched the children push and shove one another and dive to their knees as we drove off.

When we had turned the corner, Mama opened the hatbox I had put on the seat. She removed her black hat and replaced it with a blue number trimmed in fake flowers. Over her mourning dress she draped a glittery shawl in striped colors like the rainbow.

There, she said. I feel so much better now. Are you all right, Earle?

Yes, Mama, I said.

Aunt Dora.

Yes, Aunt Dora.

I wish you had a better mind, Earle. You could have paid more attention to the Doctor when he was alive. We had our disagreements, but he was smart for a man.

·　　·　　·

The train stop of La Ville was a concrete platform and a lean-to for a waiting room and no ticket-agent window. When you got off, you were looking down an alley to a glimpse of their Main Street. Main Street had a feed store, a post office, a white wooden church, a granite stone bank, a haberdasher, a town square with a four-story hotel, and in the middle of the square on the grass the statue of a Union soldier. It could all be counted because there was just one of everything. A man with a dray was willing to take us, and he drove past a few other streets where first there were some homes of substance and another church or two but then, as you moved further out from the town center, there were only worn-looking one-story shingle houses with dark porches and little garden plots and clotheslines out back with only alleys separating them. I couldn't see how, but Mama said there was a population of over three thousand living here. And then, after a couple of miles through farmland, with a silo here and there, off a straight road leading due west through fields of corn, there swung into view what I had not expected: a three-story house of red brick with a flat roof and stone steps up to the front door like something just lifted out of a street of row houses in Chicago. I couldn't believe anyone had built such a thing for a farmhouse. The sun flared in the windowpanes, and I had to shade my eyes to make sure I was seeing what I saw. But that was it in truth, our new home.

Not that I had the time to ponder, not with Mama settling in. We went to work. The house was cobwebbed and dusty and it was rank with the droppings of animal life. Blackbirds were roosting in the top floor, where I was to live. Much needed to be done, but before long she had it all organized and a parade of wagons was coming from town with the furniture she'd Expressed and no shortage of men willing to hire on for a day with hopes for more from this grand good-looking lady with the rings on several fingers. And so the fence went up for the chicken yard, and the weed fields beyond were being plowed under and the watering hole for stock was dredged and a new privy was dug, and I thought for some days Mama was the biggest employer of La Ville, Illinois.

But who would haul the well water and wash the clothes and bake the bread? A farm was a different life, and days went by when I slept under the roof of the third floor and felt the heat of the day still on my pallet as I looked through the little window at the stars and I felt unprotected as I never had in the civilization we had retreated from. Yes, I thought, we had moved backward from the world's progress, and for the first time I wondered about Mama's judgment. In all our travels from state to state and with all the various obstacles to her ambition, I had never thought to question it. But no more than this house was a farmer's house was she a farmer, and neither was I.

One evening we stood on the front steps watching the sun go down behind the low hills miles away.

Aunt Dora, I said, what are we up to here?

I know, Earle. But some things take time.

She saw me looking at her hands, how red they had gotten.

I am bringing an immigrant woman down from Wisconsin. She will sleep in that room behind the kitchen. She's to be here in a week or so.

Why? I said. There's women in La Ville, the wives of all these locals come out here for a day's work, who could surely use the money.

I will not have some woman in the house who will only take back to town what she sees and hears. Use what sense God gave you, Earle.

I am trying, Mama.

Aunt Dora, God damn it.

Aunt Dora.

Yes, she said. Especially here in the middle of nowhere and with nobody else in sight.

She had tied her thick hair behind her neck against the heat and she went about now loose in a smock without her usual women's underpinnings.

But doesn't the air smell sweet, she said. I'm going to have a screen porch built and fit it out with a settee and some rockers so we can watch the grand show of nature in comfort.

She ruffled my hair. And you don't have to pout, she said. You may not appreciate it here this moment with the air so peaceful and the birds singing and nothing much going on in any direction you can see. But we're still in business, Earle. You can trust me on that.

And so I was assured.

· · ·

By and by we acquired an old-fashioned horse and buggy to take us to La Ville and back when Aunt Dora had to go to the bank or the post office or when provisions were needed. I was the driver and horse groom. He, the horse, and I did not get along. I wouldn't give him a name. He was ugly, with a swayback and legs that trotted out splayed.

I had butchered and trimmed better-looking plugs than this in Chicago. Once in the barn when I was putting him up for the night he took a chomp in the air just off my shoulder.

Another problem was Bent, the handyman Mama had hired for the steady work. No sooner did she begin taking him upstairs of an afternoon than he was strutting around like he owned the place. This was a problem, as I saw it. Sure enough, one day he told me to do something. It was one of his own chores. I thought you was the hired one, I said to him. He was ugly, like a relation of the horse, and he was shorter than you thought he ought to be, with his long arms and big gnarled hands hanging from them.

Get on with it, I said.

Leering, he grabbed me by the shoulder and put his mouth up to my ear. I seen it all, he said. Oh yes. I seen everything a man could wish to see.

At this I found myself constructing a fate for Bent the handyman. But he was so drunkly stupid I knew Mama must have her own plan for him, or else why would she play up to someone of this ilk, and so I held my ideas in abeyance.

In fact, I was by now thinking I could wrest some hope from the wide loneliness of this farm with views of the plains as far as you could see. What had come to mind? An aroused expectancy or suspense that I recognized from times past. Yes. I had sensed that whatever was going to happen had begun. There was not only the handyman. There were the orphan children. She had contracted for three from the do-good agency in New York that took orphans off the streets and washed and dressed them and put them on the train to foster homes in the midland. Ours were comely enough children, though pale: two boys and a girl, with papers that gave their ages, six, six, and eight, and as I trotted them to the farm they sat up behind me staring at the countryside without a word. They were installed in the back bedroom on the second floor, and they were not like the miserable children from our neighborhood in the city. These were quiet children except for the weeping they were sometimes given to at night, and by and large they did as they were told. Mama had some real feeling for them, Joseph and Calvin and the girl, Sophie, in particular. There were no conditions as to what faith they were to be brought up in nor did we have any in mind. But on Sundays Mama took to showing them off to the Methodist church in La Ville in the new clothes she had bought for them. It gave her pleasure and also bespoke of her pride of position in life. Because it turned out, as I was learning, that even in the farthest reaches of the countryside you lived in society.

And in this great scheme of things my Aunt Dora required Joseph, Calvin, and Sophie to think of her as their Mama. Say Mama, she said to them. And they said it.

· · ·

Well, so here was this household of us, ready-made, as something bought from a department store. Fannie was the imported cook and housekeeper, who by Mama's design spoke no English but understood well enough what had to be done. She was heavyset, like Mama, with the strength to work hard. And besides Bent, who skulked about by the barns and fences in the sly pretense of work, there was a real farmer out beyond who was sharecropping the acreage in corn. And two mornings a week a retired county teacher woman came by to tutor the children in reading and arithmetic.

Mama said one evening, We are an honest-to-goodness enterprise here, a functioning family better off than most in these parts, but we are running at a deficit, and if we don't have something in hand before winter the only resources will be the insurance I took out on the little ones.

She lit the kerosene lamp on the desk in the parlor and wrote out a personal and read it to me: "Widow offering partnership in prime farmland to dependable man. A modest investment is required." What do you think, Earle?

It's O.K.

She read it again to herself. No, she said. It's not good enough. You've got to get them up off their ass and out of the house to the credit union and then on a train to La Ville, Illinois. That's a lot to do with just a few words. How about this: "Wanted!" That's good, it bespeaks urgency. And doesn't every male in the world think he's what is wanted? "Wanted—Recently widowed woman with a bountiful farm in God's own country has need of Nordic man of sufficient means for partnership in same."

What is Nordic? I said.

Well, that's pure cunning right there, Earle, because that is all they got in the states where we print this—Swedes and Norwegies just off the boat. But I'm letting them know a lady's preference.

All right, but what's that you say there—"of sufficient means"? What Norwegie off the boat'll know what that's all about?

This gave her pause. Good for you, Earle, you surprise me sometimes. She licked the pencil point. So we'll just say "with cash."

We placed the personal in one paper at a time in towns in Minnesota and then in South Dakota. The letters of courtship commenced, and Mama kept a ledger with the names and dates of arrival, making sure to give each candidate his sufficient time. We always advised the early-morning train, when the town was not yet up and about. Besides my regular duties, I had to take part in the family reception. Each of them would be welcomed into the parlor and Mama would serve coffee from a wheeled tray, and Joseph, Calvin, and Sophie, her children, and I, her nephew, would sit on the sofa and hear our biographies conclude with a happy ending, which was the present moment. Mama was so well spoken at these times I was as apt as the poor foreigners to be caught up in her modesty, so seemingly unconscious was she of the greatheartedness of her. They by and large did not see through to her self-congratulation. And of course she was a large handsome woman to look at. She wore her simple finery for these first impressions, a plain, pleated gray cotton skirt and a starched white shirtwaist and no jewelry but the gold cross on a chain that fell between her bosoms, and her hair was combed upward and piled atop her head in a state of fetching carelessness.

I am their dream of Heaven on earth, Mama said to me along about the third or fourth. Just to see how their eyes light up standing beside me looking out over their new land. Puffing on their pipes, giving me a glance that imagines me as available for marriage—who can say I don't give value in return?

Well, that is one way to look at it, I said.

Don't be smug, Earle. You're in no position. Tell me an easier way to God's blessed Heaven than a launch from His Heaven on earth. I don't know of one.

·　　·　　·

And so our account in the La Ville Savings Bank began to compound nicely. The late-summer rain did just the right thing for the corn, as even I could see, and it was an added few unanticipated dollars we received from the harvest. If there were any complications to worry about, it was that fool Bent. He was so dumb he was dangerous. At first, Mama indulged his jealousy; I could hear them arguing upstairs, he roaring away and she assuring him so quietly I could hardly hear what she said. But it didn't do any good. When one of the Norwegies arrived, Bent just happened to be in the yard where he could have a good look. One time there was his ugly face peering through the porch window. Mama signalled me with a slight motion of her head and I quickly got up and pulled the shade.

It was true Mama might lay it on a bit thick. She might coquette with this one, yes, just as she might affect a widow's piety with that one. It all depended on her instinct for the particular man's character. It was easy enough to make believers of them; if I had to judge them as a whole I would say they were simple men, not exactly stupid but lacking command of our language and with no wiles of their own. By whatever combination of sentiments and signatures, she never had anything personal intended but the business at hand, the step-by-step encouragement of the cash into our bank account.

The fool Bent imagined Mama looking for a husband from among these men. His pride of possession was offended. When he came to work each morning, he was often three sheets to the wind, and if she happened not to invite him upstairs for the afternoon siesta he would go home in a state, turning at the road to shake his fist and shout up at the windows before he set out for town in his crouching stride.

Mama said to me on one occasion, The damned fool has feelings.

Well, that had not occurred to me in the way she meant it, and maybe in that moment my opinion of the handyman was raised to a degree. Not that he was any less dangerous. Clearly he had never learned that the purpose of life is to improve your station in it. It was not an idea available to him. Whatever you were, that's what you would always be. So he saw these foreigners who couldn't even talk right not only as usurpers but as casting a poor light on his existence. Were I in his position, I would learn from the example of these immigrants, and think what I could do to put together a few dollars and buy some farmland for myself. Any normal person would think that. Not him. The only idea that got through his thick skull was that he lacked the hopes of even the lowest foreigner. So I would come back from the station with one of them in the buggy and the fellow would step down, his plaid suit and four-in-hand and his derby proposing him as a man of sufficient means, and it was like a shadow and sudden chilling as from a black cloud came over poor Bent, who could understand only that it was too late for him—everything, I mean, it was all too late.

And, finally, to show how dumb he was, he didn't realize it was all too late for them, too.

.   .   .

Then everything green began to fade off yellow, the summer rains were gone, and the wind off the prairie blew the dried-out topsoil into gusty swirls that rose and fell like waves in a dirt sea. At night the windows rattled. At first frost, the two little boys caught the croup.

Mama pulled the Wanted ad back from the out-of-state papers, saying she needed to catch her breath. I didn't know what was in the ledger, but her saying that meant our financial situation was improved. And now, as I supposed with all farm families, winter would be a time for rest.

Not that I was looking forward to it. How could I, with nothing to do?

I wrote a letter to my friend Winifred Czerwinska, in Chicago. I had been so busy until now I hardly had the time to be lonely. I said that I missed her and hoped before too long to come back to city life. As I wrote, a rush of pity for myself came over me and I almost sobbed at the picture in my mind of the Elevated trains and the lights of the theatre marquees and the sounds I imagined of the streetcars and even of the lowings of the abattoir where I had earned my wages. But I only said I hoped she would write me back.

I think the children felt the same way about this cold countryside. They had been displaced from a greater distance away in a city larger than Chicago. They could not have been colder huddled at some steam grate than they were now, with blankets to their chins. From the day they arrived, they wouldn't leave one another's side, and though she was not croupy herself, Sophie stayed with the two boys in their bedroom, attending to their hackings and wheezes and sleeping in an armchair in the night. Fannie cooked up oatmeal for their breakfasts and soup for their dinners, and I took it upon myself to bring the tray upstairs in order to get them talking to me, since we were all related in a sense and in their minds I would be an older boy orphan, taken in like them. But they would not talk much, only answering my friendly questions yes or no in their soft voices, looking at me all the while with some dark expectation in their eyes. I didn't like that. I knew they talked among themselves all the time. They were smart. For instance, they knew enough to stay out of Bent's way when he was drinking. But when he was sober they followed him around. And one day I had gone into the stable, to harness the horse, and found them snooping around in there, so they were not without unhealthy curiosity. Then there was the unfortunate matter of one of the boys, Joseph, the shorter, darker one—he had found a pocket watch and watch fob in the yard, and when I said it was mine he said it wasn't. Whose is it then, I said. I know it's not yours, he said as he finally handed it over. To make more of an issue of it was not wise, so I didn't, but I hadn't forgotten.

Mama and I were nothing if not prudent, discreet, and in full consideration of the feelings of others in all our ways and means, but I believe children have another sense that enables them to know something even when they can't say what it is. As a child I must have had it, but of course it leaves you as you grow up, it may be a trait children are given so that they will live long enough to grow up.

But I didn't want to think the worst. I reasoned to myself that were I plunked down so far away from my streets among strangers who I was ordered to live with as their relation, in the middle of this flat land of vast empty fields that would stir in any breast nothing but a recognition of the presiding deafness and dumbness of the natural world, I, too, would behave as these children were behaving.

.   .   .

And then, one stinging cold day in December, I went into town to pick up a package from the post office. We had to write away to Chicago for those things it would not do to order from the local merchants. The package was in, but there was also a letter addressed to me, and it was from my friend Winifred Czerwinska.

Winifred's penmanship made me smile; the letters were thin and scrawny and did not keep to a straight line but rose and fell while slanting in a downward direction, as if some of her mortal being was transferred to the letter paper. And I knew she had written from the bakery because there was some powdered sugar in the folds.

She was so glad to hear from me and to know where I was. She thought I had forgotten her. She said she missed me. She said she was bored with her job. She had saved her money and hinted that she would be glad to spend it on something interesting, like a train ticket. My ears got hot reading that. In my mind I saw Winifred squinting up at me, I could almost feel her putting her hand under my shirt to feel my heart the way she liked to do.

But on the second page she said maybe I would be interested in news from the old neighborhood. There was going to be another inquest, or maybe the same one reopened.

It took me a moment to understand she was talking about the Doctor, Mama's husband in Chicago. The Doctor's relatives had asked for his body to be dug up. Winifred found this out from the constable, who knocked on her door as he was doing with everyone. The police were trying to find out where we had gone, Mama and I.

I hadn't gotten your letter yet, Winifred said, so I didn't have to lie about not knowing where you were.

I raced home. Why did Winifred think she would otherwise have to lie? Did she believe the bad gossip about us? Was she like the rest of them? I thought she was different. I was disappointed in her, and then I was suddenly very mad at Winifred.

Mama read the letter differently. Your Miss Czerwinska is our friend, Earle. That's something higher than a lover. If I have worried about her slow eye being passed on to the children, if it shows up, we will just have to have it corrected with surgery.

What children, I said.

The children of your blessed union with Miss Czerwinska, Mama said.

Do not think Mama said this merely to keep me from worrying about the Chicago problem. She sees things before other people see them, she has plans going out through all directions of the universe, she is not a one-track mind, my Aunt Dora. I was excited by her intentions for me as if I had thought of them myself. Perhaps I had thought of them myself as my secret, but she had read my secret and was now giving her approval. Because I certainly did like Winifred Czerwinska, whose lips tasted of baked goods and who loved it so when I fucked into her. And now it was all out in the open, and Mama not only knew my feelings but expressed them for me, and it only remained for the young lady to be told that we were engaged.

I thought then her visiting us would be appropriate, especially as she was prepared to pay her own way. But Mama said, Not yet, Earle, everyone in the house knew you were loving her up, and if she was to quit her job in the bakery and pack a bag and go down to the train station even the Chicago police, as stupid as they are, they would put two and two together.

Of course, I did not argue the point, though I was of the opinion that the police would find out where we were regardless. There were indications all over the place, not anything as difficult as a clue to be discerned only by the smartest of detectives, but bank-account transfers, forwarding mail, and such. Why, even the driver who took us to the station might have picked up some remark of ours, and certainly a ticket-seller at Union Station might remember us, Mama being such an unusual-looking woman, very decorative and regal to the male eye, she would surely be remembered by a ticket-seller who would not see her like from one year to the next.

Maybe a week went by before Mama expressed an opinion about the problem. You can't trust people, she said, it's that damn sister of his who didn't even shed a tear at the grave. Why, she even told me how lucky the Doctor was to have found me so late in life.

I remember, I said.

And how I had taken such good care of him.

Which was true, I said.

Relatives are the fly in the ointment, Earle.

•   •   •

Mama's not being concerned so much as she was put out meant that we had more time than I would have thought. Our quiet lives of winter went on as before, though as I watched and waited she was obviously thinking things through. I was satisfied to wait even though she was particularly attentive to Bent, inviting him in for dinner as if he was not some hired hand but a neighboring farmer. And I had to sit across the table on the children's side and watch him struggle to hold the silver in his fist and slurp his soup and pity him the way he had pathetically combed his hair down and tucked his shirt in and the way he folded his fingers under when he happened to see the dirt under his nails. This is good eats, he said aloud to no one in particular, and even Fannie, as she served, gave a little humph, as if, despite having no English, she understood clearly enough how out of place he was here at our table.

Well, as it turned out there were things I didn't know. For instance, that the little girl, Sophie, had adopted Bent, or maybe made a pet of him as you would any dumb beast, but they had become friends of a sort and she had confided to him remarks she overheard in the household. Maybe if she was making Mama into her mama she thought she was supposed to make the wretched bum of a hired hand into her father, I don't know. Anyway, there was this alliance between them that showed to me that she would never rise above her unsavory life in the street as a vagrant child. She looked like an angel, with her little bow mouth and her pale face and gray eyes and her hair in a single long braid that Mama herself did every morning, but she had the hearing of a bat and could stand on the second-floor landing and listen all the way down the stairs to our private conversations in the front parlor. Of course, I knew that only later. It was Mama who learned that Bent was putting it about to his drinking cronies in town that the Madame Dora they thought was such a lady was his love slave and a woman on the wrong side of the law back in Chicago.

Mama, I said, I have never liked this fool, though I have been holding my ideas in abeyance for the fate I have in mind for him. But here he accepts our wages and eats our food then goes and does this?

Hush, Earle, not yet, not yet, she said. But you are a good son to me, and I can take pride that as a woman alone I have bred in you the highest sense of family honor. She saw how troubled I was. She hugged me. Are you not my very own knight of the Round Table? she said. But I was not comforted; it seemed to me that forces were massing slowly but surely against us in a most menacing way. I didn't like it. I didn't like it that we were going along as if everything was hunky-dory, even to giving a grand Christmas Eve party for the several people in La Ville whom Mama had come to know—how they all drove out in their carriages under the moon that was so bright on the plains of snow that it was like a black daytime, the local banker, the merchants, the pastor of the First Methodist church, and other such dignitaries and their wives. The spruce tree in the parlor was imported from Minnesota and all alight with candles, and the three children were dressed for the occasion and went around with cups of eggnog for the assembled guests. I knew how important it was for Mama to establish her reputation as a person of class who had flattered the community by joining it, but all these people made me nervous. I didn't think it was wise having so many rigs parked in the yard, and so many feet tromping about the house, or going out to the privy. Of course, it was a lack of self-confidence on my part, and how often was it that Mama had warned me nothing was more dangerous than that, because it was translated into the face and physique as wrongdoing, or at least defenselessness, which amounted to the same thing. But I couldn't help it. I remembered the pocket watch that the little snivelling Joseph had found and held up to me, swinging it from its fob, I sometimes made mistakes, I was human, and who knew what other mistakes lay about for someone to find and hold up to me.

But now Mama looked at me over the heads of her guests. The children's tutor had brought her harmonium and we all gathered around the fireplace for some carol singing. Given Mama's look, I sang the loudest. I have a good tenor voice and I sent it aloft to turn heads and make the La Villers smile. I imagined decking the halls with boughs of holly until there was kindling and brush enough to set the whole place ablaze.

•　　•　　•

Just after the New Year, a man appeared at our door, another Swede with his Gladstone bag in his hand. We had not run the Wanted ad all winter, and Mama was not going to be home to him, but this fellow was the brother of one of them who had responded to it the previous fall. He gave his name, Henry Lundgren, and said his brother Per Lundgren had not been heard from since leaving Wisconsin to look into the prospect here.

Mama invited him in and sat him down and had Fannie bring in some tea. The minute I looked at him I remembered the brother. Per Lundgren had been all business. He did not blush or go shy in Mama's presence, nor did he ogle. Instead he asked sound questions. He had also turned the conversation away from his own circumstances, family relations, and so on, which Mama put people through in order to learn who was back home and might be waiting. Most of the immigrants, if they had family, it was still in the Old Country, but you had to make sure. Per Lundgren was closemouthed, but he did admit to being unmarried, and so we decided to go ahead.

And here was Henry, the brother he had never mentioned, sitting stiffly in the wing chair with his arms folded and the aggrieved expression on his face. They had the same reddish fair skin, with a long jaw and thinning blond hair, and pale woeful-looking eyes with blond eyelashes. I would say Henry here was the younger by a couple of years, but he turned out to be as smart as Per, or maybe even smarter. He did not seem to be as convinced of the sincerity of Mama's expressions of concern as I would have liked. He said his brother had made the trip to La Ville with other stops planned afterward to two more business prospects, a farm some twenty miles west of us and another in Indiana. Henry had travelled to these places, which is how he learned that his brother never arrived for his appointments. He said Per had been travelling with something over two thousand dollars in his money belt.

My goodness, that is a lot of money, Mama said.

Our two savings, Henry said. He comes here to see your farm. I have the advertisement, he said, pulling a piece of newspaper from his pocket. This is the first place he comes to see.

I'm not sure he ever arrived, Mama said. We've had many inquiries.

He arrived, Henry Lundgren said. He arrived the night before so he will be on time the next morning. This is my brother. It is important to him, even if it costs money. He sleeps at the hotel in La Ville.

How could you know that? Mama said.

I know from the guestbook in the La Ville hotel, where I find his signature, Henry Lundgren said.

· · ·

Mama said, All right, Earle, we've got a lot more work to do before we get out of here.

We're leaving?

What is today, Monday. I want to be on the road Thursday the latest. I thought with the inquest matter back there we were O.K. at least to the spring. This business of a brother pushes things up a bit.

I am ready to leave.

I know you are. You have not enjoyed the farm life, have you? If that Swede had told us he had a brother, he wouldn't be where he is today. Too smart for his own good, he was. Where is Bent?

She went out to the yard. He was standing at the corner of the barn, peeing a hole in the snow. She told him to take the carriage and go to La Ville and pick up half a dozen gallon cans of kerosene at the hardware. They were to be put on our credit.

It occurred to me that we still had a goodly amount of our winter supply of kerosene. I said nothing. Mama had gone into action, and I knew from experience that everything would come clear by and by.

And then, late that night, when I was in the basement, she called downstairs to me that Bent was coming down to help.

I don't need help, thank you, Aunt Dora, I said, so astonished that my throat went dry.

At that they both clomped down the stairs and back to the potato bin, where I was working. Bent was grinning that toothy grin of his as always, to remind me he had certain privileges.

Show him, Mama said to me. Go ahead, it's all right, she assured me.

So I did, I showed him. I showed him something to hand. I opened the top of the gunnysack and he looked down it.

The fool's grin disappeared, the unshaven face went pale, and he started to breathe through his mouth. He gasped, he couldn't catch his breath, a weak cry came from him, and he looked at me in my rubber apron and his knees buckled and he fainted dead away.

Mama and I stood over him. Now he knows, I said. He will tell them.

Maybe, Mama said, but I don't think so. He's now one of us. We have just made him an accessory.

An accessory?

After the fact. But he'll be more than that by the time I get through with him, she said.

We threw some water on him and lifted him to his feet. Mama took him up to the kitchen and gave him a couple of quick swigs. Bent was thoroughly cowed, and when I came upstairs and told him to follow me he jumped out of his chair as if shot. I handed him the gunnysack. It was not that heavy for someone like him, he held it in one hand at arm's length, as if it would bite. I led him to the old dried-up well behind the house, where he dropped it down into the muck. I poured the quicklime in and then we lowered some rocks down and nailed the well cover back on, and Bent the handyman, he never said a word but just stood there shivering and waiting for me to tell him what to do next.

Mama had thought of everything. She had paid cash down for the farm but somewhere or other got the La Ville bank to give her a mortgage, and so when the house burned it was the bank's money. She had been withdrawing from the account all winter, and now that we were closing shop she mentioned to me the actual sum of our wealth for the first time. I was very moved to be confided in, like her partner.

But really it was the small touches that showed her genius. For instance, she had noted immediately of the inquiring brother, Henry, that he was in height not much taller than I am. Just as in Fannie the housekeeper she had hired a woman of a girth similar to her own. Meanwhile, at her instruction, I was letting my dark beard grow out. And at the end, before she had Bent go up and down the stairs pouring the kerosene in every room, she made sure he was good and drunk. He would sleep through the whole thing in the stable, and that's where they found him, with his arms wrapped like a lover's arms around an empty can of kerosene.

•   •   •

The plan was for me to stay behind for a few days just to keep an eye on things. We have pulled off something prodigious that will go down in the books, Mama said. But that means all sorts of people will be flocking here and you can never tell when the unexpected arises. Of course, everything will be fine, but if there's something more we have to do you will know it.

Yes, Aunt Dora.

Aunt Dora was just for here, Earle.

Yes, Mama.

Of course, even if there was no need to keep an eye out you would still have to wait for Miss Czerwinska.

This is where I didn't understand her thinking. The one bad thing in all of this is that Winifred would read the news in the Chicago papers. There was no safe way I could get in touch with her now that I was dead. That was it, that was the end of it. But Mama had said it wasn't necessary to get in touch with Winifred. This remark made me angry.

You said you liked her, I said.

I do, Mama said.

You called her our friend, I said.

She is.

I know it can't be helped, but I wanted to marry Winifred Czerwinska. What can she do now but dry her tears and maybe light a candle for me and go out and find herself another boyfriend?

Oh, Earle, Earle, Mama said, you know nothing about a woman's heart.

• • •

But anyhow I followed the plan to stay on a few days, and it wasn't that hard with a dark stubble and a different hat and a long coat. There were such crowds nobody would notice anything that wasn't what they'd come to see, that's what a fever was in these souls. Everyone was streaming down the road to see the tragedy, they were in their carriages and they were walking and standing up in drays, people were paying for anything with wheels to get them out there from town, and after the newspapers ran the story they were coming not just from La Ville and the neighboring farms but from out of state in their automobiles and on the train from Indianapolis and Chicago. And with the crowds came the hawkers to sell sandwiches and hot coffee, and peddlers with balloons and little flags and whirligigs for the children. Someone had taken photographs of the laid-out skeletons in their crusts of burlap and printed them up as postcards for mailing, and these were going like hotcakes.

The police had been inspired by the charred remains they found in the basement to look down the well and then to dig up the chicken yard and the floor of the stable. They had brought around a rowboat to dredge the water hole. They were really very thorough, they kept making their discoveries and laying out what they found in neat rows inside the barn. They had called in the county sheriff and his men to help with the crowds, and they got some kind of order going, keeping people in lines to pass them by the open barn doors so everyone would have a turn, it was the only choice the police had if they didn't want a riot, but even then the oglers went around back all the way up the road to get into the procession again—it was the two headless remains of Madame Dora and her nephew that drew the most attention, and of course the wrapped bundles of the little ones.

There was such heat from this population that the snow was gone from the ground, and on the road and in the yard and behind the house and even into the fields where the trucks and automobiles were parked everything had turned to mud so that it seemed even the season was transformed. I just stood and watched and took it all in, and it was amazing to see so many people with this happy feeling of spring, as if a population of creatures had formed up out of the mud especially for the occasion. That didn't help the smell any, though no one seemed to notice. The house itself made me sad to look at, a smoking ruin that you could see the sky through. I had become fond of that house. A piece of the floor hung down from the third story, where I had my room. I disapproved of people pulling off the loose brickwork to take home for a souvenir, there was a lot of laughing and shouting, but of course I did not say anything. In fact, I was able to rummage around the ruin without drawing attention to myself, and sure enough I found something—it was the syringe, for which I knew Mama would be thankful.

I overheard some conversation about Mama, what a terrible end for such a fine lady who loved children was the gist of it. I thought as time went on, in the history of our life of La Ville I myself would not be remembered very clearly. Mama would become famous in the papers as a tragic victim mourned for her good works, whereas I would be noted down only as a dead nephew. Even if the past caught up with her reputation and she was slandered as the suspect widow of several insured husbands, I would still be in the shadows. This seemed to me an unjust outcome considering the contribution I had made, and I found myself for a moment resentful. Who was I going to be in life now that I was dead and not even Winifred Czerwinska was there to bend over for me?

Back in town at night, I went behind the jail to the cell window where Bent was and I stood on a box and called to him softly, and when his bleary face appeared I ducked to the side where he couldn't see me and whispered these words: "Now you've seen it all, Bent. Now you have seen everything."

·　　　·　　　·

I stayed in town to meet every train that came through from Chicago. I could do that without fear—there was such a heavy traffic all around, such swirls of people, all of them too excited and thrilled to take notice of someone standing quietly in a doorway or sitting on the curb in the alley behind the station. And, as Mama told me, I knew nothing about the heart of a woman, because all at once there was Winifred Czerwinska, stepping down from the coach, her suitcase in her hand. I lost her for a moment through the steam from the locomotive blowing across the platform, but then there she was in her dark coat and a little hat and the most forlorn expression I have ever seen on a human being. I waited till the other people had drifted away before I approached her. Oh my, how grief-stricken she looked, standing by herself on the train platform with her suitcase and big tears rolling down her face. Clearly she had no idea what to do next, where to go, who to speak to. So she had not been able to help herself when she heard the terrible news. And what did that mean except that if she was drawn to me in my death she truly loved me in my life. She was so small and ordinary in appearance, how wonderful that I was the only person to know that under her clothes and inside her little rib cage the heart of a great lover was pumping away.

·　　　·　　　·

Well, there was a bad moment or two. I had to help her sit down. I am here, Winifred, it's all right, I told her over and over again, and I held my arms around her shaking, sobbing wracked body.

I wanted us to follow Mama to California, you see. I thought, given all the indications, Winifred would accept herself as an accessory after the fact.

Newsweek

FINALIST, COLUMNS AND
COMMENTARY

Playing God on No Sleep

Anna Quindlen writes with piercing honesty and intelligence about the events that touch all of us. This column takes a hard look at the sugarcoated face of motherhood. Whatever the topic, Quindlen's columns move effortlessly between the personal and the universal.

Anna Quindlen

Playing God on No Sleep

Isn't motherhood grand? Do you want the real answer or the official Hallmark-card version?

So a woman walks into a pediatrician's office. She's tired, she's hot and she's been up all night throwing sheets into the washer because the smaller of her two boys has projectile vomiting so severe it looks like a special effect from "The Exorcist." Oh, and she's nauseated, too, because since she already has two kids under the age of 5 it made perfect sense to have another, and she's four months pregnant. In the doctor's waiting room, which sounds like a cross between an orchestra tuning loudly and a 747 taking off, there is a cross-stitched sampler on the wall. It says GOD COULD NOT BE EVERYWHERE SO HE MADE MOTHERS.

This is not a joke, and that is not the punch line. Or maybe it is. The woman was me, the sampler real, and the sentiments it evoked were unforgettable: incredulity, disgust and that out-of-body feeling that is the corollary of sleep deprivation and adrenaline rush, with a soupçon of shoulder barf thrown in. I kept reliving this moment, and others like it, as I read with horrified fascination the story of Andrea Yates, a onetime nurse suffering from postpartum depression who apparently spent a recent morning drowning her five children in the bathtub. There is a part of my mind that imagines the baby, her starfish hands pink beneath the water, or the biggest boy fighting back, all wiry arms and legs, and then veers sharply away, aghast, appalled.

But there's another part of my mind, the part that remembers the end of a day in which the milk spilled phone rang one cried another hit a fever rose the medicine gone the car sputtered another cried the cable out "Sesame Street" gone all cried stomach upset full diaper no more diapers Mommy I want water Mommy my throat hurts Mommy I don't feel good. Every mother I've asked about the Yates case has the same reaction. She's appalled; she's aghast. And then she gets this look. And the look says that at some forbidden level she understands. The looks says that there are two very different kinds of horror here. There is the unimaginable idea of the killings. And then there is the entirely imaginable idea of going quietly bonkers in the house with five kids under the age of 7.

The insidious cult of motherhood is summed up by the psychic weight of the sampler on that doctor's wall. We are meant to be all things to small people, surrounded by bromides and soppy verse and smiling strangers who talk about how lucky we are. And we are lucky. My children have been the making of me as a human being, which does not mean they have not sometimes been an overwhelming and mind-boggling responsibility. That last is the love that dare not speak its name, the love that is fraught with fear and fatigue and inevitable resentment. But between the women who cannot have children and sometimes stare at our double strollers grief-stricken, and the grandmothers who make raising eight or 10 sound like a snap and insist we micromanage and overanalyze, there is no leave to talk about the dark side of being a surrogate deity, omniscient and out of milk all at the same time.

The weight was not always so heavy. Once the responsibility was spread around extended families, even entire towns. The sociologist Jessie Bernard has this to say: "The way we institutionalize motherhood in our society—assigning sole responsibility for child care to the mother, cutting her off from the easy help of others in an isolated household, requiring round-the-clock tender, loving care, and making such care her exclusive activity—is not only new and unique, but not even a good way for either women or—if we accept as a criterion the amount of maternal warmth shown—for children. It may, in fact, be the worst."

It has gotten no better since those words were written 25 years ago. Worse, perhaps, with all the competing messages about what women should do and be and feel at this particular moment in time. Women not working outside their homes feel compelled to make their job inside it seem both weighty and joyful; women who work outside their homes for pay feel no freedom to be ambivalent because of the sub rosa sense that they are cutting parenting corners. All of us are caught up in a conspiracy in which we are both the conspirators and the victims of the plot. In the face of all this "M is for the million things she gave me" mythology it becomes difficult to admit that occasionally you lock yourself in the bathroom just to be alone.

The great motherhood friendships are the ones in which women can admit this quietly to one another, over cups of tea at a table sticky with spilt apple juice and littered with markers without tops. But most of the time we keep quiet and smile. So that when someone is depressed after having a baby, when everyone is telling her that it's the happiest damn time of her life, there's no space to admit what she's really feeling. So that when someone does something as horrifying as what Andrea Yates did, there is no room for even a little bit of understanding. Yap yap yap, the world says. How could anyone do that to her children?

Well, yes. But. I'm imagining myself with five children under the age of 7, all alone after Dad goes off to work. And they're bouncing off the walls in that way little boys do, except for the baby, who needs to be fed. And fed. And fed again. And changed. The milk gets spilled. The phone rings. Mommy, can I have juice? Mommy, can I have lunch? Mommy, can I go out back? Mommy, can I come in? And I add to all that depression, mental illness, whatever was happening in that house. I'm not making excuses for Andrea Yates. I love my children more than life itself. But just because you love people doesn't mean that taking care of them day in and day out isn't often hard, and sometimes even horrible. If God made mothers because he couldn't be everywhere, maybe he could have met us halfway and eradicated vomiting, and colic too, and the hideous sugarcoating of what we are and what we do that leads to false cheer, easy lies and maybe sometimes something much, much worse, almost unimaginable. But not quite.

National Magazine Award Winners

General Excellence

1973   Business Week
1981   ARTnews
       Audubon
       Business Week
       Glamour
1982   Camera Arts
       Newsweek
       Rocky Mountain Magazine
       Science 81
1983   Harper's Magazine
       Life
       Louisiana Life
       Science 82
1984   The American Lawyer
       House & Garden
       National Geographic
       Outside
1985   American Health
       American Heritage
       Manhattan, inc.
       Time
1986   Discover
       Money
       New England Monthly
       3–2–1 Contact
1987   Common Cause
       Elle
       New England Monthly
       People Weekly
1988   Fortune
       Hippocrates
       Parents
       The Sciences
1989   American Heritage
       Sports Illustrated
       The Sciences
       Vanity Fair

1990   Metropolitan Home
       7 Days
       Sports Illustrated
       Texas Monthly
1991   Condé Nast Traveler
       Glamour
       Interview
       The New Republic
1992   Mirabella
       National Geographic
       The New Republic
       Texas Monthly
1993   American Photo
       The Atlantic Monthly
       Lingua Franca
       Newsweek
1994   Business Week
       Health
       Print
       Wired
1995   Entertainment Weekly
       I.D. Magazine
       Men's Journal
       The New Yorker
1996   Business Week
       Civilization
       Outside
       The Sciences
1997   I.D. Magazine
       Outside
       Vanity Fair
       Wired
1998   DoubleTake
       Outside
       Preservation
       Rolling Stone
1999   Condé Nast Traveler
       Fast Company

I.D. Magazine
Vanity Fair
2000   National Geographic
Nest
The New Yorker
Saveur
2001   The American Scholar
Mother Jones
The New Yorker
Teen People
2002   Entertainment Weekly
National Geographic
   Adventure
Newsweek
Print
Vibe

Personal Service

1986   Farm Journal
1987   Consumer Reports
1988   Money
1989   Good Housekeeping
1990   Consumer Reports
1991   New York
1992   Creative Classroom
1993   Good Housekeeping
1994   Fortune
1995   SmartMoney
1996   SmartMoney
1997   Glamour
1998   Men's Journal
1999   Good Housekeeping
2000   PC Computing
2001   National Geographic
   Adventure
2002   National Geographic
   Adventure

Leisure Interests (formerly Special Interests)

1986   Popular Mechanics
1987   Sports Afield
1988   Condé Nast Traveler
1989   Condé Nast Traveler
1990   Art & Antiques
1991   New York
1992   Sports Afield
1993   Philadelphia
1994   Outside
1995   GQ
1996   Saveur
1997   Smithsonian
1998   Entertainment Weekly
1999   PC Computing
2000   I.D. Magazine
2001   The New Yorker
2002   Vogue

Reporting

1970   The New Yorker
1971   The Atlantic Monthly
1972   The Atlantic Monthly
1973   New York
1974   The New Yorker
1975   The New Yorker
1976   Audubon
1977   Audubon
1978   The New Yorker
1979   Texas Monthly
1980   Mother Jones
1981   National Journal
1982   The Washingtonian
1983   Institutional Investor
1984   Vanity Fair
1985   Texas Monthly
1986   Rolling Stone

1987	Life
1988	The Washingtonian and Baltimore Magazine
1989	The New Yorker
1990	The New Yorker
1991	The New Yorker
1992	The New Republic
1993	IEEE Spectrum
1994	The New Yorker
1995	The Atlantic Monthly
1996	The New Yorker
1997	Outside
1998	Rolling Stone
1999	Newsweek
2000	Vanity Fair
2001	Esquire
2002	The Atlantic Monthly

Public Interest

1970	Life
1971	The Nation
1972	Philadelphia
1974	Scientific American
1975	Consumer Reports
1976	Business Week
1977	Philadelphia
1978	Mother Jones
1979	New West
1980	Texas Monthly
1981	Reader's Digest
1982	The Atlantic
1983	Foreign Affairs
1984	The New Yorker
1985	The Washingtonian
1986	Science85
1987	Money
1988	The Atlantic
1989	California
1990	Southern Exposure

1991	Family Circle
1992	Glamour
1993	The Family Therapy Networker
1994	Philadelphia
1995	The New Republic
1996	Texas Monthly
1997	Fortune
1998	The Atlantic Monthly
1999	Time
2000	The New Yorker
2001	Time
2002	The Atlantic Monthly

Feature Writing

1988	The Atlantic
1989	Esquire
1990	The Washingtonian
1991	U.S. News & World Report
1992	Sports Illustrated
1993	The New Yorker
1994	Harper's Magazine
1995	GQ
1996	GQ
1997	Sports Illustrated
1998	Harper's Magazine
1999	The American Scholar
2000	Sports Illustrated
2001	Rolling Stone
2002	The Atlantic Monthly

Columns and Commentary

2002	New York

Essays

2000	The Sciences
2001	The New Yorker
2002	The New Yorker

Reviews and Criticism

2000	Esquire
2001	The New Yorker
2002	Harper's Magazine

Profile Writing

2000	Sports Illustrated
2001	The New Yorker
2002	The New Yorker

Single-Topic Issue

1979	Progressive Architecture
1980	Scientific American
1981	Business Week
1982	Newsweek
1983	IEEE Spectrum
1984	Esquire
1985	American Heritage
1986	IEEE Spectrum
1987	Bulletin of the Atomic Scientists
1988	Life
1989	Hippocrates
1990	National Geographic
1991	The American Lawyer
1992	Business Week
1993	Newsweek
1994	Health
1995	Discover
1996	Bon Appétit
1997	Scientific American
1998	The Sciences
1999	The Oxford American
2002	Time

Design

1980	Geo
1981	Attenzione
1982	Nautical Quarterly
1983	New York
1984	House & Garden
1985	Forbes
1986	Time
1987	Elle
1988	Life
1989	Rolling Stone
1990	Esquire
1991	Condé Nast Traveler
1992	Vanity Fair
1993	Harper's Bazaar
1994	Allure
1995	Martha Stewart Living
1996	Wired
1997	I.D.
1998	Entertainment Weekly
1999	ESPN The Magazine
2000	Fast Company
2001	Nest
2002	Details

Photography

1985	Life
1986	Vogue
1987	National Geographic
1988	Rolling Stone
1989	National Geographic
1990	Texas Monthly
1991	National Geographic
1992	National Geographic
1993	Harper's Bazaar
1994	Martha Stewart Living
1995	Rolling Stone
1996	Saveur
1997	National Geographic
1998	W
1999	Martha Stewart Living
2000	Vanity Fair
2001	National Geographic
2002	Vanity Fair

Fiction

1978	The New Yorker
1979	The Atlantic Monthly
1980	Antaeus
1981	The North American Review
1982	The New Yorker
1983	The North American Review
1984	Seventeen
1985	Playboy
1986	The Georgia Review
1987	Esquire
1988	The Atlantic
1989	The New Yorker
1990	The New Yorker
1991	Esquire
1992	Story
1993	The New Yorker
1994	Harper's Magazine
1995	Story
1996	Harper's Magazine
1997	The New Yorker
1998	The New Yorker
1999	Harper's Magazine
2000	The New Yorker
2001	Zoetrope: All-Story
2002	The New Yorker

General Excellence Online

1997	Money
1998	The Sporting News Online
1999	Cigar Aficionado
2000	Business Week Online
2001	U.S. News Online
2002	National Geographic Magazine Online

Best Interactive Design

2001	SmartMoney.com

Essays and Criticism

1978	Esquire
1979	Life
1980	Natural History
1981	Time
1982	The Atlantic
1983	The American Lawyer
1984	The New Republic
1985	Boston Magazine
1986	The Sciences
1987	Outside
1988	Harper's Magazine
1989	Harper's Magazine
1990	Vanity Fair
1991	The Sciences
1992	The Nation
1993	The American Lawyer
1994	Harper's Magazine
1995	Harper's Magazine
1996	The New Yorker
1997	The New Yorker
1998	The New Yorker
1999	The Atlantic Monthly

Single Award

1966	Look
1967	Life
1968	Newsweek
1969	American Machinist

Specialized Journalism

1970	Philadelphia
1971	Rolling Stone
1972	Architectural Record
1973	Psychology Today
1974	Texas Monthly
1975	Medical Economics
1976	United Mine Workers Journal

1977	Architectural Record
1978	Scientific American
1979	National Journal
1980	IEEE Spectrum

1974	The New Yorker
1975	Redbook
1976	Essence
1977	Mother Jones

Visual Excellence

1970	Look
1971	Vogue
1972	Esquire
1973	Horizon
1974	Newsweek
1975	Country Journal
	National Lampoon
1976	Horticulture
1977	Rolling Stone
1978	Architectural Digest
1979	Audubon

Service to the Individual

1974	Sports Illustrated
1975	Esquire
1976	Modern Medicine
1977	Harper's Magazine
1978	Newsweek
1979	The American Journal of Nursing
1980	Saturday Review
1982	Philadelphia
1983	Sunset
1984	New York
1985	The Washingtonian

Fiction and Belles Lettres

1970	Redbook
1971	Esquire
1972	Mademoiselle
1973	The Atlantic Monthly

Special Award

| 1976 | Time |
| 1989 | Robert E. Kenyon, Jr. |

2002 National Magazine Award Finalists

NOTE: All nominated issues are dated 2001 unless otherwise specified. The editor whose name appears in connection with finalists for 2002 held that position, or was listed on the masthead, at the time the issue was published in 2001. In some cases, another editor is now in that position.

General Excellence

This category recognizes overall excellence in magazines. It honors the effectiveness with which writing, reporting, editing and design all come together to command readers' attention and fulfill the magazine's unique editorial mission.

Under 200,000 circulation

The American Scholar: Anne Fadiman, Editor, for Spring, Summer, Autumn issues.
City: John F. McDonald, Editorial Director & Publisher, for March/April, September/October, November/December issues.
MBA Jungle: Bill Shapiro, Editor-in-Chief, for May, September, November issues.
Nest: Joseph Holtzman, Editor-in-Chief and Art Director, for Summer, Fall, Winter issues.
Print: Martin Fox, Vice President & Editor, for January/February, May/June, July/August issues.

200,000 to 500,000 circulation

Details: Daniel Peres, Editor-in-Chief, for September, October, December issues.
National Geographic Adventure: John Rasmus, Editor-in-Chief, for March/April, May/June, September/October issues.
Saveur: Dorothy Kalins, Editor-in-Chief, for March issue; Colman Andrews, Editor-in-Chief, for July/August, September/October issues.
Sports Illustrated Women: Susan Casey, Managing Editor, for September, October, December/January issues.
Texas Monthly: Evan Smith, Editor, for April, July, November issues.

500,000 to 1,000,000 circulation

Gourmet: Ruth Reichl, Editor-in-Chief, for March, August, September issues.
Jane Magazine: Jane Pratt, Editor-in-Chief, for April, October, November issues.

The New Yorker: David Remnick, Editor, for February 19 & 26, September 24, December 10 issues.

Vibe: Emil Wilbekin, Editor-in-Chief, for September, November, December issues.

Wired: Katrina Heron, Editor-in-Chief, for February issue; Chris Anderson, Editor-in-Chief, for September, December issues.

1,000,000 to 2,000,000 circulation

Entertainment Weekly: James W. Seymore, Jr., Managing Editor, for June 29/July 6, November 2, December 21/December 28 issues.

ESPN: The Magazine: John Papanek, Editor-in-Chief, for March 19, August 6, September 17 issues.

Fortune: Rik Kirkland, Managing Editor, for May 14, October 1, December 24 issues.

In Style: Martha Nelson, Managing Editor, for March, May, November issues.

Vanity Fair: Graydon Carter, Editor, for October, November, December issues.

Over 2,000,000 circulation

Better Homes and Gardens: Jean LemMon, Editor-in-Chief, for March issue; Karol DeWulf Nickell, Editor-in-Chief, for November, December issues.

National Geographic: William L. Allen, Editor-in-Chief, for March, July, December issues.

Newsweek: Richard M. Smith, Chairman and Editor-in-Chief; Mark Whitaker, Editor, for September 24, October 1, October 15 issues.

O, The Oprah Magazine: Oprah Winfrey, Founder and Editorial Director; Amy Gross, Editor-in-Chief, for May, June, September issues.

Time: James Kelly, Managing Editor, for September 13, September 24, December 31/January 7 issues.

Personal Service

This category recognizes excellence in service journalism. It honors the intelligence and clarity with which a magazine presents information intended to help readers improve the quality of their personal lives.

BabyTalk: Susan Kane, Editor-in-Chief, for *Special Babies,* by Melanie Howard, February.

MBA Jungle: Bill Shapiro, Editor-in-Chief, for *Anatomy of an Interview,* by David Blend, Lisa Chudnofsky, and Maria Spinella, November.

Money Magazine: Robert Safian, Managing Editor, for *Family Matters,* by Andrea Bennett, Jean Sherman Chatzky, Borzou Daragahi, Amy Feldman, Judy Feldman, Leslie Haggin Geary, Roberta Kirwan, Penelope Wang, Cybele Weisser, September.

National Geographic Adventure: John Rasmus, Editor-in-Chief, for *Land of the Lost,*
   by Laurence Gonzales, November/December.
Worth: John Koten, Editor, for *A Gift for Giving,* by Reshma Memon Yaqub, December.

Leisure Interests

This category recognizes excellence in coverage of leisure-time pursuits. It
honors the intelligence and clarity with which a magazine presents information and advice designed to help readers enjoy specific hobbies or other
recreational interests.

Field & Stream: Slaton L. White, Editor, for *How We Hunt Deer,* by Scott Bestul, John
   Barsness, Sam Curtis, Joe Doggett, Keith McCafferty, September.
O, The Oprah Magazine: Oprah Winfrey, Founder and Editorial Director; Amy
   Gross, Editor-in-Chief, for a special section, *"Creativity,"* November.
Philadelphia Magazine: Loren Feldman, Editor, for *How to Buy Art,* by Sarah Jordan
   and Sasha Issenberg, May.
Sports Illustrated: Bill Colson, Managing Editor, for *'Ring Tossed,* by Steve Rushin,
   January 15.
Travel + Leisure: Nancy Novogrod, Editor-in-Chief, for *New Classics,* September.
Vogue: Anna Wintour, Editor-in-Chief, for three articles by Jeffrey Steingarten:
   Caviar Conundrum, March; *Salt Chic,* July; *High Steaks,* September.

Reporting

This category recognizes excellence in reporting. It honors the enterprise,
exclusive reporting and intelligent analysis that a magazine exhibits in covering a story of contemporary interest and significance.

The Atlantic Monthly: Michael Kelly, Editor, for *The Crash of EgyptAir 990,* by
   William Langewiesche, November.
Fortune: Rik Kirkland, Managing Editor, for *Is Enron Overpriced?,* by Bethany
   McLean, March 5.
The New Yorker: David Remnick, Editor, for three articles by Seymour M. Hersh:
   What Went Wrong, October 8; *King's Ransom,* October 22; *The Iran Game,*
   December 3.
Time: James Kelly, Managing Editor, for *Inside the Battle at Qala-i-Jangi,* by Alex
   Perry, December 10.
Yankee Magazine: Jim Collins, Editor, for *A Question of Life and Death,* by Geoffrey
   Douglas, September.

Public Interest

This category recognizes journalism that has the potential to affect national or local policy or lawmaking. It honors investigative reporting or groundbreaking analysis that sheds new light on an issue of public importance.

The Atlantic Monthly: Michael Kelly, Editor, for *Bystanders to Genocide,* by Samantha Power, September.

Governing: Peter A. Harkness, Editor & Publisher, for *Grading the States 2001,* by Katherine Barrett and Richard Greene with Michele Mariani, February.

San Francisco Magazine: Bruce Kelley, Editor-in-Chief, for *Trouble in the Presidio,* by Kerry Tremain, December.

Self: Lucy S. Danziger, Editor-in-Chief, for *The Big Fat Question: If Obesity Is America's Number-One Health Problem, Why Do So Many People Have to Go It Alone?* by Shannon Brownlee, December.

Sports Illustrated: Bill Colson, Managing Editor, for *Snow Job,* by Donald L. Barlett and James B. Steele, December 10.

Feature Writing

This category recognizes excellence in feature writing. Whether the piece is reported narrative or personal reflection, the award honors the stylishness and originality with which the author treats his or her subject.

The Atlantic Monthly: Michael Kelly, Editor, for *Moonrise,* by Penny Wolfson, December.

Esquire: David Granger, Editor-in-Chief, for *Gone,* by Tom Junod, December.

Los Angeles Magazine: Kit Rachlis, Editor-in-Chief, for *Valley Girl, Interrupted,* by Dave Gardetta, October.

Men's Journal: Sid Evans, Editor, for *Killing Libby,* by Mark Levine, August.

The New Yorker: David Remnick, Editor, for *Matchmaker,* by James B. Stewart, August 20 & 27.

Columns and Commentary

This category recognizes excellence in short-form political, social, economic or humorous commentary. The award honors the eloquence, force of argument, and succinctness with which the writer presents his or her views.

GQ: Arthur Cooper, Editor-in-Chief, for three columns by Terrence Rafferty: *Eminem: A Fan's Notes,* April; *Kate Winslet, Please Save Us,* May; *God Is Dead. Bob Dylan Lives,* June.

New York Magazine: Caroline Miller, Editor-in-Chief, for three columns by Michael Wolff: *Russert to Judgment,* February 12; *Sullivan's Travels,* March 5; *The Stupids,* April 9.

Newsweek: Richard M. Smith, Chairman and Editor-in-Chief; Mark Whitaker, Editor, for three columns by Anna Quindlen: *Playing God on No Sleep,* July 2; *A Good Girl, A Great Woman,* July 30; *Imagining the Hanson Family,* September 24.

Newsweek: Richard M. Smith, Chairman and Editor-in-Chief; Mark Whitaker, Editor, for three columns by Fareed Zakaria: *The End of the End of History,* September 24; *The Allies Who Made Our Foes,* October 1; *Let's Spread the Good Cheer,* November 26.

The Oxford American: Marc Smirnoff, Editor, for three columns by Hal Crowther: *Among the True Believers,* May/June; *The O Brotherhood,* Summer; *A Man of the World,* Fall.

Essays

This category recognizes excellence in essay writing. It honors the eloquence, perspective, and fresh thinking that an author brings to bear on an issue of social or political significance.

The American Scholar: Anne Fadiman, Editor, for *Moving,* by Anne Fadiman, Winter.

Harper's Magazine: Lewis H. Lapham, Editor, for *Welcome to Cancerland,* by Barbara Ehrenreich, November.

Men's Journal: Sid Evans, Editor, for *40 Years in Acapulco,* by Devin Friedman, July.

The New Yorker: David Remnick, Editor, for *My Father's Brain,* by Jonathan Franzen, September 10.

The New Yorker: David Remnick, Editor, for *The Revolt of Islam,* by Bernard Lewis, November 19.

Reviews and Criticism

This category recognizes excellence in criticism of art, movies, television, theater, music, dance, dining, fashion, products, and the like. It honors the knowledge, persuasiveness, and original voice that the critic brings to his or her reviews.

The Atlantic Monthly: Michael Kelly, Editor, for three pieces by Caitlin Flanagan: *The Wedding Merchants,* February; *The Tabloid Habit,* July/August; *Confessions of a Prep School College Counselor,* September.

Gourmet: Ruth Reichl, Editor-in-Chief, for three reviews by Jonathan Gold: *Foam Follows Function,* April; *Ticket to the World,* May; *Nothing Like a Flame,* June.

GQ: Arthur Cooper, Editor-in-Chief, for three reviews by Alan Richman: *Toro! Toro! Toro!,* March; *Slicing Up Naples,* May; *Pardon Us, Bubba . . . ,* July.

Harper's Magazine: Lewis H. Lapham, Editor, for three reviews by Lee Siegel: *Seize the Day Job,* March; *The Second Coming of Richard Yates,* July; *Cold Verities,* October.

The New Yorker: David Remnick, Editor, for three pieces by Hilton Als: *This Lonesome Place,* January 29; *In Black and White,* June 4; *Unhappy Endings,* December 3.

Profile Writing

This category recognizes excellence in profile writing. It honors the vividness and perceptiveness with which the writer brings his or her subject to life.

Esquire: David Granger, Editor-in-Chief, for *Ferran Adrià,* by Michael Paterniti, July.

GQ: Arthur Cooper, Editor-in-Chief, for *Our Man in Mexico,* by Charles Bowden, June.

Harper's Magazine: Lewis H. Lapham, Editor, for *Dr. Daedalus,* by Lauren Slater, July.

Los Angeles Magazine: Kit Rachlis, Editor-in-Chief, for *Hollywood's Information Man,* by Amy Wallace, September.

The New Yorker: David Remnick, Editor, for *The Lost Tycoon,* by Ken Auletta, April 23 & 30.

Single-Topic Issue

This category recognizes magazines that have devoted entire issues to an in-depth examination of one topic. It honors the ambition, comprehensiveness, and imagination with which a magazine treats its subject.

Cincinnati Magazine: Kitty Morgan, Editor, for *Listen to Me: Growing Up Young, Black and Male,* August.

Gourmet: Ruth Reichl, Editor-in-Chief, for its special Paris issue, March.

The Nation: Katrina vanden Heuvel, Editor, for *Death Trip: The American Way of Execution,* by Robert Sherrill, January 8/15.

The New Yorker: David Remnick, Editor, for its September 11 special issue, September 24.

Time: James Kelly, Managing Editor, for its September 11 special issue, September 13.

Design

This category recognizes excellence in magazine design. It honors the effectiveness of overall design, artwork, graphics, and typography in enhancing a magazine's unique mission and personality.

Audubon: Lisa Gosselin, Editor-in-Chief; Kevin Fisher, Art Director, for January/February; David Seideman, Editor-in-Chief, Kevin Fisher, Design Director, for March/April and November/December issues.
Details: Daniel Peres, Editor-in-Chief; Rockwell Harwood, Art Director, for September, October, November issues.
Esquire: David Granger, Editor-in-Chief; John Korpics, Design Director, for April, July, September issues.
Nest: Joseph Holtzman, Editor-in-Chief and Art Director, for Summer, Fall, Winter issues.
Surface: Riley John-donnell and Richard M. Klein, Publishers and Creative Directors; Jeremy Lin, Editorial Director, for March, September, November issues.
Time: James Kelly, Managing Editor; Arthur Hochstein, Art Director for September 13, December 24, December 31–January 7 issues.

Photography

This category recognizes excellence in magazine photography. It honors the effectiveness of photography, photojournalism and photo illustration in enhancing a magazine's unique mission and personality.

National Geographic Adventure: John Rasmus, Editor-in-Chief; Julie Curtis, Design Director; Sabine Meyer, Photo Editor; Michael Bain, Art Director, for March/April, May/June, September/October issues.
Newsweek: Richard M. Smith, Chairman and Editor-in-Chief; Mark Whitaker, Editor; Lynn Staley, Assistant Managing Editor, Design; Sarah Harbutt, Director of Photography, for September 24, November 26 issues; Alexis Gelber, Director of Special Projects; Amid Capeci, Art Director; Simon Barnett, Picture Editor, for Fall/Winter issue.
Time: James Kelly, Managing Editor; Arthur Hochstein, Art Director; Michele Stephenson, Director of Photography, for September 13, October 1, December 31/January 7 issues.
Vanity Fair: Graydon Carter, Editor; David Harris, Design Director; Susan White, Photography Director, for April, November, December issues.

Vogue: Anna Wintour, Editor-in-Chief; Charles Churchward, Design Director; Russell Labosky, Art Director; Ivan Shaw, Photo Director, for March, June, October issues.

Fiction

This category recognizes excellence in magazine fiction writing. It honors both the quality and the novelty of a publication's literary selections.

The Atlantic Monthly: Michael Kelly, Editor, for *The Hunter's Wife,* by Anthony Doerr, May; *Digging,* by Beth Lordan, September; *Popular Girls,* by Karen Shepard, October.

Harper's Magazine: Lewis H. Lapham, Editor, for *Curly Red,* by Joyce Carol Oates, April; *Revenge,* by Steven Millhauser, July; *Love and Hydrogen,* by Jim Shepard, December.

The New Yorker: David Remnick, Editor, for *What is Remembered,* by Alice Munro, February 19 & 26; *A House on the Plains,* by E. L. Doctorow, June 18 & 25; *Surrounded by Sleep,* by Akhil Sharma, December 10.

The Paris Review: George Plimpton, Editor, for *Aqua Boulevard,* by Maile Meloy, Spring/Summer; *The Caretaker,* by Anthony Doerr, Fall; *Eating Mammals,* by John Barlow, Winter.

Zoetrope: All-Story: Adrienne Brodeur, Editor-in-Chief, for *Anything for Money,* by Karen E. Bender, August; *The Evil B.B. Chow,* by Steve Almond, August; *The Affairs of Each Beast,* by David Benioff, November.

General Excellence Online

This category recognizes outstanding magazine Internet sites. It honors the use of Web technology and design to display and build on the core strengths of a site's print counterpart, if any, or to create an entirely original "magazine environment" on the web.

Beliefnet (www.beliefnet.com): Steven Waldman, Editor-in-Chief

The Chronicle of Higher Education (www.chronicle.com): Phil Semas, Editor, New Media

National Geographic Magazine Online (www.nationalgeographic.com/ngm): Valerie May, Director, New Media

RollingStone.com (www.rollingstone.com): Larry Carlat, Editor-in-Chief

Slate (www.slate.com): Michael Kinsley, Editor

Permissions